THE STRENGTH OF ROMAN WOMEN THROUGH COINS AND A FEMINIST CRITIQUE FROM THE PAST TO THE PRESENT

Editora Appris Ltda.
1.ª Edição - Copyright© 2024 da autora
Direitos de Edição Reservados à Editora Appris Ltda.

Nenhuma parte desta obra poderá ser utilizada indevidamente, sem estar de acordo com a Lei nº 9.610/98. Se incorreções forem encontradas, serão de exclusiva responsabilidade de seus organizadores. Foi realizado o Depósito Legal na Fundação Biblioteca Nacional, de acordo com as Leis nos 10.994, de 14/12/2004, e 12.192, de 14/01/2010.

Catalogação na Fonte
Elaborado por: Dayanne Leal Souza
Bibliotecária CRB 9/2162

B452s 2024	Bélo, Tais Pagoto The strength of roman women through coins and a feminist critique from the past to the present / Tais Pagoto Bélo. – 1. ed. – Curitiba: Appris, 2024. 388 p. : il. ; 23 cm. Inclui referências. ISBN 978-65-250-6146-7 1. Female power. 2. Coins. 3. Feminist consciousness. 4. Women of Antiquity. I. Bélo, Tais Pagoto. II. Título. CDD – 305.42

Livro de acordo com a normalização técnica da ABNT

This work received support from the São Paulo State Research Support Foundation (FAPESP – process numbers: 2019/06953-6; 2020/06911-9).

Appris
editora

Editora e Livraria Appris Ltda.
Av. Manoel Ribas, 2265 – Mercês
Curitiba/PR – CEP: 80810-002
Tel. (41) 3156 - 4731
www.editoraappris.com.br

Printed in Brazil
Impresso no Brasil

Tais Pagoto Bélo

THE STRENGTH OF ROMAN WOMEN THROUGH COINS AND A FEMINIST CRITIQUE FROM THE PAST TO THE PRESENT

FICHA TÉCNICA

EDITORIAL	Augusto Coelho
	Sara C. de Andrade Coelho
COMITÊ EDITORIAL	Ana El Achkar (UNIVERSO/RJ)
	Andréa Barbosa Gouveia (UFPR)
	Conrado Moreira Mendes (PUC-MG)
	Eliete Correia dos Santos (UEPB)
	Fabiano Santos (UERJ/IESP)
	Francinete Fernandes de Sousa (UEPB)
	Francisco Carlos Duarte (PUCPR)
	Francisco de Assis (Fiam-Faam, SP, Brasil)
	Jacques de Lima Ferreira (UP)
	Juliana Reichert Assunção Tonelli (UEL)
	Maria Aparecida Barbosa (USP)
	Maria Helena Zamora (PUC-Rio)
	Maria Margarida de Andrade (Umack)
	Marilda Aparecida Behrens (PUCPR)
	Marli Caetano
	Roque Ismael da Costa Güllich (UFFS)
	Toni Reis (UFPR)
	Valdomiro de Oliveira (UFPR)
	Valério Brusamolin (IFPR)
SUPERVISOR DA PRODUÇÃO	Renata Cristina Lopes Miccelli
PRODUÇÃO EDITORIAL	Bruna Holmen
REVISÃO	Monalisa Morais Gobetti
DIAGRAMAÇÃO	Andrezza Libel
CAPA	Eneo Lage
BOOK COVER IMAGE	© The Trustees of the British Museum Available at: https://www.britishmuseum.org/collection/object/C_R-6361, accessed in:16/05/2024

To all of us, women.

Acknowledgements

To the Research Support Foundation of the State of São Paulo (FAPESP); to Prof Vagner Carvalheiro Porto (MAE/USP); to Prof François de Callataÿ (ULB/KBR); to Prof Pedro Paulo A. Funari (UNICAMP); to Prof Maria Cristina Nicolau Kormikiari Passos (MAE/USP); to Prof Sarah Fernandes Lino de Azevedo (USP); to Prof Diogo Leite; to Prof Juarez Oliveira; to Prof Kenneth Bertrams (ULB); to Prof François Blary (ULB); to Zoë-Joy Vangansewinkel (KBR); to Jaqueline Van Driessche (KBR); to Fran Stroobant (KBR); Walkiria Schneider (MAE/USP); to Fábio Batista dos Santos; to the study groups: Messalina, Medusa, Ancient Numismatics and Provincial Roman Archaeology Laboratory (LARP); and to the loves of my life, Danna ✶, Lara ♥, Nico and Alecrim.

"All rape is an exercise in power, but some rapists have an edge that is more than physical. They operate within an institutionalised setting that works to their advantage and in which a victim has little chance to redress her grievances. Rape in slavery and rape in wartime are two such examples. But rapists may also operate within an emotional setting or within a dependent relationship that provides a hierarchical, authoritarian structure of its own that weakens a victim's resistance, distorts her perspective and confounds her will".

(Brownmiller, 1975, p. 256)

Preface 1

After a book on Boudica, the "warrior-queen" whose subtitle was rather programmatic (*The female facets over time: nationalism, feminism, power and the collective memory*),[1] Tais Pagoto Bélo is back with another engaging monograph: *The strength of Roman women through coins and a feminist critique from the past to the present*.

As indicated by the title, the aim of the book is double: to consider how Roman empresses were represented on coins and, in so doing, engage a debate about feminism old and new. The angle is original and pertinent as well. Original since, although there is certainly no shortage of literature on Roman empresses and even on Roman empresses' coins, nobody seems to have really tackled so far the topic with an assumed feminist perspective. Pertinent since coins are well known to be especially useful considering built identities. At the difference of literary sources, largely posterior and heavily biased most of the time, coins indicate how the issuing power has consciously searched to be represented through a kind of objects produced in industrial numbers.

As the purpose is methodological, not all the Roman empresses have been considered. Five of them have been selected, from the end of the Republic to the high Roman Empire: Fulvia, Octavia, Livia, Agrippina Major and Agrippina Minor. Generally speaking, coin images are images produced under strict control and constraints exercized by men. So, it is the male vision of the ideal woman which is at stake, especially when, as it is the case of Livia and Agrippina Minor, this vision is aimed to proclaim domestic values.

Tais Pagoto Belo's book takes a committed approach, regularly moving back and forth between ancient Rome and the present day, opening up perspectives that go far beyond Roman coinage and calling on philosophers and gender studies specialists alike. Her view of an ancient world is fully placed at the service of a modern struggle, stating in her conclusion: "It should be emphasised that the Roman female position proves to be an important

---

[1] BELO, Tais Pagoto. **Boudica and the female facets over time**: nationalism, feminism, power and the collective memory. São Paulo: Alexa Cultural, 2019.

instructive resource to be explored to raise awareness of current male and female agencies". As such, it should be of interest to a wide audience, many of whom we hope will be male.

François de Callataÿ
Royal Library of Belgium
École Pratique des Hautes Etudes, Sciences Historiques et Philologiques
Université Libre de Bruxelles

Preface 2

The study of Roman empresses under a gender perspective

The study of Roman empresses on coins is a fascinating field of numismatics and historical research. Seemingly embryonic, the first studies on Roman empresses on coins can be traced back to the first numismatic and historical works that focused on the representations of empresses on coins from the Roman Empire. Although numismatics has a long history as a discipline, the specific study of representations of empresses and reflections on gender have yet to be further developed. The present work *The strength of Roman women through coins and a feminist critique from the past to the present*, written by Tais Pagoto Bélo, offers a relevant contribution to both fields: the presence and agency of Roman empresses in Roman society as a whole, and the resulting gender reflections.

Historically, academic production included the cataloguing of Roman coins, which at first was no more than a simple referencing of the coins (the fact that women were included in these catalogues had nothing to do with their choice of iconography, they were included because their effigies, busts and legends were on the coveted coins). In this regard, we highlight Joseph Hilarius Eckhel (1737-1798), an Austrian Jesuit scholar and numismatist. Eckhel is often considered one of the pioneers in the study of Roman coins and their historical context. In his monumental work *Doctrina Numorum Veterum* (published at the end of the 18th century), Eckhel extensively catalogued and described Roman coins, including those with empresses. His work laid the foundations for the systematic study of numismatics.

The 19th century saw the flourishing of several numismatic studies of relevance to the subject, among them the work *Description historique des monnaies frappées sous l'Empire romain communément appelées, médailles impériales*, written by Henry Cohen in 1859. At this time, the cataloguing of pieces with Fulvia, Octavia, Livia, Agrippina Major and Agrippina Minor followed the protocol of being there simply because they were of interest to the collection.

Moving into the 20th century, we find important reference works for collectors and scholars of Roman coins. Over the years, various numismatists, historians and archaeologists have continued to study and write about Roman empresses on coins. However, research in this field was still in its infancy, and even with scholars using advanced techniques and resources to gain a deeper understanding of the role of empresses in the Roman Empire, such study remained somewhat neglected until the work of Tais Pagoto Bélo.

From the 1920s, we would highlight *The Roman Imperial Coinage*, written by Harold Mattingly and Edward Allen Sydenham (1926). This is a classic work on Roman coins and includes valuable information on the representation of Roman empresses on coins.

The post-World War II period saw the publication of Roman Coins and Their Values (1964) by David R. Sear. This work endeavoured, albeit timidly, to include information about Roman empresses on coins, their titles and the historical context in which they were minted.

The book *Roman Silver Coins: The Republic to Augustus*, written by Herbert Allen Seaby in 1987, covers a wide variety of Roman coins, including those with empresses, and provides us with valuable context.

A few years later, the book *Handbook of Roman Imperial Coins: A Complete Guide to the History, Types, Symbols and Artistry of Roman Imperial Coinage*, written by David Can Meter in 1991, proved to be a practical guide for collectors and researchers interested in Roman imperial coins, including those with empresses.

In 1999, Martin Goodman wrote *The Roman World 44 BC-AD 180*. This work traces the impact of imperial politics on the life of the city of Rome itself and on the rest of the empire, arguing that despite long periods of apparent peace, this was a society controlled as much by fear of state violence as by consent. Although it doesn't focus on coins, this book provides an overview of the history of the Roman Empire and the role of the empresses.

First published in 2001, *Coinage and History of the Roman Empire* by David L. Vagi is an invaluable study in the field of Roman history. Vagi is an invaluable study in the fields of Roman history and numismatics. This book provides relevant insights into the historical and political context of Roman coinage, including the role of empresses.

William E. Metcalf released *The Oxford Handbook of Greek and Roman Coinage* in 2012. Although the author focuses on Greek and Roman coinage more broadly, it contains sections on imperial women and their representation on coins.

All these works that have been written over the last few decades, in one way or another, provide information about the Roman empresses, but only in a tangential and terse way.

As for the study of the gender perspective in ancient coins, it is important to consider that this is still a very narrow but fascinating field of numismatics. Although the main focus of ancient coins is often on their historical and economic aspects, scholars have also examined how these small objects reflect and sometimes mould gender roles, identities and representations in the societies that produced them. Therefore, we can assure you that "The Strength of Roman Women" is the great ace up its sleeves in the development of the field.

Some themes have emerged on this horizon, such as studies on the portraits of female rulers on coins. These reflect gender perspectives through the representation and strength of female rulers, such as Cleopatra in Egypt or Julia Domna in Rome. Studies on iconography and symbolism: the symbols and motifs on coins can often have gender-specific meanings, and this, among many other things, is what Pagoto Bélo seeks to show throughout her work. Studies on the imperial family and forms of dynastic politics can also be highlighted. In this case, the coins of Ancient Rome show how the roles and attributes of empresses and other female members of the family can be studied through their numismatic representations. Studies of women in economic contexts have also been the focus of concern for scholars over time. Women's agency in economic activities, such as trade or financial management, political influence, their actions as philanthropists and sponsors, their role in patronage and clientelism relationships have acquired proportions that are only now, thanks to the concerns of gender studies, beginning to be better observed.

Although there is ongoing research in this field, specific studies may vary depending on the region and period of interest. Numismatists, archaeologists and historians often collaborate to analyse and interpret the gender perspective on ancient coins, contributing to our understanding of how gender roles and representations have evolved throughout history.

Tais Bélo contributes to the debate by analysing the public image of Roman imperial women through coins during the Julio-Claudian family. Starting with an iconographic analysis of the coins, she sought to highlight issues linked to Roman patronage, as well as issues linked to the imperial cult, always taking as her starting point the political and daily life of the women of the imperial family.

The author also discusses the spheres of private and domestic life of Roman women in the context of the *patria potestas*, which were significant and marked the power relations within the Roman family. Her research highlights the achievements of Roman imperial women who, among many feats, had their memory preserved by having their names remembered on statues, plaques and coins.

Tais Pagoto Bélo's research at the Museum of Archaeology and Ethnology of the University of São Paulo (MAE-USP), as well as at the Coin and Medal Cabinet of the Royal National Library (KBR) and the Université Libre de Bruxelles (ULB), has sharpened her knowledge and enabled her to produce this absolutely relevant work on the agency of Roman empresses in ancient Roman society, and on the role of gender studies in Antiquity. The coin, in her work, is the vehicle with which we can access "the strength of Roman women"; as well as inviting us to reflect on the role of these women in the past and present.

Vagner Carvalheiro Porto
Museum of Archaeology and Ethnology
University of São Paulo

Presentation

This work aims to expose the public image of Roman women such as Fulvia, Octavia, Livia, Agrippina Major and Agrippina Minor, including the Late Republic and Early Empire (84 BC - AD 59), through coin samples and written sources that exemplify their lives. The objective is to illustrate how these women improved their public images through duties linked to the imperial family, Patronage, religion, and imperial propaganda.

The written sources gave visions of values and showed social relations, the principles of property, individual rights, and their duties in Roman society. These sources also confirmed that Roman women of this time were embedded in a hierarchy of power marked by boasting male rule. In the written sources, they were described in domestic environments, but with exceptions and malcontents, forming an opposition between the public and private worlds.

The material sources, the coins with these women's portraits, composed a formidable working tool, as they justified positions and consolidated powers within an aristocratic context of competition. As a movable monument, such objects promoted a wide audience, even far from the elite. They demonstrated that elite women achieved an "apparent" prominence, building a social life that led to a certain political openness, which contributed to them to be important authors of Rome's history. Women's changes at that time may have ensured a social change in all categories, especially in cultural constructions and political performances. This fact led Roman society to mould itself into a tangle of circumstances, in which the divisions of male and female became intertwined, demonstrating a social and gender complexity.

However, the purpose of this work was to explain through iconographic analysis what these objects wanted to communicate politically and in an identity manner. That said, the question was raised about the power and place of action of the feminine, since the "sexual *habitus*" could have marked the values between the genders. Both the material culture and the written sources analysed together were essential to prove this problematic, since literature made the gender relations of the emperors and their women very explicit. Material culture, by demonstrating male power, also highlighted female power.

In this way, the major importance of this work is an invitation to a reflection of the perception of the reality of the present, through an analytical approach in relation to the improved conditions of the Women's Studies of Antiquity, with a purpose capable of managing conscience and coherence of current feminine factors in contrast to the existence of a variety and similarity about the woman of the past.

Lista of figures

Figure 1 – Quinarius, from Lugdunum, 43 - 42 BC 137

Figure 2 – Silver denarius, Rome, 42 BC 140

Figure 3 – Denarius, Julius Caesar, Rome, 46 BC 141

Figure 4 – Bronze coin, Julius Caesar, 45 BC 142

Figure 5 – Denarius, from an uncertain mint, 32 - 29 BC 143

Figure 6 – Aureus minted by C. Numonius Vaala, Rome, 41 BC 145

Figure 7 – Bronze coin from Tripolis, 42/41 BC 147

Figure 8 – Coin of Fulvia, Phrygia, Eumeneia, 41 - 40 BC 149

Figure 9 – Phrygia coin, city of Eumeneia, 41 - 40 BC 150

Figure 10 – Aureus, from 40/39 BC 165

Figure 11 – Aureus, dated 38 BC 167

Figure 12 – Silver cistophoric tridrachm, from 39 BC 170

Figure 13 – Cistophoric tridrachm, silver, 39 BC 172

Figure 14 – Copper alloy As, from 36 - 35 BC 177

Figure 15 – Copper alloy dupondius, from 38 - 37 BC 178

Figure 16 – Copper alloy sestertius, from 36 - 35 BC 179

Figure 17 – Tremissis (three asses) from 38 BC. - 32 BC 181

Figure 18 – Silver tetradrachm, circa 36 BC 183

Figure 19 – Copper alloy coin, minted in Alexandria, Egypt, 51 - 30 BC 185

Figure 20 – Copper alloy coin, with Cleopatra VII on obverse, 51 - 30 BC 186

Figure 21 – Copper alloy dupondius, from 9 - 3 BC 190

Figure 22 – Augustus and Livia coin, 27 BC 202

Figure 23 – Coin from Alabanda, Asia, dated 27 BC - AD 14 203

Figure 24 – Coin of Mysia, Pergamum, dated 10 BC - AD 2 204

Figure 25 – Bronze coin with lead, Smyrna, 10 BC 205

Figure 26 – Bronze coin with lead, Smyrna, AD 4 - 14 205

Figure 27 – Silver denarius, dated 13 BC 210

Figure 28 – Coin of a metal melting type, 27 BC to AD 14 212

Figure 29 – Bronze sestertius from Rome, AD 97 214

Figure 30 – Bronze dupondius, AD 22 - 23 225

Figure 31 – Bronze dupondius with veiled bust, from AD 22 - 23 226

Figure 32 – Bronze dupondius, AD 22 - 23 227

Figure 33 – Copper alloy sestertius, dated AD 22 - 23 229

Figure 34 – Silver tetradrachm, from AD 14 - 37 231

Figure 35 – Copper alloy as, Rome, AD 40 - 41 232

Figure 36 – Aureus, Roman Empire, Lugdunum, dated AD 13 - 14 238

Figure 37 – Aureus, AD 14 - 37 239

Figure 38 – Denarius, AD 14 - 37 240

Figure 39 – Coin, 15 - 16 BC 241

Figure 40 – Dupondius from *Colonia Romula*, Spain, dated AD 15 - 16 244

Figure 41 – Silver coin from Byzantium, AD 20 - 29 248

Figure 42 – Dupondius dated AD 41 - 50 251

Figure 43 – Bronze As, AD 41 - 50 252

Figure 44 – Bronze sestertius, AD 41 - 50 252

Figure 45 – Bronze dupondius, AD 41 - 50 253

Figure 46 – Coin with bust of Claudius on the left on the obverse 254

Figure 47 – Silver denarius, from Catalonia, city of Tarraco, Spain 258

Figure 48 – Aureus, AD 68-69 259

Figure 49 – Bronze dupondius, AD 68-69 259

Figure 50 – Bronze sestertius, AD 68 - 69 260

Figure 51 – Aureus, Rome, AD 75 to 79 261

Figure 52 – Dupondius, in copper alloy, AD 80 - 81 262

Figure 53 – Dupondius, copper alloy coin, AD 80 - 81 263

Figure 54 – Bronze sestertius, AD 79 - 81 264

Figure 55 – Caesarea Panias. Bronze 265

Figure 56 – Bronze sestertius, 37 - 41 BC 280

Figure 57 – Aureus, Rome, AD 40 281

Figure 58 – Silver tetradrachm, dated AD 37 - 38 282

Figure 59 – Smyrna mint coin, 37-38 BC 283

Figure 60 – Copper alloy sestertius, dated AD 50 - 54 284

Figure 61 – Copper alloy sestertius, dated AD 80 - 81 285

Figure 62 – Bronze sestertius, 37-38 BC 290

Figure 63 – Aureus, AD 50 - 54 293

Figure 64 – Silver cistophoric tridrachm, AD 50 - 51 294

Figure 65 – Sestertius, AD 50 - 54, Rome 294

Figure 66 – Silver cistophoric tridrachm, minted in Ephesus, AD 51 296

Figure 67 – Copper alloy coin, AD 41 - 54 297

Figure 68 – Silver drachm, Crete 298

Figure 69 – Æ Diobol (two obols) of alloy, dated AD 41 - 54 299

Figure 70 – Metal alloy coin, from AD 41 - 54 300

Figure 71 – Copper alloy prutah, AD 54 - 55 301

Figure 72 – Copper alloy prutah, AD 54 - 55 302

Figure 73 – Silver Didrachm, from the government of Claudius, AD 50 - 54 303

Figure 74 – Silver denarius, minted in Rome, AD 50 - 54 304

Figure 75 – Silver denarius with Nero and Agrippina Minor, Rome, AD 54 313

Figure 76 – Aureus, 7.63g, dated AD 54 314

Figure 77 – Aureus, AD 55 315

Figure 78 – Aureus minted in Lyon 316

Figure 79 – Aureus, AD 64 - 65 317

Figure 80 – Silver Didrachm, AD 58 - 59 318

Figure 81 – Silver drachm, AD 58 - 59 319

Figure 82 – Silver As, AD 58 - 59 320

Figure 83 – Silver tetradrachm, AD 56 - 57 321

Figure 84 – Brass coin, minted in Eumeneia 322

Figure 85 – Aureus, AD 58 - 68 323

List of tables

Table 1 – The main denominations of the denarius system after 141/140 BC. 379

Table 2 – The main denominations of the Roman monetary system under Augustus. 379

Table 3 – Andrew Meadows' denominational system for Greek coins. 380

Tables of contents

Introduction 27
    The importance of this work for nowadays 27
    What to expect from this work..36

CHAPTER 1
Roman women from the late Republic to the early Empire 49
    1.1. Roman structural patriarchy..56
        1.1.1. Religious discourse 58
        1.1.2. The historical discourse..59
        1.1.2.1. The rape of Rhea Silvia 59
        1.1.2.2. The abduction of Sabine women 61
        1.1.2.3. The rape of Lucretia...62
        1.1.2.4. The attempt to rape Verginia..63
        1.1.2.5. Aspects of the origin myths and the Roman *stuprum*....................65
        1.1.3. The female position and legal discourse 76

CHAPTER 2
Women's representations, Patronage, propaganda and coins 93
    2.1. Coins and propaganda..105
    2.2. Images of roman women on provincial and roman coins 121

CHAPTER 3
Fulvia, the bloodthirsty..125
    3.1. The importance of Fulvia and her coins 128

CHAPTER 4
Octavia, the ideal roman matron 157
    4.1. The life and coins of Octavia..163
    4.2. Octavia and Cleopatra: between rivals...194

CHAPTER 5
Livia: power, agency, and representations of prosperity 199
    5.1. Livia's life and coins 201
        5.1.1. Livia and Augustus 210
        5.1.2 Livia and Tiberius 216
        5.1.3. Livia and Claudius 250
        5.1.4. Livia and other rulers 257

CHAPTER 6
Agrippina Major and her posthumous importance 269

CHAPTER 7
Agrippina Minor and the dream of being Augusta 289

Conclusion 327

Bibliography 343

APPENDICES

Appendix 1 379

Appendix 2 381

Appendix 3 383

Appendix 4 387

Introduction

The importance of this work for nowadays[2]

> "[...] in Western culture, the present epoch is the first period in which men are discovering that they are men themselves, in other words, they possess a problematic "masculinity". In previous eras, men assumed that their activities constituted "history", while women existed almost timelessly, doing the same thing they have always done".
>
> (Giddens, 1992, p. 70).

Even today, the opposition between "women's studies" and "gender studies" is common, and the confusion between "gender" and "woman" is frequent, which is understandable when we consider the history of feminist thought. The concept of gender developed within the framework of women's studies and came to share many of its assumptions. However, the formation of the concept of gender sought to overcome problems related to the use of some of the central categories in women's studies (Piscitelli, 2002, p. 16).

Thus, "gender studies" encompasses "women's studies" and even "women's history". It is important to realise that the concept of "gender" developed as an alternative to works on patriarchy, which was the product of the same feminist concern relating to the causes of women's oppression. However, the development of this concept is linked to the realisation of the need to associate this political problem with a better understanding of how "gender" operates in societies, which required thinking about power in different times and places in a more complex way. The feminist perspectives which began the work on "gender" maintain an essential interest in the situation of women, although they do not limit their analyses to the study of them (Piscitelli, 2002, p. 21).

Women's history is no longer a discrete subdisciplinary area of research, because it has become clear that broader gender issues are on the agenda in women's studies (Bahrani, 2005, p. 7). However, for Antiquity, it is prominent. In this perspective, the approach of this paper is tied to feminist

---

[2] Throughout this work there are digressions from aspects of the present, as a stimulus for a comparison with the past. In addition, there are quotations from several authors working with the present that have been adjusted for interpreting the past.

and postmodern concerns, and to the extent of material and written sources, and anthropological issues, which offer an interdisciplinary approach.

Women's history has been understood as a narrative within the broader narrative of world history or human history, known as the history of men. Therefore, it is often presented as a parallel and opposing history to the androcentric one. Sometimes, women's history is simply understood as any historical approach or methodology as long as it is written or taught by female scholars. Perhaps more often, women's history is understood as investigations concerned with what are conceived as intrinsically or essentially female worries. This division occurs because the categorisation of women is intrinsic to the domain of a powerful axiom of historical scholarship, and thus the categories of woman and man are taken as self-evident (Bahrani, 2005, p. 8-9).

For this study, it is important to note what has already been commented to date on the term patriarchy. This concept has already been useful for political mobilisation, portraying problems regarding the historicity of the female condition. It was relevant while distinguishing forces for the maintenance of sexism, in the feminist attempt to show female subordination. However, if patriarchy had a beginning, it could have an end. Feminist thought looked to patriarchy for the idea of an origin, or when the history of oppression of women began. The conditions set by the term could cause problems, as they prevent clarifying the gender relations of any group under study, since the concept already demonstrates the pre-existence of masculine domination in all societies. Thus, it is criticised for its generality or for universalising a form of masculine domination situated in different times and spaces, adding the fact that it always considers the physical difference between men and women as an invariable universal aspect (Piscitelli, 2002, p. 15-16).

Saffioti, when talking about Brazilian culture and most of the world's population, mentions that they are described as patriarchal. In her understanding, patriarchy would be a form of social organisation and domination linked to the exploitation of men over women (Saffioti, 2004). The author describes masculine domination as present in all social dynamics, such as in the family, at work, in the media, in politics and in the subtle controls of variables unknown to men and women (Freitas; Morais, 2019, p. 111).

In this conceptualisation, Saffioti seems to generalise the term, as Piscitelli criticises. This may be a view of contemporary society on women, a view that is not very comprehensive, since women in past societies, known as "barbarians", could have a much more comprehensive feminine adequacy, without certain prerogatives existing in today's world. For this reason, there is a great need to study other societies and social groups that may present other configurations of power. In this work, the concept of masculine domination is not considered in a universal way, but specifically for the study of a group that lived between the Republic and the beginning of the Roman Empire, which belonged to the Roman elite. It should be noted that, in the existence of groups within the same society, these could present different characteristics, marking the existence of a social complexity. What is refuted is that vague and imprecise ideas about this term do not allow us to discover basic aspects of what gender relations were like. Moreover, the universalisation of male dominance is not appropriate when studying the "barbarians", for example, since there is no evidence that these peoples dichotomised their worlds based on domains of power (Piscitelli, 2002, p. 21).

Thus, it is important for this study to think about patriarchy in the case of the Roman past, in which gender assumptions were fundamental to the construction of the basis of the formation of this society, with devices that confirmed a structural patriarchy. The similarities and divergences between this patriarchy and the current one indicate attenuating temporal contingencies, which do not allow them to be confronted, but provide a primordial reflection on both of them. In this respect, the consideration of comparison can result in a provocation to the incomparable. The singularity of each place and time, with its particular characteristics, should be noted, but it points to something broader and of beneficial use to this study. The search for similarities with the past may be intrinsic to the observation of the present. With this, the comparison would not be to compose general thoughts, but to understand and become aware of human cultural varieties and thought mechanisms. All this explanation turns to elucidate how much the comparison is still controversial and that this can be an obstacle in elucidating the past. The comparison of the past with the present is nothing more than the composition of a history or archaeology of the present.

The similarities between the patriarchy of different times show that it operates institutionally and discursively. It shows its variations over time and space, but with almost timeless characteristics. For example, it can be understood as a phenomenon that favours men's access to deliberative institutions. Institutionally, patriarchy acts discursively and symbolically, through narratives that legitimise power structures. In Ancient Rome, this becomes evident through narratives such as that of Livy, who presents stories that were part of Roman social memory, such as those of Lucretia and Verginia, which tell about the formation of Roman institutions during the period of the Republic (Azevedo, 2023, p. 127).

In relation to women's studies, classicists have engaged with issues of gender and sexuality since the late 1960s. Many have successfully incorporated postmodern, feminist, and psychoanalytic theories, even contributing to the field of *queer* theory, which started to be developed during the 1990s (Bahrani, 2005, p. 9).

The "first academic feminist wave" emerged from the feminist political movements of the 1960s and was concerned with combating androcentric bias and with locating and documenting women in sources. The interest was in a feminist revisionism, achieved by reading accounts in search of any information that could be obtained about women's lives, using legal texts and economic documents, which were re-read to define women's social position. From this perspective, the identification of women's contributions for history has become an important goal (Bahrani, 2005, p. 14).

In this way, classicists have been developing the issue of gender and sexuality since the late 1960s, with queer theory in the same field since the early 1990s (Bahrani, 2005, p. 9). In 1993, Skinner mentioned that gender studies in Antiquity were still very conservative, hierarchical, and patriarchal (Skinner, 1993) and that they used to rely on empiricist readings of textual sources, based on common sense. In this sense, Funari proposed that this type of approach should be avoided, since *"only a critical analysis allows us to understand 'masculine' and 'feminine' as social constructions that vary in terms of social class, gender and ethnicity, in different historical periods and in different societies"* (Morgan, 1993, p. 194; Funari, 1995, p. 179-180 apud Bélo, 2018, p. 37). Currently, these studies have undergone a great increase since the 2010s, which is allowing these themes to develop and update, bringing other perspectives and new criticisms.

In the Classical world, the starting point for women's studies began in 1965, when Finley published a paper entitled *"The Silent Women of Ancient Rome"*, arguing that the sources for women's studies were scarce and therefore a faithful picture of them could not be proposed. Consequently, the number of papers on the subject increased, with the aim of showing new ways of studying them, and conditions were developed to better interpret the sources. In this way, various types of expanded studies were able to encompass women: the study of the Roman family, which shows how was the man's relationship with his wife; the domestic services performed by her and the inclusion of Patronage, which eventually involved women in economic and social life; the study of women's professions, legal texts; and representations of women in art, literature and funerary inscriptions, which revealed personal relationships, especially of the mother with the father and with children. Sexuality and eroticism also encouraged scholars to look at the Roman world with a new point of view (Rawson, 2006, p. 324).

It can also be added that written sources, such as *The Law of the Twelve Tablets*, the oldest Roman codification, were able to give insights into Roman values, social relations, property principles and individual rights and duties. Several episodes from the history of Rome can be cited in the writings of authors such as Sallustius, who commented on Sempronia[3], a woman of the elite who became involved in Catilina's conspiracy to acquire power in AD 63. Cicero, with his letters, which dealt with women's activities in society, as well as speeches and legal commentaries, which have survived in the last compilation of the *Digest*; Catullus, with his poetry, which explored the world of sex, marriage and society; Lucretius, with his philosophy, which undertook the themes of human emotions; Aurelia Philematium and her husband, with the inscription of the year I; and the statues of individual women (Rawson, 2006, p. 325), which were and continue to be inspirations for the study of women in Antiquity (Bélo, 2018, p. 37-38).

Gender studies in archaeology had already been discussed since the mid- 1970s, but it was with Conkey and Spector's 1984 work, entitled *Archaeology and the study of gender*, that this type of research began to grow. Severe criticisms of androcentrism were presented, with emphasis on the search for women in archaeological records and their contribution to the past (Voss, 2008 apud Bélo, 2019, p. 30). In 1991, there was also the publication of the work by Gero and Conkey, entitled *Engendering Archaeology: women and prehistory*, which was influenced by feminist contributions from Anthropology (Meskell, 1999). According to Wylie (1991), gender archaeology is divided into three parts: the first criticises androcentrism; the second looks for women, calling it "the discovery of women", not only prehistoric women, but also archaeologists, who have been erased from our history;

---

[3] Sempronia appears to have been married to D. Junius Brutus and was the mother or stepmother of D. Junius Brutus Albinus, one of Caesar's assassins. Syme (1964) suggests that she was the daughter of a Sempronius Tuditanus, making her the aunt of Fulvia, wife of Clodius, Curius and Mark Antony, but this is just a hypothesis (Syme, 1964, p. 133-135; Hemelrijk, 1999, p. 277).

and the third, finally, makes a fundamental review of concepts (Meskell, 1999; Bélo, 2014, p. 28 apud Bélo, 2018, p. 35).

The "second academic feminist wave", generally considered to begin in the late 1970s, showed interest in issues beyond revising the silence on women in the historical record, to consider broader issues of gender construction. The second phase notably criticised the first, for not recognising gender subordination, and was a period of finding women in sources to point to their oppressed status and form alternative methods of defining gender relations in society. This was a time marked by feminists making explicit the difference between re-establishing women as agents of history and making gender a central category of analysis. The notion of gender or gender roles was taken as socially constructed identities imposed on biological sex, an essential identity located in the natural body. In this way, sex would have an ontological status, while gender would be variable. This movement sought to find a cause for the subordinate status of the female gender (Bahrani, 2005, p. 15).

Following the third feminist wave[4], marked by the year 1980, gender studies linked to age, sexual orientation and ethnicity began, given that gender identity should have been conceived as something complex, classified by a network of meanings, varying from individual to individual over time, joining other networks of symbolic practices located in the concepts of class and race. It was thus defined that female exploitation varies according to the social class, race, and ethnic division in which a woman is inserted (Meskell, 1999; Bélo, 2014, p. 29 apud Bélo, 2018, p. 36).

The "third wave of academic feminism" began in the mid-1980s, according to most estimates. This movement sought a broader framework for thinking about the complex processes already pointed out by some second-wave feminists. In the separation done of home and work, family and marriage, among other aspects, were analysed as the domain of women. However, this was not enough to understand the complexity of gender relations, which also perpetuated the binary structure of male/female hierarchies. Feminists therefore began to problematise these structures in power relations. Concepts such as oppression, patriarchy, sexuality, and identity, used by white middle-class feminists, were increasingly challenged by a new feminist association with cultural theory and postmodernism,

---

[4] To learn more about feminist waves, read: CUDD, A. E.; ANDREASEN, R. O. **Feminist Theory**. Oxford: Blackell Publishing, 2005.

especially post-structuralism (Brooks, 1997, p. 29-68; Barrett, 1992, p. 201 apud Bahrani, 2005, p. 18-19).

During the 1980s and early 1990s, there was a growing body of research on family in Antiquity, such as the works of Suzanne Dixon, *The Roman Mother,* 1988, and *The Roman Family,* 1992; Susan Treggiari (1991), who also contributed to *Roman Marriage,* which studied the institution of marriage throughout Roman history; Keith Bradley (1991), who contributed with the work *Discovering the Roman Family,* pointing out legal and social relevance in relation to family; and, demonstrating a political aspect of women, Richard Bauman (1992) proved that they were not passive, in the work *Women and politics in Ancient Rome* (Moore, 2017, p. 3).

Studies on the image of Roman imperial women appeared timidly, as it was a new subject in 1962, through the work of Balsdon. The feminist and revolutionary look came with the work *Goddesses, whores, wives and slaves,* by Pomeroy, published in 1975. In 1980, even with all the turmoil of the feminist movement, a large *corpus* of imperial portraits was assembled, called *Das römische Herrscherbild,* in which the emperors had a long section, and their women were exemplified only at the end. Roman women began to stand out in academic works when Fittschen and Zanker published in 1983 a catalogue on portraits of the people of Rome in the Capitonile Museums of Rome, and the volume on women was the first to be published.

The year 1996 was a remarkable one, as Barrett published a biography of Agrippina Minor; Rose (1997) promulgated a study of imperial family groups, not failing to emphasise the importance of women for dynastic transmission; and Winkes (1995) produced a monograph on Livia, Octavia Minor and Julia. It is essential to mention that there was a work on imperial and common women in Rome called *I Claudia: Women in Ancient Rome,* edited by Diana Kleiner and Susan Matheson (1996), which portrayed the image of these women in material culture, including them on coins, and other themes, such as Patronage and gendered domestic spaces (Wood, 1999, p. 3-4). Elizabeth Bartman (1999) produced a monograph called *Portraits of Livia,* which comprised a catalogue of images associated with the Roman empress.

In the next decade, studies such as *Imperial women,* by Susan Wood's (2000) appeared, which has great extent and richness of material culture from the Julio- Claudian dynasty (Moore, 2017, p. 3). Barrett (2002) published his *Livia: first lady of Imperial Rome* and Elaine Fantham (2006) launched

Julia Augusti. These dealt with historical sources and material culture. In addition, Cleopatra eventually received the same treatments in Duane Roller's (2010) work *Cleopatra: a biography*; Treggiari's (2007) work *Terentia, Tullia, and Publilia* analysed textual evidence, placing such women in a broader context of their contemporaneity; and Josiah Osgood's (2014) *Turia* reveals a similar analysis of a woman whose name has been lost in history (Moore, 2017, p. 3-4).

Within this historical-bibliographical context of ancient women's studies, there is a valorisation of English-speaking authors. Most of the works have been published by publishers that overlap with world publications, creating a shadow that obfuscates small or foreign publishers, which also have exemplary works in the field of ancient women's studies. This fact emphasises the idea that there are other non-English language works that are not being discussed. When they are, there is an academic effort from the "centre" to devalue these authors.

However, within the global framework, women's research has always been reluctant to be accepted, as Eleonor Scott demonstrated in 1995. The scholar indicated that women's studies were still being suppressed by academia. Firstly, by their very exclusion, women are completely ignored due to the narratives of the Roman world, which were concentrated in activities where men were dominant, such as politics in Rome and the provinces. Secondly, the author claims that there is a pseudo-inclusion, that is when women are included, they only appear when they are anomalous to male norms. Thirdly, inclusion occurs through alienation, when women are only considered in relation to men or when they threaten the male view of their "correct" behaviour (Scott, 1995, p. 176-179). The difficulty arises from the Roman sources themselves, which were used to build hierarchies on an idealised discourse rather than providing a true narrative showing the lives of children, women, or slaves. Like material culture, these sources are part of the meanings by which the Romans defined their "minorities" (Revell, 2016, p. 2-3).

In Eleonor Scott's view, the difficulty would be more restricted to a theoretical-methodological context than to a researcher's challenge to be recognised for her work. However, the biggest current problem is not being able to continue the research. In addition to the difficulties of the research itself, the female researchers reach a limit point in their academic development, which prevents them from continuing to develop their work, given that university professorships are mostly awarded to men. Even though the number of publications of women's research is higher than that of male researchers, they are little read and cited.

Narro, in 2014, had already collected some statistics regarding women as professors/researchers in Brazil. These data revealed that, in positions considered to have greater purchasing power and social prestige in the area of being professors and researchers, only 14 per cent of full professorships in universities in Latin America, Portugal and Spain are filled by women (Narro, 2014). Such results refer to the thought that men have greater power to manipulate particular sets of variables and operate more successfully (Freitas; Morais, 2019, p. 112). In this sense, the statistical and qualitative results, even within university groups, usually led by men, in which people should be aware of social and gender discrepancies, demonstrate that discourses on social diversity work as a camouflage, so that behavioural patterns linked to gender assumptions are still common. This fact contributes to the maintenance of male dominance, through the division of gender roles, in addition to continuing the symbolic oppression of intellectual women.

Considering a global context, there is a restriction on the acceptance of works by female researchers who are not native English speakers, but who can write in English, because the works that gain global repercussion are still restricted to the "centre", which mainly conglomerates authors native from the United States of America and England. This "centre" was formed within a colonial vision, but today it wants to soften the colonising past with demagogic speeches, to mitigate such surviving ideals that still in the minds of intellectuals from these countries, which perpetuates the assumptions of gender, race, and ethnicity.

However, this situation can be shaken by technology or contribute to the fact that some assumptions still exist within online events, such as the non-acceptance of works that are not by women from the "centre", evidencing the fear of disseminating works by non-Anglo-Saxon authors. The ease of repercussion and propagation has resulted in the fourth feminist wave, marked as beginning in 2010 and ongoing at the time of writing this paper. This movement has brought about a new agenda of young women, who are seeking to point out, speak out and challenge global injustices towards women in general, for even though there are multiple feminisms, they all strive for gender equality. This latest wave is mainly evidenced by activism through the internet, which has been accentuated in recent times due to the difficulties faced during the Covid-19 pandemic.

These young feminist women are professors, researchers, doctoral students, master's students, and undergraduates who are interweaving Women's History and participating in virtual events to publicise their works. These events include national and international congresses, lectures and symposia that are bringing together scholars from all over the world in a Google Meet room, for example; classes and other events that are available on YouTube through platforms such as StreamYard; in addition to podcasts, in which academic content is also being disseminated through interviews with researchers. Technology has also facilitated the translation of texts, by DeepL, an alternative for non-English language texts to be translated and read, demonstrating that there is no longer any excuse for not reading authors from outside the Anglo-Saxon world and quoting them.

All of these avenues of communication are facilitating the dissemination of work by researchers from different backgrounds on the subject of women and gender in Antiquity. Women's studies today are enabling a comparison of women's experience and new criticisms of past and present patriarchy. Thus, the proposal of this work is not disconnected from contemporaneity, considering that it is through the current point of view, through values, beliefs and behaviours experienced, in addition to the problematic on present women's issues, that this knowledge was sought, since this study had as its essential theme perspectives of independence and female leadership. That said, the reconstruction of the past is fundamentally located within the context of the present and the politics and social issues of the present impact on the reconstruction of past societies (Shanks; Tilley, 1992 apud Revell, 2016, p. 5).

Therefore, this work is relevant because it is characterised as a reflection of the perception of the reality of the present through an analytical approach to the improved conditions of women's studies of Antiquity. It is thus able to generate awareness and coherence of the present female reality as opposed to the existence of a past female variety and sameness.

What to expect from this work

Any ordinary person in imperial Rome would be familiar with the members of the emperor's family, even if they had never seen them in person. Walking around Rome, in a basilica or in a square, there would be statues, frescoes and plaques of deified imperial figures for the public to appreciate it. In addition, the images of these people circulated daily through a very common object: the coin[5]. It was a reflection of the reality of its time, with a side of the perception of power which reflected what the person did or was going to do (Tunner, 2007, p. 5), in addition to its value, since coin's captions explained the importance of the minted subject in the power structure, indicating its attributions. Above all, coins were not ephemeral, because they circulated even after the death of the emperor who had minted them and could continue circulating for more than a hundred years afterwards (Porto, 2018, p. 142).

Many of these familiar faces were of women connected to the imperial family, for example: the emperor's mother, wife, daughters and even his sisters. The consideration of being able to remember someone for eternity marked the esteem of memory for that society, as well as being a marker of family status. The memory of Roman characters was linked to the cult of ancestors in Rome and was a strong element of religiosity that manifested itself in many ways, such as in funeral processions, in portrait exhibitions in the courtyards of senatorial residences, etc. Monetary iconography was another way to show family power and status in society (Florenzano, 2015, p. 16). Roman women were always remembered as appropriate examples of wives. Their figure on coins, for example, expressed that they supported imperial prosperity, marital virtue, security, loyalty, and other characteristics.

Rome, especially with Augustus, was regulated by the visibility of imposing people, but this visualisation did not fail to stigmatise and define the notion of gender in that society, which leads to questioning the purposes and conditions under which these Roman women appeared in public and in their various representations. The agency of power over the sampling of governmental force may have defined female performance, or female agency itself deliberated them in the public sphere, since the emperor was the one who appropriated the public space, in addition to having control over it and maintaining limitations on public expressions, with the idea

---

[5] Coins from 49 BC to AD 14 have been collected in two reference works. Republican coins from before the battle of Actium, 31 BC can be found in Crawford's work, *Roman Republican Coinage* (RRC). Coins from after AD 31 can be found in the first volume *The Roman Imperial Coinage* and the second edition (RIC 1²). The coins of the provincial cities, from after 44 BC, have been catalogued in the *Roman Provincial Coinage series* (RPC 1). RRC organises the coins chronologically, with each group of coins called a series (e.g., 344), followed by another number, which refers to an individual coin within the series (e.g., RRC 344/1, 344/2). RIC separates coins by emperors and mints, with each coin type signed by a different number (e.g., RIC 1² 56). RPC is organised by geographical regions, mint and chronologically, with each coin type signed by a unique number (e.g., RPC 1 456). The dates signalled by Crawford in RRC are based on the combination of data coming from metrology (weight and denominational system). It should be noted that the coins do not have a precise indication of their dates and the years given by Crawford are suggestions that have been well accepted nowadays (Rowan, 2019, p. 20).

that no one should be more visible than himself. However, it must be taken to account the fact that imperial women took on activities within the Patronage that were essential to maintaining the image of the imperial family and that, consequently, gave them greater visibility, freedom of expression and presence, which may even have led to tensions. These could have resulted in a different view of women's performance, which may have led to changes in standards that were no longer appropriate in the face of new female performances.

Thus, the purpose of this work was to carry out a study on the public force of Roman women who composed the social elite, within the period of the Late Republic and Early Empire (84 BC - AD 59), through the analysis of the monetary images of Fulvia, Octavia, Livia, Agrippina Major and Agrippina Minor, together with information from textual sources. The minting of coins with their portraits makes up a formidable working tool today, since it brings information about these characters, which are not in written documents. Howgego believes that the coin is the most deliberate of all symbols within a public identity, in that identity is not eternal, but something actively constructed and contested, within a particular historical context, and based on a subjective rather than an objective criterion. Moreover, for everything that is contingently constructed, identity is a powerful guide to action. Coins demonstrate a huge range of self-definition and explicit representations of public, official, communal and, above all, civic identity. Material culture allows to avoid costly problems associated with externally defined, implicit and private identities. In addition, questions can be asked about public identity, resistance, self-definition, and promotion (Howgego, 2005, p. 1), such as propaganda.

Material culture is not value-free, but provides symbolic meaning for specific contexts (Hodder, 1986 apud Shanks; Tilley, 1992). These meanings are formed according to the social construction that exists between relationships, which influences how people in the past maintain their positions of power within a society.

Specifically, coins feature their own combination of image and text, unusual for other media categories. The monetary captions often name the issuing authority, a ruler's name or another person of importance to power. Consequently, this materiality has an advantage over vases and sculptures in terms of documentary contextualisation. Coins turn out to be better dated than any other category of artefacts. They often circulated for a long time, which multiplied the potential for viewers (Callataÿ, 2022, p. 249 and 252).

The coins combine images, texts, and materiality. They were produced by authorities who ensured their value. They demonstrate aspects of the representations of the group that produces them, communication and economic decisions made. However, they are everyday objects and were found in the Ancient world in treasuries, settlement excavations and religious sites. Coins are both historical documents and archaeological objects and have the ability to link social structures and individual agency (Kemmers, 2019, p. 3).

Regarding the most common captions, on the obverse the names and titles of the emperors were written in the nominative or dative (after S P Q R, from the Senate and the people of Rome to the Emperor); and on the reverse, a god or goddess commonly appears, often anonymous or with their names also in the nominative, basically with AUG, meaning AVGVSTA or AVGUSTI. This type of caption appears repetitively (Williams, 2007b, p. 60-61), but can occur in other types as well.

The coin brings in its small space the opportunity to legitimise a power, since by itself this object can be considered a public place of governmental expression, multiplied by its own capacity and function to spread and disseminate a discourse, which gains strength by having great repercussions. This can also be limited, depending on the governmental power, the territory and the acceptance of the symbols that this material culture carries. Consequently, the coin legitimises the power of the one who mints it and carries it, spreading its meaning as far as the limit of where the object is used. The currency has an agency that is built from who chooses the elements and symbols that will be minted on it to its manufacture and the realisation of its existence, as well as the communication, not only of the economic value[6], but also of the symbolic understanding, which must be understood by those who made it and those who received it.

The symbolism surrounding the images and texts on coins can refer to an understanding within social relations and the ideals, standards and values involved. In this way, coins could be used to spread an ideology. By disseminating various types of messages and various ideological types, the coin reached different audiences (Manders, 2008, p. 10-11). However, the elements on a coin had to be chosen for a purpose and should not be trivial symbols.

According to Rowan, the coin was a mode of self-exhibition and communication, used alongside texts, buildings, and other monuments to

---

[6] For currency values and nomenclatures, see Appendix 1.

justify positions and consolidate power within an aristocratic context of competition. However, more than monuments such as those of the forum or the Arc de Triomphe, the coin was a mobile monument, promoting a wider audience and one that was not just designed for the elite. This object was a source that could attest to political alliances and ideologies (Rowan, 2019, p. 23). That said, the representations of power on the coins had the purpose of legitimisation, information and glorification, which were often associated with religiosity, such as the fact that some emperors identified themselves with some deity and used it for self-glorification (Manders, 2008, p. 32), in addition to the fact that the divine could be something that everyone recognised and understood.

To add, coins go beyond exchange value. In the Roman world, this object was like a "monument in miniature". Taking into account what he wanted to communicate. It was also a means of identity formation, as well as a material culture that could have been present in diverse activities, such as religious, present in cults and social life (Rowan, 2019, p. 4).

In order to delve deeper into the issues of the communication elements of the coins, iconography becomes the most compelling means to be followed. Such iconographic elements were probably chosen for the self-legitimisation of an elite. In this sense, symbols have more meaning for those who forged them than for those who passively accepted them. Even with a small scope of monetary circulation, iconography was important to represent the collective political identity of the elite (Barker, 2020, p. 17). However, for monetary analysis, consideration was given to where, when and by whom the coins were minted (Callataÿ, 2022, p. 253).

Jones (1956, p. 14-15), like Michael Crawford and Ted Buttrey, believed that coins were financial rather than political instruments, but in 1980 things began to change. Paul Zanker and Niels Hannestad systematically included the visual part of coins in their studies, composing them together with Roman art, and were not afraid to use the word "propaganda" to explain imperial communication intentions and purposes (Zanker, 1987; Hannestad, 1986). Tonio Hölscher, in a more theoretical work, emphasised that the language of the images of the Roman Empire formed a coherent semantic system, which allowed their repetition in the media (Hölscher, 1987).

Andrew Wallace-Hadrill has pointed out that in the period of transition to Augustus' rule, the appearance of the portrait on the obverse combined the image of victory, triumph, and abundance for the legitimisation of the coin itself, as it was something of the State and the legitimisation of the ruler (Wallace-Hadrill, 1986, p. 84-85). Reinhard Wolters was able to show that literary sources had an awareness and relevance of the images on coins more often than previously thought, evidencing that some coins were selected for ritualistic activities (Wolters, 1999, p. 308-340). These works opened the field for the increased study of coins as instruments of political communication (Kemmers, 2019, p. 16-17).

Andrew Meadows and Jonathan Williams promoted the notion of "monumentality" to understand the coin types of the late Republic. For them, "propaganda" would not be the best term to put on coins, as these objects did not persuade the population, but reminded people of a certain aspect or event. However, the authors never denied the "communication message" that coins presented (Meadows; Williams, 2001; Hekster, 2003, p. 3). According to Williams, Roman coins were monuments that brought to mind past events and characters during the Republic. Meanwhile, during the Empire, Romans commemorated the *fame, res gestae* and *virtutes* of the reigning emperor and his family (Williams, 2007b, p. 60).

The word *moeda* (coin) was tied to the ancient etymological origin of the Latin verb *moneo*, meaning "to warn" and "to caution", which could be understood as "to remind" or "to make think", and its infinitive would be *monere*. Otherwise, the word is also linked to the goddess Juno Moneta, with the epithet *Moneta* derived from the same verb (Glare, 2012, p. 1243-1234; Meadows; Williams, 2001, p. 27-49). However, another word linked to the verb *moneo* is *monumentum*, understood by Meadows and Williams (2001) as a Roman convention related to memory and monument. In this sense, coins would have the function of acting as a reviver of collective memory (Halbwachs, 1992; Assman; Czaplicka, 1995 apud Sales, 2022, p. 60-61).

As far as a monument is concerned, it would not just be a tomb, but anything that refers to memory, for "remembering" (*meminisse*) is like drawing from memory (*memoria*) which comes from the same root as *monere* ("to remember") and *monet* (those who remember). Things that are made to preserve memory are monuments (*monimenta*). In Latin, anything related to the memory of a person or event is a *monumentum*, such as a historical work, a poem, an inscription, a building, or a statue. These words are also related to *Moneta* and the Greek *Mnemosyne*, who is the divine personification of memory. That said, coins would be "monuments on a small scale". The competitiveness among members of the Greek aristocracy, in the 2nd century BC, would have favoured these characteristics for monetary coinage (Meadows; Williams, 2001, p. 27-49 apud Sales, 2022, p. 61).

The association of *coin* with Juno Moneta permeates both lexicons, bringing the temple of the goddess closer to the house of coins and the deity's relationship with *memoria* (Galinsky, 2014, p. 1). The goddess was related to the qualities of *concordia*, *libertas* and *pietas*, being also associated with memory and the ability to recall and remember. In the *Odyssey*, Livy Andronicus translated the name of the Greek goddess Μνημοσυνη into Latin as Moneta, where in Greek *Mnemosyne* was the goddess of memory (Meadows; Williams, 2001, p. 33). Thus, memory would be linked to the temple of Juno Moneta (Sales, 2022, p. 63-64).

Moreover, coin is part of a stratagem of power, since power is not an institution, a structure, and a universal law, but is the name given to a complex strategic situation in a given society. The effects of domination are dispositions of manoeuvres, tactics and techniques within a network of tense relations, which are always in activity, which shows that among the relations of power there are presuppositions of domination and repression present in civil society (Foucault, 2001 apud Filho; Vasconcelos, 2007, p. 11-12) and the coin is just an object that reflects this system.

Therefore, through iconography, this work is based on the elucidation that coins are skilful objects for the demonstration of power relations, considering Wolf's concept (1990), which emphasises that power must be hierarchical, involving dominance and subordination, and that it always causes resistance. Kent (1984) mentions that power is an access to control over other people or means. Yet, for Western's business or military society, power is tied to control and command and has been projected according to past cultures as the only kind of power. From this perspective, feminists have criticised the infiltrating male bias which results in hierarchical androcentric power (Spencer-Wood, 1999, p. 178-179). Feitosa notes that it is possible to have a male-dominated stance and obscure oneself in terms of the perception of different powers, defining gender relations as relations of power or prestige, which also complement each other (Feitosa, 2005). The connection with power can be seen as a phenomenon of institutional reflexivity in constant movement. In this way, it is considered to be institutional because it is the basic structural element of social activity; and it is reflexive in the way that it is introduced to describe social life, which can be transformed - not in a mechanical way, nor in a controlled way, but as part of configurations of actions employed by individuals or groups (Giddens, 1992, p. 39).

As women's representations on coins, in general, had to initially pass through the approval of the emperor, the Senate and the local provincial elites, relying on their limits of expressions, this work will demonstrate how the opportunity for visibility of these women was often developed as a tool for a male gender discourse. Furthermore, it indicates, through material culture, how the female gender was characterised, tested, defined, flaunted, and dominated through circumstances that could favour the maintenance of a power relationship, and consequently a gender relationship, between the emperors and their women. It should be borne in mind that the images do not reflect the truth of everyday life, but an idealisation, which does not fail to consider gender relations and their influence on power structures. However, by analysing coins with female figures, attitudes about gender control and power can be calculated. Another factor to think about is how the minting of these images of women on coins could be important for government success.

Regarding numismatic analysis, this work does not follow the traditional precepts, which would be linked to economic aspects such as monetary circulation, value, various types of transactions, payments of war soldiers, etc., but to what coins intend to communicate, which may include gender relations. The coin has been studied from the perspective of a commodity and an object of exchange. Social history has looked at the effects that monetary change has had on society, in terms of wages, the cost of living and collective behaviour in society. The scholar of coins has been concerned with the social and economic body that the coin served and the metal with which it was produced. Structurally, currency went beyond the geographical limits of the power that issued it and ideologically defined a people and a civilisation to which this object belonged (Carlan, 2008 apud Sales, 2022, p. 60).

This caveat is made since ancient coins were monetary instruments and served to an economic function. However, they were also providers of identity and/or political communication (Elkins, 2019, p. 105). Roman imperial coins communicated messages that were visualised, but the authority, purpose, and reason for minting coins with certain images on them have always been studied. However, numismatic studies may overemphasise coinage as a means of political communication because people were not supposed to pay much attention to such elements (Elkins, 2017, p. 4).

However, the government should have had a reason for coining certain elements that could show the cultural dynamics of Roman society, such as gender strategies. It is questioned, then, how Roman women were presented to the public, counting that their images were constructed to refer appropriate messages to the public consumption according to the interests of the State, given that the emperor had considerable control over the coinage, and he was not obligated to include his women in his coins. Thus, when analysing a coin, it was considered that it has two sides and that these sides interact with each other (Callataÿ, 2022, p. 248).

However, more than the Roman people, the elite should understand the imagery meanings. Indeed, the people and even those from the provinces were expected to despise images of elements that were not of their world. Elkins mentions that coins offered internal evidence that suggested outsiders understood them. Many coins were chosen to be minted as elements of the plebs, such as bronze imperial coins and as *quadrans* that first circulated in Rome. However, typically in imperial coin images, the elements drawn belonged to a common vocabulary to various artistic forms, suggesting that the symbols, gestures, and figures were understood by a foreign audience. That said, Roman coinage was one of the most important communicative media of the Roman Empire, compared to monuments and relief sculptures, reinforcing political rhetoric (Elkins, 2017, p. 4-6).

The iconography of coins and their captions could indicate messages to a specific audience not only of the Senate, but also of the people. All coins show that they are embedded with political messages that could affect certain types of social groups, such as the female figures with branches of grains, which apparently point to a female role model of the elite, as well as demonstrating fertility, productivity, prosperity and, most importantly, food distribution. This suggests that coins carried images and texts that supported ideological messages, indicating that communication was an important function for Rome.

From this perspective, coins offer a remarkable mirror of constructed identities. They show how the issuing powers wished to be seen and perceived. Moreover, they appear as deliberate witnesses of their time and are much more reliable than later literary and partisan sources (Callataÿ, 2022, p. 244-245).

However, depending on the female figure that was chosen to be visible in this kind of material culture, the ruler was able to present the virtues of his family and his descendants, as well as make a good propaganda of his government, starting with Augustus, who was copied by later Roman emperors. Nevertheless, there were those like Tiberius who restricted the honours paid to his mother, Livia. In this way, the material culture constituted by coins can be fundamental to prove the status and authority over the female figure, evidencing an ideological and legal aspect of the ruler and the women around him. In this regard, it can be observed that the messages on the coins conveyed a combination of words and images. Generally, these are imperial figures and of people linked to the emperor or of the elite associated with the ruler which presupposes a hierarchical structure. This must be analysed through the details, because coins and their tributes, especially the titles, will be fundamental for future generations, as it was the title of *Augusta* (Brubaker; Tobler, 2000, p. 573-575), which was given from the emperor to women such as Livia and Agrippina Minor.

Coins opened the doors for the emperor's propaganda, counting that its two sides were useful and served as suitable ammunition for this kind of communication. The obverse bears the most prominent figure, while the reverse, a secondary figure, mythological or other images, which the ruler could use to boast his power. Regarding women on coins, many appear alongside the emperor or alone, but with captions indicating them, with the criterion of being used as support for the government in a political context invoking female domestic virtues. Generally, the women chosen have important positions at the emperor's side, such as his mother, sister or wife, but there are also exceptions to this model.

During the rule of Augustus and Tiberius, there were official mints in Rome and Lugdunum, but many provincial cities continued to strike coins independently, which caused them to produce a large amount of coins with images of the emperor's family, which did not fail to spread an imperial ideology. Another fact is that most of the coins minted in Rome were with images of the emperor himself and those with imperial women ended up being minted in the provinces (Harvey, 2020, p. 107 and 121).

Coins minted in provincial towns carried both local and Roman references. The provinces often brought a new conception of the imperial family and the emperor. Livia and other members of the imperial family were more commonly depicted on provincial coins, and the emperor was usually associated with a local deity. Different regions had distinct images of Augustus, demonstrating that his public image should be seen as a collaborative process involving multiple authors (Rowan, 2019, p. 149).

However, in Augustus' time, gold and silver coins that were officially Roman continued to be struck in the provinces, with a decentralised coinage from the civil war period remaining. Burnett mentions that since Augustus had officialised his resignation from the consulship, he should no longer have constitutional power to control coinage in Rome. Yet, having minted precious coins in the provinces, Augustus could maintain direct control of the process through his proconsular power (Burnett, 1977). This explains why Gaul and Iberia might have been more convenient for paying soldiers (Rowan, 2019, p. 150).

The archaeological remains reveal that the circulation of official coins was common alongside older coins, imitations, and other types of coins. This suggests that the daily monetary experience was different from one city to another, and the impression given by the artificial division into RRC (*Roman Republic Coins*), RIC (*Roman Imperial Coins*) and RPC (*Roman Provincial Coins*), appearing that cities did not need to develop their local solutions (Rowan, 2019, p. 184).

In view of this, this work is based on an understanding that presents new assumptions, which are open to the study of the symbolic and especially to the study of society, individuals, power relations and gender, that considers social relations, being concerned with the historical and social context. In addition, it reflects the subjectivity and commitment of social groups (Funari, 2003), also demonstrating that the individual is part of the social changes and the material culture that surrounds him. It thus considers the dilemmas of present society based on the past, criticising social injustices and oppressions.

Specifically, the concern of the study will be on how the coins could demonstrate the power of the emperor through female images; how this power appears through the symbolic elements of the coin; how the women minted on coins were used to highlight the functions they had socially; how they could appear as mothers, daughters, wives, personified and with their virtues. The most interesting thing about these coins is to understand the representations and changes in government power.

Following this thought, it was necessary to clarify in chapter 1 what life was like in general for Roman women in the Late Republic and Early Empire. The explanation ranges from their involvement in religion and aspects of *pudicitia* to their family position, to being part of a system within a structural patriarchy, based on religious, historical, and legal discourse.

Before explaining the life and coins of Fulvia, Octavia, Livia, Agrippina Major, and Agrippina Minor, in chapter 2 it is demonstrated how the image of these women reached the public and how such materialities were important to compose a repertoire of these women's lives.

After such explanatory chapters, the work goes into each character. Thus, chapter 3 is dedicated to Fulvia's life, her coins and how coins iconography was related to her actions, facing the purpose of territorial expansion done by her husband, Mark Antony.

After a woman of attitude like Fulvia, the life and coins of Octavia, Octavian's sister, are presented in Chapter 4. The chapter involves all the obstacles Octavia had to make to support her brother when she was married to Mark Antony. Her iconography was only entered during the period of her marriage, showing her to have been a woman who was in the balance between two rivals and who had almost no autonomy. However, she was an example of the ideal Roman matron, as delineated by some ancient authors.

Chapter 5 emphasises how important Livia was for the public evidence of imperial women. This part of the work is based on the public issue of women, confirmed after Livia's agency. Her performance did not make her cease to be seen as an ideal matron, since her monetary iconography always related her to prosperity, fertility, dynastic success and to goddesses linked to these virtues.

Chapter 6 is devoted to Agrippina Major, a woman who spent her life preparing to be an empress, but whose destiny was deflected by Tiberius. Agrippina Major, like Fulvia, displayed the character of a military leader by acting in favour of the survival of Roman soldiers against Germanic groups. Her and her husband's deaths were honoured by the future emperor, Caligula, who arranged coins to be minted to celebrate the lives of his parents.

Chapter 7 explains the life and coins of Agrippina Minor. The title of the chapter is a metaphor to the life that Livia had, as if Agrippina wished to follow in her footsteps and become a woman of great power. Her life was outlined by some ancient authors as full of stratagems so that she would arrive, together with her son, at the most glorious point of power. Her monetary iconography brought back ancestral memories, such as that of her mother, Agrippina Major, and she was minted with the emperors who were around her too, such as both of her husband, Claudius, and her son, Nero. Like Livia, her coins also featured virtues related to prosperity, fertility, dynastic success, and goddesses who carried such symbolism.

The conclusion finishes the work with the aspects of the lives and monetary coinages of these women, and delves into a discussion of their place of action and how the public and private places are currently interpreted. Through this work, such a pattern of analysis, with various criticisms, was decoded in a more complex way, since the written sources delimit such divisions, but with so many exceptions that it is suggested that it should be seen with a broader look, and not divided in a binary way. And finally, the position of these women of the past is compared and contrasted with the position of women of nowadays.

Chapter 1

Roman women from the Late Republic to the Early Empire[7]

> "[...] in 1918 in London, interviewed in an oral history study by Joy Melville, recalls that her mother whispered to her every night when she went to sleep that she should not have sex before marriage, or she would go mad. She didn't question why single mothers were put in asylums; she just thought: 'Well, they deserved it; they had sex and went mad'".
> (Melville, 1991, p. 2 apud Giddens, 1992, p. 70)

The Mental Deficiency Act, sanctioned in 1913 in the United Kingdom, allowed local authorities to prosecute and imprison unmarried pregnant women who were poor, destitute, or just "immoral". It was believed that illegitimate pregnancy was in itself a sign of subnormality. Elite unmarried women who became pregnant could have illegal abortions, as the poor ones, but these last ones at greater risk. Consequently, this was the result of a society that was ignorant about sex and reproduction and assumed women to be abnormal by these standards (Giddens, 1992, p. 90). In the week of 20th June 2023, *Time Out London* published on its *Instagram* page that thousands of protesters marched through London in opposition to an 1861 law, which still criminalises abortion in the UK. Referring to this law, UK legislation puts:

> Every woman, being with child, who, with intent to procure her own miscarriage, shall unlawfully administer to herself any poison or other noxious thing, or shall unlawfully use any instrument or other means whatsoever with the like intent, and whosoever, with intent to procure the miscarriage of any woman, whether she be or not with child, shall unlawfully administer to her or cause to be taken by her any poison or other noxious thing, or shall unlawfully use any instrument or other means whatsoever with the like intent, shall be guilty

---

[7] For the purpose of this work, the studied period is from the date of Fulvia's birth (84 BC) to the death of Agrippina Minor (AD 59). However, coins of Livia minted in later governments are also discussed.

of felony, and being convicted thereof shall be liable... to be kept in penal servitude for life.

Whosoever shall unlawfully supply or procure any poison or other noxious thing, or any instrument or thing whatsoever, knowing that the same is intended to be unlawfully used or employed with intent to procure the miscarriage of any woman, whether she be or be not with child, shall be guilty of a misdemeanor, and being convicted thereof shall be liable... to be kept in penal servitude[8].

When thinking about the women of the Roman elite, the sources that refer to the home and the family are always taken into account, since the documents about them, both written and material, refer to this path. Thus, by giving importance to the feminine, in this time, society and social status, the male opposition is pondered, which recognised women as the "others", left to the plane of otherness and submissive in the face of social reality and in symbolic terms. Ancient Rome provided several examples of matrons, characterised as wives, mothers and procreators, and created feminine patterns that were part of the gender assumptions, which lasted in the Roman collective consciousness for centuries. Many of these feminine models would refer to pudor (*pudicitia*), which could have made them cover their bodies, act as modest, possess self-control, chastity, severity, firmness, in addition to spending their lives preparing to wait for a husband (Cid López, 2011, p. 55-56).

In general terms, *pudicitia* would be related to sexual virtue. Its adjective would be *pudicus* and other similar words in Latin would be: *castitas, sanctitas, abstinentia, continentia* and *verecundia, modestia* (Langlands, 2006, p. I). *Pudicitia* was also a deity related to modesty and charity, who appeared holding a sceptre and was commonly veiled (Sear, 2000, p. 40).

Pudicitia has always been linked to sexual behaviour, yet it was the only term related to pride in political philosophy. It was a virtue that empowered both men and women, but its expectation could mitigate the differences between them. It was a Roman concept, without a Greek equivalent, developed separately from traditional Greek philosophy, but related to the Greek concept of *sophrosyne* (self-control) and *aidos* (shame). *Pudicitia* governed individual sexuality and relationships with other people and society as a whole, which implied non-sexual behaviour. Sexual morality

---

[8] Available at: https://www.legislation.gov.uk/ukpga/Vict/24-25/100/crossheading/attempts-to-procure-abortion. Accessed: 2 July 2023.

promoted the opportunity to examine the public virtue of Rome's society and individual ethical development. *Pudicitia* is derived from the word *pudor*, but the former has a narrower field of meaning, which is associated more with sexual relations than with social relations. The relationship with *pudicitia* varied according to relationships with other people and according to the ownership of one's own body, just as the free individual had responsibility for his own body and a slave was a mere instrument of his master's needs. Most often, the term is translated as "chastity", but chastity would be more associated with a Christian root of sexual abstinence and repression of desire (Langlands, 2006, p. 2, 5, 19, 22 and 30).

In other contexts, *pudicitia* is translated as "a sense of decency" or "self- respect", emphasising aspects of the individual's morality, as if it were a social protocol for living in community. It can also appear as linked to modesty, purity, and sexual integrity. *Pudicitia* was something also associated with appearance, especially of married women. The commitment of a *univira* woman, who was a widow and had no other man, was also linked with *pudicitia*. Roman women were concerned with three things: beauty (*forma*), their conduct or morality (*mores*) and their reputation (*bona fama*) (Langlands, 2006, p. 31, 37, 46 and 67).

In view of this, one criterion that should be questioned is the use of gender assumptions or stereotypes as an academic facility, which are often used for a general image, so that the reader immediately understands the relationship of the character of women and the men to which they were linked. Generally, this criterion divided them into "good" and "bad". Thus, the good woman would be the ideal matron, of good character, with attributes of beauty, chastity, and loyalty, who wove, who was fertile, modest, generous, among other attributes. Meanwhile, men were to assert their masculinities through courage, *virtus* and other characteristics (McCullough, 2007, p. 78). The deity Virtus was related to valour and courage and was represented in armour, holding Victoria or parazonium[9] and a spear, or with a spear and a shield. It could appear with another male personification, such as Honos (Sear, 2000, p. 42).

Feminine virtue could be linked to *pudicitia*, which would place such a virtuous woman of the Roman elite as the one who should refuse sexual temptation, which would be supported by various institutional protections (Giddens, 1992, p. 16), such as tutelage, family, and religion.

---

[9] Type of dagger. Available at: http://www.perseus.tufts.edu/hopper/text?doc=Perseus%3Atext%3A1999.04.0059%3Aentry%3Dparazonium. Accessed: 23 May 2022.

Consequently, by taking this position, the Roman woman was placing herself in relation to others in society, with inter-relationships with other individuals - intersubjectivities - that would also determine the positions assumed. The agencies and choices of women in the Roman elite were related to issues of institutional power in dominant discourses, with many benefits to be gained from building themselves as a particular type of person, interacting with other people in a specific way. It is added that investment was a matter not only of emotional satisfaction, but also of real material, social and economic benefits, which were attributed to the respectable man, the good wife, the powerful mother, or the well-behaved daughter (Moore, 2000, p. 37).

Dominant discourses and the different individuals' positions that these discourses confer on women and men assign to them strategies that they must trace (Moore, 2000, p. 40). In societies such as the Roman, dominant gender discourses constructed categories such as "woman" and "man" as exclusive and hierarchically related, creating a highly sexualised violence that is inseparable from the notion of gender, linked directly to gender difference, and can be a mode of maintaining certain fantasies of identity and power (Moore, 2000, p. 43-44).

However, it should be noted that gender assumptions arise in different cultural and historical contexts, establishing standards for the role of men and women and being constituted through educational and familiar ways. Gender patterns, therefore, are social constructions that occur in different cultures and historical moments (Mead, 1969; Whitaker, 1995; Nolasco, 1993; Maia, 2005; Reis; Maia, 2009, p. 137). They are linked to society itself, which shares the same thinking, within the same culture, and reinforces them through education (Pereira, 2002, p. 52; Reis; Maia, 2009, p. 137).

Gender assumptions are a set of beliefs fixed according to the behaviour and sexual characteristics acquired in the process of socialisation with the family, education and other means that transmit values and convictions (Zenhas, 2007; Reis; Maia, 2009, p. 138). Consequently, society ends up reinforcing the sexist process, establishing "natural" conceptions, in which the family, religion, the education and the media determine actions, concepts and establish absolute truths, which reproduce these assumptions (Souza, 2006; Reis; Maia, 2009, p. 138).

This is because the act of communication depends on a common or ideological discourse about what is expected of members of a certain identity.

These activities are performed under a repetitive basis and become part of repeated routines. Normative actions and roles are reinforced through the consent of other members of society, in general, for the individual to be accepted into the social group. The approval of others becomes one of the ways in which activities are constructed. Routines are enacted under and through repetitive bases, by which the group internalises various aspects of its identity. Even the smallest of actions performed, done without thinking, are somehow products of social norms and within these aspects there are identifying elements of identity (Revell, 2016, p. 11).

Following this thought, Roman literary texts tended to convey the image that their women were passive, subordinate and in need of protection. However, if they performed other behaviours, they were described as dangerous, adulterous and in need of male control (Dieleman, 1998; Matić, 2021a; Orriols-Llonch, 2007 apud Matić, 2021b, p. 5).

One example was Cornelia[10], who lived in the second century BC. She was a model of a matron, who was married to Tiberius Sempronius and after the death of her husband she decided not to marry again (*univira*), spending her life worrying about the education of her sons, Tiberius and Gaius Gracchi. She was thus honoured with a bronze statue. Therefore, the women who were said to be respectable were those loving wives venerated by their husbands, those who sacrificed their lives for their

---

[10] Cornelia was the daughter of Publius Cornelius Scipio Africanus, conqueror of Hannibal and one of the most prosperous and powerful men of his time, knowledgeable in Greek culture; and her mother was Aemilia of the prosperous *Aemilii Paulli* family. She married Tiberius Sempronius Gracchus in about 175 BC and was a devoted mother of twelve children. Unlike other women of the Roman elite, who were confined to spinning, weaving and other domestic activities, she was educated and fluent in the Greek language. Her uncle, Lucius Aemilius Paullus Macedonicus, was the first Roman to bring an entire library from Greece to Rome, which he used to educate his children, but it seems that other relatives also took advantage of this collection. Cornelia also received instruction in Latin rhetoric and was noted for her excellent oratory and writing style, having her letters published and admired. Education was undergoing rapid changes in her time and the teaching of rhetoric had not yet been institutionalised, in other words, there was no Latin school. Future politicians learnt the art of public speaking during the *tirocinium fori*, which were rhetoric courses, in which women were excluded. Cornelia, as well as Sempronia, who could have been her daughter - who was part of Catilina's Conspiracy, but her role is not clear (Sall. *Cat.* 25 and 40.5) - were part of a small group of gifted women of the Roman elite during the Late Republic and Early Empire. It can be added that her role as a widow and intellectual was able to educate her sons, Tiberius and Gaius, without the intervention of any tutor and it was during this period that her intellectual qualities were outstanding. However, it seems that her sons had Greek tutors well chosen by her. However, in Roman society, female education was viewed with both admiration and criticism (Helmelrijk, 1999, p. 22, 61-62, 71 and 80). Cornelia probably married with *manus*, which was customary during the 2nd century BC, and remained under her husband's *potestas*. However, after his death, she became *sui iuris* and legally able to own and manage her property, but still needed the consent of a *tutor* for certain legal transactions, not to mention the repossession of her dowry. Also, as her sons died before her, she must also have inherited part of their fortunes. However, after this part of her life, she was able to control a great deal of wealth and have some independence (Helmelrijk, 1999, p. 96-97).

family, those who were sociable, urbane, educated and morally impeccable (Riess, 2012, p. 492).

Cornelia's sons turned out to be notable Roman politicians, but they were assassinated for trying to put measures in place that had no social or political consensus. According to Cid López, there is no doubt that there was an interest in Seneca to make a biography of Cornelia to serve as an example for the other aristocratic women. However, Cornelia also took an interest in politics to boost her sons' careers (Cid López, 2011, p. 60), which was not well regarded and led to her being characterised as a controversial figure who was also active in patronage (Hemelrijk, 1999, p. 61).

With this, it can be mentioned that Roman society ended up creating influential women, but who were linked to a religious discourse, and that their norms of conduct were led to the elaboration of regulations present in Roman law, which demonstrated that legal procedures exemplified the demand for male control over the female population. This led these institutions, both religious and legislative, to become tools that configured and legitimised a social organisation that gave male dominance power over the female population, configuring a patriarchal society. Male dominance is a particular form of symbolic violence. For the analysis of masculine dominance, bodies are considered in the way they are used and brains in the form of principles of perception of the bodies of others, which consequently leads to the circularity of relations of symbolic dominance. This makes it not easy to get rid of this symbolic dominance, which exists objectively in the form of objective divisions and mental structures that organise the perception of these objective divisions between man and woman, for example. When a world is realised as constructed through subjectivity and in accordance with objectivities, everything seems evident. For all of this to work, objectivities must be able to reproduce themselves in mentalities. In this sense, in order for this to be changed, it is necessary to transform the environment together with psychosomatic actions that tend to profoundly transform mentalities and corporealities (Bourdieu, 1996a, p. 30-31).

Following the same line of reasoning, it should be borne in mind that Roman society assigned to women maternal work combined with the functions of their bodies and ultimately their gender, which was formulated throughout history and by family, educational and religious discourses, since these discourses became essential to the social reality that portrayed them

(Giddens, 1992, p. 39). For this reason, gender should not be thought of as a simple cultural inscription of meanings about sex, which is considered as "given", but should be seen as the result of a production apparatus, developed by the discursive/cultural milieu, in which "natural" sex would also be produced and established as pre-discursive (Butler, 1990, p. 6-7 apud Piscitelli, 2002, p. 27). Therefore, it should be thought that conceptions of biological difference vary between and within cultures over time. For this reason, this type of study always deals with historically specific forms of masculinity or femininity, as well as with other notions of individuality and identity (Bahrani, 2005, p. 9).

Consequently, gender identity is constructed and lived (Moore, 2000, p. 15), since the relationship between the individual and the social must be considered, with individuals leading collective lives related to power and domination. However, identity is not entirely passive and acquired only through socialisation. Identities are diverse and forged by practical engagement in lived lives, but have both individual and collective dimensions. Social representations of gender can affect subjective constructions and social constructions. Individuals are born into cultures and become members of them by processes of learning and socialisation, but as units they exist prior to their contact with the social, being singular entities that require a cultural imprint. From this perspective, gender is ambiguous, as it is not fully defined by cultural categorisations and normative understandings. When gender identity is seen as an enigma or something that requires explanation, both from a subjective and a collective point of view, the inadequacy of the standard category (Moore, 2000, p. 21-22) for such an individual within society becomes obvious, once women with leadership attitudes, politicians and who went to war were described by ancient authors as inadequate or a model not to be followed, such as Fulvia, Cleopatra, Livia, Agrippina Major and Agrippina Minor.

The attitude of these women confirms that individuals are multiply constituted and can assume diverse character positions within a range of discourses and social practices. The large number of women connected to men of power or who were in the public spotlight who received criticism in literary texts is noticeable, as at different times most of them were made to represent a variety of positions and had to construct their social practices. Such practices could have been subversive, as they could contradict a competing set of discourses about what it was to be a "woman". As a result, women and men could have different understandings of themselves as gendered people, because they would have different positions in relation to discourses concerning gender and sexuality, resulting in different positions for them within these discourses (Moore, 2000, p. 23, 25 and 36).

Therefore, it can be mentioned that societies do not have a single model of gender, but a multiplicity of discourses on gender, which can vary both contextually and biographically (Moore, 2000, p. 24).

1.1. Roman structural patriarchy

Gender assumptions create major social problematisations. In the Roman case, they were present at the base of the formation of society, with structuring devices for the existence of a structural patriarchy, which were especially outlined on account of three bases: the discourse, which would involve the educational, familiar and, mainly, the religious discourse, which seems to have influenced both of the first ones; the historical one, considering the "myths of origin", once history was taken as experience; and, finally, the legal one, which was formed according to religious norms and as a consequence of historical events, which let it be understood that women should be protected in some way.

In this society, the matron was seen as a fruitful, prolific being who cared for her offspring and was faithful to her husband. However, there were exceptions, in addition to the fact that the matron was not the only example of a woman, insofar as, as a whole, they should be much more complex than this set belonging only to the Roman elite, who were differently educated to exercise their role as wives and reproducers (Cid López, 2011, p. 56 and 58).

The purposes of female roles were disseminated through family, education, and other modes of communication, such as religion, which contributed to perpetuate these traditional models. However, religion was very effective in this role because deities legitimised social practices and the ideological propaganda of the state. Goddesses who emphasised procreation took on a special significance by idealising female functions (Cid López, 2011, p. 56). These discourses were tied to sexuality and gender, constructing women and men as different types of individuals, who differed in principles of agency, but men were portrayed as active, aggressive, imposing, and powerful and women as passive, weak, submissive, and receptive. Such discourses offer accurate descriptions of social practices and experiences that assign gender to men and women and define them as people based on difference, which is the result of the operation of discourse meaning, producing a gender categorisation (Moore, 2000, p. 16-17).

1.1.1. Religious discourse

The religious discourse was essential to Roman society since the divine sphere had to be in accord with the human one. The *pax deorum* and the *pax hominum* were at the centre of the understanding of Roman religion. Rituals and cults were central to the maintenance and success of Rome. When Rome had problems, they were dealt with by the religious sphere and the reintegration of the pax *deorum* and *pax hominum* was crucial. However, when a woman or a Vestal[11] behaved inappropriately, the Roman system could break down and the resolution would involve politico-religious action by the elite, the Senate, and the priests (Takács, 2008, p. 90).

Religion and law were apparatuses that produced "truths" that masked other realities, ready to sustain a discourse of this "truth" about such a society. From this perspective, the production of "truth" was articulated according to the religious-legal model. The juridical could serve to represent an essential power that did not function through the law itself, but through normalisation and control, going beyond the essence of the State and its apparatuses (Foucault, 1988, p. 55, 62, 63 and 85). However, women's rights travelled through the domestic or private sphere, while the masculine, within the public. This difference, obviously, implied a disparity, affecting all women, independently of social status (Cid López, 2011, p. 57).

According to this social model that discriminated women, which was spread and preserved by religious conceptions and practices, on the one hand, and by legal norms on the other, it is important to think about its scope and effectiveness for these Roman women. They were expected to assume what religion had idealised about the feminine and which was subsequently legitimised by the law. According to some characteristics, it can be mentioned that, among the women mentioned here, Fulvia would have the character most outside this ideal and, sometimes, Agrippina Major. In the history of Rome, there have been other women with similar characteristics, who have been identified as rebels for occupying public places, such as

---
[11] On the Vestal Virgins, see Appendix 2.

Livia, or who have usurped male spaces of power. With such behaviours, some characters still appeared as paradoxical images but many ancient writers, due to such acts, placed them as active in defending, supposedly, their rights as mothers and wives (Cid López, 2011, p. 57) to soften their behavioural transgression.

1.1.2. The historical discourse

> *"In a survey, women were asked what they were most afraid of. They answered that they were afraid of being raped and murdered. Men, on the other hand, answered that they were most afraid of being ridiculed, in other words, that people would laugh at them".*
> (Noble, 1992, p. 105-106 apud Kimmel, 2016, p. 115)

This work will attempt to clarify aspects of Roman women, especially those of the elite. However, such incursions seem to be distant and even non-existent from the perspective of the present day. Since 2011, the Brazilian Ministry of Health's Notifiable Diseases Information System (SINAN) has been recording the characteristics of victims and perpetrators of sexual violence. Of the 12,087 cases recorded that year, the majority of victims were female of all age groups, 81.2% of children; 93.6% of adolescents; and 97.5% of adults (IPEA, 2014a). In all age groups of victims, the aggressors were men in more than 90% of cases, characterising sexual violence as gender-based violence (Freitas; Morais, 2019, p. 113).

Going back to Antiquity, it can be observed that another factor that contributed to the formation of the patriarchal structural basis of this society was the historical one, which also included the "myths of origin", which demarcated events in the formation of Rome as if they were experiential data, proliferating in the Roman collective consciousness. As the "myth of origins" has their fictional side, these "stories" (because there is a doubt whether they are real) were essential to Roman history and society. They contained an underlying discourse to explain and perpetuate Rome and an ideal within morality, used to highlight behaviours that should be imitated or rejected (Takács, 2008, p. xx, 9). The information about rape events against women is highlighted in these origin myths, demonstrating that sexual and violent behaviours appear together, which may confirm a patriarchal culture by the high frequency of these acts.

1.1.2.1. The rape of Rhea Silvia

> *"People often ask what the classic Greek myths reveal about rape. Actually, they reveal very little. For one thing, myths about any given god or goddess are often contradictory and impossible to date; and for another, it is far too easy to retell a Greek myth to fit any interpretation one chooses. It does seem evident that up there on Olympus and down here on earth and in the sea and below, the male gods, Zeus, Poseidon, Apollo, Hades and Pan, raped with zest, trickery and frequency. Yet on the other hand, the goddesses and mortal women who were victim to these rapes, Hera, Io, Europa, Cassandra, Leda, rarely suffered serious consequences beyond getting pregnant and bearing a child, which served to move the story line forward. Hera, Zeus's sister, wife or consort, had a foolproof method of recovery. She would bathe yearly in a river to restore her virginity and be none the worse for wear. Aphrodite was a champion seducer in her own right".*
>
> (Brownmiller, 1975, p. 283)

The first such event considered here and the most important one to be commented on is the rape of Rhea Silvia, also known as Ilia (Takács, 2008, p. 7), which led to the birth of Romulus and Remus. Her uncle, Amulius, expelled his brother, Numitor, and killed his nephews for power, making his niece become a Vestal Virgin, under the pretext of trying to honour her by depriving her of all expectations in life. She was eventually raped and gave birth to twins. However, she said that her rapist was the god Mars. This must have been something she herself wanted to believe or the "fault" - as Livy puts it, with a dubious sense that this "fault" could have been hers or all rape was considered the woman's fault - might seem less heinous if a deity was the cause. Livy adds that neither gods nor men protected her and her babies from the king's cruelty, as she ended up in prison and the children were ordered to be thrown into the river (Livy, *History of Rome* 1.4).

When the uncle of the Vestal Virgin learnt of her pregnancy, Ilia could no longer perform her duties, because the sentence for her would be death, together with her children. According to an ancient law, a Vestal who had transgressed the customs had to be buried alive or thrown off the Tarpeian rock, located in the south-west of the Capitoline hill. Antho, her cousin, made an appeal on her behalf and the sentence was changed to solitary confinement (Takács, 2008, p. 7).

Arieti comments that if a god was responsible for the rape of the girl, the act would be ennobled or perhaps the density of the rape would be softened. The author's choice of the god Mars could also have had a special meaning since he was the god of war. On these occasions of rape, the guilt fell on the woman, but since it was with a god, her crime would be lighter, and the violence of the god would bring something that would give pride to the Romans or something that was great (Arieti, 2002, p. 210-211) to the history of Rome, as well as the origin of the most important city of the future empire. It can also be noticed the fact that religiosity is directly present in this episode.

The circumstance that it was a god or that sexual violence had a positive outcome, such as the origin of Rome, makes seemingly harmless cultural practices contribute to the maintenance of men and women in gender roles of domination and submission, respectively. It thus leads to an acceptance of violent and abusive practices, which contribute to the maintenance of sexual violence to varying degrees (Freitas; Morais, 2019, p. 119).

In Augustus' time, when this event was written, it was encouraging to remember the origins of the *princeps* himself: the *gens Iulia* was believed to be descended from Iulus, son of Aeneas, and Romulus. Julius Caesar believed he was descended from the two creator gods of Rome. Consequently, Augustus built a temple commemorating the origins and martial virtues of the people of Rome, the temple of Mars Ultor, near the forum of Augustus. The temple was promised by the emperor when he fought against Caesar's assassins in the city of Philippi. Inside the temple was a statue of the god Mars, Venus Genetrix and Julius Caesar. In addition, the Ara Pacis, which was an altar of peace, was built in the Campus Martius, an area with military significance, in 9 BC. In some panels or friezes of the altar, there are images with military connotations. However, in one of the panels there is the she-wolf breastfeeding Romulus and Remus, while Mars, their father, and Faustulus, the peasant who adopted them, are looking on. A demonstration of this scene on an altar of peace corroborates a principle of harmonisation. However, Mars and Romulus are associated with war. This reveals that Augustus certainly wanted his connection with Mars[12] and Venus, to have divine progenitors, since if he were descended from one god, he would be

---

[12] God of war was a popular deity in Rome. He appears with a spear and shield or with a trophy as an indication of success in battle. He is usually depicted naked, except for his helmet and cloak, or in armour. When given the title of PACIFER, he appears as an olive branch of peace. Other titles are also associated with him, such as: CONSERVATOR, PROPVGNATOR (the victor of Rome), VLTOR (the Avenger) and VICTOR (Sear, 2000, p. 31).

a hero, but since he was descended from two gods, he would be doubly a hero (Arieti, 2002, p. 225) or a god.

1.1.2.2. The abduction of Sabine women

The sequence of a tragedy resulting in something gained or positive for the Romans is repeated in the other rape events, as if a girl's virtue had to be sacrificed for the Romans to prosper. However, another rape story, also related to the origin of Rome, was the abduction of the Sabine women, an event that marked nothing more than the beginning of the formation of Rome, by a collective rape. This episode was mentioned by Cicero (Cic. *Rep.* 2.11-12), Virgil (Virg. *Aen.* 8.635-38), Titus Livius (Liv. 1.8-1.9) and Ovid (Ov. *Ars* 1.101-32).

According to Titus Livius, Romulus planned an increase in the number of inhabitants of the city (Livy, *History of Rome* 1.8), which was strong, but without prospects for growth, because it did not have a sufficient number of women to give birth to a new generation. With the advice of the Senate, Romulus sent emissaries to the neighbouring peoples to request alliances through marriage for the formation of a new people. However, the emissaries were rejected, as these groups feared for their descendants, due to the great power that was being formed. This attitude was seen as an insult by these representatives, and it was sure to end in violence. In response, Romulus arranged the *Consualia*, which was a festival of games to celebrate the harvest and invited the neighbouring groups to see the new city and join in the feast, among them the Sabines. When the show began and everyone was paying attention to it, the attacks began. Romulus' men caught and took the guests' wives to their homes. At the end of the games, the women's parents noticed and accused the Romans of violating their religion and honour. Romulus went to them and mentioned that it was their pride that was the cause of such an act, for not accepting to marry their daughters. Hersilia, Romulus' wife, insisted that he forgive the parents and welcome them in harmony, which was accepted by him, but not by the groups that suffered such disrespect, hence going to war. The last and greatest attack was that of the Sabines. Titus Livius accused the Sabines of having started the war and further said that, having lost the sense of their disgrace, they dared to intermingle in the war to separate the hostile forces. They expressed that sons-in-law and fathers-in-law could not be party to ungodly bloodshed nor pollute with parricide the suppliant children, grandchildren of one party and children of another. In a lengthy speech that brought the war to a halt, the Sabines clamoured that they were to blame, that it would be better for them to turn their anger against them and that it was preferable for them to die (Livy, *History of Rome* 1.9-13).

This episode marked the beginning of the formation of the city of Rome and was evidenced as an extraordinary women's tale, a type of rhetoric that was used when describing women who went out on the battlefield to avoid a war or when facing an enemy, as in the case of Agrippina Major. The abduction of the Sabine women portrayed an example of the peace making woman, recurrent in the history of Rome (Cid López, 2011, p. 60). However, it is important to emphasise that the rape of them ensured the population continuity of a new city and, later, an alliance with the Sabines. In this way, the act of violence may have been considered highly successful. Moreover, the act of peace that was concluded by the intervention of the Sabines mitigated the crime (Arieti, 2002, p. 209 and 212).

1.1.2.3. The rape of Lucretia

The rape of Lucretia was another controversial episode that eventually marked the end of the Monarchy and the expulsion of the Etruscan dynasty for the beginning of the Republic. The event of Lucretia took place during the 6th century BC, more precisely in 509 BC, during the reign of Tarquinius Superbus or the Arrogant, and enshrined the feminine ideal of chastity in honour of Roman women determined to die for their *pudicitia*. The event began when the very wealthy city of Ardea was invaded by the Roman king, intent on repairing his own depleted fortunes. However, his tyranny had already produced discontent. As the city of Ardea was under siege, and the troops were stationed, the men of higher rank could easily ask for permission to leave the place. The same men spent their time in entertainment, such as the wine feast given by Sextus Tarquinius, son of the king, at which Collatinus was present, when a conversation began about their wives and each started to speak of the virtues of their wives. Collatinus suggested that they go and find out how superior Lucretia, his wife, was to the others. So, they went to visit their wives to see how they were doing. They ended up in Rome and then went on to Collatia, Collatinus' town, where they met Lucretia. Unlike the king's daughters-in-law, who were in banquets and lust, she was found at her woollen work and welcomed her husband and companions, who invited them to stay (Livy, *History of Rome*, 1.57.1-1.57.9).

Sextus Tarquinius, the king's son, was immediately enamoured of Lucretia's beauty and purity. Then they returned to camp. However, after a few days Sextus Tarquinius returned to Collatia and was received with hospitality. After dinner, he went to Lucretia's room, told her to be silent and threatened her with a sword, saying that if she uttered a word she would die. Tarquinius spoke of his passion, begged her, threatened her, and said anything to sway a female heart, but he saw that she was adamant. Finally, he threatened her with death and reported that he would place her body next to a slave corpse and denounce her for adultery. With this terrible threat to her honour, he succeeded (Livy, *History of Rome*, 1.57.9-1.58.5).

Lucretia then called her father in Rome and her husband in Ardea. Surius Lucretius arrived with Publius Valerius and Collatinus arrived with Lucius Junius Brutus, so that she could tell them all about what had happened and ask them to promise her that the adulterer would not go unpunished. They all gave her their words. Titus Livius says that the husband was trying to shift the blame from the victim of the outrage to the perpetrator, which was dubious, since the perpetrator blamed the victim for the act. Lucretia went on to say that although she would rid herself of the sin, she would not rid herself of the penalty, that no impure woman would live henceforth and that she would beg for her example. At that moment she drew a knife from her dress and plunged it into her chest, falling dead. Brutus took the bloody knife and swore to drive out Lucius Tarquinius Soberbus, with his wife and children. All the noblemen followed him to abolish the Monarchy and gathered a mob, in which they obtained armed volunteers. The king's sons were expelled and two of them followed their father into exile among the Etruscans at Caere. Sextus Tarquinius was killed at Gabii, in revenge for old disputes, marking the end of the Tarquinians (Livy, *History of Rome*, 1.57-60).

This event is all based on the virtue of Roman women, from the symbolic meaning of Lucretia spinning. Such spinning instruments eventually became part of the marriage of the matrons, who would appear carrying the spindle and the wool. In addition, the rapist's challenge to destroy the girl's virtue stands out (Arieti, 2002, p. 213).

1.1.2.4. The attempt to rape Verginia

Rape was also a major factor in Verginia's history, which led to the dissolution of the Second Decemvirate, provoking political reform, and resulting in the reestablishment of the Republic (Arieti, 2002, p. 209; Takács, 2008, p. 14). This episode is attributed to the 5th century BC, which presents Verginia as the most defenceless of women of high social status, but with an "independent" character, such as Lucretia's. This event was told by Titus Livius; Dionysius of Halicarnassus, in Book IV, sections 64 - 85; and Cassius Dio. In order not to go through the social shame of the raped daughter and to free her, her father decided to take her life (Rawson, 2006, p. 326-327).

Titus Livius characterises this event as an atrocity and the result of brutal lust. The episode began when Appius Claudius (Livy, *History of Rome,* 3.44), an officer duly elected by the people (Arieti, 2002, p. 2016), fell in love with Verginia, who was of plebeian birth and the daughter of L. Verginius, who held a high rank in the army at Algidus. Her father was an exemplary man and his wife was brought up with equally high principles as his children. Verginius had promised his daughter's hand to L. Icilius, who had been a tribune and was active, energetic, and courageous. The young girl excited Appian's passions and he tried to buy her with gifts and promises. When he found that her virtue was proof against all temptations, he resorted to unscrupulous and brutal violence. Appian hired a client, M. Claudius, to claim the girl as his slave and to retain possession of her until the case was tried, since with the absence of her father, who was on army duty, he would have an opportunity for such illegal action (Livy, *History of Rome* 3.44.1-3.44.5).

As she was going to school, the pimp of the decemvir put his hand on her, declaring that she was the daughter of one of his slaves, so she would be a slave too. He forced her to follow him and threatened her if she hesitated. The girl's maid began to scream, and in consideration of her father and her fiancé, a crowd came to support the maiden. The man who took her said that he was proceeding according to the law and the case ended up in the court of Appius. The complainant rehearsed a story already familiar to the judge, as he was the author of the plot himself, which mentioned that the girl had been born in his house and had been stolen and taken to Verginio's house. The girl's defenders insisted that she wait for her father to return. The judge, Appius, decided that her father should be summoned and during that time the girl should stay with the man who claimed his right to take her, which was contested by the crowd. Her fiancé appeared to defend her, as he was determined to marry a chaste girl. Appius asked M. Claudius to waive his right to take her and allowed the girl to remain in the custody of his friends until the next day. On his arrival, Verginius went with his daughter and several matrons to the forum and there he appealed to the people to help him (Livy, *History of Rome* 3.45.4-3.47.1).

Appius made the court and the accuser began his brief protest, which was interrupted by Appius himself, who declared that the girl was a slave. Verginius cursed that it was to Icilius and not to Appius that he had promised his daughter. When the master went to take possession of his slave, the people retreated and Verginius, seeing no way out, turned to the court, asked Appius for his pardon for being a father, took the girl to the temple of Venus Cloacina and stuck a knife in her breast, telling her that it was the only way to get her freedom. He also dedicated Appian's head to the infernal gods. Appius immediately ordered Verginius' arrest (Livy, *History of Rome* 3.44-48.4).

What is most striking about this fact is that the sexual violence against Verginia was done through threats and that she was killed by her own father, in other words, it was not done by the rapist or by herself. Appius used tortuous means to misapply the law, using his power as a legislator to subvert legal principles (Arieti, 2002, p. 216).

1.1.2.5. Aspects of the origin myths and the Roman *stuprum*

> "A man may agree with friends who say that a woman was at fault for being raped in order to receive attention from others, or even to avoid aversive consequences of the response of disagreeing, such as receiving less attention in future conversation, not being asked to go out with these colleagues, or even being teased about his masculinity. In this regard, in an experiment, it was shown that men under the circumstance of having their masculinity threatened are more likely to say that the victim was at fault for being raped".
> (Munsch; Wiler, 2012 apud Freitas; Morais, 2019, p. 115)

In nowadays society, verbal behaviours are emitted and maintained, which make the ideas of discourses suffer a social reinforcement through men and women, in an attempt to follow a rule maintained through a negative effort and that would hardly receive a verbal stimulus of repression, for behaving in a certain way. In this perspective, many women end up agreeing with some aspects in relation to women victims of sexual violence, assuring the idea that, by taking due care, violence will not happen to them. In an analysis in Brazil [3810] (IPEA, 2014b), 58.5% of the people interviewed agreed that if women knew how to behave there would be fewer rapes; and 26% agreed that women who wear provocative clothes deserve to be attacked (Freitas, 2019, p. 115-116). It is essential to point out how much rape and other violence against women are still present in our daily lives, especially in the context of a pandemic. Social isolation, taken as a measure to prevent the contagion of the Covid-19 virus, has brought alarming indications about domestic violence committed against women, demonstrating that the home can be an unsafe environment for women trapped with their aggressors.

However, to understand these aspects in the Roman world, it is necessary to define *stuprum* in order to delimit the extent of such acts and the social imprint of such histories in that society. The verb would be *stuprare* (*constuprare*) and the agent noun *stuprator*. *Stuprum* itself could also have the meaning of fornication. The verb fornicate is intransitive and can have a feminine subject, while the verb *stuprare* is transitive and requires a masculine subject. *Stuprum,* thus, covers both fornication and sodomy. Within the meaning, the notion of penetration as an assault that harms the woman/boy/man penetrated is taken into account (Fantham, 2011, p. 118-119).

There are records of public and private punishments for the offence of *stuprum* from the earliest times of Rome, when the word originally had a much wider reference, denoting any public disgrace or infamous act, and was only secondarily applied to unsanctioned sexual intercourse. In the midthird century BC, *Naevius' Bellum Punicum* used *stuprum* to stigmatise the military disgrace of desertion or cowardice, but also to denote the shame of seduction upon the unmarried *Danae* in his tragedy. *Danae Naevius* used a euphemism parallel, *probrum* (reproach). Within a generation, however, *stuprum* was replacing *probrum* as the euphemism for unlawful intercourse and, after Plautus, it became so much the *vox propria* that it is no longer found with any other reference (Fantham, 2011, p. 117-118).

Most uses of the noun *stuprum* in republican authors treat it as a form of corruption or violation of the passive partner by the penetrator or (when the passive partner is accused of reproach) of self-corruption. Neither society nor the law recognised slaves as legal people: they belonged to their master, who could use them for his own sexual needs or rent them out for the pleasure of others. Similarly, in practice foreigners had no legal standing to do so, and even citizens, women or men, who once accepted gifts in exchange for sexual favours were considered removed from the protection of the law. Examples of rapes not involving relations with male or female citizens cannot be found, because the Romans would have seen nothing improper in such acts. The Roman law considered the young man or woman who was still in the father's house as not *sui iuris*, but as individuals under his consent, demonstrating that the concept of "sexual consent" was very different from today. Moreover, popular gender assumptions tolerated or admired the growing man's sexual initiatives but, at the same time, regarded shyness as a defensive virtue of the woman. Thus, unpremeditated rape, since it was rectified by subsequent marriage, gave more credit to men (Fantham, 2011, p. 118-119).

Stuprum is conceptualised by Mommsen as a category of injuries against women's modesty. Together with *adulterium*, the two terms indicate in ancient sources illicit sexual relations, which were subject to punishment, such as sex between a married woman and a man other than her husband or sexual intercourse without consent by one of the pairs - which would be a more current conception of the word "rape" (*stuprum per vim*). Thus, *stuprum* becomes something peculiar, encompassing adultery and other forms of illicit sexual relations (Azevedo, 2014, p. 117).

In the present days, the World Health Organisation (WHO, 2014), with information from 133 countries, reported that one in five women under the age of 18 had already been victims of sexual violence or rape. For the present, the WHO (2002) conceptualises rape as any type of penetration, either superficial, or physically forced, or by means of coercion, of the vulva or anus, or with the penis, or other part of the body, or object (WHO, 2002, p. 149). In the more specific case of Brazil, the concept of rape is defined by article 213 as being something linked to constraining someone by violence or serious threat to have carnal conjunction. "Carnal conjunction" is associated with vaginal penile penetration, while "other libidinous act" is a broad expression, making it possible, or not, to couple a greater diversity of acts than the WHO definition. Rape is understood when a sexual act is practised by touching the sexual organ of another person by means of any part of the perpetrator's body or object, with or without penetration, but without the consent of the victim. It is important to mention the concept within the Maria da Penha Law (Brazil, 2006):

> [...] any conduct that compels her to witness, maintain or participate in an unwanted sexual relationship, by means of intimidation, threat, coercion or use of force; that induces her to commercialise or use her sexuality in any way, that prevents her from using any contraceptive method or that forces her into marriage, pregnancy, abortion or prostitution, by means of coercion, blackmail, bribery or manipulation; or that limits or cancels the exercise of her sexual and reproductive rights (art. 7, subparagraph III; Freitas, 2019, p. 4).

The existence of sexual violence comprises several behaviours created by a set of contingencies, which encourage and/or are permissive in the face of violent and abusive sexual practices existing in a society. Such aspects frame what is now known as "rape culture" (Buchwald; Fletcher; Roth, 1995; Connel; Wilson, 1974 apud Freitas; Morais, 2019, p. 110). Briefly, the concept of "rape culture" involves a complex set of beliefs that facilitate male sexual aggression and violence against women; it includes sexual comments, sexual contact, and rape, as well as physical and psychological aggression. However, in a "rape culture", society assumes that sexual violence is something from everyday life and, hence, inevitable. Consequently, many things that is accepted as inevitable may be the expression of values and attitudes that could be changed (Buchwald; Fletcher; Roth, 1995, p. XI). As these practices and beliefs have been well entrenched in society, modifying them would require a cultural intervention (Freitas; Morais, 2019, p. 119), which would not occur quickly. Such characteristics and practices contribute to the maintenance of masculine domination and thus to a structurally patriarchal society.

In the case of the Roman origin myths, the first rape, of Rhea Silvia, a sacred woman, brought glory to Rome, enabling the city to call for a divine ancestry. His son founded Rome and became a god after his death. In addition, the rape of the Sabine women was essential for the settlement and growth of the city itself, providing for the first generation of Romans.

The third rape of Lucretia, brought shame to the Roman Monarchy and the establishment of the Republic (Arieti, 2002, p. 214). Lucretia revealed her victimisation in a family council before killing herself, causing authors such as Cicero and others from the time of Augustus to value this event for its political consequences (Fantham, 2011, p. 125). She blames herself for the rape because according to Roman Law, this was the only possible place she could be, since women had no access to legal mechanisms as they were excluded from deliberative instances. However, this would be considered exemplary behaviour as she invites the men in her family to take the law into their own hands (Azevedo, 2023, p. 123).

She was seen as a model of a chaste woman and, consequently, an attraction for Sextus Tarquinius' desire. In other words, it is her very adequacy to the male ideal of feminine virtue that is placed as an inciting factor, something to think about of the victim blaming, making an apology for the punishment of adulteresses, which would reflect a subjective strategy of an oppression that legitimised gender hierarchies (Azevedo, 2023, p. 124-126). In this way, Lucretia became a model of virtue for her gesture of integrity. However, if she had stayed alive, she would have proved an example of *impudicitia* to other women, as they could not have sex with other men besides their husbands and then claim that they were forced to do such an act against their will (Langlands, 2006, p. 94-95).

The fourth event, Verginia's rape attempt, besides being prevented and not occurring, dissolved the Decemvirate (Arieti, 2002, p. 214 and 218) and put in doubt the legal action, its laws, and its legislators. As she was a potential wife, she should be *pudica*. What is interesting is to realise Verginia's passive status while she was objectified as a reward, as a prize for which men were fighting. She simply waited her fate (Langlands, 2006, p. 102), as a woman in her position would have no way of even acting to defend herself within a society that would not accept such an act. Thus, with all the inconveniences already caused, whether Verginia had taken any action, she would be seen as a transgressor, which could demoralise her. *Pudicitia* was so important to the Romans that Verginius preferred to kill his own daughter rather than let her live with future disturbances that would recall that occasion, since her *pudicitia* could always be questioned again socially.

Verginia's fate highlights the sense of honour of her father, Verginius, a mere plebeian with a patrician spirit. It shows a free girl of good repute who could not be seduced with legal impunity: thus, in Titus Livius' version, the lustful Decemvian, Appius Claudius, needed not only to obtain the girl in his possession, but also to obtain her status as a free person, annulled by the law, since she was considered a slave. Thus, Appius' man claimed her as his slave in the absence of her father, but she regained her right to remain free until the court decision, with the argument that even a brief period outside the paternal home would destroy her reputation. In a second phase, Appius' men claimed that Verginius had stolen a slave girl and was falsely claiming her as his daughter. As Appius was the presiding magistrate, he decided the case himself, and Verginius then demonstrated his convictions by publicly stabbing his daughter to death as the only way to defend not her chastity but her freedom, which was for her legal protection against sexual abuse. The father's role as head of his family was to protect his wife, children, and other dependants and to ensure his daughter's fitness to serve the community and to defend her for a future marriage as a mother of legitimate children. The role of the community was to guarantee the power of the heads of the family, and Appius' violation of this right justified the popular uprising that overthrew the regime of the Decemvirate (Fantham, 2011, p. 125-126).

The event with Verginia displays the crimes of *iniuria* and *adulterium/stuprum,* adding Rome's aristocratic conflicts between senators, equestrians, and Augustus. However, it is illuminating in terms of justice and the idealisation of the Roman citizen and institutions, making explicit patterns of gender and power relations. These elements provide important aspects for thinking about the reality of Rome in the Late Republic and Early Empire. The crime of *iniuria* is evidenced when Verginius accuses Appius of claiming the guardianship of Verginia using a false will, in addition to demonstrating the intention of misconduct in relation to the guardian agent. In other words, Appius claims her guardianship to maintain relations configured as *stuprum* (Bryen, 2016, p. 331 apud Azevedo, 2023, p. 119-120).

There is a pattern in the episodes of Lucretia and Verginia: the women are killed and the men, politicians and legislators who abuse power, are expelled from the cities; *pudicitia* is avenged, with changes in the power structure. Regarding gender, there is the presence of sexual offences, confirming the legitimacy of legislation for the killing of women. Such deaths are definitive, while the aspects of political and legal changes could be temporary, showing respect and preservation of their lives over the lives of women (Azevedo, 2023, p. 122).

To add to this, in both events men monopolised judicial mechanisms, physical violence and aggression, common in the face of a belligerent power that highlighted an ideal of masculinity. This power naturalised violent behaviour, as if this type of action were the only answer to everyday challenges. These women did not claim power or question the structure, they only called on men to do justice. Therefore, the victimisation of women appears as a patriarchal discourse related to the female experience (Azevedo, 2023, p. 123 and 126).

The most interesting thing about the events is that a political and constitutional importance is always shown as a consequence. However, it is worth noting that when these episodes were written it was the period of Augustus, when it was believed that there was a resurgence and revival of ideas from ancient Rome (Arieti, 2002, p. 218), not to mention the manipulation of new laws produced for women in this period and even the encouragement for them to procreate as in the past. The idea of an eternal city, recurrent in the period of Augustus, appears in Cicero (*Pro Marcello* 22) and three times in Livy (*History of Rome* 4.4.4, 5.7.10 and 28.28.11 apud Arieti, 2002, p. 224).

Titus Livius demonstrated his textual, sexual, and political concerns, as well as placing freedom, social status, abuse of power and the vulnerability of sexual integrity as vital to overall social well-being. Otherwise, the Roman "origin myths" also emphasised that such physical violence corrupts a man's mind, since he may subsequently commit worse acts. However, men should also be protected, so that they could be adequate protectors of Roman society (Langlands, 2006, p. 121-122).

In this sense, it is noted that religiosity is part of these events once again, as a whole, demonstrating that it was of great importance to Roman society, since, according to Arieti, these episodes offer a mixture in the meanings of the actions of Mars and Venus, in other words, they are violent, forceful and destructive, but otherwise produce something positive. Such gods can represent Rome, being the two progenitors of that people, combining the opposite forms of the universe: destruction and creation, and providing competing forces that made up Rome (Arieti, 2002, p. 2019). The positive side of such stories could soften acts of violence.

Titus Livius (*History of Rome*, 1.5-9), Cicero (*Rep.* 2.25.46) and Juvenal (*Satires* 10.193-5) used these accounts to allude to the position of women in society. In addition to their political interest, these events perpetuated the idea of female chastity. Therefore, if a woman acted independently, the men of that society would be criticised for not exercising control over her (Rawson, 2006, p. 326-327). Lucretia's act of taking her own life can also be seen as an act of independence, because she was the one who took the decision to execute her own death.

According to Riess (2012), Titus Livius praised Lucretia's chastity (*castitas*) as well as her feminine pride (*decus muliebris*). In order to save his daughter from being raped, Verginius, her father, killed her with his own hands (Livy, *History of Rome,* 3.44-58; Cic. *Rep.* 2.63).

The rape or seduction of girls who were still under the protection of the paternal home was under the control of the father, extended by the consultation of the family council (Fantham, 2011, p. 135). In Verginia's case, the father is constrained to kill his daughter, which seems to be the correct behaviour for an exemplary citizen, as he acts legitimately, exercising over his daughter the *ius occidendi* (right to kill), conferred by the *patria potestas*, which confirms the domestic jurisdiction existing during the Republic over his tutelage (Bryen, 2016, p. 331). However, the reaffirmation of *patria postestas* could reveal that it was threatened, since the legislation of 18 BC transferred the punishment for *adulterium/stuprum* from domestic to public jurisdiction, which generated a reaction from the Roman aristocracy. The *Lex Iulia de Adulteriis* proves such prerogatives by the fact that it had the function of limiting the actions of the father and husband in the face of the punishment for adultery (Azevedo, 2023, p. 93 and 120).

Moreover, Livy and Cicero praised Verginia's chastity in terms similar to those of Lucretia. In both cases, the chastity and purity of Roman women, as well as sexual inviolability, symbolised the invulnerability of Rome itself. Such events show that the honour of the female body supported the political body of Rome as a whole, for the sense of devotion (*pietas*), which was seen as essential to Rome's political and social cohesion. The violence inflicted against these women can be understood as a foundational violence. However, before this classification, it is necessary to incorporate these acts into gender-based violence. In other words, it has a gendered basis, given that violence itself is understood as behaviour involving physical force with the intention of hurting, damaging, or killing someone; and gender is commonly understood as a sociocultural interpretation between individuals of different sexes (Díaz-Andreu, 2005, p. 15 apud Matić, 2021a, p. 1). Regarding the act of violence, the woman and the social environment are strangers to each other, in an instable series of hierarchical determinations (Moore, 2000, p. 21).

These "origins myth" created parameters of female conduct in the Roman imagination (Riess, 2012, p. 492), and such events led the raped victims to opt for suicide and a father to kill his own daughter, out of the extreme eagerness to preserve chastity and virginity, in addition to the harm that she could have illegitimate offspring (Cid López, 2011, p. 59). These myths were described in a masculine language, which expressed both deprivation and domination (Chodorow, 1978 apud Giddens, 1992, p. 129), resulting in narratives configured according to the cultural origin of Roman society, which was understood within a social order dominated by the masculine principle. This fact made the constitutive opposition between nature and culture and between the "sexuality" of nature and the "sexuality" of culture consider the female place and the initiative of the woman as a perverse initiator, who was "naturally" instructed for the things of the house. Domesticity was to be performed at the demand of men, in accordance with the order of things and the fundamental hierarchy of the social order and carried out by the legitimate domination of the masculine principle over the feminine, which symbolised male supremacy (Bourdieu, 1998, p. 28-29).

The coexistence of multiple discourses for different genders produces hierarchically ordered discourses (Moore, 2000, p. 28). Consequently, the sexual differences become naturalised through practices continuously performed by gender acts, which society prescribes as normative for the different sexes. According to this thinking, practices that could be done by both sexes become prescribed and natural for one sex and inappropriate for the other (Butler, 1990, p. 43-44 apud Matić, 2021, p. 2).

It is assumed that women were used as objects in the social construction of Rome, which defined them as social statuses and objects of exchange between families, projected to contribute to male continuity and success. The exchanges of these "objects" between men comprised equal communication between them, so that women were symbolic instruments of male politics, intended to be fiduciary signs and to establish relations between men, being reduced to the condition of instruments of production or reproduction of symbolic and social capital. This demonstrates a symbolic violence that rested on these women, but which also legitimised them as chaste women bound to *pudicitia*. Since the practices subtly structure gender relations and power hierarchies, privileging a specific gender, they are known as symbolic violence or structural (Žižek, 2008, p. 1-2).

Bourdieu defines symbolic violence as a "soft violence", imperceptible and invisible even to the victims, exercised largely through purely symbolic channels of communication and cognition (Bourdieu, 2001, p. 1-2). With regard to gender, its understanding as symbolic violence can be exemplified by the fact that the dominated assume the categories of the dominant as natural (Matić, 2021a, p. 2). However, it is understood that there was a hidden dimension to the politics of the marriage transaction (Bourdieu, 1998, p. 56), which, when such a matrimonial exchange was not possible, often the response was physical violence through rape, which was also a way of taking away the honour of such women and compromising an entire family generation.

For Giddens, violence is a frustrated attempt at domination (Giddens, 1992, p. 15). Frustration can be understood as the inability to maintain or assume a gendered social subject position, resulting in a crisis, real or imagined, of self-representation and/or social evaluation. Frustration may lie in a failure in sexual relations or even in economic provisions and may characterise the inability to receive the expected satisfactions or retributions for assuming a gendered individual position or a manner of subjectivity marked by gender. However, it is not necessary to be aware of what the individual's satisfactions or retributions should be in order to experience frustration. Thus, it is the perpetrator of violence who experiences frustration (Moore, 2000, p. 39-40).

One of the great examples of frustration was that of Tarquinius. Sex with Lucretia was an assertion of power over her, after he had been humiliated when his family demonstrated the lack of basic moral qualities that the other men possessed, especially Collatinus (Langlands, 2006, p. 88).

The response of violence, including rape, is based on the understanding that such occurrence appears when masculinity does not achieve sexual control of men over women, which seems to have been more an incidental feature of Roman social life. Anger can come from non-consent and when control begins to fail, revealing a compulsive male sexual character created within that society. When that control is in decline, it can also generate an increasing flow of violence towards women (Giddens, 1992, p. 11).

The concept of "consent" in relation to societies and historical time must be considered complex and diverse, since the consent from Antiquity, for example, should take place between the male parties, and not like the current female consent, which was not expected by Roman society. What was expected of the woman was that she fulfils her role as subordinate, often having to be complacent with the forced sexual act within marriage, for example. In Roman society, women were seen as the property of men, who could be their husbands or, before marriage, their fathers, which suggests that rape could have arisen to punish those who took something that belonged to another man, as in the case of Tarquinius. In this context, it mattered little whether the woman consented to have sex with her husband or even if she had consented to marry such a man, since the possibility of rape in marriage was neither conceived nor questioned (Freitas; Morais, 2019, p. 118).

Comparing this fact with the present, in Brazil, rape within marriage was not legally recognised until the law n. 11.340, commonly known as Maria da Penha Law. In 1990, the jurist Noronha said that the husband could not be accused of rape by his own wife, because the Civil Code presented the duty of the spouses to maintain sexual relations. Consequently, the woman's sexual refusal could cause the husband to force her to do the act without answering for the crime of rape. Even today, with the recognition of sexual violence in marriage and the creation of Women's Defence Police Stations (DDM), the effects on justice processes are still precarious. There are various reasons why women do not report their aggressors, such as fear of reprisals, the need to keep the aggression as a personal matter and the protection of the aggressor. The closer the relationship between victims and perpetrators is, the more likely it is that violence will go unreported (Tjaden; Thoennes, 2006).

To add, Vargas (2007) pointed out that 71% of the police reports in the city of Campinas (Brazil) were filed and only 9% of the reported cases were legally punished. According to Andrade (2005), the Criminal Justice System (SJC) continues to maintain patriarchal practices that only indict non-white, low-income men, while women who are victims are categorised as "honest" or "dishonest". There is also a lack of adequate reception for victims, which includes humiliation and moral judgement, causing them to suffer further psychological violence by the State (Bueno *et al.*, 2016, p. 13 apud Freitas; Morais, 2019, p. 117).

Force and violence are part of all known types of domination and violence is only resorted to when the legitimate order collapses. Sexual violence against women, especially rape, is the mainstay of men's control over women (Griffin, 1973; Brownmiller, 1973). Rape shows the reality of the phallus' rule and is a violence that is part of the ancient male oppression over women. Such violence leads to an emphasis on the fact that women must be protected, especially in the public sphere, where men themselves subject each other to violence. However, violence against women can rarely be directly linked to them, but to the men with whom they are associated.

In this way, violence is pronounced and rape is an activity involving men who are seen as destroyers or as destroyed. Violence may also be a reaction to the decline of complicity with the feminine (Giddens, 1992, p. 136-138).

In this context, the "origin myths" brought conflicts that encompassed the concept of *pudicitia* in the entanglement between male and female subjective consciousness, between body and mind, between internal and external moral control, and between the need to see virtue and the potential for deceptive signs (Langlands, 2006, p. 93).

1.1.3. The female position and legal discourse

According to these Roman principles, it is noted that the family was the basis of Roman social organisation, composed of father, mother, children, as well as slaves, animals, and the property itself, where the father exercised dominion over all and decided their destinies (Sampaio; Venturini, 2009, p. 2). The word *familia* for the Romans had the same meaning as house and included all members, including slaves, who would be under a legal power (*potestas*) of the man of the house. The concept of *domus* would be more linked to the meaning we have of family in contemporary times (Grubbs, 2002, p. 17).

At the beginning of the Republic, everything remained under the power (*potestas*) of the father, the *paterfamilias*, who could be the grandfather or even the great-grandfather, who possessed the *potestas* of some people (Gardner, 1990, p. 5), such as his wife and children. The power of the *pater* over the *familia* has its primitive origins in Roman society, when the protection of the group depended on his own efforts and not on the rules of the law (Gardner, 1990, p. 6). Upon the death of the *pater*, his children and wife had to remain under the control of another guardian (*alieni iuris*) or independent, under the protection of the state justice. The adult son became the *paterfamilias* and the mother, the *materfamilias* (married under *manus*) (Gardner, 1990, p. 6-7). The term *materfamilias* has some interesting meanings, as at first it described a wife who was married *in manu*, in other words, who would be under the legal power of her husband. When this type of marriage became obsolete, the term came to refer to a respectable matron, married or not. The defining factor would be the woman's behaviour, especially her social propriety and what would concern her sexual honour (Grubbs, 2002, p. 19).

It was the paternal family that severely defined children's identity, inheritance ties, as well as name, cult and residence. In practice, brothers and sisters were considered equal before the will. However, each brother, upon the death of the *pater*, became *pater* of his own *familia*, with absolute control over his property and the finances of those under his *potestas* (Gardner, 1990, p. 172), as well as the sister, when she was not married, as she needed a protector to guard her dowry. If the daughter was an only child, it was perfectly legal for the father to appoint an heir from outside, even leaving her a legacy of up to half of his property (Gardner, 1990, p. 174). On the other hand, the mother's family, with no institutional ties, established more tender relationships with her godchildren, grandchildren, and nephews (Funari, 1995, p. 44). Fathers had the power to decide the fate of women and children, who were considered their property, as were animals and crops (Omena, 2007; Sampaio; Venturini, 2009, p. 2). In the case of impurity of daughters, for example, the *pater* could condemn them to death (Gardner, 1990, p. 7), something that lasted until the end of the Republic.

Daughters could not own property or sign a contract. After their father's death, they became independent (*sui iuris*) but, in any case, they were subject to a guardian (Rawson, 2006, p. 332) and remained under male tutelage. The *tutela muliebris* over elite women came to be known as *patria potestas*, in which powers were granted to the eldest men in a family (Cid López, 2011, p. 64). What can be seen is that the *patria potestas* was significant and marked the father's power relations within the Roman family, classifying women as unequal to men, as well as children. The ideology through each gender identity was legitimised differently, with unequal values between men and women, which was accepted by both groups and internalised through everyday activities.

The husband could marry his wife in the form of a *manus*, which in Latin literally means "hand" and which corresponded to a type of marriage agreement in which the wife was in the power (*potestas*) of her husband. She had the same rights as her husband's children when he did not make a testament before his death. However, the husband's power over her was more limited than over the children, and he did not have the right of life, death or sale over the wife (as in the *coemptio*[13], another type of marriage settlement which stated that when the wife was sold, all her property went

---

[13] *Coemptio fiduciae causa*, a way of selling a woman with the guardian's consent to a man of her choice, who became the guardian *fiduciarius*. This meant the end of *potestas*, ending the *pater* as guardian, becoming a *tutor legitimus*, who protected his family in relation to succession rights without a testament (Gardner, 1990, p. 17).

with her, even her debts). The *lex Voconia* of 169 BC, which took place in a period of conquest and prosperity, forbade women to receive an inheritance, except when it was the will of the deceased father to leave something to his daughter (Gardner, 1990, p. 164-170). As a result, women could not own property and everything they received as a gift or betrothal, for example, was invested by their husbands, with the exception of some rights to their dowries. What they received from their husbands' will depended on their generosity (Gardner, 1990, p. 11-15).

Women were seen as beings who needed support, which led this society to impose their seclusion in the *domus*, and the mandatory presence of a guardian, considered as a protector for their entire life. This meant that, in order to marry or divorce at any age or condition, they had to ask his permission, receive or transmit inheritance and control or dispose of their property (Cid López, 2011, p. 64). However, in societies such as the Roman, constructed virility brought about masculine domination over the female, keeping women as symbolic objects and placing them in a permanent state of bodily insecurity or symbolic dependence. Actions were expected of them, which should also be socially constructed, and they should be feminine, loyal, submissive, fertile and conform to a *pudicitia*. Otherwise, everything would depend on the social status of that woman. In the case of the woman of the Roman elite, who is referred to in this work, she was exposed to all the effects of anxiety in relation to the social gaze, reaching the extreme form of symbolic alienation, in other words, the effects of her social position, which could reinforce gender consequences or attenuate them, but never annul them (Bourdieu, 1998, p. 82-83).

This rule of women's seclusion illustrated precisely the consolidation of a patriarchal society (Cid López, 2011, p. 57). The only ones who were free from the *tutela muliebris* were the Vestals, some imperial princesses and, from Augustus' government, citizens women who had more than three children or freed women with four or more children, according to the *ius trium liberorum*, which reduced the power of the guardian and gave women effective control over their property (Hemelrijk, 1999, p. 97). Thus, this measure, from the time of Augustus, was not designed to help women in any way, but to enhance a pro-natality policy, which emphasised the role of motherhood for women (Cid López, 2011, p. 64) and the warlike role for those born male.

In this sense, when a woman was under the *postestas* of a *paterfamilias*, she could gain relative independence after his death, as she became *sui iuris*. Moreover, it could happen that the *paterfamilias* released her from his *potestas* voluntarily, at any time he considered it beneficial, but this was not a common practice. In any case, the woman had to be under a guardian (*tutela mulierum*). During the Republic, the guardian (*tutor*) was commonly a relative, such as a paternal uncle. The tutor became the legal and business guardian on behalf of the woman. This fact did not mean that they lived together (Berdowski, 2007, p. 285).

Daughters had no legalised independence, even when they reached adulthood, which in the republican period was when a woman turned 12 or when she married. The father, exercising the *patria potestas*, was free to sell his daughter into slavery, choose whom she would marry, impose a divorce or even kill her if caught in adultery. With Augustus, this judgement left the private sphere, becoming a law called *lex Iulia de adulteriis*. After marriage, it was the husband who performed the same function or, if there were any problems, the closest relatives, such as a brother or children, took over (Cid López, 2011, p. 65). Later, female domestic life in Augustus' time took the path of a deep ideology and of reactionary elements. However, its effects transformed what Roman politics understood about the feminine meaning (Milnor, 2005, p. 34).

In Romulus' time, to enshrine a man's right to divorce, his wife had to be caught using magic or (presumably abortifacient) drugs without his consent or caught in adultery (Lefkowitz; Fant, 1992, p. 9). Adultery was judged by relatives and both adultery and drinking wine were punishable by death. The same order forbade a woman to divorce her husband. In 166 BC, the consul Valerius Maximus was able to divorce his wife because she appeared outside the house without a headscarf. This case shows how much Roman law could vary. Ulpianus, writing *On Adultery 1* in the *Digest* (48.5.24), comments that jurists had previously specified that the couple guilty of adultery had to be caught in the act to confirm the action. However, in the time of Augustus, divorce would not be a public offence if the husband did not take action to divorce his wife (Tac. *Ann.* 2.85.3).

Before Augustus, only women who had no family were punished by the state. Moreover, the poisoning of husbands circulated in the collective consciousness as being related to adultery. Records examined by Fantham, show that citizen women were dealt with by the courts in the first instance. Added to this is the fact that if their behaviour caused a public scandal, women without relatives were summoned for *aedile* trial. If a generalised public crisis provoked a senatorial investigation, women incriminated and found guilty would be returned to their families for punishment and would only be dealt with by the state when they had no family. As most cases had sexual implications, the discipline of women was a good factor to take into consideration by public and private male authorities. However, there is no evidence of any laws that authorised criminal charges against adultery by the husband or the father of the woman, but there is evidence from the third century BC that there was a law that referred to the restitution of the dowry to the wife's family in case of divorce (Fantham, 2011, p. 133-134).

Fragments of the speeches of Cato the Censor from the 2nd century BC attest to the emphasis placed on civil proceedings between the wife's family and her ex-husband after divorce and the evaluation of a system of deductions from the sum in question for the fault of both sides. In the last century of the Republic, the jurist Servius Sulpicius devoted an entire book to dowry law issues. There is much more substantial evidence of the Roman courts' interest in dowry during the Late Republic than of any concern with punishing adultery or seduction as such. However, the same Cato, as an arbitrator of a divorce case, reported a case that was assessed as a penalty to be paid by the wife for drinking wine and thus committing a shameful act to her husband. Moreover, it also reaffirmed the husband's right to kill his wife if he caught her in the act (Fantham, 2011, p. 135).

It is concluded that in this period there was a continued recognition of adultery as a private offence, which justified extreme action by the wronged husband against his wife, but not by the criminal court. Otherwise, the civil courts showed that the concern of their actions was with the financial aspect of marriage, which involved the transfer of property between families (Fantham, 2011, p. 134).

Augustus promulgated the *lex Iulia de adulteriis* in 18 BC, twenty years after he divorced Scribonia, when she had just had her daughter, Julia, so that he could marry Livia, wife of Tiberius Claudius Nero, who was six months pregnant with the former's son, Drusus. This was the first law to make adultery a crime subject to public prosecution, which had previously been a family matter (Fantham, 2011, p. 115). Augustus made adultery a public crime and established a new criminal court for sexual offences (Barrett, 2002, p. 123).

Under this law, a husband confronted with his wife's infidelity did not have the option of forgiving or ignoring her offence. He or his wife's father had sixty days to initiate adultery proceedings. The husband, the lover, upon obtaining his conviction, and the "ex-wife", in the absence of the husband or father, were encouraged to bring charges against the lover, the wife and the husband himself for their complicity. The woman's father was authorised to kill the lover caught in the act in the paternal or marital home, since he also killed his daughter on the same occasion. The husband's rights were more limited. He had the right to kill his wife and could also kill his lover if he had surprised him in the couple's home and if the man was of ill-repute *status*. Adulterers found guilty were sentenced to confiscation of a substantial part of their property and sent to an island (Fantham, 2011, p. 115-116).

The *lex Iulia de adulteriis* defined adultery as a sexual relationship between a married woman and a man who was not her husband. Both were incriminated, as it was understood that they had committed an offence against the woman's husband. Condemned, they would be sent to different islands and parts of their property were confiscated. This law was part of a reform of a moral and political nature, which was initiated by Augustus at the end of the Civil Wars of 31 BC. It was part of a larger project, with the purpose of restructuring Roman politics to legitimise a new form of government, which would be based on dynastic ideals, and, consequently, to complete the transition from the Republic to the Empire (Azevedo, 2014, p. 1-2). The *lex Iulia de maritandis ordinibus*, which also took place in the same period, regulated the validity of marriages between different social classes (Barrett, 2002, p. 123). The development of an imperial dynasty made sexual association with princesses a form of high treason, something that was established as the purpose of the *lex Iulia de adulteriis* (Fantham, 2011, p. 121-122).

The most famous victim of the *lex Iulia de adulteriis* was Augustus' daughter Julia, condemned in a private trial but publicly denounced to an embarrassed Senate. She was disinherited and sent to the barren island of Pandataria, without permission to return to Rome or re-enter normal civilian life. It was not surprising to find in the adultery of severely punished wives the approval of their murder at the hands of their own father (Fatham, 2017, p. 116).

In this way, adultery judged by relatives should have been overcome by the time of Augustus, but in AD 17 Tiberius placed the responsibility for punishment for Appuleia Varilla's adultery in the hands of her relatives, just as Nero placed Pomponia Graecina in the hands of her husband and his family when she was accused of superstition (Tac. *Ann.* 2.50.3 apud Levick,

2012, p. 101). However, the same law applied to a much smaller number of women not yet, or no longer, married, whose sexual activity was designated as *stuprum*: the basic prohibition was that no one should commit fornication or adultery intentionally or with premeditated malice (*Digest* 48.5.13). Both the adultery of a wife and the sexual activity of an unmarried woman of respectable status were viewed under the term *stuprum* (Fantham, 2011, p. 116 and 119).

The *lex Iulia de adulteriis*, like other laws of the Augustan period, seems to have been promulgated by an appeal to ancient customs (*mos maiorum*) for the legitimisation of power, with time-honoured principles, traditional models, and appropriate laws of conduct. Augustus implemented an extraordinary programme on marriage and morality. Part of the legacy of the Republic seems to have fallen to him for his own legitimisation as Julius Caesar's heir. In this way, he won the loyalty of Caesar's soldiers and supporters (Barker, 2020, p. 6).

There was a male concern about the control of offspring, called "custody of the womb", which showed that the woman was treated as a mere receptacle, to produce offspring, of which the father was the owner (Cid López, 2011, p. 58). This control was linked to the fact that rape and adultery could disrupt the kinship continuum of society (Matić, 2021, p. 7). The interest of controlling offspring was one of the reasons for the seclusion women throughout Roman history, with the excuse of protecting them from the dangers of the outside. One of the jobs to keep them at home was weaving, so the female symbol for excellence became the spindle. Female aristocrats also worked to care for the sick people, as well as receiving instruction to educate their children, especially the male child, under the control of the *pater* (Cid López, 2011, p. 59).

The point of honour was the principle of the system of reproduction strategies by which men, who had a monopoly on the instruments of production and reproduction of symbolic capital, aimed to ensure the conservation of the strategies of fecundation, marriage, education, economics, and succession, oriented towards the transmission of power and inherited privileges. The result was the exclusion of women from all public places where all the games of honour were played (Bourdieu, 1998, p. 62).

For the Roman elite, being a man, in the sense of *vir*, implied certain duties linked to *virtus*, similar to nobility and honour, which were socially constructed and took on dispositions apparently from the *habitus*. These dispositions could normally be seen in the posture of the body, when standing upright, when raising the head or in their attitudes, their way of thinking, their beliefs, in other words, in their *éthos*. However, the one who ruled, regardless of status or rank, lower or higher, was the man of honour. Honour functioned as a leader of thoughts and practices, as if it were a force, but without automatically compelling him. This force guided his action, which was linked to a logical necessity, as if that man could not act in another way. This force led him to perform acts inevitably, which would be seen by others as impossible or unthinkable, as if a social transcendence had seized him, functioning as *amor fati* or love of fate, in which the body performs something that is in accordance with an identity constructed within a social essence, which thus becomes its destiny, as was the case with Verginio's action against his daughter, Verginia. Nobility and/or honour are the result of a social work of nomination and inculcation, in which a social identity has been constructed, so that it has been known and recognised by everyone in that society, becoming a *habitus* or a socially incorporated law (Bourdieu, 1998, p. 63-64).

According to these criteria, the link between sexual practice and social practice in the formation of Roman masculinity established that the aristocratic man's body was as if it were inviolable and his sexual role was idealised in order to legitimise an active and domineering stance. This idealisation was related to a projection of social practice that attributed to him the command and maintenance of the prevailing order associated to conquest, domination and authority over other individuals and peoples (Feitosa, 2008). This explains that the ideal of masculinity was associated with the public performance of Roman men, who used it as a way to negotiate power (Azevedo, 2023, p. 129-130).

In relation to the formation of masculinity, it is necessary to know that it is not static, nor timeless, but historical, just like femininity. It is not a manifestation of an internal essence, but socially constructed. It does not arise in the consciousness of the human being through biological constitution, but it is culturally created. Masculinity has different meanings at different times to different people, and Roman masculinity may be distinct from 19th century masculinity or have some similarities. What must be taken into account is that masculinity is constantly changing, being materialised in a space where relationships between women and other men take place (Kimmel, 2016, p. 99).

Masculinity can be equated with power over women and over other men. From a perspective of comparing the past with the present, it is important to consider the aspects of current feminist women in relation to power. According to Kimmel, they have theorised that masculinity is about the drive for domination, for power and for conquest. This view is how women experience masculinity. Feminists generally note that women as a group do not hold power. Individually, women do not feel powerful. What they feel is fear because they perceive themselves as vulnerable. In another way, feminism also reminds us of the fact that men as a group are in power (Kimmel, 2016).

However, Kimmel points out that feminism has tended to assume that individual men should feel powerful (Kimmel, 2016, p. 118). Hannah Arendt mentions that power corresponds to the human ability not to act alone, but together. Consequently, power is not the property of an individual, but of a group. That said, power only continues to exist if such a group continues together. When someone is in power, that person is empowered by a certain number of people, who act in their favour (Arendt, 1970, p. 44 apud Kimmel, 2016, p. 120). This proposition by Kimmel cannot be taken as an absolute truth, since he considers the male and female issue as equal for all feminisms, tangent to a "global feminism". However, the fact that men act in groups is something relevant to pay attention to and observe the trend of such behaviour.

That said, male privilege can also be a trap, as it imposes on men the duty to affirm themselves, in any and all circumstances, through their virility. Moreover, virility has to be validated by other men, within the truth of society, being violent, or powerful, attested and recognised by a group, which has the ability to judge the "real men". Men find their beginning in the fear of losing the esteem or consideration of the group and are thus consigned to the categories of the feminine, of the weak and/or the delicate. However, what is recognised as "courage" often has its origins in a form of cowardice, in the face of acts such as killing, torture or violence, which are based on the "manly" fear of being left out of the "man's world" - that place without weakness and the space for the tough. Consequently, virility is constructed within a relational notion in front of other men and for other men, against femininity, as a kind of fear of the feminine, elaborated initially within themselves (Bourdieu, 1998, p. 64-67). This approach is valid both for the present as well as the Roman past.

The heterosexual[14] relationship itself, present in marriage among the Roman social elite, was linked to procreation and heredity, in which women were subjected to a social construction, elaborated as a universal standard for women of the Roman elite. This was a labour guaranteed by institutions such as the family, religion, and politics, to affirm the reproduction of masculine domination and vision, as well as ensuring the divisions of functions between the sexes. This system contained a family morality, patriarchal values, and, above all, a belief in the inferiority of women. All of these were constructed historically in the collective unconscious and by communicated signs, certifying trust in patriarchal assumptions, which initially served to justify a family hierarchy (Bourdieu, 1998, p. 103-104).

However, it should be noted that female subordination varies according to the historical period and the place in the world where these women lived. It should not be thought of as universal, as if it occurred everywhere and in all historical periods (Piscitelli, 2002, p. 9). However, the social disciplinary production of gender gives rise to false stabilities for the interests of heterosexual construction and the regulation of a sexuality within a reproductive domain (Butler, 1990, p. 134-139).

This system was what organised the social world of the Roman elite, which involved categories of kinship, mythical-ritual, reproduction, games, and access to social reproduction, guaranteed by a type of exchange aimed at accumulating genealogical status, lineage, or ancestral names, which were components of symbolic capital and were related to lasting powers and rights over people. Exchanges between men were thus linked to honour and hence to domination. Women were sometimes seen not as agents, but only as the place, the occasion and the support, condemned to remain ignored, and their actions were usually worked out of sight, in the obscurity of the home, since their public performance could be contradictory. Men were given a monopoly on all official, public activities, representation, exchanges of honour, exchanges of words, exchanges of gifts, exchanges of women, exchanges of challenges and deaths. It was on account of these investments that men earned their honour and virility, with all their duties submitted to themselves, which had to be fulfilled in order to be acting correctly and to be worthy, according to a constructed *habitus* (Bourdieu, 1998, p. 58-61).

---

[14] It should be borne in mind that such a term was not used during Antiquity, but is used here for an explanation and to have a didactic understanding of the situation experienced in the past by women of the Roman elite, which does not deny the fact of possible homosexual relations outside marriage.

The marriage of the Roman elite woman placed her in the only acceptable position that society allowed her and involved important transfers of property through the dowry law (Fantham, 2011, p. 116-117). In this sense, the transmission of property was also something of concern in this society, which demarcated the authority of the *pater* and the desire to always keep the *familia* property as intact as possible. The request for consent to marriage and dowry revealed a whole origin in relation to the Roman control of property between families. The dowry was basically a way for the wife's family to help the husband with expenses of home and to maintain a social status. In other words, it was an agreement between families, not between individuals. When a woman entered in a marriage through *manus*, all her property was absorbed by her husband or his *pater*, even though the latter was still under his *potestate*. Thus, upon the death of the father, the dowry went directly to the husband (Gardner, 1990, p. 13-18, 97-98 and 108).

The declaration of the dowry could be made by the woman herself, her father, her paternal ancestor or a third person who was indebted to the woman. The promise of dowry could be made by others who were connected to the woman or her father, but it was the *pater* of the future husband who questioned whether the parties of the woman promised to give a certain amount for the dowry. However, as much as the dowry was considered property under the protection of the husband, its purpose was for the maintenance of the wife. In the event of a dissolution of marriage, the wife's family had the right to claim and have the dowry returned, which led to restrictions on its use. The wife's father was the one who claimed the dowry back, when he was still alive, but he could only do so with the consent of the daughter. For Gardner, Ulpian emphasised that the dowry was the daughter's property; Tryphoninus, a Roman jurist, mentioned that the dowry was part of the husband's property, although it belonged to the wife (Gardner, 1990, p. 99, 102 and 112).

In contrast, Saller works with another point of view of the *patria postestas*. He argues that, firstly, it must not have been employed for a long time, as it is considered, and points out the side of the *pater*'s sons. According to the scholar, Gaius, a Roman jurist of the 2nd century AD, *patria postestas* was a special characteristic of the Roman citizen according to his virtue. His sons would not have this power and, in the imperial period, women no longer passed into the power of their husband, but, like their brothers, remained under the power of their father until the end of his life. After the father's death, his children became *sui iuris*, under their own control or power. However, Saller recognises that the *patria postestas* gave a strong, authoritarian, and patriarchal character to the Roman family (Saller, 1986, p. 7). Because of the *patria potestas'* oppression, many sons committed parricide[15]. The lucky Roman would be the one whose father died early (Veyne, 1978), since elders could maintain their political dominance indirectly, by using *patria postestas* against disobedient sons (Daube, 1969). A son who refused to follow the father's guidance in public life could be disinherited or could have his political career suspended by withholding resources, which made these fathers prevent any weakening of the *patria potestas* (Saller, 1986, p. 9-11).

Within this system, matrons probably used religion as a pretext to leave the *domus* and gather with other women, as an opening to be able to attend spectacles, which was something reprehensible (Cid López, 2011, p. 63). In addition, they could have fun in the religious context, entertain themselves with music and drink wine without water (*temetum*), which was reserved for gods and men. They were allowed to drink this sacrificial wine during festivals, as they were in a position of worship, their actions being symbolic, which ensured fertility and the continuation of life, like the Vestals throughout their mandates (Takács, 2008, p. 110).

For these women, it was not respectable to leave the house, unless if it was to do pious work. Another fact is that the rituals and even their organisations ended up giving them their own spaces outside the *domus*. In this way, religious activities possibly favoured the organisation of matrons to claim some rights from men, since they had gained experience with the cultural tasks, which they performed to honour the deities. This gave rise to protests that led to the revision of laws, which implied the deprivation of the exercise of political activities and the control of their lives and fortunes, in addition to showing themselves against the subordinate position they had in relation to men (Cid López, 2011, p. 63).

One of the protests took place in 195 BC and reached the forum, the place par excellence of men and their political discussions, when men were criticised for not taking care of their wives (Livy, *History of Rome* 34.1-8). The matrons showed their repudiation regarding the *lex Oppia*, which was declared after a period of war in 215 BC. This law served to check women's extravagances in relation to inheritance and forbade them to wear jewellery

---

[15] There is small evidence on parricide (Saller, 1986, p. 19).

and flashy dresses. The tribune L. Valerius argued that the law was intended to limit the amount of gold a woman could own, the colour of her dresses and the use of the chariot, except at religious festivals (Levick, 2012, p. 102). Its abolition was in 195 BC, after there was an opening for women to show their status in a time of austerity and crisis, but soon after this episode ended and when everything was overcome, it was considered that women should return to normality in Rome, considering that the act of squandering prosperity was to hide the crisis. However, with the law, their precious objects had to be returned to the hands of men, their protectors, and women could not stand out or show off. However, they wanted to continue to show off their privileged social positions and thus achieved their goal. Nevertheless, what they wanted was to continue to show off their privileged social positions and thus they achieved their goal (Cid López, 2011, p. 68; Takács, 2008, p. 16).

Another episode of protest took place in 48 BC, when the wealthiest women came out to claim the high price of the taxes they paid. They came to the forum to ask for a reduction because they could not even manage public affairs or intervene in decisions that affected them. In the end, they were partially successful in getting their taxes reduced. What is striking about these events is the lack of political rights, such as the inability to go to war, to hold a public office, among others. These protests were made by the aristocrats, characterised as *axitiosae,* who went to defend their economic interests and to demonstrate their social position. There were certainly other episodes of social conflict (Cid López, 2011, p. 68) between women and men, but they must not have been written down by the ancient historians, who narrated their documents according to the interests of the male elite, as well as favouring the models of matrons to be followed.

To add to this, women of the Roman elite instituted the *ordo matronarum,* which was an "ordo of matrons", created in analogy or imitation of the male ordo, but was not a formal order and was not well defined. Its origins date back to the early Republic, characterising it as an insignia representing a women's organisation, an ordo that came to the fore mainly during the Empire. It was used freely in the written sources to denote upper-class married women acting in a public group, unlike the women of the lower "orders" (Hemelrijk, 1999, p. 11).

The criterion for being part of the *ordo matronarum* was to be an elite, prosperous and married woman, characteristics very similar to the male senatorial order, in addition to moral excellence, which was also present in the male order. In addition, they had a distinctive way of dressing, which was with *stola*, *vittae* and the use of the colour purple, equivalent to *the toga* and *latus clavus* of the male senatorial layer. They also used certain chariots, such as the *carpentum*, which was two-wheeled; and the *pilentum*, four-wheeled and more luxurious (Hemelrijk, 1999, p. 11).

During the Empire, the use of *carpentum* in the city of Rome was a special mark of social distinction, allowed to be worn only by certain matrons, mainly of the imperial family. There was a hierarchy within the order that was based on the husband's birth, prosperity, career, and social *status*. In addition, during the Empire, there was the *conventus matronarum*, which was an assembly of matrons and there was great competition to be part of it. The *ordo* and the *conventus* met for religious purposes and other things connected to festive days, special occasions, and distinct matters of female importance (Hemelrijk, 1999, p. 11-12).

The activities of women, which were linked to wealth and prominence, demonstrated that this limitation to *domus* was more theoretical than real and control could always be avoided by various devices, such as appeal to a magistrate. Even formal restrictions on women who had given birth to three children were eventually removed by Augustus (Barrett, 2002, p. 116). However, in the Late Republic and Early Empire, *tutela mulierum* diminished in importance, due to the right instituted by Augustus in 9 AD, *ius (trium) liberorum*, which freed a woman from *tutela mulierum* if she had borne three or four children. In the case of free women, the right would only apply when the child had been born after it was instituted. Emperor Claudius abolished the *tutela legitima* to completely free women to do business. *Tutela mulierum* only disappeared from legal texts in the early 4th century and the last source to mention it was *Rules of Ulpian* and a collection of legal sources known as *Fragmenta Vaticana* (Evans Grubbs, 2002, p. 43-46; Arjava, 1996, p. 143-156 apud Berdowski, 2007, p. 286).

This delay in writing laws was due to the fact that for the Romans custom (*mos*) was strong and had the power to establish rights (*iura*). Such customs would be culturally established, intrinsic to that society and should not be easy to abolish, but could be affirmed by law, edited by a magistrate, or decreed by the Senate (*senatus consultum*). Consequently, law and custom were directly linked to the norms that ensured order. Tacitus made a pronouncement in one of his works, *Germania*, on the sexual relations of "barbarians", in which he mentions that good conduct (*mores*) would be more effective than good law anywhere (Tac. *Germania*, 19.1).

With the empire, these manners ceased to exist because of the emperor's decisions, which had a profound impact on the people. Advice and interpretations were provided by authoritative jurist-consultants for three centuries, starting in the middle of the first century before the Christian era: for example, the *Institutes* of Gaius, from the middle of the second century, and the *Digest*, published in AD 533, as part of Justinian's codification. However, women were seen as enemies of order and those who required control, since the Romans believed that Romulus had already decreed a single law that would lead women to prudence and orderly conduct (Lefkowitz; Fant, 1992, p. 95 apud Levick, 2012, p. 96-97).

It was only in the High Empire, with the jurist Ulpian, that the legal situation of women's public life was outlined on paper. The jurist contended in AD II that women were barred from all civic and public life and went on to say that they could not be judged, hold a magistracy, speak for someone else or be a representative in a trial. However, the way in which these women developed public influence and honour was certainly quite complex. One thing that women did achieve in the Republic was in relation to the concept of nobility, whereby the surname of the family ancestor began to be passed on by both men and women (Brennan, 2012, p. 362 and 363).

However, even at the end of the Republic and the beginning of the Empire, women could marry *cum manu* or *sine manu*. A *cum manu* marriage was one in which the *potestas* of the woman's father passed to the husband, who would become the *paterfamilias*. However, this type of marriage fell into disuse around the 1st century BC. Marriage *sine manu* meant that the woman remained under the *potestas* of her father, retaining her rights in the intestate succession of her birth family. She continued to be unable to own property, but upon her father's death she became *sui iuris*, requiring a guardian to authorise her to make certain transactions, although she could manage and have control of her property (Hemelrijk, 1999, p. 97). Otherwise, in marriage *cum manu*, the woman could not own property or even share property with her husband (Gardner, 1990 apud Evans Grubbs, 2002, p. 20-21).

For the woman to pass into marriage in *manus* form, the husband depended on her continuous "use" (*usocapio*). This could be avoided, to the advantage of the Roman father's property, if the woman abstained three nights of each year, which took the name of *trinoctium*, which was made obsolete by Gaius (Gaius, *Institutes* 1.111). Consequently, the *manus* form of marriage declined and one that did not involve the transfer of *potestas* prevailed. However, Gaius' view of this behaviour was that women would not be so unruly (Gaius, *Institutes* 1.144f., 190f), and in his day *tutela* was something merely formal. Similarly, instituted by the *Institutes of Justinian*, it was said that women could not adopt because of the fact that they did not have power over their own children (Justinian, *Institutes* 1.11pr), however, with the emperor's indulgence, they could adopt for consolation if the woman had lost a child (Levick, 2012, p. 99).

During the Empire, women generally no longer transferred authority from their fathers to their husbands by marriage, incorporating *sine manu* marriages. They became independent property owners and received a substantial amount of resources because of the father's death, and gifts between husband and wife became forbidden by law, enabling women to have an independent financial life in agrarian society. An unusual practice was to make sons or daughters independent by the *paterfamilias*, through a ritual of fictitious sale provided by law (Saller, 1986, p. 15-16).

With the images of Roman women and their names remembered through statues, plaques, and coins, it could be noted that men and women might have constructed different meanings about the dominant gender ideology and material culture. The fact that Roman women of the elite were depicted on coins, for example, as well as in other ways, was of great esteem to their public lives, and that, from the later period of the Republic, they rarely entered the domain of their husbands' power (*manus*) or received possessions when they died. Thus, this study demonstrates that women not only lived under male dominance, but were also social agents, who attempted to create their own identities and ideologies (Spencer-Wood, 1999).

From this perspective, women never ceased to be an adornment for their husbands and families, so that their attitudes could not overshadow the man's masculinity but should enrich it in the best possible way. Therefore, activities such as the Patronage could have helped them to reach new positions and consequently caused tensions and modifications in the strategies of the powers. However, men, especially emperors like Augustus, adjusted them to these new positions through Livia, with the aim of government propaganda.

Tensions arose because these women began to have greater control over their economies. Thus, it was necessary to accept that multiple aspects of an individual's identity come together with another individual's, allowing us to emphasise that a woman of the Roman elite, for example, could take ownership of elements of masculine identity, creating levels of tensions within the social hierarchy of Rome (Revell, 2016, p. 15).

This means that with greater economic access, women of the Roman elite began to occupy themselves with other activities that, in a way, were connected with the family business, for example, with Patronage. As a result, they began to have their own images in the form of statues, cameos, coins, and other kinds of arts. This new position led them to utilise both public and private spaces, in a way. However, this division of public/private must be put in doubt, since the allegation that one was male and the other female contradicts gender negotiations, limiting the Roman view through this division as a key factor in delineating, defining and measuring both masculine and feminine. It should be kept in mind that power is inherently unstable and constantly being worked on (Foucault, 1979 apud Revell, 2016, p. 15).

The discourse of practice, which creates a sense of identity, was also used in an ongoing revelation and renegotiation of social power for each individual (Revell, 2016, p. 15). Power was exercised at numerous points and within unequal and instable relations. Generally, power relations are not as exposed as other types of relations, such as economic, knowledge or sexual. Power relations are the immediate effects of the parts, the inequalities and the imbalances that have been produced in the relationship itself, inasmuch as, to understand power relations, it must be considered that these kinds of relations are not in the position of supra-structures, with the simple role of prohibition or reconduction, but have a directly productive role where they are activated. These relations are intentional and are in no way subjective, and can cause resistance, which is present throughout the power network and can transform power itself (Foucault, 1988, p. 89-91). However, it is important to reflect on who controls the different cultural gender roles and relationships, as power is not a static hierarchy but a dynamic negotiation between individuals (Spencer-Wood, 1999).

In conclusion, the aim of this chapter was to demonstrate in which context of life the women covered in this work lived, their cultural backgrounds, their lifestyles, how they were integrated into society, their social roles, their relationships and responsibilities, their customs, and obligations, so in this way, the material culture discussed here can be understood. From this perspective, the coins minted with the images of these women present elements and symbols pertinent to the entire milieu of life and how they were viewed in Rome and provincial societies.

Chapter 2

Women's representations, Patronage, propaganda and coins

> *"[...] relations between political enemies stand for relations between men and women".*
> (Strathern, 2016, p. 21)

Because of the symbolic categories of "woman" and "man" created in Roman society, the difference inscribed within and between them are linked to representations and self-representations, as well as to the everyday practices of individuals. These reproductions were marked by gender categories, produced through the outcome of dominant discourses and practices.

What gave rise to some representations of women was Patronage, which was one of Rome's own characteristics and primarily specific to men. Although, Patronage is recognised as a typical activity of the Republic, it came to exist in both the Republic and the Empire. There were two forms of Patronage: the first concerned a rich and powerful individual in the community who was regarded as *patronus* and who offered legal protection or money for public constructions, such as a bath house, an amphitheatre, a harbour and so on. For such a performance, he was honoured by the community with a statue or an inscription in which he was called *patronus*, in the sense of "protector" or "benefactor" (Hemelrijk, 1999, p. 93-94).

The second type of Patronage was from one individual to another individual, where there had to be a relationship between two people of different status, which was called personal Patronage. However, these people had to be free and they had to have a friendship between them and reciprocal exchanges of goods and services. The patron would utilise his power, status, and superior prosperity to help his client's career through his political influence and advice, by offering legal assistance and protection, or by supporting him financially. In return for the *beneficium*, the client would offer his *gratia*, which could be demonstrated by divulging the patron's benefits, resulting in an increase in his reputation. This could also be done by following his advice, by being loyalty to him (in the republican period it was often expressed by voting), by attending the morning greeting or even by being at his disposal all day (Hemelrijk, 1999, p. 94).

During the Augustan period, politicians engaged in a system of Patronage and nepotism (Syme, 1939, p. 386), whereby the emperor was expected to intervene in the affairs of prominent citizens in need of aid and assistance. In this way, he was expected to show generosity on a large scale to the Roman people and army. This subsidy became a Roman tradition. When a prominent family experienced difficulty, contributions would commonly be made by the father's friends (Barrett, 2002, p. 188).

As far as Patronage was concerned, women were slow to join the activity due to the reclusive life they were expected to follow and the conflict that the activity designated with public life, in addition to the restriction of some women regarding the control of their property. Consequently, those who followed the activity of matrons had to deal with the conflict between the public role of Patronage and traditional feminine values. Thus, as they had no legal or political support, their Patronage was limited, restricted to material rewards and literary encouragement, with less effect on women of the imperial family. The link with the emperor brought a certain power and as the emperor's intermediaries, they secured good rewards, since the emperor himself was the universal patron and connections with him were vital for political success. Due to their close position to the emperor, they were regarded as public figures, so that birthdays, weddings, as well as births of children were celebrated in verse according to an existing cultural Patronage. However, poems could only be reciprocated with gifts of money, property, or literary encouragement (Hemelrijk, 1999, p. 95-96, 98 and 137-138).

Portraiture of their own image had a close connection with Patronage, especially after the second century AD, when the demand for public affairs for imperial and non- imperial women increased. Women who donated funds for public buildings, public festivals and games received as a reward a portrait of themselves in a prominent place in the city (Meyers, 2012, p. 453). Compared to the emperor's Patronage, theirs was quite limited. However, the Patronage of non-imperial women was even more limited and they could not receive rewards equivalent to a powerful public position (Hemelrijk, 1999, p. 138).

Regardless of the limits, from the middle to Late Republic and Early Empire, it was recognised that women could "freely" be useful in giving private advice to men in their families and being a familiar influence on friends. In the turbulent period of the triumvirate, several women were recruited to help their husbands or sons. Moreover, they could intervene in some matters in place of their relatives through the *amicitia* (Barrett, 2002, p. 186-187). However, the representations and appearances of these women in public or within activities such as the Patronage still singularised a posture that should be contained and dominated, deprived of properties that, for the most part, qualified such agencies within the male sphere. This could range from the proper name, which came from a *paterfamilias,* to a restricted image reproduction, with an appeal of norms to be followed for such disclosure and other restrictions. In this period, the construction of female identity was still rooted in the internalisation of women in norms enunciated by male discourses (Chartier, 1995, p. 40).

However, the restriction did not contain the fact that in the Late Republic women exercised Patronage and used this position to influence the men in their families in political matters. This activity was tolerable and in accordance with the ideal, because the circumstances concerned family matters (Dixon, 1983; Fischler, 1994, p. 118). Thus, it cannot be denied that this gave rise to a more complex series of interactions that would have to be constantly negotiated and cared for (Giddens, 1992, p. 17).

The conquest of the public space probably happened because women like Livia and Agrippina often had to deal with demands for activities that were outside the limits of household chores to fulfil family responsibilities, at which time they came into contact with domestic and public affairs (Fischler, 1994, p. 122). Women's consent to work in this sphere demonstrates their acquiescence to the dominant representations of gender difference. Even taking up new activities, the division of attributions and spaces, legal inferiority, the inculcation of social roles and exclusion from the public sphere distanced them from the real and from having only male figures in the imaginary, contributing to the female inferiority, tirelessly repeated and demonstrated, which was inscribed in the thoughts and bodies of one and other women (Chartier, 1995, p. 40).

Differentiation in women's activities does not mean that the new spheres have removed manipulation. Recognising the mechanisms, limits and uses of consent are good strategies for correcting the privilege that women's history has largely accorded to "victims or rebels", "active or actors of their destiny", to the detriment of "passive women", who are too easily seen as consenting to their situations, even though the question of consent is central to the functioning of a system of power, whether social or sexual. It is of utmost importance to realise that not all the fissures that erode forms of masculine domination take the form of spectacular tears, nor are they expressed by the eruption of a discourse of refusal or rejection. They are usually born within consent itself when the incorporation of the language of domination is reemployed to mark a resistance. In this context, the submission imposed on women as symbolic violence helps us to understand how the relationship of domination is affirmed, radical, irreducible and universal. For that reason, domination has historical configurations and mechanisms that announce agencies and representations as "natural", therefore biological, which stems from a social and thus historical division of roles and functions (Chartier, 1995, p. 42), framing patriarchy as structural, just as it already was in Rome.

The sexual difference is constructed by the discourse that founds and legitimises itself. This is how the gender division of labour has been produced by all the discourses, such as economic, political, legislative, state and other types of discourse, which entrench the opposition between domestic and public activity or between reproductive and productive work. These discourses provoke a sexual division of labour, bringing women together in certain activities and placing them ever lower in the professional hierarchy (Scott, 1991, p. 428 apud Chartier, 1995, p. 43). However, such a proposition is not in line with a "biological determinism", which postulates a direct relationship between biology, aspects of personality and behaviour, in which biology would determine personality and individual behaviour (Piscitelli, 2002, p. 35), since the division of labour by sex is made by various societies to camouflage an essentially cultural phenomenon.

The fact that patriarchalism in Rome is structural is linked to the difficulty of perceiving the specific articulations in such history, referring it to the inertia, in the long durations, of the representations that found the essence of strangeness, inferiority and female exclusion. These representations inspire speeches of several centuries, which are models of understanding with restricted variations and tireless repetitions, which only change when the entire social world is transformed, otherwise the feminine powers will always be in a situation of subjection and inferiority, holding a limited sphere. In this regard, it is observed that female culture is built within a system of unequal relations and reactive to conflicts, framing times and spaces in their social relations (Chartier, 1995, p. 45-47).

Consequently, women's new activities and the right to have their names remembered by means of statues, plaques and coins was something recent, which misinformed and camouflaged a symbolic dominance during the Late Republic and Early Empire. The new activities were mostly established through Patronage, that is, when an individual provided a donation from their wealth for the benefit of the city or a small group within it (Meyers, 2012, p. 461) and received a tribute in return. However, those who were elevated to high positions but proved unworthy of their honours, as was the case of Messalina, could be erased from the memory of the Roman people[16] (Bélo; Funari, 2017, p. 79), having their works destroyed or eliminated in some way.

The first scholar to use the terms "Patronage" and "voluntary solidarity" was Fustel de Coulanges (1890), who described relationships of mutual obligation, such as *fides* (trust in another), which was the most common. Both favours (*beneficia*) and services or marks of gratitude (*officia*) necessarily implied an ethic of reciprocity that influenced people's involvement and reputation, which was measured according to their respective private obligations and abilities in preserving the patrons' networks of relations, passing this act from generation to generation. The exchange of services and benefits belonged not only to private morality, but also to Rome's public morality (Deniaux, 2006, p. 401-402).

Thus, the concept of evergetism and Patronage in Antiquity would be associated with the practice of receiving gifts or reciprocity. Reciprocity would be the basis of Greek and Roman Patronage, influencing religious and civic "giving". The concept of evergetism would be linked to the transliteration of the word *évergétisme*, which would be a neologism from the modern appropriation of the Greek εὐεργετέω, meaning "I do good works" (Hornblower; Spawforth; Eidinow, 2014, p. 293). The word is designated to define a phenomenon of voluntary benefaction to an ancient community, such as a construction, donation of grain, an honorific monument or rebuilding for the benefit of the community (Perissato, 2018, p. 116 apud Sales, 2022, p. 55).

The concept of "Patronage" (from Latin *patronus*, patron) is linked to a support given by an influential person. Not having an equivalent of this word in Greek, the closest term would be *"euergetism"* (from Greek *euergetes,* benefactor) or evergetism, which means all acts of goodwill by

---

[16] This practice was called *damnatio memoriae*, "the erasure of memory", by the disappearance of all references to the existence of that being passing through the face of the Earth. Excluding any reference to the dead was like leaving their corpse unburied, one of the worst things that could happen to the Romans, as their souls would be left without harbour and direction (Gonçalves, 2014, p. 12-13).

an individual to other citizens. The term describes the public role done by an individual rooted in a masculine reference system. These terms are difficult to apply to women, because in Latin the word *patrona* is derived from the masculine *patronus*, which is formed from *pater* and essentially refers to male authority (Bielman, 2012, p. 239).

Gift exchanges in the Homeric period preceded Hellenistic evergetism and expanded in that period to eastern regions, while in the Roman period they were maintained by the economic, social, and political needs of the Empire. During the Hellenistic period, with long-standing religious and social reciprocity, the use of political and economic reciprocity made evergetism an element for hierarchical legitimisation. In this way, Hellenistic evergetism may have influenced the Roman Patronage in some way[17] (Sales, 2022, p. 55).

In mentioning the action of Patronage, Hermelrijk comments "civic munificence" as something common to "good" Roman people. Civic munificence was generally seen as involving two parties: the benefactor, who provided the community with buildings, entertainments, and other services; and the beneficiaries, who expressed their gratitude with an honourable reward and privileges. Different motives have been suggested for civic beneficence, namely competition among the elite, the gain of social prestige, financial pressure from the cities, and legitimisation of elite political laws, all of which have shown that civic munificence was a complex phenomenon that served many purposes, such as promoting civic unity, lessening the tension between the prosperous elite and those who were not of the elite (Hermelrijk, 2015, p. 112).

Civic munificence contributed to the stability and attractiveness of civic life. The benefits could range from the beautification of cities, public buildings or infrastructure works such as roads and aqueducts. These acts of generosity contributed to the appearance and ease of cities, and there were many public buildings financed by women, as well as religious buildings such as temples. In addition, infrastructure work was carried out, such as water supplies, roads, bridges, city walls, gates, arches, the paving of public areas, structures for entertainment, as well as theatres, amphitheatres, squares, utility buildings and other facilities, which include bath houses, bookstores, harbours, basilicas, *chalcidica* (galleries), *curiae* (building where the Senate met) and others. According to the study made by Hermelrijk, it was possible to see that most of the buildings that received sponsorship from women were

---

[17] For more on reciprocity see: MAUSS, M. The Gift: the form and reason for exchange in Archaic societies. *In*: MAUSS, M. **Sociology and Antropology**. London and New York: Routledge, 1950. p. 224.

religious constructions, as well as temples and sanctuaries of various types and sizes, in addition to the donation of statues of deities to these places and a whole structure linked to the temple, such as kitchens, ports, halls with furniture, extension of rooms, furniture, columns, altars, pavements, doors, benches and other equipment (Hermelrijk, 2015, p. 112-119).

It is interesting that in the Republic, donations from women were restricted to the religious field, but this restriction ceased to exist during the Empire, when women donated a large proportion to public buildings. In the case of temples, they were used for various purposes and were mostly financed by private money. Temples served as repositories for treasures and valuable goods. They were also used to store treaties and other documents; to hold sacred banquets; to function as local senates (*collegia*) of some cities for their social and political affairs; to provide centres of commercial activities in their surroundings, among others. Temples were the heart of religion and social life in Roman cities and donors attracted a lot of attention (Hermelrijk, 2015, p. 120).

The extreme form of response to the benefit of rulers was the offering of adorations, in other words, those who received benefits exalted their patrons as worthy of the honours destined for the deities. Adding to this is the fact, the Patronage relationship in the provinces involved the need for the local elite to preserve their properties and privileges, contributing for leaders to always be favourable to peace and, therefore, to Rome (Sales, 2018, p. 41 apud Sales, 2022, p. 56).

The munificence was not static, but a dynamic process in which women received public esteem and recognition, as well as bringing them into the public arena, with the gain of social distinction and some privileges, demonstrating their integration into civic society with distinction (Hemelrijk, 2015, p. 179). Benefits to donors could take the form of statues or even plaques of honour. These statues tended to celebrate the individuals of family connections, but imperial women received some physical characteristic from the emperor, since they owed their position to the family member who held the imperial office, which evidenced a cohesion of the imperial family and the project of dynastic continuation, as well as themes such as motherhood, happiness, and fertility. Women's public activity contributed to the life of their cities through office work, donations of money or other resources, subsidising public entertainment and the construction of buildings (Meyers, 2012, p. 460-461).

Beneficiaries were also commemorated for their actions of public generosity through honorary inscriptions, in which the explanation of why the benefit was made was omitted. For women, this process was more intense in the imperial period, when they began to accumulate large sums of money, which were often passed on to their children or paternal inheritance. However, there were those who decided to invest in public acts of generosity. The return of the benefit usually made a memorable impact, from the smallest ones, such as a name plaque for having donated oil to a bath house, to the largest ones, such as the construction of a building in the town with the donor's name in giant size on the façade, to be remembered for generations. This also helped mould a personality of the donor (Meyers, 2012, p. 463). In most of the terminologies used on tribute plaques, it is not clear what renovation activities were done by the benefactor. The honour plaques usually said that the donors had paid for the renovation or other activity with their own money (Hermelrijk, 2015, p. 117-119).

Hermeldijk, in studying the women donors of some Roman provinces, highlights some terms that were used to recall their merits in providing an important civic contribution, but the reasons that proved this honour are generally vague. The most concrete terms presented are: *munificentia, liberalitas, beneficia*; the most common are: *merita, munificentia, liberalitas* and *beneficia*; there are also sayings of close relatives, such as the husband and the father, but no extra information; still, the terms are reinforced by superlatives corresponding to merit, generosity and honour; there are moral (*pudicitia, castitas, pudicissima*), civic and religious virtues, such as integrity, prudence, *piety* or devotion (*innocentia, sapientia, pietas*); in addition to her emotions and social distinction (*honestissima*). Other terms are even more vague, such as simply speaking of their merits (*merita*) and the combination of *ob merita et beneficia*, and *munificentiam*. However, these inscriptions were imprecise (Hermelrijk, 2015, p. 155-156), which suggests that the fact of not knowing for sure the actions of such women seems to cover up actions for political and gender reasons.

This last hypothesis agrees with Hermelrijk's work, when the scholar mentions that there would be gender conventions that would lead to the conciseness of the inscriptions and dedications to women donors. In addition, she points out that, for larger female inscriptions, the names of male members were placed together, such as the names of husbands, something that may refer to the perseverance of male dominance and the use of artifices to gain greater space for male success. Moreover, these longer sayings also enumerated how much work they had already done. To add to this, mentioning the male members of their families was also linked to the importance of emphasising their origins. Other sayings made it clear that the money donated was directly theirs. However, for these honours to exist, there would have to be the consent of the Senate or the local consul. They also decided what kind of merit was to be used for the donor and how it was to be demonstrated, as well as determining the material, costs, and wording (Hermelrijk, 2015, p. 157-158).

Women often had partners as donors, meaning that they were usually family members, such as a husband, father, brother, or grandfather. And there was a hierarchy of names in the honorary inscriptions, since the names of male donors always appear in the first instance than the name of the female donor. In the event that the names of all the donor's family members appeared, there was the sequence of the male name first, followed by the donor's name, the adolescent children and lastly the children. The fact happened because *sine manu* marriages were strictly separated, the donation of this type of couple was seen as a joint business, not as a gift from the husband to his wife, and there was co-operation between fathers and daughters. However, a woman with a living father would be under his *potestas* and unable to own property (Hermelrijk, 2015, p. 131).

Almost all munificent women were supposed to be *sui iuris*, which could indicate that they would have received earnings through wills made by their parents or grandparents. Thus, due to the separation of property between husband and wife in *sine manu* marriages, these *sui iuris* women would mostly contribute to their own possessions. The money used for donations for the construction of buildings, for example, would be deducted from part of the children's inheritance. Consequently, the honorary plaques remembered the generosity of these people, but were also part of a favourable advertisement for the entire family involved (Hermelrijk, 2015, p. 131).

Placing statues of themselves and other family members in public spaces reinforced the family's place in the city's history, communicating their ideas and beliefs to visitors and residents. Women began to perform this type of activity because they may have had the same desire as men to receive glory by participating in public life. Moreover, it may have been a way of reacting to the system of division, which formed a traditionalism between the "public" and the "private" and which allowed them to enter urban affairs in the same way as men. These events of the Augustan period contributed to changes in Roman culture, giving such women the opportunity to be acclaimed and to be seen as examples for other women. These actions were essential for the continuation of the dynastic lineage of the families to which they belonged (Meyers, 2012, p. 464-465), as such acts kept the esteem and value of a certain family.

In general, a public statue was erected for religious reasons, to show loyalty to the emperor, for honour or to commemorate someone notable of the place. Financed with public or private money, the choice of placing a statue and its location was up to the power of the local Senate. As long as the statue was a beautification to the city, this act was taken as a civic benefit. A public statue not only conferred a recognition of the person, but also brought prestige to those who were named together with the honorary inscription (Hermelrijk, 2015, p. 134 and 161).

Munificence brought several openings for women of that time because they were considered to be disqualified from civic office and from the gaining of public honour. However, the reason for this act could be more complex, involving differences of family prosperity, social *status*, ambition, family tradition, religious feelings, and others, but honour seems to be the most important. In this sense, many members of families known for their custom of giving, must have felt pressurised to do so, since munificence guaranteed the family reputation. In relation to women donors, in addition to maintaining the family reputation, it seems that there was a dispute between them, since some of them became role models for other women to follow. Thus, munificence was essential for honour and public recognition, aiming to achieve posthumous fame. In Rome, this space was taken by women linked to the imperial family, while in the provinces this group could include free women and those who were part of the local elite. However, the status of such women was not indicated (Hemelrijk, 2015, p. 165-176) in the sayings.

However, the promotion of these women to the imperial body encouraged the attitude of linking them to the state, which helped explain their appearance in literature. What appears is that active women, such as Fulvia, who organised summit conferences, commanded armies and implemented prohibition policies, and others who were even less politically active, seem to have been pursued by ancient authors, such as Tacitus and Suetonius, in order to warn Roman men of their disturbances and threats to the political order (Hallett, 1984, p. 10).

From this perspective, the wives and mothers of discredited emperors were represented as those who had everything to be "good" and became "bad". However, this type of interpretation resulting from bilateralism can be considered obsolete academically. Nonetheless, these representations, pointed out by scholars, can demonstrate in a simplified way a tension generated within Roman society itself about the status of women, about the role they played and about whether such roles were accepted by society. Both the elite and the emperors felt ambivalent about the ideal place for imperial women, so their representation in literature was a reaction to this tension and the contradictory product of the nature of the imperial woman's role (Fischler, 1994, p. 129-130).

The activities involving imperial women became category standards that were used by these authors to qualify emperors, thus portraying the quality and nature of the "bad" ruler. For the Romans, "good" emperors had wives and mothers whom they could control and who would never overstep their bounds. However, because of their traditional activities, they were subject to reinterpretation when they were executed by imperial women. Inherently, these women were part of the empire and were seen by elite men as threats to a "good" governor. For this reason, writers such as Tacitus and Cassius Dio used "bad" imperial women as synonyms for a state in disorder (Fischler, 1994, p. 127-128). However, dividing such women into "good" or "bad" and the emperors into "good" or "bad" seems to limit how these people were described, as an interpretation restricted to a dual perspective, even taking into account the point of view of the authors who characterised them.

In this context, the law, such as the *lex Oppia*, was accepted, because female heirs of great wealth were seen as threats to the Roman patriarchal social structure. They would be in a strong position to make decisions regarding the family publicly and ultimately influence family interactions with Roman society (Hallett, 1984 apud Gardner, 1990, p. 171).

As for women of provincial origin, they were seen as embarrassing members of Rome's senatorial elite, but they were synonymous with patriotic pride in their homelands, for both men and women. They usually came from senatorial or equestrian families, where the male member had a career in Rome. Cities honoured them with public statues and hoped to take advantage of their high social positions. This kind of honorary status was impossible to achieve in the capital, where honours went directly to the imperial family. Thus, in the capital there is practically no trace of these women who were not imperial. However, honours were more common in the provinces of North Africa, Italy, Spain, Gaul, Gallia Narbonensis,

Upper Germania, Dalmatia and the provinces of the Alps; nothing has been found in the provinces of Britannia, Belgian Gaul, and Lower Germania (Hemelrijk, 2012, p. 156, 478-479 and 487).

However, ancient authors paid almost no attention to women outside of Rome, except for the more moralistic ones who were linked to the senatorial elite and their families. Provincial women generally copied those of the capital and some testimonies show their public life as civic benefactors, associated with priesthood, "mothers of the city" and linked to associations (*collegia*), generally in cities of Italy and Latin provinces in the first three centuries after Christ. They financed public buildings, as well as held festivals, games, donations to the city and others in exchange for great public prestige. Their status ranged from the senatorial elite, free women from ancient Roman families, to those who had achieved Roman citizenship. They could also derive from a decurial or subdecurial elite. The cult for the priesthood could also bring great social advancement, which was usually practised out of a sense of social and moral obligation. Most important was the protection of the interest of the city or *collegium* with the local authorities or Roman ones, for their social connections (Hemelrijk, 2012, p. 479-481).

An acceptance of the Patronage of the city of origin would bring the benefits and consideration of a worthy citizen. The titles *mater municipii* and *coloniae* were of great honour and merit for (sub)decurial women, but seem to have been restricted to central Italian cities. The highest degree of honour was when a statue of the person was built, which ultimately stimulated and influenced other members of the town. The prestige and perpetual remembrance of the public statue was a guarantee of covetousness. Few of these statues in the provinces have been preserved and few belonged to families who were not from Rome or who had recently received Roman citizenship, which indicates that these women were from a special group (Hemelrijk, 2012, p. 482-485).

In this light, the application of Roman laws to Roman citizens must have enabled the increase in the number of female citizens in provincial cities and the ease of inheritance and of owning, managing, and controlling a vast amount of property with almost no male interference. It was difficult to neglect these women, who, along with the legal ability of control, were welcomed, especially when cities were in financial difficulties, acquiring, in this way, a public face (Hemelrijk, 2012, p. 488).

The reward to the man or woman donor was demonstrated through mentions on plaques accompanying statues, for example, as Hermelrijk (2015) points out. Nevertheless, this is not seen on the coins, in other words, the coins captions do not clarify the correlation between the minting of the female image coins and Patronage, suggesting that coins might not be directly linked to Patronage, but that it would have a greater propagandistic link in favour of the emperor. Finally, these women could be patrons and their images on coins would increase the public reception of their figures. In this way, the disclosure of a female figure who had contributed to the benefit of the city would also be something honourable and worthy of pride for the emperor, especially if she was part of the imperial family, and thus would allow the granting of her face on coins. Differently, in the provinces, female images on coins seem to be a way of celebrating their acts performed by Patronage and a celebration of the emperor's wife, sister or mother.

2.1. Coins and propaganda

In order to demonstrate the public image of Roman women through coins, throughout the period covering the Late Republic and Early Empire, this work illustrates how, in this context, women of five generations managed to improve their visibility in public life through responsibilities linked to the imperial family, which led them to Patronage. Consequently, they were part of imperial propaganda, which included their own image on coins, which was a way of demonstrating power, since there is no doubt that the Romans used symbols, captions, and images on coins to promote political ideas, social and religious events, and military or economic messages (Porto, 2014).

In addition, striking coins was a sign of authority and the right to do so was disputed either by the Senate, by generals who pursued imperial power, or by provinces that wanted to be independent from the central power. Furthermore, the emperors, the main agents of Roman power, used the space on the coins to reinforce their authority, publicising their military conquests, their virtues and the ways in which they benefited the population (Florenzano, 2015, p. 17-18)

Initially, being in public and maintaining a public image were a crucial projection for the ideal of masculinity and were part of the definition of being male. The emperor not only had control over the public space, but also forced aristocrats to respond to this masculinity through other alternatives, such as military service, which became one of the Roman ideals of virtue (*virtus*), strength, courage, and glory. Oratory was also an aspect of masculinity, in addition to the vestments and the toga, which symbolised the Roman ideal of the *vir,* and the figure of the citizen was to appear in the Forum and surrounding areas, which were part of the heart of Rome's politics and social life. Augustus, in turn, moulded an image of dominance, identity and masculinity, delineating and reinforcing the male gender in proportion to his responsibilities and using an appropriate figure of the Roman male, which included his look, gestures, walk and speech. Consecutively, the effeminate man was also determined by their visual appearance, feminine qualities and other aspects concerning power, described as *mollitia,* a term denoting softness of body, character, weakness, and effeminacy (McCullough, 2007, p. 13-18).

Despite the position these women found themselves in and having to deal with the patriarchy of the time, they achieved a certain public scope, which is marked in the material culture of that society. Imperial women knew the value of image to promote themselves, since the practice of placing an individual's image on coins comes from before the Romans themselves started this activity in the last decades of the Republic. This was a practice already started by successors of Alexander the Great, who had been doing it for a century and a half, but Julius Caesar started the practice in Rome in 44 BC (Harvey, 2020, p. 18-19).

In Hellenistic Greece, not only governors had their images on coins, but also women, a practice incorporated by the Romans in the same way. The images on Hellenistic coins were designed with characteristics of gods or goddesses, but with some elements to show who the person represented was. An example is the series of coins of the Ptolemies. Coins with women on them could feature clothing and hair styles similar to those of goddesses such as Aphrodite and Demeter, a fact that sometimes makes identification difficult. Sculptures served as models for the definition of faces on coins and also helped numismatists identify the faces on the coins themselves when the name was not identified. It was customary at the beginning of coinage in Greece, in the 6th and 5th centuries BC, to place images of the patron deity of the city as a mark of identity and authority, suggesting that later Hellenistic kings did not want to break this tradition entirely, making the images hybrid and usually with an idealised beauty (Harvey, 2020, p. 20-26).

In general, the image of a person was important in a society where most of the population could not read or write. In addition, images on coins had great power and impact. The ideas and information embedded in the images that circulated in such societies reached the users directly and effectively. The agents producing these objects were well aware of these mechanisms that turned coins into important elements of political propaganda and sought to make the most of them (Florenzano, 2015, p. 18).

To add to this, the oldest known coin hoard from Classical Antiquity was found hidden in a pot buried in the foundations of the temple of Artemis at Ephesus, in the mid-6th century BC. Deities and their attributes regularly adorned the coins of Greek cities. Even in the early coinage of the Hellenistic kings, the mythical ancestors Zeus and Hercules were the ones who dominated the silver coins and Athena and Nike (Victoria) the gold ones. Even before Alexander, some Persian provincial governors and other rulers of Asia Minor suggestively usurped the place of divine portraits, supplanting them on the obverse with their own likenesses. Moreover, Greek iconography was the same for centuries, varying only in style or detail over time. The earliest Roman coin types, from the late 4th and early 3rd centuries BC, drew heavily on the Greek repertoire, mainly with gods such as Mars, Hercules or Apollo and symbols that were also linked to religion, such as the tripod, the eagle, the thunderbolt, the caduceus and other elements (Williams, 2007a, p. 143).

Only in the mid-2nd century BC did the figures of women on coins begin to gain more individualised attributions, removing some of the goddess aspect, which could evidence an increase of them in political activities. Regarding coins with faces minted in Rome, the individualised use of the face became a norm during the Late Republic (Harvey, 2020, p. 18-26), where the figures of elite Roman women were shown for the purpose of propaganda about the imperial family.

In Rome, coinage was an important medium for imperial propaganda, which helped to form Augustus' image as a ruler (Bruun, 1999, p. 26). Authorities relied primarily on dynastic competence to influence social minds, but messages on coins were part of a legitimisation of power. Symbols were validated by the fact that they presented images that led to respect, since rulers claimed it (Levick, 1999, p. 44-45). The wives of emperors played an important role in legitimising their husbands. They became important to be seen in statue groups, dedications, festivals, and imperial coins. It was also important that their ancestors had been emperors or prominent members of the imperial ruling family (Claes, 2013, p. 125).

In keeping with the proposed theme, it is interesting to note that the term *propaganda* comes from the Latin verb *propagare* and the noun *propagatio*, which means to enlarge, extend, spread, implant, or extend times. *Propagator* was the title of a magistrate, who had the function outlined as one of the epithets of Jupiter, in other words, the one who enlarges, magnifies, and conquers the Empire (Busino, 1980, p. 275-276; Gonçalves, 2002, p. 69). According to Huici Módenes, propaganda is an activity that has been almost consubstantial with politics since the dawn of humanity and seems to have been born at the same time as the appearance of the first concepts of organisation and social hierarchy. Thus, propaganda has been asserting its persuasion techniques, which can range from extreme physical intimidation to the most elaborate verbal constructions through rhetoric. However, persuasion is not always synonymous with manipulation, but with convincing and resulting in certain behaviours constructed on reality (Huici Módenes, 1996, p. 21-42 apud Gonçalves, 2002, p. 70-71).

For Marta Sordi, propaganda is always done in a hidden way, through surreptitious persuasion. It is not a simple dissemination of news, but also of gestures, actions, speeches, images, writings, and other artistic representations, which are intended to exert psychological pressure on a group to emphasise or discredit an idea, a person, a product, a policy, or a religiosity, in order to obtain consensus (Sordi, 1974, p. 5). According to Busino, propaganda is a way of formulating, disseminating, and propagating biased messages, aiming to conquer and/or maintain hegemony through persuasion, for the use of power (Busino, 1980, p. 276). According to Godechot, propaganda is the art of persuasion and its greatest characteristic is that it is a temporary process (Godechot, 1952, p. 515). For Bobbio, it is a systematic and conscious effort to influence opinions (Bobbio; Matteucci; Pasquino, 1986, p. 1018 apud Gonçalves, 2002, p. 71-74).

In Antiquity, existing symbols were already articulated to create an image of themselves for their people, which should be in accordance with the cultural standards accepted by that society. Images required calculated communication, with precise effects, which unveiled a part of reality, because power also owes its existence to the appropriation of information and knowledge to govern, manage and dominate (Balandier, 1980, p. 13). Through propaganda, Roman emperors achieved prestige, consideration, loyalty, adherence, and obedience (Busino, 1980, p. 276 apud Gonçalves, 2002, p. 58-60).

Such images were not made for agitation propaganda, which aims to change attitudes, but for integration propaganda, which aimed to reinforce ideologies, in other words, to stabilise the social body as an instrument of the government. This explains why the government cared about the communication of ideas and values associated with the emperor and his legitimisation. In view of this, propaganda was of positive value to the emperor's rules, with a degree of persuasion, even if it was only implicit. However, the result of this resource would have to be a motivation to idealise the emperor through a series of ideals and values associated with him (Noreña, 2011, p. 18 apud Elkins, 2019, p. 111).

Propaganda helped justify the rule by one person and his prominence over other human beings. Moreover, the justification of power was derived from the law, the constitutional structure guaranteed by the plebs and the Senate, and the nature that the sovereign demonstrated to have. The sense was that the emperor should show himself to be better to his subjects and hold divine consent for their worship (Mazza, 1970, p. 3-93). Practising the virtues and publicising this practice became important propagandistic actions, which gave cohesion to the public sense, propagating the continuity of the imperial system and its values, as well as the prince's connection with the subjects and gods (Hidalgo de la Vega, 1995, p. 19-25 and 108-125 apud Gonçalves, 2002, p. 59-60).

Images carry power and the sovereign uses them as an obligation to substantiate his own power. Politics, however, generates effects of order and security, and ends up imposing itself not only through coercion, but also through images, which are capable of reinforcing adherence and setting people in motion. Through acts and images, the ruler shows his greatness and qualities, acting according to the rules of virtue, such as competence in governing (Balandier, 1997, p. 15 and 110). In this way, he feels compelled to show himself according to his position and function, notifying the population of his identity, with the advent of his authority, who he is and what he should be (Bourdieu, 1997, p. 101). The creation of images and symbols is done on behalf of the sovereign and those around him, because what will be revealed and explained by images and symbols is created and organised (Balandier, 1997, p. 62) with the aim of establishing an image of permanence, continuity and tradition. Thus, force must be kept inactive while the sovereign uses his symbolic power (Luttwak, 1999, p. 266-267). These ways of persuasion through communication are explained by the intention of maintaining command, as there may be social tensions (Elias, 2001, p. 140-151 apud Gonçalves, 2002, p. 60-62).

The symbolic is used as a power to make us see and believe, which confirms and can transform our world view and our actions on the world, consequently, modifying the world itself through a specific mobilisation effect (Bourdieu, 1989, p. 14-15). For the reception of these symbols, its knowledge is presumed. In other words, for a symbolic exchange to work, both parties must have equal categories of perception and evaluation (Bourdieu, 1996b, p. 168). However, there is an enormous variability and plurality of understandings or misunderstandings of ancient representations (Chartier, 1990, p. 21). Symbolic systems act within knowledge and communication (Bourdieu, 1989, p. 9).

Symbols transport messages that help human beings to demonstrate their vision of their own position in the world. Hence, the vision of their social identity makes politics the place par excellence of symbolic efficacy, since ideas about the social world are subordinated to the logic of the conquest of power. The symbolic process fulfils the function of legitimising and justifying power by providing it with the symbols necessary for its expression, making the maintenance of the symbolic order contribute to the maintenance of the political order, with involvement in the relations of production, circulation, and consumption, which help in the ordering of social relations (Bourdieu, 1999, p. 69, 99, 159, 175 and 354).

However, authority is often confused with legitimacy, which are closely related. Power often becomes the central criterion for authority, while success serves as legitimacy. Earned authority helps to legitimise power and the ability to issue communications, elaborated for convincing reasons, securing the position of ruler (Friedrich, 1974, p. 94-100). To legitimise the ruler, it is necessary to disseminate his image through propaganda (Gonçalves, 2002, p. 62-65).

The legitimacy of political power rested not only on taxes and the army, but also on the beliefs of human beings. The imperial population saw the idealised ruler, who symbolised an unchanging order of the world (Hopkins, 1978, p. 232). For the ruler to achieve his designs, propaganda must convey positive information; the message must inform the existence of power; easily, people must identify who issues it; the attributes of the ruler must be shown; the achievements of those in charge must be demonstrated. Thus, analysing power also means considering the imaginary and the symbolic (Balandier *et al.*, 1989, p. 147-153). That said, manipulating political symbols is a form of propaganda (Kaplan; Lasswell, 1979, p. 148). In the Roman Empire, the ruler needed support, so much so that relationships were established such as Patronage, clientele, among other alliances that helped in this regard (Gonçalves, 2002, p. 66-67).

However, the images, symbols and allegories had to be clear and understandable representations to the population, with due control. Some members of the local aristocracy who wanted to honour the emperor would dedicate a statue to him, but the representation had to be accepted by the ruler. To this end, since the Republic, there were rules (*ius imaginum*) regulating the right to publicly display individual portraits, which were generally placed in public places such as forums, sanctuaries, and others, for propaganda purposes and to exalt the family of the person represented. With the establishment of the dynastic cult[18] by Augustus, portraits of the prince and his family increased (Gonçalves, 2002, p. 76). According to Tacitus, no honour was left to the gods when Augustus chose to be worshipped with temples and statues, like the deities, and with priests (Tac. *Ann.* I.10). The cult of the emperor constituted a ceremony or a ritual that gave a divine aura to this human being, represented as a god on earth. In theory, his authority was unlimited and the notion of *divus augustus* developed until Byzantine times (Brubaker; Tobler, 2000, p. 574).

Augustus was the first to be concerned with the systematisation of images together with politics, seeking to publicly expose his military qualities as *divi filius* and his merits of the State (Gonçalves, 2001, p. 57), by putting aesthetics at the service of politics (Porto, 2012, p. 17; Porto, 2018, p. 141). Associated with the image of the god Apollo, Augustus made himself grow, since the divine was superior to any human being, which was perfected after his death and with his deification. Even alive, from 27 BC, Rome saw the emergence of the imperial cult, a rite born of reverence for the *manes* of the ancestors and linked to the private sphere, which revered the strength of the ruler. However, Octavian became a "public" *paterfamilias* after the institutionalisation of the imperial cult (Martins, 2011, p. 69-72). He built his public image based on his conquests, which were linked to his *cursus honorum,* including his civil, military, political and religious activities, which built the characteristics of his representation, which at the end of his rule added up in a way that could only be synthesised through divinisation (Martins, 2011, p. 69-72 and 179).

---

[18] On the deification of the emperor and the dynastic cult, see Appendix 3.

In the West, after Caesar's death and his proclamation of himself as his adopted son, Augustus had to implement a policy of encouraging the cult of the deified Julius and the cult of his own *Genius*, in which the gratitude and reverence of the people over their leader brought back peace and prosperity. Livia was never officially included in the cult of *Genius Augusti*, but she was related to Juno, as the other part of a family's *Genius* would be in the mother, who would be Juno (Grether, 1946, p. 224-225). *Genius* would be associated with the spirit, who could appear holding a cornucopia and a *patera*, sometimes with an altar at his feet. He was often linked to the *Genius* of the Roman people (GENIVS POPVLI ROMANI) and represented in various ways, such as *Genius* of the Senate (with beard and toga), *Genius* of the Emperors (and Caesars) and *Genius* of the Army (as the standard military example) (Sear, 2000, p. 41).

The dissemination of imperial images was essential to the spread of the imperial cult. With Augustus, several cities in the West erected temples and statues in honour of the ruler's *Genius,* while in the East the honour was paid to the person of the emperor himself. In several cities, there were places dedicated to the cult of the imperial house, and different temples could be erected for each member of the imperial family. By honouring the prince, the financiers could appear before the emperor, a way for the municipal elites to have direct access to the ruler (Lintott, 1993, p. 171-185), which brought the feeling of belonging to the empire. The cult was not a ritual of simple submission and fidelity, but the cities ended up transforming it into great public ceremonies, games, processions, among others. All this activity served to attract the attention of the sovereign and as an opportunity for the elite to show the strength of their munificence (Zanker, 1989, p. 319-321 apud Gonçalves, 2002, p. 79-80).

Augustan symbols can be found on coins, which were directly or indirectly linked to the imperial cult, related to *pax deorum,* the peace between the gods and the citizens, as well as *signa imperii,* signs and symbols of Augustus (Porto, 2018, p. 139). Since 27 BC, the symbols of Augustus were combined in various ways and with symbols of victory or salvation (Zanker, 1992, p. 74, 87) to honour, for example, the battle of Actium (31 BC), which was significant for Augustus' rule (Silva, 2013, p. 37 apud Porto, 2018, p. 139).

The imperial cult was a reappropriation by Augustus of a cult already known, which was introduced in his government at the time of the *restoratio augustana,* which involved changes in cultural, legal, political, and religious aspects. The initial cult was in devotion to the Lares gods and, from 7 BC, there was the inclusion of Augustus' divinity, *Genius Augusti,* and it was renamed *Lares Augusti* (Scheid, 2003, p. 163-165). In this sense, Augustus was to be an example both for citizens and for the future rulers of the empire (Porto, 2018, p. 140).

In the East, there was a tradition of veneration of power, but in the West the cult was imposed by Rome (Porto, 2012, p. 17). In the East, the cult was differentiated, since there was interaction with the local gods (Beard; North; Price, 1998, p. 334 *apud* Porto, 2018, p. 141). To add to this, Augustus propagated his cult through coins, with symbolic elements that characterised him, which made him guarantee merit and prestige to his government (Zanker, 1992, p. 18).

It was the coins that provided the faces and proclaimed, before other arts, the publicity and values of those who ruled the Roman world. However, for the reality of the empire, it must be admitted that coins were essentially important for their primary role, which was linked to circulation, in particular among soldiers, while in the late empire they circulated among bureaucrats (Brennan, 2007, p. 8). This fact may suggest that these groups were the ones on whom propaganda should be in the first instance and whom the facet of power should be aimed at reaching.

Coins of cheaper materials, such as copper, were seen as a vehicle for disseminating state-approved ideas to a broad popular base. However, gold ones, for example, had a more restricted audience, covering specific elite groups (Brubaker; Tobler, 2000, p. 573), although it is not confirmed that there were specifically coins that circulated more in one group than another.

In the Republic, the decision to strike a Roman coin and its quantity was probably made by the Senate. Three officials or a moneyer were responsible for the production of these objects and it seems that they were elected for this (Burnett, 1987, p. 17). They were the *tresviri*, a title that was represented by the abbreviation III VIR or III VIR A.A.A.F.F. The moneyers of the Republic were usually from stable families of Rome and were at the beginning of their political careers. They were like minor officials, from the lower part of the *cursus honorum* or traditional path, followed by men of the Roman elite (Crawford, 1974, p. 598-599). It seems that the moneyers worked like the *quaestors*, who were officials connected with the treasury. In the Republic and Early Empire, there were moneyers who signed their coins, however, later, these names disappeared from the coinage (Rowan, 2019, p. 14).

Regarding the choice of the subject of a coin or who decided the minting of such a coin, Levick (1982) and Wallace-Hadrill (1986) agree that coins should be chosen by government officials (*tresviri monetales,* three magistrates of coinage), by a secretary (*a rationibus,* the financial minister in charge of the imperial treasury) or by other high officials who wished to honour the emperor. Rome began producing its own coins following Greek models at the end of the 4th century BC. Rome's place of minting was administered by *triumviri monetales*, which were the same three minting magistrates, who were responsible for the model, design and issue of coins. They were selected by the consuls, who usually chose relatives or clients. The choice of coin types in the Republic was very conservative, adhering to the intention of promoting Rome, with its female personification as a city-state and with gods and goddesses of the Roman pantheon. At the beginning of the 2nd century BC, these minting magistrates began to want to promote themselves by putting their names on Roman silver denarii. In the same century, coins began to bear not only their names but also those of famous ancestors and gods associated with their families (Harvey, 2020, p. 33).

Sutherland (1986) does not agree with this position in relation to the *tresviri monetales,* pointing out that this task should have been done by an officer of higher rank and should have had an audience with the Senate and the army for this type of choice. Probably, in the provinces, this responsibility would be left to the local elites and the coinage magistrates, with the intention of the representation being accepted by the government of Rome to flatter the emperor (Harvey, 2020, p. 10-11). In this regard, Harvey (2020) cites this theme as if there was still no definitive conclusion among scholars as well as regarding who was responsible for such choices.

The *tresviri* were the annual magistrates responsible for Roman coinage, but the mint also had a wider network of workers. The *familia monetalis*, as they were called, consisted of inspectors and superintendents, such as *officionatores* or sector workers. They were a mixture of free and slave labourers (Burnett, 1987, p. 29). The mint was also expected to hire the moulders, because three people were needed to strike a coin: one to hold the hammer and strike the mould (*malliator*); another to hold the metal between the two moulds; and another to hold the upper die, which would give origin to the reverse. Provincial cities that did not produce coins regularly probably made use of travelling coin minters and coin beaters (Rowan, 2019, p. 16).

Rowan is also uncertain about who chose the themes of coins in the Late Republic and Early Empire, but emphasises that it must have been a high-status official who understood the official imperial ideology and had the ability to produce an image for a particular individual and/or an event. The scholar compares the coin with monuments, which were not made by the emperor himself, but by those who knew the emperor's ideological perception (Rowan, 2019, p. 15-16). Otherwise, the emperor should have agents, to whom he could present his wills and such artists would reproduce his ideas.

In fact, very little or nothing is known about the mechanisms of how monetary iconography was made. It is curious that in the field of art the term propaganda was abandoned, implying the use of "persuasion", "convincing" from a certain political point of view and a government agency or even the direct involvement of the emperor (Zanker, 1988, p. 3; Zanker, 2010, p. 108-112 apud Steward, 2008, p. 112). Otherwise, it is thought that the image was formulated at the mint (Wolters, 1999, p. 290-308 apud Cheung, 1988-1989, p. 58-60). Moreover, when planning provincial coins, it is suggested that local traditions influenced the agency of the mints (Elkins, 2013 apud Elkins, 2019, p. 111).

Extra money often had to be produced and the decision was made by the Senate, which was represented on coins by the captions S C (*senatus consultum*) or EX S C (*ex senatus consulto*), meaning "by the consent of the Senate". However, the need to mark coins in this way suggests that these objects could be made outside of Rome without the approval of the Senate and could be illegal. Even if this were the case, treasures of these types have been found alongside denarii legally in Rome, which suggests that these coins had a practical activity and were socially accepted (Rowan, 2019, p. 14-15).

There are doubts whether in the Empire coins had the consent of the Senate to be minted or whether this was something that only the emperor could decide. However, if the Senate was outside of this consent, it would hardly be possible to find a reason for these letters to continue to be minted. Konrada Kraft (1969) mentions that the S C could allude to honours to the *princeps*, but such letters began to be used very deliberately. On the one hand, Burnett (1977) suggests that if the Senate had openness to decide on coins, this would create a diarchy of authority, but otherwise this could cause senatorial preservation (Levick, 1999, p. 50). On the other hand, if the consent was in the hands of the emperor, the letters S C could be used to legitimise the coins by a governmental power, showing that they were minted by an official mint; or, simply, the letters were used because they were already being minted in this manner by an official mint employed for many years, as a *habitus*. According to King, monetary designers were not innovators in the development of the coinage style (King, 1999, p. 127) and its elements.

For Elkins, images and messages were formulated to persuade or manipulate the population. The Romans did not have ministers of propaganda and the emperor was too busy administering the empire. However, it seems that the individual responsible for formulating the coins should have been close to the emperor, since, as in addition to propaganda, they legitimised the government and were linked to imperial expectations and positive relations between constituent groups (Elkins, 2017, p. 7 and 10).

It seemed that the emperor had an audience to be glorified through imagery, and several images were related to his power base, such as the Senate, the *praetorians*, the military, the urban mass of Rome, and the inhabitants of Italy and provinces. In addition, many coins featured the emperor as a patron and a benefactor of these groups, bearing their titles and showing them on the obverse. In return, these groups always showed a reciprocity to the emperor, such as praising him, making sacrifices to him, dedications and honouring him in inscriptions and monuments. Many coins honoured the emperor for what he had done or what he was expected to do. These objects served as a reminder of the positive benefits of the relationship with the emperor. Even with the doubt about who chose the elements of the coins, it can be seen that the mint had an imperial agency to select the images and their meaning, with the effect of glorifying the emperor (Elkins, 2017, p. 10-11).

However, the types of coins and the shapes, and how the female characters were portrayed, become essential to constitute a monetary classification together with the political contemporaneity in which the material was elaborated. Much of what was happening at the time may be related to the production of the object, for example, the image reproduced on the coin should be something acceptable to the standards of representation that the public would expect, in other words, the type of figure would have to be something that demonstrated that the imperial family was well cultivated or successful. In the specific case of women, they should be reported as showing their domestic virtues. Therefore, it is important to consider who generated these images and for which audience.

In Livia's case, her images legitimised her with power and status, but otherwise the production also carried symbols of male power, which also legitimised the government under which the coins were minted. Some emperors even commemorated mothers who had already died, as Caligula did. Such an act was not only a demonstration of *pietas*, but of legitimising themselves through the maternal lineage (Claes, 2013, p. 94). These images reflected the desire and interest of dominant groups (Harvey, 2020, p. 157), with Rome's coinage being directly linked to the emperor, while those of the provinces followed the Roman coins models and/or honoured the emperor and his family. Roman symbolic motifs generally referred to good fortune, peace, abundance, order, and prosperity, which was believed to derive from both the divine favour obtained by Roman piety and the secular success of Roman arms, including symbols such as the caduceus, cornucopia, rudder, and ears of corn, which appear both alone and often in combination with each other and as attributes of various appropriate deities. The personifications generally fell into two categories: those that referred to the virtues of the emperors: Aequitas (Justice), Clementia (Mercy), Liberalitas (Generosity), Pietas (Religiosity) and so on; and those that referred to the qualities or attributes desired by the empire as a whole: Salus (Welfare), Spes (Hope), Securitas (Security), Felicitas (Prosperity), Hilaritas (Joy) etc. (Williams, 2007a, p. 155-156).

Duncan-Jones (1999) posits that many reverses that feature personifications of gods and goddesses are related to the structure of the mint and lack propaganda content, suggesting a questionable interpretation. According to Elkins, it is not because the image does not denote a specific historical or political event that it does not communicate something or that it does not have an ideological value. Roman art is full of personifications, with their meanings, which can encompass a larger number of social categories (Elkins, 2017, p. 23).

For Elkins, personifications and emblems were the most successful modes of communication, due to their non-specific character, making the empire and its population available to give their own meanings, but with a central power and the benefits that the imperial population received from the emperor (Elkins, 2017, p. 103).

Personification is closely linked to religiosity and Callataÿ, when dealing with Greek coins with gods and goddesses, mentions that these deities were important as they were the final guarantors of the exchange, contributing to the non-deception of trade, since merchants would be making their exchanges under the eyes of revered authorities (Callataÿ, 2022, p. 246). The personified human figures gained a meaning through a visual format and a concrete body, for a wide variety of abstract ideas (Noreña, 2001, p. 153). Moreover, every personification was honoured in cults and considered a deity (Manders, 2008, p. 33).

Roman coins were not treated as religious objects, although they were often decorated with images of gods, emperors and other symbols of Roman religion and worship. In fact, coins were usually described in legal contexts as public things, not sacred. The elements chosen to represent the public type were part of what made the coins something public and identified them as Roman. However, religion provided most of the key motifs that constituted such a public type. Coins were one of the most defining symbols of public identity in Antiquity and religion was absolutely fundamental (Williams, 2007b, p. 163) to these objects. In another way, it is not possible to completely separate the coin from the religious aspect, because, in addition to being an instrument of exchange and measure of value, they were objects impregnated with magical or religious functions, working as amulets around the neck and other purposes. They were left in sacred places, and they also fulfilled the role of pacifying some deity for good luck and/or protection. In most human societies, objects of exchange, such as stones, feathers, seeds and other materialities, become indispensable to life and were seen as manifestations of power and special strength (Florenzano, 1995, p. 223-228).

Regarding the aesthetics of imperial women in public representations, Julia, for example, would have the freedom to choose her clothes and hair, but it was her father who controlled the ultimate approval of her representations, with the intention of ensuring that her images survived. In this way, she always appeared with the same severely modest hair type as her stepmother Livia (Wood, 1999, p. 20). Hair type linked women to a certain period and connected individuals to a generic classicism and a conservative sense of social worth. However, it is understood that honour identities were constructed by the look and by short texts, which were repeated since the former had functioned socially. Confidence was thus built about that type, resulting in replication and constant repetition, as long as they were elaborated in a way that supported social preferences and categorised these women as being from the imperial family. They were unified in an ideology of the elite, which clamoured for a shared set of values and legitimacy of government categories (Trimble, 2011, p. 192-202).

The hairstyles of the Hellenistic queens on coins were similar to those of the hairstyles of the goddesses, in other words, that hair curled in a loose curve with a bun at the back. These more reserved hairstyles could have been used to convey the impression of the morality of the woman depicted, of a high status, and to link them to a specific social and political role. Sometimes, however, the hair was not similar to the goddesses', but rather had unique characteristics, perhaps for the woman to be truly identified. One type of hair that was a mark of the ideal Roman matron was the *nodus*, which only Roman women wore, marking a mortal rather than divine character of the figure represented there (Harvey, 2020, p. 48).

In addition to their hairstyles, these women displayed other varieties of attributes, including the sceptre and other symbols, which would have divine associations and which would later be taken up by the figure of Livia on coins, for example. Many of these Hellenistic female figures were influenced by images of Hera, Aphrodite, and Demeter. Several Greek women would have been deified and then compared to the goddesses (2nd-1st century BC) (Harvey, 2020, p. 26-30). What it suggests is that this was a formula found so that Greek women could appear publicly, since the women of the elite of Athens, for example, rarely appeared in political history and were not demonstrated in the male social environment, which made their social invisibility create difficulties to study them. In Rome, women would not be politically involved unless they were elite and had a male family member with authority and prestige (Hallett, 1984, p. 12 and 35).

However, the image might not correspond to what the person was in themselves. Physical or moral qualities were attributed that could have been enhanced or tarnished, changeable, transformed, and full of meanings given to them according to memories, which were established, but also linked to the imaginary. This could be mobilising and evoking images, using the symbolic, which presupposed the imaginary capacity. The image could be formed from a real axis, and the imaginary would translate the mental representation in which the exterior was perceived (Laplantine; Trindade, 1997 apud Gonçalves, 2002, p. 57).

The immediate conclusion is that there was a visual construction of identity, and that these representations of women, both in statues, on coins and other art, should not be understood as they really were in their essence. They would correspond to the demonstration of their virtues, such as chastity and sexual virtue, suggesting the maintenance of an honorary purpose within a network of public relations equivalent to high social position, being representatives of families of the imperial elite and civic benefactors. Representations took shape according to the gender construction of that society (Trimble, 2011, p. 153-154).

In relation to the representations of ancient women, gender is not a stable identity or a locus of agency from which various acts emerge, but it is an identity tenuously constituted in time, an identity instituted through a stylised repetition of acts. Moreover, gender is constituted through the stylisation of the body and consequently should be understood as a mundane way in which bodily gestures, movements and their varieties constitute the illusion of the permanence of gender itself. This thought is in line with the basic conception of the substantial model for that which requires the conception that constitutes a social temporality. Significantly, if gender is instituted by acts, which are internally discontinuous, the substance of the appearance is precisely that of the constructed identity, a performative realisation in which the mundane-social audience, including the actors themselves, comes to believe and effect a model of opinion. If the foundation of gender identity is the stylised repetition of acts through time, rather than an apparently perfect identity, the possibilities of gender transformations are to be found in an arbitrary relationship between its acts, in the possibility of different kinds of repetitions, and in the subversive breaking or repetition of that style (Butler, 1990 apud Trimble, 2011, p. 155).

It is as if there were two dimensions in society that are active at the same time and space: one would be that in which conservatism applauds and affirms a moulded gender constitution that must be followed and represented in artistic manifestations; while the second would be reality, with its distribution of gender variety existing within a group. It is thus always a society of friction between the collective thought and beliefs regarding the idealised gender, against transmutation and the existing reality of gender. This tension can cause common adversities in society involving gender bias and a dictatorial imposition by the parties sharing the first dimension.

As much as the reproductions of these women show some distinguishing feature, we have no idea how they actually looked, since their features would be tied to a formula, which would be linked to an honour-oriented figuration. However, it is understandable that the first coins with female faces would be associated with religion, when priesthood was a central part of the honour of elite women (Trimble, 2011, p. 157-165). It is therefore suggested that the female representations would be orientated towards an agency fully linked to public and civil activities, which would be correlated to a gender identity orientated towards the values of the group.

In addition to the figurative representations of women, it should be taken into account the coin captions when they exist and detect their characteristics. They can present individual characteristics, such as name and to which emperor they were linked; as well as generic aspects, associated with religion or mythology, and writings of praise for the emperor and family connections, with the possibility of relating the image to the text. Unfortunately, the real characteristics of these women in these objects are poor or nil, favouring aspects of the aristocracy evidenced from an exclusively elite point of view, accepted by the public. However, gender in representation is constructed through similar interactions and their effects, demonstrating that it is constructed as a social and collective aspect of identity (Trimble, 2011, p. 191). In this way, the coins and their captions oscillate between poles of individuality and collectivity, which should have been consciously acted upon in relation to the honour of the person to the privilege of the ruler.

2.2. Images of roman women on provincial and roman coins

The iconography of the coins analysed can show the gender dispositions regarding the woman represented. This aspect will be exemplified by the relevance of the figurative elements that accompany her, as well as those related to mythology, gods, goddesses and other attributes, in addition to the sayings in the captions of the coins, in other words, whether the woman's name is mentioned alone, accompanied by her titles or titles of male figures and the relationships of these women with such titles, relying on the framing of the gender relationship, when accompanied by a male figure, of the gender role and its social status, as far as possible.

Kampen (1991) noted in Roman art that gendered iconography had been used on Roman coins to express programmatic concerns of the state and the emperor. Harvey is also convinced that the representations of Livia on coins show that the images of Roman imperial women were part of a complex ideology of gender and power, communicating to the Roman Empire the purposes of social and political maintenance of power structures. For this interpretation, the scholar ended up analysing in the female figures of Livia the style of hair, the facial features, dress, body position, among others, as well as tracing image patterns (Harvey, 2020, p. 64).

The last years of the Republic were composed by civil wars in Rome, first between Julius Caesar and Pompey and then between Mark Antony and Octavian. The images on coins were used by them to promote themselves as icons of power, to gain governmental authority and to grow the empire. In the 40s BC, they began to put their relatives and wives on coins for the promotion of their own family. Antony coined Cleopatra VII; and Octavian his sister, Octavia, as whether they had already a public place, becoming symbols of power and authority. In this way, these female members of the imperial family were utilised as key individuals to perpetuate the dynasty (Harvey, 2020, p. 33-34). The first female donors of public buildings were from the last decades of the Republic, with a peak in the early second century AD, followed by a decline in the third. Since the Emperor and his family were formed in Rome, they gradually monopolised work on public buildings and honorary statues (Hermelrijk, 2015, p. 127).

Imperial women were generally connected with the idea of motherhood and the virtue of fertility or personified forms of deities linked to these aspects, such as Ceres, Diana (Lucifera), Juno (Lucinae) and Venus (Genetrix). The virtue of chastity, *pudicitia*, was also attributed to them. This virtue communicated the genuine blood relationship between the emperor and his heir, which was an important element in the transfer of imperial power. When the heir was adopted, chastity was not as idealised, but it had *concordia* within the family according to the pure female character (Claes, 2013, p. 188).

In this way, the role of the imperial woman was also seen as that of a protector, who could guarantee peace, *corcordia*, well-being and contentment to the Roman state. Therefore, she would be directly linked to the "idea of fertility", as bearing a child would be an act of ensuring the succession of the emperor and a peaceful transition of power. Moreover, their *pudicitia* was also related to philanthropic acts, which came from their own finances, including charity projects or public buildings inside and outside Rome (Claes, 2013, p. 188).

However, it seems that the emperors used the female figures of their families to claim power or to legitimise their kingdoms. To do so, they would need a media, which would be the coins, for everybody to know the greatness of imperial power. The spread of emperor's family members was influenced by the historical circumstances, showing, in the case of women, how they were entering public life. Historical circumstances provoked the dissemination of persuasive messages on coins, especially when the emperor or the candidate for emperor needed instruments to legitimise his rule or power (Claes, 2013, p. 236-237).

Emperors of the 1st, 2nd and 3rd centuries used a retrospective of posthumous relatives as messages to legitimise their reigns, along with historical circumstances on coins. In the Julio-Claudian family, retrospective messages were used to legitimise succession after Augustus, claiming descent and employing captions such as *divi filius* or *divi pronepos*, which referred to Augustus or someone in his family line (Claes, 2013, p. 238). Therefore, imperial women were also included on these types of coins, which featured female ancestors of the emperor, such as his mother, grandmother, wife, and others. Many emperors used the retrospective and descent of women from the Julio-Claudian and Flavian families to legitimise their positions. Women, as mothers, wives, and sisters, were placed in the messages as benefactors, but above all to elucidate family harmony (Claes, 2013, p. 241).

Chapter 3

Fulvia, the bloodthirsty

Fulvia (84 BC - 40 BC), who appears to have been born in Tusculum, was the only daughter of Marcus Fulvius Bambalio (Cic. *Phil.* 3.16) and Sempronia, daughter of Sempronius Tuditanus (Asc. *Mil.* 35). It is not clear which Sempronia was her mother (Welch, 1995, p. 197), but it is still possible that Fulvia's mother was the sister of the Sempronia of the Conspiracy of Catiline (Bauman, 1992, p. 83). The Sempronia of Catiline's Conspiracy, like Fulvia, was portrayed as one who adopted inappropriate gender roles. She committed crimes of masculine audacity, repudiated her debts, and took the initiative in sexual matters, without any regard for the "feminine" virtues of modesty, chastity, and sobriety (Hemelrijk, 1999, p. 86). With regard to her father's family, *Fulvii* was a distinguished family, which had Lucius Fulvius Curvus as consul in 322 BC. His father, Bambalio, who was an orator and politician, was dismissed by Marcus Tullius Cicero, being considered as an insignificant man (Cic. *Phil.* 3.16 apud Weir, 2007, p. 3).

Fulvia has often been described as a politically aggressive woman and domineering wife. However, according to Babcock (1965), it would be a view of modern scholars to cast the prominence of Fulvia as the wife of Antony in the first phase of the Second Triumvirate[19] and to limit the fact that only with this marriage did she launch into the political field. This thought may have come from the fact that women such as Tanaquil, Cornelia and Fulvia herself were the ones who began to have more freedom, due to the promotions won by their husbands, in other words, none of them had an autonomous power to promote themselves (Zager, 2014, p. 36). Thus, they became active participants in the glorification of their families, so that the recording of their images on coins and other representations was a way of honouring them and boasting their families.

Babcock questioned how she managed to have three important marriages and be influential. He demonstrates that all three of Fulvia's husbands were from consular families and had distinguished prospects

---

[19] The second triumvirate began after Julius Caesar's death, when Octavian took the region of Italy to deal with the veterans; Antony took the eastern provinces; and Lepidus took North Africa (Moore, 2017, p. 72).

(Babcock, 1965, p. 3). Firstly, Fulvia was the widow of Publius Clodius Pulcher, the demagogue, with whom she had a daughter, who was Octavian Caesar's first wife, Clodia. She took a large sum of money for the dowry of her marriage to P. Clodius Pulcher (Brennan, 2012, p. 357), whose *transitio ad plebem* only emphasised his patrician origin through his connection with the Claudian family. He was the son and grandson of a consul, the grandson of a judge and the brother of a future consul judge, and his three sisters had married consuls (Babcock, 1965, p. 3).

Clodius became tribune in 58 BC (Weir, 2007, p. 2) and was an extremely popular politician among the people (Val. Max. 3.5.3). Consequently, he was considered a demagogue (Plut. *Ant.* 10.1), and one of his laws passed was the *lex Clodia frumentaria* (Lintott, 1967, p. 163; Tatum, 1999, p. 151), which provided free corn for all plebeians. However, the negative view before he was famous, was that he had desecrated a sacred Bona Dea ritual in 62 BC, which was exclusively for women (Cic. *Mil.* 72). On that occasion, he dressed up as a woman and robbed Caesar's house during the ritual in order to seduce his wife (Plut. *Cic.* 28.2; Cic. *Att.* 1.12.3). However, Caesar refused to press charges (App. B. Civ. 2.2.14; Cass. Dio, *Roman History* 37.45.1; Plut. *Cic.* 29.9; Plut. *Caes.* 10.10; Suet. *Iul.* 74), since he did not want to make trouble, which could affect Clodius' popularity.

Another law that made him famous was the *lex de capite civis Romani* (Tatum, 1999, p. 153), which was made directly against Cicero. It punished anyone who declared the death of a Roman citizen without trial by sending the person into exile, for Cicero had ordered the execution without trial of the conspirators of Catilinia, among whom was Antony's stepfather, Publius Cornelius Lentulus Sura. Another law of his authorship was the *lex Clodia de exsilio Ciceronis*, which confirmed Cicero's punishment of being exiled after he had fled Rome because of the accusation arising from the previous law (Tatum, 1999, p. 156 apud Weir, 2007, p. 4-5).

Tensions with Milo began in 52 BC, with his candidature for praetor. After Clodius died violently at the hands of his political opponent in the same year, Fulvia, with two children, managed a funeral that remained in social memory for many years, in which his body was taken to the Senatorial house, cremated in a pyre (Brennan, 2012, p. 357) and she wailed dramatically. This was Fulvia's first public appearance. At the trial of Clodius' death, Ascanius recalled that Fulvia's act caused disorder. Later, she brought evidence to the trial of Milo when Cicero recognised her and expressed that she had not left her husband's side in life before the event (Cic. *Mil.*

28.55), implying that it was Clodius who had plotted against Milo and, in order to kill him, he had to do it without his wife. On the other hand, it is possible to understand that if Fulvia was always with him, she could have been considered an accomplice in his actions. However, as the widow of a popular leader, Fulvia gained a prestigious position among the people (Weir, 2007, p. 35-37).

After being widowed, she married Gaius Scribonius Curio, around 51 or 49 BC, who was also popular among the plebs and had come from a family that had reached the consulship only with his father in 76 BC (Babcock, 1965, p. 3), and was a tribune in 50 BC. He played a crucial role in the civil war with Caesar. In addition, he was a tribune in North Africa during the civil conflict, following Caesar (Brennan, 2012, p. 357). Probably, Curio had a connection with Clodius, since Cicero wrote to him in 53 BC asking for support in the case of Milo's election to the Consulship (Cic. *Fam.* 2.6.3), but Curio was already supporting Clodius (Cic. *Att.* 2.12.2; Cass. Dio, *Roman History* 38.16.4). Curio was killed by the army of Juba, king of Numidia, while fighting for Caesar in Africa in 49 BC (App. *B. Civ.* 2.7.45). Cicero proclaimed that both Clodius and Curio died for the sake of Fulvia (Cic. *Phil.* 2.1).

She then married Mark Antony - around 45 BC, according to Babcock (1965), or 46 BC, according to Weir (2007) - who was also a friend of Clodius (Cic. *Phil.* 2.48) and Curio (Cic. *Phil.* 2.45; Huzar, 1978, p. 26; Tatum, 1999, p. 116 apud Weir, 2007, p. 7), and Cicero ended up having a rivalry with him as well (Weir, 2007, p. 37). Antony had ancient and obscure origins and seems to have come from a family of plebeian nobility, which had regained strength in the early first century (Babcock, 1965, p. 3). He had already become tribune before his marriage in 49 BC, commanded Caesar's army at Pharsalus in 48 BC, and became Master of Horse in 47 BC, co-consul with Julius Caesar in 45 BC (Moore, 2017, p. 53), and consul in 44 BC (Weir, 2007, p. 2 and 7).

What it appears is that he had a maternal grandmother who was from the Fulvia family (Brennan, 2012, p. 357), two consular grandfathers, one of whom was a judge, as well as two uncles, one of whom also became a judge (Babcock, 1965, p. 3). Fulvia had two sons with Antony: Marcus Antony Antyllu, who was chosen by Octavian to marry his daughter Julia in 36 BC, but was killed in 31 BC; and Iullus Antony, who married Marcella, Augustus' niece, reaching the consulship in 10 BC, but was killed in 2 BC (Brennan, 2012, p. 357). All of Fulvia's husbands had promising careers, given that their family connections would lead her to good marriages (Babcock, 1965, p. 3).

Just as Clodius and Curio, Antony had run-ins with Cicero. In addition to the issue with his stepfather, he began to oppose Cicero after the latter failed to show up for an appointment required by Antony, which was to be a meeting in the Senate to vote on a measure in Caesar's honour, which Cicero considered shameful and skipped in order not to have to vote (Cic. *Phil.* 1.12; 5.19). Cicero responded to Antony's offences and the latter mentioned that he was insulted and suggested that he had betrayed Caesar's legacy (Wier, 2007, p. 39).

Babcock (1965) emphasises that Fulvia's family was one of the most distinguished of the Republican plebeian nobility. However, no consul of her family was recognised since 125 BC. It is significant that her father, M. Fulvius Bambalio, possibly the last of his line, married the last daughter of another noble plebeian family, the *Sempronii Tuditani*, whose name is portrayed by Fulvia's grandfather, who does not seem to have had a good career. He was the son and uncle of a consul in 129 BC, through his sister's marriage to Quintus Hortensius Hortalus, the orator. These are not characteristics that seem to have favoured Fulvia for a marriage with a good dowry. However, Babcock believes that she was wealthy and mentions a passage in which Cicero claimed that her grandfather Tuditanus appeared mad in the Forum, badly dressed and scattering money to the people, in addition to the fact that he was probably the only heir, which could have led Fulvia to have had a good amount of money, since she was the only daughter of the family of Fulvia and Sempronia. She was the daughter of M. Fulvius Bambalio and Sempronia, being the last of the Sempronius Taditanus (Brennan, 2012, p. 357), in other words, the last of each of these lineages, *Fulvii* and *Sempronii Tuditani*. Consequently, her heritage would not be despised by any young nobleman of expensive habits and meagre income (Babcock, 1965, p. 3-5). To add, Cicero describes her as a good woman and certainly a wealthy one (Cic. *Phil.* 3.16). Weirs characterises this passage as sarcastic, since it seems that Cicero was suggesting that Antony married her because of her wealth (Babcock, 1965, p. 4 apud Weir, 1965, 2007, p. 57).

3.1. The importance of Fulvia and her coins

Fulvia took on a political role after Caesar's assassination in 44 BC. She had to represent Antony's interests in Rome while he warred in the East and started a relationship with Cleopatra (Brennan, 2012, p. 358). Fulvia ended up having a special role in the plots of her husband, Mark

Antony. Seen as the one who had a constant presence at the side of her dead husband, Clodius, she was also known for her multiple interferences in Antony's actions. After her marriage to the triumvir, she was covered with discontent at her presence in the political sphere. This may have been due to her actions in a troubled time, in which she had to demonstrate a feminine authority in representing her absent husband, so as not to let his interests to be succumbed to (Rohr Vio, 2015, p. 62-63).

It was in the context of Fulvia's marriage to Antony, in 44 BC, that she first supported her husband against Cicero, who was trying to convince the Senate that Antony was an enemy of the State, with despotic designs (App. *B. Civ.* 3.8.51). In the same year, she had her first brush with the military world, when Antony had to face the sedition of two legions in Brundisium, the IV and the Marzia. Octavian invested considerable sums of money in an attempt to obtain the defection of these troops in his favour (Cass. Dio, *Roman History* 45.12.1). However, Antony opted for the hard line and, in compliance with the military code, having ordered the delivery of the legions' records to identify the rioters, proceeded to decimate them (Cristofoli; Galimberti; Rohr Vio, 2014 apud Rohr Vio, 2015, p. 64).

Cicero and Cassius Dio state that Fulvia witnessed such execution (Cic. *Phil.* 5.22; Cass. Dio, *Roman History* 45.35.3). This episode contributed to crediting Fulvia with the characteristic of a cruel and bloodthirsty woman and to paying attention to the occasions when she interfered in her husband's politics, Cicero characterising her as the most ambitious and cruel woman (Cic. *Phil.* 2.113, 2.95, 6.4 and 13.18), as he did with his enemy Antony (Cic. *Phil.* 5.2), adding that he defiled her (Weirs, 2007, p. 59). However, she was only a spectator of such an act by Antony, which took place within a *domus*, a traditional place for women, which led to the development of the thought that Antony inappropriately mixed private life with his public duties (Rohr Vio, 2015, p. 66-67). In fact, the *domus* and the performance of the woman in this space was ambiguous, since the woman would have a position of authority in this place, in addition to her participation in the social life that surrounded it. There were some rooms, such as the *atrium*, which was the central and most public part of the house, where the husband received his guests, and which was also where the wife supervised the work of slaves on different occasions. In addition, the wedding itself would provide the woman with participation in social life, as women were expected to entertain their husbands' guests and accompany them on social visits and to dinner parties (Hemelrijk, 1999, p. 8).

However, the integration of women in the home and in the social life of the family is still interpreted academically in an uncomplicated or diverse way, through a gendered division of social tasks and activities, pointing to a segregation of husband and wife in part or for the most part of their daily activities. This separation is something that such a society also believed to exist, but in practice the functionality of the *domus* could be different, even totally distinct. Cicero demonstrated an example of how the house could be used in the Late Republic. It was considered a potent material and discursive symbol of a man's position in his private life (Milnor, 2005, p. 67), which suggests arguments against the division between public and private, which has been taken narrowly, without taking into account the complexity of spatial and gendered subjectivity.

It is assumed that the couple received guests and the wife, mother, daughter, or sister acted as hostesses to the women guests. However, it was inappropriate for the husband to receive guests of both sexes. The wife spent her time in the *domus,* usually at her toilet, supervising household work, caring for the children, her husband's needs or any sick relative, while the husband might engage in discussions of his public, political and intellectual career with friends, at which their wives might be present. Moreover, they were not confined to the home or bound only to domestic activities, especially when they were prosperous, as their elevated positions as daughters, wives and mothers obscured their social lives and within politics, but they could exercise such activities indirectly. In this way, their positions were uncertain, as they were part of a social stratum that ruled and had power but were subordinate. They did share prestige and distinction in society, but at the same time they were socially inferior to men in the same social sphere. They were linked to senatorial, equestrian and decurial orders through the men of the family or their husbands (Hemelrijk, 1999, p. 8-10).

Faced with this point of view, Cicero criticised Antony for taking state business to his home (Cic. *Phil.* 2.95; 3.10; 5.11), taking the opportunity to blaspheme that it was not Antony, but his wife, who was conducting the business (Skinner, 1983, p. 276). Plutarch already mentioned that Antony's mother restricted his father's philanthropic acts, because he was a rich man, showing the balance between his mother and his father's charitable acts (Plut. *Ant.* 1) and proving that Antony could have learnt to obey a woman from his own mother. The author states that Cleopatra should thank Fulvia for teaching him to obey her (Plut. *Ant.* 10.1). With this, Cicero ended up suggesting that Antony was weak and not even in control of himself (Weir, 2007, p. 40-41).

Cicero further stated that the closeness of Antony and Curio suggested a homosexual relationship, which would make Antony a passive, subjugated by another man, having the *status* of a woman (Cic. *Phil.* 2.44; Butler, 2002, p. 121 apud Weir, 2007, p. 41), which reinforced Cicero's malediction about the subjugation of Antony by Fulvia. This type of argument was common among enemies, noting a feminisation attributed by Cicero towards his opponent. This situation was constantly reinforced by the use of popular metaphors, which combined defamation with the loss of sexual potency and masculinity, such as emasculation, castration and impotence (Moore, 2000, p. 32). This was because sexuality was closely linked to power, such that power and strength themselves were sexualised, in other words, they were inscribed in gender difference and hierarchy (Moore, 2000, p. 35). Fantham also reaffirms this issue, as she mentions that Romans easily resorted to accusations of effeminacy when they wanted to insult each other or discredit the other's oratory and political position (Fantham, 2011, p. 141).

The characteristics that Cicero attributed to Antony show that he was linked to lust, levity, insanity and that he was a drunkard. This description served to indicate that Antony would be submissive, especially to his wife (Cic. *Phil.* 6.4; Craig, 2004, p. 191). Most of the invocations about Fulvia in Cicero were to show Antony's weakness, as well as that Fulvia was performing a masculine role, rather than the traditional one of a woman, when dealing with business in the spinning room (Cic. *Phil.* 3.10). Cicero also claimed that her transactions were illicit (Cic. *Phil.* 2.95 apud Weir, 2007, p. 42, 46 and 59). Often, women who distinguished themselves by performing masculine roles were called masculine or seen as masculinised. However, if masculine characteristics were desirable in a woman, she would have to exhibit key feminine virtues as well. Moreover, masculinity in a woman was not seen as flattering. Women in whom masculinity was not balanced by feminine virtues and who publicly crossed the masculine field or employed what was considered a masculine bad habit were seen as "different" (Hemelrijk, 1999, p. 84-85). In this way, Fulvia did not escape the common stigmas given by Roman society when performing such roles, even though she contributed as a mother and wife to her wifely virtues.

Fulvia was also described as perverse and bloodthirsty during the proscriptions that followed the creation of the Second Triumvirate in 43/42 BC (App. *B. Civ.* 4.4.29; Cass. Dio, *Roman History* 47.8.2), with Mark Antony, Lepidus, and Augustus. After Caesar's assassination in 44 BC, Rome faced a civil war, since the first action of the triumvirs was proscription, which eliminated 130 senators and 2000 *equites*, who were knights of the second social order of Rome. The choice of those proscribed and killed was directly linked to the three men. The material gains from the proscriptions went to finance the war efforts against Caesar's assassins, Marcus Iunius Brutus, and Marcus Licinius Crassus (Takács, 2008, p. 21).

Taxes were also levied on the landowning classes, with one tax being instituted on wealthy women. Consequently, women, under the leadership of Hortensia, daughter of one of the most prominent orators, rose up in defiance. First, the rebellious women sought the help of the relatives of the triumvirs. Octavia, Augustus' sister, and Julia, Antony's mother, welcomed them. However, Fulvia snubbed them. The women, led by Hortensia, then did a protest in the forum and went to the court. There, Hortensia made a manifestation, but they were expelled. However, their protests reduced the number of women to be taxed from 1,000 to 400, while men in possession of over 100,000 drachmas were taxed. It is interesting to note that Antony's mother, Julia, did not oppose the protesters, although her daughter-in-law, Fulvia, did (Takács, 2008, p. 21).

Brennan accuses Apian and Plutarch of characterising her as a cruel and greedy woman in the absence of her husband, adding her role in the proscriptions and in the beheading of Cicero (Brennan, 2012, p. 358). Fulvia had become a prime target of Antony's enemies, first by Cicero (44 - 43 BC) and then by Octavian (42 - 41 BC) (Weir, 2007, p. 8), who used the strategy of insulting Fulvia to target Antony. Cicero's letters to and about Terentia and other Republican matrons, as well as those from the beginning of Fulvia's career, are evidence that women during and at the end of the Republic were far from apathetic or relegated to the private domain. However, such documents present them in the background (Moore, 2017, p. 132).

When speaking of the proscriptions, Cassius Dio recalls those of Sulla, aimed at those who betrayed the state, and gives more reason for this than to the most recent one (Cass. Dio, *Roman History* 47.4.1). The author places Lepidus and Antonius as the articulators of the slaughter (Cass. Dio, *Roman History* 47.7.1), since their rhetoric must have been designed to flatter Octavian, softening his participation in the proscriptions. The author goes on to report that Caesar saved many lives, while mentioning that Antony was merciless and a savage, adding that he loved to see the heads of the dead, even if he was eating, and indulged in their unholy and pitiful sight. He mentions that Fulvia also caused the death of many and took satisfaction in the end of her enemies, aiming to gain wealth, and often with dead people her husband did not even know the face of. During this activity, Cicero's head was also brought to them. The author cites that Antony spoke bitter words to it and ordered it to be displayed as prominently as possible, in a place where Cicero was often heard making statements against Antony, along with his severed hand.

Before that, Cassius Dio points out that Fulvia took his head in her hands, put it on her knees, spat on it, opened his mouth and pulled out his tongue, piercing it with pins she wore in her hair and uttering brutal words (Cass. Dio, *Roman History* 47.8.1-4). She was satisfied with revenge against Cicero and all the words he had spoken against her and her husbands. Appian notes that it was Laena, a centurion of Antony, who hunted Cicero down and he himself removed his tongue and hands to present to Antony, gaining some favour in return (App. *B. Civ.* 4.4.19-20). Plutarch does not mention Fulvia and states that it was Antony who wanted revenge (Plut. *Ant.* 20.3 apud Weir, 2007, p. 105).

Apian cites another episode that reveals Fulvia's brutality and greed. The author recounts that she had the desire to possess her neighbour's house, which caused her to have him proscribed. In this sense, she ordered him to be beheaded in front of her house in the Palatine, evidencing her desire for revenge against Rufus, for not fulfilling her wishes immediately. What it seems is that this act was a public warning to those who wanted to cross her path and Appian demonstrates that Fulvia also added names to the list of proscribed men (App, *B. Civ.* 4.3.15-16), suggesting that she also participated in the proscriptions so that she could take revenge on people who persecuted her family. However, Cassius Dio reports directly that she killed many (Cass. Dio, *Roman History* 47.8.2-3).

According to Plutarch, while Cleopatra managed to captivate Antony completely, his wife Fulvia, around 41 BC, led a rebellion against Octavian Caesar to defend her husband's interests (Plut. *Ant.* 28.1). Plutarch, just as he did with Octavia (Plut. *Ant.* 53.5), always placed Mark Antony's wives in opposition, as if they were acting out of jealousy of him (Plut. *Ant.* 30.1, 53.2 and 57.1). In comparison to Fulvia, women such as Cleopatra, Agrippina Major and Agrippina Minor seem to have been delegitimised as women by ancient writers, which seemed canonical in the face of the repetition of such arguments in relation to matrons close to men of power, by the allegation of inappropriate interference (Rohr Vio, 2015, p. 79). Another reaction of contemporary orators, such as Cicero, and ancient writers was to insult the wives, with the intention of dishonouring and targeting the man. Cicero was no exception, as he needed to insinuate that Fulvia was an adulteress to attack Antony (Kennedy, 1972, p. 271; Wier, 2007, p. 34). However, the adultery would be with Antony himself, during the period when she was married to Clodius and Curio (Cic. *Phil.* 2.48) and Antony, with Antonia, when he accused his wife of infidelity in order to divorce her, marrying Fulvia soon after (Weir, 2007, p. 61).

Fulvia was an influential woman who would have shown leadership traits and who was involved in military affairs while in Gaul. She played an active role in managing Antony's policies after he took control of affairs in the East. In addition, she supported her husband's cause in Italy, along with Antony's brother, Lucius, during the Perusine War (41 - 40 BC), in which she had considerable political and military influence, launching attacks on Rome. Barrett mentions that she took up a sword, issued slogans, made a speech to soldiers, and gave war advice to senators and knights. This last action was interpreted as her worst move in interfering with the loyalty of the troops (Barrett, 2002, p. 117).

According to Brennan, her behaviour was extremely transgressive. According to Cassius Dio, Fulvia had become accustomed to conducting all her deliberations with the help of Antony and his brother, Lucius, as well as to send orders wherever they were needed. At this point, no one should have been surprised by her, because she was already arming herself with a sword, giving orders, and addressing the soldiers (Brennan, 2012, p. 360). Moreover, she went to this war with her children, armed herself and issued military orders (Cass. Dio, *Roman History* 48.10).

When referring to Fulvia, Plutarch criticised her manners, as she seemed to have no interest in spinning, managing the household or even dominating a husband who had no ambition for public life. Her real desire, according to the author, would have been to dominate those who ruled or those who commanded. Plutarch demonstrates that Fulvia was a model of an elite woman who should not be followed. However, he does not make it clear that women of this period, as wives of rulers, played a crucial role in the economic sphere, as they had to manage the finances of their families and homes, and that they would undoubtedly have a political impact in some way, far from the usual centres. However, it was natural for such women to represent their husbands' interests in Rome in the face of any absence of their husbands (Brennan, 2012, p. 359).

Fulvia's attitude proves the existence of a plurality of femininities (Connell, 1987, p. 177) in Roman society, as well as transgressive attitudes within the feminine assumption of loyalty to the husband. It is by engaging with positions offered by social discourses that "women" and "men" individually are able to reproduce the dominant cultural discourse, while remaining distant from the categories of that discourse. Otherwise, each individual has his or her own personal history, and it is at the intersection of history, situations, discourses and collective identities that the problematic between the social and the individual resides, so that resistance - or acting differently from what is expected - and obedience are not only types of agencies but also forms or aspects of subjectivity (Moore, 2000, p. 16, 29 and 31).

From the very beginning, in Caesar's time, when Cassius Dio describes Fulvia, he already mentions her imposingly, commenting that when Publius Servilius and Lucius Antonius became consuls, Mark Antony and she were the ones who were active. The author goes on to describe her as Caesar's[20] mother-in-law and states that she had no respect for Lepidus, due to her laziness. For this reason, she ended up managing the business herself, making sure that neither the Senate nor the other merchants went against her will. In 41 BC, when she interfered in a military context (Rohr Vio, 2015, p. 67), Fulvia's power was already respected even by the victors, since Lucius had defeated certain peoples of the Alps and she, for a time, did not grant him the triumph. In this case, this triumph was only granted as if it had been won by Antony and it seems that it was Fulvia who granted it to her husband, an act that suggests high importance to her, since she had the power to choose who would be the triumphant one. According to the author, the presence of Fulvia was so imposing that she was the one who seemed to give the show, while Lucius put on the triumphal costume, climbed into the chariot, and performed the expected rituals (Cass. Dio, *Roman History* 48.4.1-5).

After the Brundisium episode, Fulvia moved closer to the military sphere and suffered a delegitimization of the matron model, especially with the Perusine War, when she acquired an operational role in the field. During this war, which took place in the years 41 to 40 BC, she assumed the traits of a true *dux femina,* being a matron, who appropriated the role of soldier, officer, and commander of the army (Rohr Vio, 2015, p. 68-69). Cassius Dio characterises her with all the elements of a *dux femina*, but does not classify her with a particular Greek word that could correspond to the same meaning. In Plutarch and other authors, she could also have been close to a *vir militaris* or a matron active in a scenario of armed men, and her feminine expression was classified as an anti-model, but the exceptionalities of the political-institutional conditions legitimised behaviour that was not traditional. She was a matron who had become a commander on the battlefield and a woman who was driven by the need to act militarily by being careful, in collaboration with her husband and in place of heirs who were still very young, such as Antillus and Iullus Antony (Rohr Vio, 2015, p. 78-79).

---

[20] For Cassius Dio, Caesar was Octavian at that time. This information is not to be confused with Julius Caesar. Octavian had been betrothed to Servilia, daughter of Publius Servilius Isauricus, and then, with a reconciliation with Antony, married his goddaughter, Claudia (or Clodia), daughter of Fulvia and Publius Clodius, only reaching nubility, and, then permanently married Scribonia, with whom he had Julia, but separated and later kidnapped Livia, pregnant by her husband Tiberius Nero (Tac. *Ann.* 5.1).

Fulvia's importance could have led her to be the first Roman woman to have her image depicted on coins, soon after Julius Caesar appeared minted in 44th century BC. Her figure first appeared under the personification of Victoria/Nike, however, the identification, whether or not it is Fulvia, is questionable (Harvey, 2020, p. 18). It is possible that Fulvia may have been minted through this personification, since it was customary to use the image of goddesses to commemorate achievements and because no woman had ever been minted on coins before. Considering the *pudicitia* and the fact that women were not used to appearing in public, it may have been an attempt to camouflage the image of Fulvia, but at the same time to honour her or her husband, using the fact that, at that time, the female images that appeared on coins were only of goddesses.

The goddess Victoria was first and foremost the Greek Nike, in other words, both are goddesses of victory, but one is Roman and the other Greek. Nike was the daughter of Titan Pallas and Styx, the nymph present in the river of the underworld. She was recognised by her wings and by holding a laurel wreath in her left hand and a palm branch in her right. In the sculptures of Antiquity, she was usually connected with the colossal statues of Zeus or Pallas-Athena, being represented life-size, on top of a ball and on the open palm of the deity who accompanied her. She was sometimes attached to victory inscriptions on the shields of conquerors, with her right foot slightly raised. Nike was highly honoured as Victoria by the Romans, who linked her to their conquests. The goddess' main shrine was the Capitoline Hill, where it was common for generals, after success in battle, to erect statues to her in commemoration of their victories, one of them being the one built by Augustus after the battle of Actium (Berens, 2009, p. 98-99). Victoria usually appeared winged, holding a garland and a palm branch; sometimes she appeared holding a shield, which showed inscriptions or erecting a trophy (Sear, 2000, p. 41).

Coins appeared minted in Lugdunum around 40 BC with the name of Antony on the reverse and with a winged bust of a female figure on the obverse. On this type of coin, the female image had *nodus-like* hair, which could suggest a mortal woman, possibly Fulvia, wife of Mark Antony, because she was linked to the conquests of Gaul. In the same period, mints in Rome started to make the same bust of Victoria with *nodus* hair, seemingly inspired by the Lugdunum type (Barrett, 2002, p. 140).

The next coin is a quinarius[21], minted at Lugdunum in 43 and/or 42 BC. This series of coins sometimes appears struck with the name of the *colonia* or with the name of Antony (Rowan, 2019, p. 82). He could have used Fulvia as a model for Victoria's face on the obverse, being this quinarius taken as the first coin image of a woman. On the reverse is a lion, symbolising Antony's birth (Brennan, 2012, p. 358), who was celebrating his forty-first birthday. If Lugdunum's civic elite was responsible for the monetary types, this one was chosen to honour Antony's wife. However, the fact that the coins bear Antony's name suggests that he was the authority to choose the coinage according to Rome's ideal type. For Rowan, the lion would be more closely linked to the silver coins of Gaul, but within the Roman system. This animal appeared on the oldest Greek coins before the Late Republic of the same city (Rowan, 2019, p. 82-83).

Figure 1 – Quinarius,[22] of Lugdunum, 43 - 42 BC. Obverse: bust of Fulvia as a personification of Victoria facing right. Caption: III-VIR-R-P-C (*Triumviri Rei Publicae Constituandae* = Triumviri for the Restoration of Government[23]). Reverse: a lion walking, with a dot border. Caption: ANTONI IMP XLI (*Antoni Anno quarantegesimus unus Imperator*[24] = Commander Antony, [celebrating] his forty-first [birthday][25])[26]

Source: Courtesy of the American Numismatic Society

---

[21] The silver quinarius was not struck during the Julio-Claudian period, but was revived in AD 68 during Galba's rule and continued during the Flavian period (Sear, 2000, p. 20).

[22] Reference: RPC 1 513 = RRC: 489/6, available at: http://numismatics.org/collection/1944.100.4491, accessed 21 July 2021. The coin has been catalogued in both RRC and PRC, showing it to be both a provincial example and from a Rome series. Both the division between provincial and Rome coins can be taken as somewhat artificial and not helpful (Rowan, 2019, p. 82). CRI 126, BMCRR Gaul 48. RSC 3.

[23] Available at: https://en.numista.com/catalogue/pieces66597.html. Accessed: 29 June 2021.

[24] *Imperator*, which appears as IMP in coin captions, is a title that originally meant "commander" and was used to describe victories. The title was used in imperial periods as the *praenomen* or personal name of the emperor by virtue of his supreme command over the legions, auxiliaries, and naval officers. Another use of the title would be to enumerate the victories during the emperor's reign. When there was any successful battle, the emperor was acclaimed, even if he was not present. The number of these acclamations was usually placed on coin inscriptions (Sear, 2000, p. 72-73).

[25] Available at: https://en.numista.com/catalogue/pieces58848.html. Accessed: 11 July 2021.

[26] Available at: http://numismatics.org/crro/results?q=489%2F6. Accessed: 29 June 2021.

On all the coins that possibly depicted the image of Fulvia, but with the personification of Victoria, she appears with a bun at the back of her head and a large, full tuft above her forehead, formed by combing a wide section of hair forward along the middle of the head, sweeping it into the hairline and then pulling it back in a braid that went along the centre of the top of the head. This hairstyle appears in many public and private portraits of women of the Late Republic and Early Empire and is commonly known as *nodus* hairstyle, because it seems to correspond to the fashion that Ovid recommended for women with short and round faces, which he described as an *exiguus nodus*. The name may or may not be appropriate, since Kockel believes that Ovid was describing an older fashion, in which the wearer pulls the hair up from the back of the head and twists it into a small tuft at the crown of the head (Ov. *ArsAm*. 3.139-140; Kockel, 1993, p. 37-38 apud Wood, 2001, p. 42).

That said, the relationship of the coins to the life of Fulvia was understandable, due to her actions in the military sphere. The Perusine War occurred because Lucius and Fulvia counted on their kinship with Caesar to be partners in the supremacy (Cass. Dio, *Roman History* 48. 5. 1), which already demonstrated a strategic malice on the part of Fulvia, according to Cassius Dio. In addition to acting in the public sphere, Fulvia had a political dynamic as matron, in other words, she had the positions of wife of Antony and mother-in-law of Octavian, which were presented in such a way that she exceeded the limits of female activity (Rohr Vio, 2015, p. 69).

However, according to the same author, Lucius and Fulvia quarrelled because they did not secure the portion of land that belonged to Antony and Caesar. Consequently, their kinship by marriage was dissolved and they were drawn into open warfare. Caesar could not stand his mother-in-law's difficult temperament and used this to demonstrate that he was at disagreement with her rather than Antony, as well as appearing to dislike both Clodia and, especially, Fulvia. In this sense, he sent Fulvia's daughter back, with the remark that she was still a virgin, something he confirmed by oath. However, this was difficult to imagine, as the question arises as to why she remained a virgin in his house for so long or whether this may have been planned in advance to prepare for the future. After this event, relations cooled down and Lucius, together with Fulvia, tried to take control of the business, making it seem as if it was in Antony's name and stating that they would not surrender to Caesar at any time. In addition, Lucius, in devotion to his brother Antony, began to use the cognomen, Pietas. Cunningly, Caesar had not made any accusation against Antony, since he was in command of the provinces of Asia, but he accused Lucius and Fulvia and took action against them, with the argument that they were acting in every respect contrary to Antony's wish and were aiming at their own supremacies (Cass. Dio, *Roman History* 48. 5. 2-5).

There was a great dispute over the distribution of land, so that Caesar wanted to act on his own in the distribution of territory and together with those who had campaigned with him and Antony. However, Cassius Dio mentions that Lucius and Fulvia claimed the right to cede to their troops the lands that they were entitled to gain and to colonise the cities, in order to appropriate to the influence of the colonies, since this seemed to both sides to be the simplest method of giving territorial possessions to the troops that had fought (Cass. Dio, *Roman History* 48.6.1-4).

Lucius and Fulvia were winning over these people who had problems with their land and at the same time they were not in conflict with Caesar's supporters, because instead of pretending that there was no need for the soldiers to receive their rewards, they tried to show that the goods of those who fought against them were sufficient for the soldiers (Cass. Dio, *Roman History* 48.7-5). What can be realised through the writings of Cassius Dio is that there was dispute over the best prizes between the war veterans, the senators, and the landowners, but what it seems is that Caesar could not stick to either side (Cass. Dio, *Roman History* 48.8.1).

In all directions, Lucius went about organising those who had lost their lands and separating all from Caesar, while Fulvia occupied *Praeneste* and, with senators and knights, as her associates to conduct all her deliberations, sent orders to any points that required them. Caesar had no means of defeating his opponents, being far inferior to them not only in troops, but also in regards to the goodwill of the citizens, for he was causing distress to many, while Fulvia and Lucius filled all with hope (Cass. Dio, *Roman History* 48.10.1-4 and 48.11.1-4). The veterans gathered at the Capitol in Rome and ordered the pact between Antony and Caesar to be read. They wished to ratify the agreement, as well as voting that they themselves should be considered arbitrators of the differences between them, and gave orders to Caesar and the other party, by means of an embassy, to present themselves for judgement at Gabii on a day appointed (Cass. Dio, *Roman History* 48.12.1-5).

This led both Caesar, Lucius and Fulvia to gather forces for a war (Cass. Dio, *Roman History* 48.13.1). After several moves on both sides, Lucius withdrew from Rome and set out for Gaul, but found his way blocked and returned to Perusine, an Etruscan city, where he was besieged by Caesar and his men. Many came to Lucius' defence, leading to several attacks. The leader and others were pardoned, but most of the senators and knights were condemned to death, led to the altar consecrated to the former Caesar and sacrificed there (three hundred knights and many senators). The city itself, except for the temple of Vulcan and the statue of Juno, was destroyed completely by fire (Cass. Dio, *Roman History* 48.14.1-5).

After the capture in Perusia, the other places in Italy also came under Caesar's rule, partly as a result of force and partly of their own free will. For this reason, Fulvia fled with her children to find her husband and many of the most important men followed her, some of them going to Antony and some to Sextus in Sicily. Julia, the mother of the *Antonii*, was received by Sextus with extreme kindness; then she was sent by him to his son Marcus, bringing him proposals of friendship, emissaries, and Tiberius Claudius Nero. The latter was in command of a garrison in Campania, and when Caesar's party won, he withdrew with his wife Livia Drusilla and his son Tiberius Claudius Nero. Livia, who then fled from Caesar, later married him. Tiberius, son of Livia and Tiberius, who then fled with his parents, succeeded Caesar as emperor (Cass. Dio, *Roman History* 48.15.1-4).

Just before the Perusine war, the coin that apparently could be Fulvia began to appear in Rome. The female figure never appeared in a purely idealised representation of a goddess or a personification. This "Victoria", who could be Fulvia, also seems to have some human identity. Moreover, her face invariably shows signs of middle age, notably drooping cheeks and chin lines, as well as physical features such as an arched nose and receding lower lip, which would not appear in the ideal image of a goddess (Wood, 2001, p. 42).

Figure 2 – Silver denarius[27], Rome, from 42 BC. Obverse: bust of Victoria or Fulvia, with punctuated borders. Reverse: Victoria on a chariot, holding the reins of two horses with her hands, and punctuated border. Inscription: L-MVSSIDIVS LONGVS (*Lucius Mussidius Longus*[28])

Source: Courtesy of the American Numismatic Society

---

[27] Reference: RRC 494/40, CRI 186, BMCRR 4229, RSC Mussidia 4.
Available at: http://numismatics.org/crro/results?q=494%2F40. Accessed: 29 June 2021.

[28] It would probably be the name of the mint, named after the owner of the mint or the family, who would have such activity for generations. The *gens* Mussidia was a little-known family, except for the coins of Rome minted during the last days of the Republic. Available at: https://en.numista.com/catalogue/pieces66660.html. Accessed: 11 July 2021.

This denarius, which was minted by an official mint of Rome, as indicated by the caption on the reverse of the object, L-MVSSIDIVS LONGVS, has a winged and draped female bust on the obverse, which may be of Fulvia, and on the reverse appears the goddess Victoria on a chariot, holding the reins of two horses with her hands. This mint struck coins in honour of the three triumvirs, but the provincial coins offer evidence that if the Victoria depicted was a real individual, she could be a woman from Antony's family (Wood, 2001, p. 41). The difference of this coin from others that may also be of Fulvia is that she has jewellery, such as the necklace and pearl earring, as goddesses used to appear. However, the jewellery of this image is not the same as the standard jewellery that Victoria/Nike present, and the hair is also different from that of the deity, suggesting that this coin image could be of a mortal.

Figure 3 – Denarius[29], Julius Caesar, Rome, 46 BC, 3.48 g, 18.4 mm diameter. Obverse: draped bust of goddess Victoria facing right with pearl borders and earrings, S.C (*Senatus Consultum*). Victoria in four-horse chariot on right, reins in left hand, crown in right hand, T. CARIS(IUS) (*Titus Carisius*[30] = *Titus Carisius*[31])

Source: © KBR *cabinet des monnais et médailles*

This last denarius, from the time of Julius Caesar, shows how common it was for such rulers to use the goddess Victoria to present their conquests. As it can be seen, once again, the figure of Victoria appears with a different type of hair from that instituted for the personification of Fulvia as Victoria, in addition to the jewellery, which is commonly indicated on figures of goddesses other than Fulvia's, as well as the image of the goddess

---

[29] Provenance: Vente E. Muschietti, List of February 1965, no. 175; RRC 464/5, Inv. II, 53.383; 2B22 / 33. Available at: https://opac.kbr.be/LIBRARY/doc/SYRACUSE/10042078. Accessed: 13 May 2022.
[30] Name of the coinage. Available at: http://numismatics.org/crro/id/rrc-464.5?lang=pl and https://ikmk.smb.museum/ndp/person/1938. Accessed: 13 Oct. 2022.
[31] Translation made by the author.

herself, which seems more artificial than that of a mortal. The figure on the reverse is similar to the coin minted by L-MVSSIDIVS LONGVS, with some differentiations, in which Victoria appears in a chariot or cart, with an object in her right hand and the reins in her left hand with three horses; probably the coin maker was Titus Carisius.

Figure 4 – Bronze coin[32], Julius Caesar, 45 BC, 13.86 g, 29 mm diameter. Obverse: draped bust of Victoria, with star on left and punctuated border, CAESAR. DIC. TER (*Caesar Dictator Tertium* = Caesar Dictator for the third time[33]). Reverse: appears to be Athena or Minerva, C. CLOVI - PRAEF (Gaius Clovius Praefectus = The Gaius Clovius Prefect[34])

Source: © KBR *cabinet des monnais et médailles*

Again, in the Caesar period, a coin featuring the goddess Victoria on its obverse appears to commemorate the ruler's achievements. On its reverse, it appears to be Athena holding a shield with her left arm. However, according to the KBR, it would be Minerva standing facing left, holding a trophy over her shoulder with her right hand, as well as a spear and shield in her left hand. The shield is decorated with *gorgoneion*[35] and ribbons, snake on the left, pearl rim, with caption C. CLOVI - PRAEF, which would probably be the indication of the mint by which the object was minted.

The coin shows a similarity with the coin in which Fulvia stands as the personification of Victoria and on its obverse there is the presence of Athena, which was minted in the city of Eumeneia, demonstrating two goddesses linked to conquests. Barbato emphasises that Victoria was linked to Venus in the Caesarian context (Barbato, 2015 apud Rowan,

---

[32] Bibliography: RRC 476/1b. Catalogue number: 2B22 / 44. Available at: https://opac.kbr.be/LIBRARY/doc/SYRACUSE/10042138. Accessed: 28 July 2022.
[33] Translation made by the author.
[34] Available at: https://en.numista.com/catalogue/pieces67085.htm. Accessed: 3 Oct. 2022.
[35] A representation of the face of a gorgon, frequent as an apotropaic symbol in Greek art. Available at: https://www.merriam-webster.com/dictionary/gorgoneion. Accessed: 28 July 2022.

2019, p. 20). That said, the reverse figure is often interpreted as Venus, not Athena.

However, it should be noted that Venus was the goddess of beauty and love, who was also common on Republican coinage. She usually appeared on titles of CAELESTIS, FELIX, GENETRIX and VICTRIX, with clothing or almost entirely with clothing. She could appear holding an apple, with an occasional helmet, and a sceptre, as well as sometimes appearing with a cupid. When she appeared half-naked, she was shown from the back. The only relation to Victoria was that Julius Caesar, who claimed to be a descendant of the goddess, represented her on several of his coins, commonly holding a small figure of Victoria (Sear, 2000, p. 35).

Figure 5 – Denarius[36], from an uncertain mint, 32 - 29 BC, 3.59 g, 20.4 mm diameter. Obverse: bust of winged Victoria. Reverse: Octavian as Neptune (?), with right foot on a globe holding *aplustrum*[37] and a centre, CAESAR DIVI F (*Caesar Divi Filius* = son of the deified Caesar[38])

Source: © KBR *cabinet des monnais et médailles*

On this last coin, the bust of the goddess Victoria is shown on the right, with open wings, in order to make a comparison with the other coins that may represent Fulvia. One of the first elements to be noticed is the difference in the type of hair and the use of cross-shaped earrings, as well as the garment falling to the shoulders. Zanker interprets the reverse as if it were the personification of Octavian as the divine or, more clearly, as the

---

[36] RIC I² 256; BMC 615. Available at: https://opac.kbr.be/LIBRARY/doc/SYRACUSE/20734095, accessed. Accessed: 28 July 2022.

[37] The curved stern of a ship, with its ornaments (ribbons, banners, and flags on a mast). Available at: http://www.perseus.tufts.edu/hopper/text?doc=Perseus:text:1999.04.0059:entry=aplustre, accessed. Accessed: 24 AugustAug. 2022.

[38] Translation made by the author. In January 42 BC, Caesar was officially divinized, and this made Octavian the son of a God (Koortbojian, 2013, p. 8). And between 41 and 39 BC, Octavian began to use the title DIVI IVLI F (son of the deified Julius) on his coins (Alfödi; Giard, 1984 apud Rowan, 2005, p. 61).

god Neptune. It seems that this coin assimilates him with the divine, both from the image and the caption, CAESAR DIVI F. It is suggested that this image represents a statue erected by Octavian after his victory over Sextus Pompey at the battle of Naulochus (Zanker, 1988, p. 39-40), but there is no evidence for its existence. The personification of Octavian as Neptune could be an allusion to Pompey, who previously appeared on denarii as Pompey the Great, with the personification of Neptune. The image could also refer to the iconography of Hellenistic coins of the third century BC (Pollini, 1990, p. 347). The similarities are in the *aplustre* and the globe and the difference is that the sceptre is in the place of the trident, showing that the figure was modified to present a naval victory of Octavian (Rowan, 2019, p. 119-120).

Octavian could have been inspired by contemporary ideologies because it was common in his time to portray himself not only as the son of a god, but also as a god in his own right. Directly and indirectly, Octavian' assimilation with the divine is seen later in the IMP CAESAR series coins (Rowan, 2019, p. 120). Regarding Mark Antony, he could have used Fulvia as a model to represent his victories, since she was involved with his conquests; and used her as the personification of Victoria/Nike by the conquerors' custom to glorify this goddess.

In 41 BC, an aureus was minted by *C. Numonius Vaala* with an image similar to that of Lugdunum (Harvey, 2020, p. 35-36). This type of coin seems to have echoed in the East (Barrett, 2002, p. 140).

Figure 6 – Aureus[39] coined by C. Numonius Vaala, Rome, 41 BC, 8.1g. Bust accepted as if it is Fulvia as Victoria on the obverse. Reverse caption: C. NUMONIUS VAALA (*Gaius Numonius Vaala*[40])

Source: © The Trustees of the British Museum

    This aureus has on its obverse the bust of a winged female figure, which is an attribute of the goddess Victoria. The features of the face and the iconography are the opposite of those of a goddess, made with a significant beauty, but not a divine beauty. The hairstyle is that of the Roman *nodus* type worn by matrons, identifying her as a Roman woman. Grueber (1910), who dated this coin to 40 BC, does not believe that it is Fulvia, because in the period when it was minted Antony had not received this honour, since in Cisalpine and Transalpine Gaul they began to mint coins of him around 43 BC and in Rome around 42 BC (Harvey, 2020, p. 36-37). Sydenham, unlike Grueber (1910), dated this coin to 43 BC and that of the *Longus* mint to 42 BC (Sydenham, 1952, p. 180). However, that of the *Vaala* mint has a problem with this date, because in 43 BC Antony was at war with the Senate, meaning that the coins of Rome were being struck to pay the troops that were fighting against him. For Crawford, 42 BC would be more likely, but he does not believe that the female figure would be Fulvia and states that it could be any other woman (Crawford, 1974, p. 100, 742 apud Wood, 2001, p. 43). However, whether it is Fulvia, the fact that it was minted on a gold coin and in Rome brings it great importance and power.

---

[39] Registration number: R.9272; C&M catalogue number: RR1p570.4215; museum number: R.9272. RR1 / Coins of the Roman Republic in the British Museum: vol. 1 aes rude, aes signatum, aes grave, and coinage of Rome from B.C. 268. (4215, p. 570), RRC / Roman Republican Coinage (514/1). Available at: https://www.britishmuseum.org/collection/object/C_R-9272. Accessed: 24 Aug. 2022.
Ghey, Leins & Crawford 2010 / A catalogue of the Roman Republican Coins in the British Museum, with descriptions and chronology based on M.H. Crawford, Roman Republican Coinage (1974) (514.1.1)
Available at: https://research.britishmuseum.org/research/collection_online/collection_object_details.aspx?objectId=3071501&partId=1&searchText=Vaala&page=1. Accessed: 18 Jan. 2020.

[40] Translation made by the author.

The aureus was minted by *C. Numonius Vaala*, which was an official mint of Rome. Like others, it had a long tradition of selecting types that illustrated the highlights of its family history. On the reverse, there is a soldier fighting, known as a *promachos,* who is in the first line of battle, or would be a soldier running or pushing against a "wall", holding a shield with his left hand and a sword with his right, against two soldiers who are holding a shield with their left hand and raising swords with their right hand. The inscription *C. Numonius Vaala* would be the name of the owner of the mint, who minted it in Gaul. Thus, presumably, this illustration could be a tribute to the act of heroism of an ancestor, since the cognomen *Vaala* comes from *vallum*[41] (Crawford, 1975a, p. 523). It seems that the reverse has no direct connection with the obverse illustration or with the deeds of Fulvia, as this design appears on other coinage, which is not linked to Fulvia. The coins of the Republic represent a type of competitive series of monumental images, which were intended to recall a personality or an event from the past of the family to which the monetary magistrate in design belonged to (Williams, 2007b, p. 58).

The owners of the mint of *C. Numonius Vaala*, or even *Lucius Mussidius Longus*, from one of the coins mentioned above, could have been moneyers (*tresviri monetales*) who might have been considered junior magistrates, who used the images on the coins to show the needs of their ancestors and link their families to Rome's mythical and legendary past. The coins were favourable in this respect because of the mint's connection to the goddess Juno Moneta (Meadows; Williams, 2001). The deity guaranteed the quality and authenticity of weights, measures, and coins, authenticating their messages as well, which made coins a useful political instrument during the civil wars of I BC and in the transition from Republic to Empire (Kemmers, 2019, p. 19-20).

The use of Victoria/Nike on coins demonstrates the emphasis on militarism, characterising such coins as of the military type, common during the Republic and Empire. These coins could appear with allegories ranging from naval fleets to quadriga. Commanders such as Antony and Octavian commonly depicted on their coins armed forces in military campaigns, military expeditions in different cities, the departure to war, and the emperor's emphasis on the superior position of the empire as military commander. The image of Victoria/Nike or the inscription of her name in coin captions continued to

---

[41] The meaning of *vallum*, according to the online Latin dictionary, *Perseus Digital Library*, would be a line of palisades, palisaded wall, circumvallation. Available at: http://www.perseus.tufts.edu/hopper/resolveform?type=exact&lookup=vallum&lang=la. Accessed: 29 Dec. 2021.

appear later on coinage of emperors such as Septimus Severus, Elagabalus, Gordian III, Gallienus, Probus, Carus and others (Manders, 2008, p. 84 and 90).

Figure 7 – Bronze coin[42] from Tripolis, from 42/41 BC, 20 mm in diameter. Obverse: head of Antony. Reverse: female bust which appears to be Fulvia, ΤΡΙΠΟΛΙΤΩΝ LTK (from Tripolis LTK[43]).

Source: (Rowan, 2019, p. 108)

The previous coin with Antony on the obverse and a female bust, which appears to be Fulvia, on the reverse may be the only one to be found without her as the personification of Victoria/Nike, and the only coin on which she appears together with Antony. It is interesting that in 36/35 BC a coin appears in the same place with Cleopatra on the obverse (RPC 1 4510) and the reverse with Nike on a bow holding a wreath. It seems that Antony's wives were honoured more than once at this area.

Coins showing the bust of a woman with the personification of the goddess Victoria, but with some individualised features, have been attributed to an assimilation with Fulvia. The lack of an identifying caption can lead to a range of interpretations (Harvey, 2020, p. 39) and there is no concrete deliberation and agreement that it is indeed Fulvia. If the bust is indeed of Fulvia, this marks the first female depiction on Roman coins, representing an innovation, as even triumvirs only appeared on coins in the mid-forties BC (Barrett, 2002, p. 140; Kahrstedt, 1910, p. 291-292; Kleiner, 1992, p. 358-360; Wood, 1999, p. 41; Bartman, 1999, p. 37 and 58). The explanation that Fulvia may have appeared as the personification of Victoria would be due to her actions, which would reflect in her political influence and the loyalty of the troops and magistrates for Antony, an attitude that opened space for other women in the public sphere (Harvey, 2020, p. 39).

---

[42] RPC 1 4509.

[43] Translation by Juarez Oliveira. The caption seems to denote a coalition of three Phoenician cities, where the letters LTK may be their initials.

The coins that showed Fulvia were also minted in the province of Phrygia, the city of Eumeneia (*Ishekli*), which was founded by *Attalus II* of Pergamum around 159 - 138 BC, to counterbalance the neighbouring city *Peltae*, which was a Seleucid stronghold. The founder named it after his brother, Eumenes. The territory of this city consisted of a rich plain between the lower *Glaucus* and its junction with the upper *Maeander*. On this plain, there was, in *Attanassos*, the *Hieron* of one of the native gods of Phrygia. The first coins minted in Eumeneia were bronze, from the second century BC (Head, 1906, p. lx). The fact that the same iconography appears in different territories, which Antony was conquering, suggests that the image was indeed of Fulvia and that it came from a Roman source. Otherwise, Antony, through the representation of Fulvia as Victoria/Nike, could have been evoking the custom of the time to use these goddesses and to draw the attention of Augustus, since both the latter and Julius Caesar used the deity to exalt their glories. In addition, images of women on coins appeared first in the provinces and then in Rome (Rowan, 2019, p. 83).

Eumeneia changed its name in honour of Fulvia (Zager, 2014; Harvey, 2020; Barrett, 2002, p. 140). This information is found in works such as Zager's (2014) and Harvey's (2020), without further explanation of how the name of the city in question was changed. What appears is that Antony was the one who gave the name of his wife, Fulvia, to the city of Eumeneia (Head, 1906, p. 213). For Brennan, Antony supported the change of the name of the city to "Fulviana" in honour of his wife, an act that was the first one done for a woman. After this name change, local coins began to be minted with the name "Fulviana" and a countermark with the old name, Eumeneia (Brennan, 2012, p. 358). With this change of city names and after a century and a half of minting local coins with the caption EVMENEΩN, the caption became ΦΟΥΛΟVΙΑΝΩΝ (Head, 1906, p. lxi), and this minting of coins of Fulvia took place around 41 BC.

Figure 8 – Coin of Fulvia,[44] Phrygia, Eumeneia, 41 - 40 BC, 4.83 g, 17 mm diameter. Obverse: draped bust of Fulvia as Victoria/Nike. Reverse: crown of Hera, [F]OULOUI/ANWN/ZMEPTOPI (Zmertorix of fulvians[45])

Source: Courtesy of WildWinds

The figure above is a coin minted in provincial Rome, in the region of Phrygia, more specifically in the city of Eumeneia, dating from around 4-40 BC, which shows on the obverse a female figure with her bust turned to the right and which appears to be the representation of Fulvia as Nike/Victoria. On its reverse is a crown of Hera and in its centre the caption [F]OULOUI/ANWN/ZMEPTOPI.

Therefore, this is a proof of the ennoblement that Fulvia obtained. What appears is that these coins were struck to flatter Mark Antony (Grether, 1946, p. 223). Even Livia, at the beginning of Augustus' rule, never had her coins struck in Rome, but in eastern provinces, which already had the habit of commemorating Hellenistic royal women on coins from the period of IV to II BC, which may have influenced the beginning of the coinage of women on Roman coins (Harvey, 2020, p. 18).

---

[44] Reference: RPC I 3140; SNG Cop -; SNG von Aulock 8367; BMC Phrygia. Available at: https://www.wildwinds.com/coins/imp/fulvia/i.html; https://www.wildwinds.com/coins/imp/fulvia/RPC_3140.jpg; and https://www.wildwinds.com/coins/imp/fulvia/RPC_3140.txt. Accessed: 30 June 2021.

[45] Translation by Juarez Oliveira, who says that due to the plural genitive, it seems to designate the citizens of Fulvia.

Figure 9 – Phrygian coin,[46] Eumeneia, 41 - 40 BC, 3,19 g, 14 mm of diameter. Obverse: winged female figure. Reverse: Athena, [Z]ΜΕΡΤΟΡΙΓΟΣ/[Φ]ΙΛΩΝΙΔΟΥ (Zmertorix, son of Filonides[47])

Source: Courtesy of the Classical Numismatic Group

  This is another coin minted in Eumeneia, a city in Phrygia, Galatea, dated to around 41- 40 BC, which shows on the obverse a female figure, with the bust turned to the right and repeating the representation of Fulvia as Nike/Victoria. On the reverse is another female figure, who may be Athena, walking on the right, holding a shield with her left arm and a spear with her right hand, and the caption: [Z]ΜΕΡΤΟΡΙΓΟΣ/[Φ]ΙΛΩΝΙΔΟΥ. The name Zmertorix is of Celtic origin, which makes the translation of the caption to be "Zmertorix, son of Philonides". This information is important, as it shows that the Greek coin did not bear the name of the polis, but that of the citizens of the city, in this case the Phrygians. Valerius Zmertorix seems to have been a magistrate, under whom the coin was minted[48].

  In addition, Victoria's face has been found on medals from Philomelium, a city between the border of Phrygia and Galatia, as well as on medals from Déiotarus, king of Galatia. This suggests that Fulvia sometimes appeared in parts of East Phrygia and that some cities in this part of Asia coined her name in her honour because she was Mark Antony's wife. Fulvia's actions are relevant to the representations dedicated to her on these coins, such as Victoria/Nike and Athena. On another example with Athena on the reverse of the same series, the caption of the right, which on this coin is cut off, was ΦΟΥΛΟΥΙΑΝΩΝ (Waddington, 1853, p. 248), which would be Fulvia's name and which could have been cut off or erased intentionally, suggesting

---

[46] ID: 79000614. Denomination AE14. References: RPC 1 3139, SNG München - cop - *Classical Numismátic Group*. Available at: http://www.cngcoins.com/Coin.aspx?CoinID=127125 and http://www.coinproject.com/coin_detail.php?coin=247324. Accessed: 30 June 2021.

[47] Translation by Juarez Oliveira.

[48] Information available at: https://www.numisbids.com/n.php?p=lot&sid=4683&lot=575. Accessed: 23 Aug. 2022.

that her name could have been dropped almost immediately (Head, 1906, p. 213). This attitude also suggests that the change of name of the city could demonstrate something that would not have been well accepted by the population, in other words, that it could have contributed to an identity destabilisation, a consequence of an imposition to this change.

In relation to the iconography of this coin, Athena was the daughter of Zeus, who in Mythology has always shown herself to be in agreement with her father or on his side, being loyal to him but also as an instrument to him, being seen as daughter and father in one being and taking her best advice from him. She was a goddess known as a reconciler between men and gods, men and women. In both Hesiod's *Theogony* (924 - 926) and the Homeric hymn to Athena, she was born from Zeus' swollen head, already dressed in his battle gear. Athena's appearance was as potent as Zeus' weapon, so that the two of them together were invincible. Athena was treated as Zeus' beloved son in epic literature, meaning she was armed with helmet, spear, and shield. Like a king, she resided the palace of Erechtheus. She was adept at manly skills, taming horses, casting bronze, tending the earth's olive trees, and she drove a chariot and fought on her father's side in the battle against the giants. She guided the heroes from the land of the sun to the underworld and was able to make them immortal. She was usually invoked after her father and before Apollo. These three deities were the ones who could use the *aegis*[49] and swing it to produce fear in the Iliad, as well as representing the extreme manifestation of patriarchy (Harrison, 1912). As the daughter of Zeus and Metis, she was endowed with an extra dose of wisdom that enabled her to restrain herself and not get lost in the world. In Greek art in general, Athena does not fail to appear with helmet, spear, shield and ready for war. She was, for the most part, accompanied in the arts by Zeus (Neils, 2001, p. 219-220 and 223), which, in the case of her accompanying Fulvia, differs from Mark Antony deities, since he was always linked to Dionysus.

The representation of Athena on Fulvia's coins may mark her warlike leadership or that of her husband, who could have a dubious appearance, feminine or masculine, in his conceptions. The characteristics of Athena are mostly masculine, as are weapons, leadership, intelligence, and bellicosity, which in the East could be accepted as feminine, different from the centre thought, that of Rome. However, loyalty and the gift of reconciliation were

---

[49] A shield or breastplate emblematic of majesty that was associated with Zeus and Athena. Available at: https://www.merriam-webster.com/dictionary/aegis. Accessed: 28 June 2021.

extremely feminine characteristics for Rome but tied to the woman within her marriage. The image of Athena on Fulvia's coins could demonstrate the strength, determination and power she brought while she was in a dispute with Octavian or the strength of Mark Antony in conquering regions of the East. These characteristics may sometimes elucidate who she was and not emphasise the masculine or feminine issue of such a character, but the coin was first and foremost a tribute to Fulvia.

It is customary to think of female deities as beings almost always linked to women's tasks, such as motherhood and marriage. However, when this conception is imposed, it means that an interpretation of a patriarchal social model is already entrenched, in which the roles of men and women are fully defined (Cid López, 2011, p. 61). However, the presence of gender assumptions in a society is not about how such women really are, but about what the majority of that society thinks it is right to be. From this perspective, it should bear in mind that it is important to realise that even the Roman elite were part of a complex group of people and that they did not all act in the same way.

The representations of Fulvia on coins are very different from other representations of women, such as those of Livia, for example, who was always linked to the deities that characterised the matron, the wife, the mother and so on. Everywhere she was minted she was represented as the personification of Victoria/Nike, as well as accentuating some behavioural characters, unlike the matron, with the image of Athena on the reverse, on coins from the East. Her deities, on the other hand, are linked to warlike and powerful activities, linked to the exercise of sovereignty and conquest, which were commonly linked to the Roman man, the *vir* or *uir*, and would not suitable for a woman.

Since the beginning of Roman times, goddesses had attributes that resembled these examples of idealised women, that is, female stereotypes. There were goddesses linked to war, power, and leadership, but the more they gained male power, the more they lost strength, so that war and guardianship became attributes of the gods, almost exclusively. In the meantime, new goddesses emerged, whose cult was linked to maternal activities, that was disassociated from the old female deities to reduce them to the protection of women in labour and domestic functions (Cid López, 2011, p. 61).

Another aspect that draws attention in the coins that could be of Fulvia is that her image always appears alone on the obverse, without the presence of a male, showing that the tribute is directly to her person and her actions, without considering Mark Antony and his position, with the exception of the one from Tripolis and the one on the reverse with the caption ANTONI. Generally, in Rome, the coin celebrated the male individual first and on the reverse, for example, or on his side; moreover, it was common for the captions to emphasise male titles rather than female ones. However, the actions of imperial women linked to the Patronage, for example, which favoured these regions, could have been instrumental in honouring them and consequently minting them on coins.

However, Fulvia's actions could have contributed to her figure appearing as the personification of the goddess Victoria, since this characterisation would bring the human person closer to a respect and to a *pudicitia* in relation to her representation. In addition, the mark of Victoria has always been a masculine symbol, linked to triumph and *virtus*, a characteristic that could be associated with the act of courage and decision of this woman, and not to the consensus of the ideal Roman matron. This ideal carries in its representations symbols of fertility, security and dynastic stability, since it was expected that their role would be to guarantee heirs, take care of the house and the husband's things, in addition to loyalty.

In the light of the common ideological criteria of Roman society, Fulvia was characterised as a loyal woman who did everything to secure her husband's political future and who watched over her marriage, defending her husband against Octavian. Even knowing about Cleopatra and Antony's affair, she fulfilled her role with honour and was thus honoured. However, this does not mean that Fulvia's actions were not criticised. At the end of her life, she was described as a power-mad shrew (Barrett, 2002, p. 117).

However, what can be affirmed, considering that the personification of Victoria is indeed Fulvia, is that during the Second Triumvirate both Mark Antony and Octavian began a campaign of self-promotion, publicly experimenting with the values of their women, represented through different arts and expressions. Like the coins of Fulvia, whose minting began around 43 to 40 BC, there were also those of Octavia, whose minting began around 40 BC and/or 39 BC.

It is important to keep in mind that these coins were mostly minted not in Rome, but in provincial cities, mainly in Hellenistic cities of the East, probably to kindle the spirits of conquest of the populations of the region, suggesting that Antony's presence in this area encouraged the minting of the figures of his wives. The appearance of the figure of these women, linked to Roman rulers, on coins and in other types of representations, such as statues, shows a change in female roles, as much as the attainment of a political influence and a new social status (Harvey, 2020, p. 6).

According to Plutarch, Antony received news that his brother, Lucius, and Fulvia had joined forces against Octavian, but were defeated and expelled from Italy. As he was about to defeat Labienus, the commander of the Parthian army and who was becoming the master of Asia, Antony received news from Fulvia, full of lamentations, which made him change his plans and go to meet her. On his way, Antony learnt that the cause of all the trouble with Octavian was Fulvia's fault. Plutarch calls her stubborn and states that she loved to interfere in political affairs, as well as stating that the only way Fulvia could make Antony leave Cleopatra would be by causing hostilities, marking once again a conflict between women, which demonstrates that jealousy between women would signal unbalanced attitudes of their part. However, Fulvia fell ill on her way to meet Antony in Sicyon. This event led to a reconciliation between Octavian and Antony, and the author reproduces the fact as if everything had been the fault of Fulvia, because before Antony was sure that Octavian was the one to blame for the war. Consequently, the result was an agreement in which Octavian gave the territories of the East to Antony, the provinces of Africa to Lepidus and he himself kept the rest (Plut. *Ant.* 30.1).

The death of Fulvia was also described by Cassius Dio, who reported that while the leaders were in a state of guard, Fulvia died in Sicyon, where she was staying. Cassius Dio blames Fulvia for the civil war and states that, as much as Antony felt responsible for her death, because of his involvement with Cleopatra and his debauchery, when this news was announced, both sides laid down their arms and effected a reconciliation, because, in the author's words, Fulvia was really the cause of all the disagreement until then. However, the author himself mentions that it was perhaps preferable to make her death an excuse, in view of the fear which each inspired in the other, inasmuch as the forces they possessed, as well as their ambitions, were equally matched, Caesar being left with Sardinia, Dalmatia, Spain, and Gaul; Antony with all the districts which belonged to the Romans across the Ionian Sea, both in Europe and Asia; Lepidus with the provinces of Africa; and Sextus with Sicily (Cass. Dio, *Roman History* 48.2-4).

The interpretation of ancient writers is that Fulvia contained several ingredients of an ambitious woman, such as avarice, cruelty, subordination of troops and, finally, ingratitude from her husband, Antony, for whom she made great sacrifices. Moreover, all the disagreements between Octavian and Antony became Fulvia's responsibility from the outbreak of the war, according to Plutarch and Cassius Dio. They demonstrated a rhetoric aimed at damaging the female image to the detriment of the male one, something that also occurs with Cleopatra in the speeches of the same authors. This suggests that it would be much more pertinent for Octavian to go against such women in order to target Antony than to miss the opportunity to reconcile with him in order to keep alive the agreement between the triumvirs, which would mark a potentially useful attitude for his politics.

Such arguments would have the effect of minimising the actions of these women, giving them a less privileged place, as well as classifying them as rash, as Tacitus also characterises Boudica in his work *Annals*, demonstrating in other narratives the recurrence of this type of hostile treatment aimed at women with power. The representation of Antony by Fulvia in the face of his affairs is used by these authors as an excuse for them to judge such an attitude in a woman, considering that her behaviour would go beyond the limits outlined for her gender. However, this was tempered, as Fulvia's actions were placed as being activities that would protect her husband and consequently her family, which would be acceptable for a loyal wife. Fulvia is qualified with a behaviour that would be suitable only for a man, going against the characteristics of a matron (Rohr Vio, 2015, p. 76).

She died accused of having been responsible for the disagreements between Octavian and Antony and of being the cause of all the mistakes of the Perusine War. This also shows the result of a partial manipulation of the memory of this woman, through the emphasis on decontextualised facts, demonstrating a delegitimization of the matron so that the authors could shape a history that was in line with their contingent interests and adjusted to their political (Rohr Vio, 2015, p. 77) and gender views. However, gender issues are less heated, but used to maintain a political agreement.

According to Cassius Dio, as much as the people were pleased with the reconciliation of Antony and Caesar, with the hope of harmony between these men, they were still unhappy with the war they were waging against Sextus (Cass. Dio, *Roman History* 48. 31.2). Antony married Octavia, Caesar's sister, who had just been widowed while pregnant (Cass. Dio, *Roman History* 48.31.3-4). Plutarch characterised her as the ideal Roman matron. However, years after the Perusine War, Octavia had had to deal with troops a few times, mediating such a task between her husband and his brother at Tarentum;

she had negotiated exchanges of supplies in 35 BC; and she had brought two thousand men to Athens for Antony at Octavian's behest. However, none of these activities damaged her image (App. *Civ.* V 94; Plut. *Ant.* 35, 2 and 4; Cass. Dio, *Roman History* 49.33. 4 apud Rohr Vio, 2015, p. 81).

The marriage between Antony and Octavia sealed a new agreement between him and Octavian, while the image of Fulvia was depreciated, with socially negative characteristics, strongly signalled by gender inequality, improperly marking her memory. However, it ended up enriching a propaganda designed to contemplate the pact between the two triumvirs.

Chapter 4

Octavia, the ideal roman matron

Octavia (69/66 BC - 11 BC) was the elder sister of Octavian, whose parents were Atia and her first husband, Gaius Octavius. She later had a stepfather, who was Lucius Marcius Philippus. Atia was the daughter of Julia, sister of Julius Caesar and Marcus Atius Balbus, who came from Aricia and was related to Pompey by his mother's family. He came from the senatorial layer to which his family belonged. However, he was never a consul, he was one of the twenty men selected for the commission of the *lex Iulia agraria* to distribute land in Campania (Suet. *Aug.* 4.1). Atia's mother was the daughter of Gaius Julius Caesar and Aurelia, of the *Aurelii Cottae* family, who were of the old plebeian nobility. Octavia's father had previously been married to Ancharia, with whom he had Octavia Major. In 61 BC, he became *praetor* and was assigned the government of Macedonia. In 58 BC, before becoming consul, he died suddenly. Atia, in turn, in 57 BC, remarried Philippus, associating him with Pompey and Julius Caesar. He came from a family of plebeian nobility, *Marcii Philippii*, whose father had been consul in 91 BC. His family was composed of multiple consuls and *praetor*s (Moore, 2017, p. 12-15).

Probably in 54 BC, Octavia, aged fifteen, had been offered by Gaius Julius Caesar as a probable bride for Gnaeus Pompeius Magnus, which shows that her birth could have been in 69 BC (Suet. *Iul.* 27 apud Wood, 2000, p. 30-35). This indicates that she could not have had Marcellus until 42 BC, as twenty-seven years seems late for a woman who had five children who survived to adulthood. She could have been born in 66 BC and had Marcellus in 42 BC, when she was twenty-four and when she was offered to be Pompey' bride, bringing her closer to her brother's age (Moore, 2017, p. 8-10). This was a typical attitude in Roman politics, in other words, both men and women of the elite would often had to dissolve existing unions in favour of desirable dynastic combinations. In this case, Pompey refused Caesar's offer and Octavia remained married to Claudius Marcellus until his death (Wood, 2001, p. 31).

Octavia's first marriage was in 54 BC, to Gaius Claudius Marcellus, of the *Claudii Marcelli* family of plebeian nobility. He was a correspondent of Cicero, consul and a political opponent of his wife's family in 50 BC. His mother-in-law, Junia, was also an example of a matron to follow (Moore, 2017, p. 27-28). The eldest daughter of the couple was Claudia Marcella Major, who married Agrippa in 28 BC (Cass. Dio, *Roman History* 53.1.2), had children with him (Suet. *Aug.* 63.1), but divorced him in 21 BC, so that her cousin, Julia, could marry him (Cass. Dio, *Roman History* 54.6.5; Plut. *Ant.* 87.4; Vell. Pat. 2.100.4). Later, Marcella Major married Antony and Fulvia's youngest son, Iullus, in 21 BC, having Lucius Antonius and another daughter (Syme, 1986, p. 144). It appears that Iullus committed adultery with Octavian's daughter, Julia, and was eventually killed or committed suicide (Moore, 2017, p. 147).

Octavia's second son with Gaius Claudius Marcellus was Marcus Claudius Marcellus. He was promised at the age of three to the daughter of Sextus Pompey (Cass. Dio *Roman History* 48.38.5), but this marriage never took place. He died aged 19 in 23 BC, just two years after marrying Julia, Augustus' daughter, removing the prospect of him being one of his heirs. This episode left Octavia distraught Marcellus, in 24 BC, was given the ability by the Senate to become Senator and to represent the consulate years earlier than usual (Moore, 2017, p. 137). Octavian gave his nephew and son-in-law a public funeral and took him to be buried in his mausoleum, as well as asking for a golden image of Marcellus to be made with a crown that was also golden, requesting that this image be placed on the stage for the *aedile* games, which Marcellus himself was to have presided over (Cass. Dio, *Roman History* 53.30.4-6). After Marcellus' death, Octavia herself suggested that Julia marry Agrippa, but he would have to divorce her daughter, Marcella Major (Plut. *Ant.* 87.2-3; Suet. *Aug.* 63.1), who would then marry Iullus, the youngest son of Antony and Fulvia. These marriages eventually took place in 21 BC (Cass. Dio *Roman History* 54.6.5; Plut. *Ant.* 87.4; Vell. Pat. 2.100.4).

However, the figure of Octavia as a virtuous wife who was grieving may have concealed a woman who had been educated and maintained the Patronage activity (Hemelrijik, 1999, p. 99-100). She dedicated an entire library to the memory of Marcellus, with the separation of Greek and Latin works. The construction was done within the enclosure of the *Porticus Octaviae*, which Augustus built in honour of his sister (Plut. *Ant.* 30.6). According to Cassius Dio, both the library and the *Porticus Octaviae* were built by Augustus in 33 BC in honour of Octavia, with the war earnings from the Dalmatian campaign (Cass. Dio, *Roman History* 49.43.8).

Augustus built the Theatre of *Marcellus* and the *Porticus Octaviae* to honour his sister and nephew. These constructions were part of Augustus' policy of creating public places (Barrett, 2002, p. 199-201). Marcellus was Octavian's closest male relative, so the privileges granted to him marked him as someone of utmost importance to his uncle (Moore, 2017, p. 133). The construction of the *Porticus Octaviae* began in the mid-20s BC, probably to celebrate Marcellus' magistracy in 23 BC, but it could have taken place earlier, in 27 BC. This portico was restored over the old *Porticus Metellus*, built in 146 BC by general Metellus, who had gone on the Macedonian campaign (Vell. Pat. 1.11.3). The new portico was designed to have the two temples of the old portico, in which *Juno Regina* and *Jupiter Strator* were celebrated.

In this period, the *Campus Martius* was the focus area of Octavian's building programme in 33 BC, in which he restored the *Porticus Gn. Octavius* and began the elaboration of his mausoleum. Octavian also resumed the construction of a theatre begun by Julius Caesar, which was later dedicated to Marcellus and renamed the Theatre of Marcellus. In Octavian's portico, nothing of the original survived, since the building was damaged by fire twice, in AD 80 and in AD 191, when it was repaired by Septimus Severus and then by his son, Caracalla in AD 203 (Moore, 2017, p. 166-168). This portico ended up being part of a set of Roman imperial propaganda, since it was named after Octavian's sister and dedicated to Marcellus.

Regarding Patronage, Octavia seems to have financed some artists, because according to Plutarch, Athenodorus of Tarsus, a Stoic philosopher who lived as an advisor to Augustus, dedicated a book to her in honour of the death of her son. This type of work was called a *consolatio*, which was produced for women who were grieving for their children (Plut. *Publ.* 17.5). This fact shows that Octavia, or even Augustus, may have given the author money or some gift in exchange for his book addressed to her or perhaps his work was dedicated to her to repay some past *beneficium*. Seneca the Younger, in his work *Ad Marciam*, described Octavia as inconsolable, as if she had never left the funeral of her son. The author states that she hated all mothers and could not hear of her son's name (Sen. *Ad Marc.* 2.1-4).

Augustus granted her the right to dismiss the guardian who was in control of her finances so that she could spend her money at will (Cass. Dio, *Roman History* 49.38.1; Purcell, 1986; Flory, 1993 apud Helmelrijk, 1999, p. 101-102). This attitude may have facilitated her entry into benefactress activity, as Octavia's benefactorship was closely linked to her status as the emperor's sister (Helmerijk, 1999, p. 102), functioning as a way of propagandising the imperial family.

The youngest daughter of Octavia and Gaius Marcellus was Claudia Marcella Minor, who was born around 40 or 39 BC. She seems to have married twice: first to Messalla Appianus, who was consul in 12 BC and with whom she had two children, Claudia Pulchra and Massalla Barbatus. His son seems to have married Domitia Lepida Minor, who appears to have been the parents of the famous Valeria Messalina, wife of Emperor Claudius, accused of having committed adultery (Balsdon, 1962, p. 97-107; Syme, 1986, p. 182-184). Later, Marcella seems to have married Paullus Aemilius Regillus (Moore, 2017, p. 148).

Octavia's second marriage was to Mark Antony in 40 BC, who was her brother Octavian's greatest rival. He had also been the husband of Fulvia and had a connection with Cleopatra (Moore, 2017, p. 5). The couple's eldest daughter was Julia Antonia Major, who was born in 39 BC, just before the couple left to live in Athens, where they lived for a few years, returning, after the Treaty of Tarentum, to Rome in 37 BC. She never saw her father again after he went to the East. Octavian eventually granted Antonia Major and her sister, Antonia Minor, part of their father's properties after his death (Cass. Dio *Roman History* 51.15.7). Antonia Major was promised to Lucius Domitius Ahenobarbus to seal the Treaty of Tarentum of 37 BC, which gave rise to Domitia Lepida Major, Domitia Lepida Minor and Gnaeus Domitius Ahenobarbus. Domitia Lepida Minor was the mother of Valeria Messalina with her cousin, Messalla Barbatus, the son of Marcella Minor. In addition, Gnaeus Domitius Ahenobarbus married Agrippina Minor, granddaughter of Antonia Minor, giving rise to Nero, who would later become emperor (Barrett, 1996; Ginsburg, 2006). Antonia Major, Antonia Minor and Marcella Major never remarried after the deaths of their husbands (Moore, 2017, p. 149).

The couple's second daughter was Julia Antonia Minor, who was born in 36 BC, shortly after the Treaty of Tarentum, followed by Octavia's return to Rome. As her father had gone to the East, she never met him. She married Livia's youngest son, Nero Claudius Drusus, with whom she had Germanicus Julius Caesar, Claudia Livia Julia (Livilla) and Tiberius Claudius Drusus. Her son Germanicus later married Agrippina Major, having as daughter Agrippina Minor, the emperor Caligula, and other children, such as Nero Julius Caesar, Drusus Caesar, Julia Drusilla, and Julia Livilla. After her husband Drusus died in 9 BC, she did not remarry (Bauman, 1992, p. 138-156; Moore, 2017, p. 150). Antonia Minor was strong, influential and with a modesty like her mother's (Hemelrijk, 1999, p. 102-103).

Iullius Antonius, son of Fulvia and Antony, who was born around 43 BC, was only three years old when his mother died. Together with his older brother Marcus Antonius Antyllus, he became Octavia's stepson in 40 BC when she married Antony. Iullus received support from Octavia as if he were her own son, Marcellus, and was brought up on the same pattern, coming to be only after Agrippa and Livia's sons in esteem to Octavian (Plut. Ant. 87). He married Marcella Major in 21 BC. He followed a political career and became *praetor* in 13 BC (Cass. Dio, *Roman History* 54.26), consul in 10 BC and proconsul of Asia in 7 BC (Vell. Pat. 2.100.4). However, in 2 BC, he was accused of adultery with Octavian's daughter Julia, an event that caused him to commit suicide or forced him to commit suicide (Fantham, 2006; Hallett, 2006; Moore, 2017, p. 152). According to Velleius Paterculus, Iullus committed suicide, but according to Tacitus he was executed for adultery. Cassius Dio mentions that Augustus had executed Iullus on the basis that he had plans for the monarchy, but both authors wrote after Paterculus, whose account seems more reliable (Vell. Pat. 2.100.4; Tac. *Ann.* 4.44; Cass. Dio, *Roman History* 55.10.15).

Another daughter that Octavia had to bring up was Cleopatra Selene, Cleopatra VII's daughter. She grew up in her house and later married Juba II. The latter was kept in Italy as a guarantee of the good behaviour of his father, Juba I, after his defeat by Julius Caesar. The two young royals returned to Juba II's homeland of Mauritania in Africa, where they built an impressive library (Moore, 2017, p. 153).

Octavia was never placed in the category of women who were ill-spoken of by ancient writers, nor was ever accused of adultery, of having poisoned a rival, of having attitudes "that were not feminine" (Moore, 2017, p. 1) or of having interfered in political actions. She never desired public glory or any kind of notoriety. However, this must have been due to the fact that she was the sister of Augustus. She was characterised by Plutarch as a wonderful, beautiful, dignified woman of good sense, who had been the widow of Gaius Marcellus (Plut. *Ant.* 31.1). Most of the time she was described together with Livia, which meant that there was no extensive analysis of her person. The descriptions were of a woman who was not troublesome (Moore, 2017, p. 7) and fit the pattern considered by the ancients as that of the ideal Roman matron.

The matron was that woman of the Roman elite associated with traditional feminine values such as beauty and fertility; who took care of the house; who did charity; who was modest; who was linked to *pietas*, severity, simplicity, sobriety, and self-restraint; who was reserved, domesticable and had total devotion to her husband and children. These women were expected to live a life of seclusion, to be chaste, devoted wives and mothers, and to marry only once, in other words, *univirae,* being faithful widows after the death of their husband, which had already changed by the time of Octavia. The emphasis on moral qualities was linked to the education of both boys and girls, but for girls the perspective was marriage and motherhood (Hemelrijk, 1999, p. 13, 57-58).

Appropriate examples of Roman women of the Late Republic have changed greatly, but they still had to fulfil being devoted to their children, like Cornelia, and obedient, fulfilling their *pietas*. As women could not have roles directly linked to politics, they were honoured by being mothers (Moore, 2017, p. 14). When they were in public, they wore a special outfit, as they were allowed to wear the *stola* or *instita*, a long overcoat that covered their ankles. In their hair they wore *vittae,* which were fillets or bands of wool. Such garments went out of fashion in the Augustan period and were worn on special occasions. Thus, the *stola, instita, vittae* and *matrona* were used to denote the married Roman citizen woman (Hemelrijk, 1999, p. 13).

When describing Sempronia, who was not a model to be followed, Sallustius emphasises that she had all the characteristics, such as beauty, wealth, and fertility, to be an ideal matron, although she did not know how to use them. In this way, he characterises her as the ideal opposite, exposing that she was weak, immoral, and wanted to overthrow the State (Fischler, 1994, p. 118-119). It cannot fail to consider the opposite role manifested in these women of Rome's imperial elite in the ancient texts, which suggests that the woman who did not follow the standards imposed by society was also a common cultural construction, in the same way as the ideal matron (Fischler, 1994, p. 118). However, the ideal matron was a social idealisation, which was used to construct criticism of other women.

Some matrons might have received an education, although in Roman society education and study were typically masculine. Knowledge of literary culture and the arts was generally reserved for the men of the elite. For them, education was valuable for the political career, which was a field of competition and an instrument of social differentiation (Hemelrijk, 1999, p. 6).

The term *matrona docta*, which would be an educated matron, was often not taken as a compliment. The Roman woman of the elite passed through different stages, from daughter, wife[50], mother and widow; there

---

[50] Women of the Roman elite were married in their teens. The minimum age under Augustus was twelve. However, girls outside the elite married later. Marriage was the biggest transition in the lives of these girls, where they became *matrons*; on the eve of the wedding, they would dedicate their dolls to Venus. Marriage was arranged by the father and was often a pairing between relatives. Formal consent was given at the age of fifteen. They had to do the bidding of their families. In the first marriage, the husband had to be around ten years older than her (Hemelrijk, 1999, p. 8).

were prescribed norms of behaviour that they had to follow. However, the position of these women was marked by ambiguities, the result of contradictory demands of status and gender. Conversely, their lives were circumscribed by their family origins and the various roles they were expected to perform within the family during the different stages of their lives. The age of the husband and wife in a woman's second or third marriage, as in the case of Octavia, should be close, since the woman would probably be less compliant and submissive at this stage than during her first marriage (Hemelrijk, 1999, p. 6-7).

4.1. The life and coins of Octavia

After Fulvia's death, Antony reconciled with Octavian. The latter saw that a marriage between Antony and his sister, Octavia, would be a way to seal this harmony, framing such an agreement with the famous Pact of Brundisium of 40 BC. In this period, men of the Roman elite exploited the marriage of their female relatives as a way to establish a political bond between allies, through the union of mature men with inexperienced girls full of life and energy, which was not the case with Octavia, as she had already gone through a marriage and was of a certain age. This element demonstrates that such types of arrangements also reverberated among older women. On the other hand, less mature women, when marrying in such circumstances, would end up being caught in the temptation of adulterous elopement (Fantham, 2011, p. 141), which was not the case for Octavia either, as her position as an ideal Roman matron did not characterise her along these lines. Octavia was expected to be married to someone her brother arranged to fulfil his political needs. Political alliances were made as a matter of course to ensure loyalty between families and to protect the mutual interest in the children of that marriage (Wood, 2001, p. 27).

It is understood that these women were used as tools in Rome's politics, contributing to dynastic continuation and political agreements, and that they were meant to act to fulfil male relevance and development. Such position contributed to the understanding among men of a signed agreement, resulting in them being reduced to manipulable instruments of treaties between male individuals and reproductive apparatuses, ensuring the next generation and the continuity of the system. This positioning also guaranteed them a social position, even if they were subject to a gender hierarchy, being the ideal victims of symbolic violence (Bourdieu, 2001, p. 1-2) for the maintenance of this system.

She was not named on any coin on which her face appeared, but the context of the object allowed the link to her character. There are many coins that unquestionably depicted her by circumstantial evidence. All her images are associated with the figures of Antony or Antony and Octavian, and they are all dated from the 40s to 36 BC (Erhart, 1980, p. 125). Coins with Octavia's portrait only appeared after she married Antony, in the cities and territories he controlled, probably Greek cities of Asia Minor, in the heart of the Hellenistic world, an area that embraced the concept of divine kingship, with celebrations and tributes to the royal couple. According to Wood, such coins could have served as propaganda for her husband, and not her brother (Wood, 2001, p. 32 and 41). However, even though her coin was minted in Antony's territories, it conveyed the peace concluded by Antony and Octavian through such a marriage, therefore being an advertisement for her brother as well.

Portraits of Octavia arguably existed from 35 BC onwards, when the Senate formally voted *sacrosanctitas* honours for her and Livia, along with other important rights. However, the scarcity of surviving inscriptions implies that such portraits were never plentiful. The Senate's authorisation for these portraits to be made suggests the unprecedented nature of such public honours for women in 35 BC. However, these figures served as propaganda objects, which allowed Octavian to honour the Roman wives of the triumvirs. After the establishment of Augustus as *princeps*, portraits of the male members of his family could legitimately be distributed and displayed, since men generally held public offices that made such public presentation appropriate, unlike the depictions of women, which might have seemed too open a declaration of dynastic intent. Augustus wished members of his own family to eventually inherit his powers, knowing that they should rest on constitutional offices and be established under the traditions of the Republic, which he claimed to have restored (Wood, 2001, p. 27-29).

In her depictions, Octavia was identified with the role of a good mother, an example of a proper matron, which was a trait to be celebrated by the empire. Her highly praised position as a moral role model was hardly elusive, since even coins bearing her image were minted only during Antony's lifetime. In fact, coins bearing her portrait were only minted in eastern Greece (Harvey, 2020, p. 39).

Most interestingly, the coins were minted to honour the union of Mark Antony and Octavia, as this union represented the end of the disagreements between the triumvirs. However, coins of the couple began to be minted after the Pact of Brundisium in 40 BC and the Treaty of Tarentum in 37 BC. This is an example of how women of the Roman elite, such as Octavia, were often placed to be married to men simply to fulfil alliances in political negotiations. However, even on these occasions, the parties marrying them desired harmony and affection (Hemelrijk, 1999, p. 8).

Figure 10 – Aureus[51], 40 - 39 BC, Rome, 8.01 g; 22 mm diameter. Obverse: Mark Antony: M ANTONIVS IMP III VIR R P C (*Marcus Antonius Imperator Triumviri Rei Publicae Constituandae* = Commander Mark Antony, Triumvir for the Constitutional Republic[52]). And Octavia on the reverse. Named piece: *De Quelen Aureus*

Source: © Photo: *Münzkabinett der Staatlichen Museen zu Berlin - Preußischer Kulturbesitz Photograf/in: Dirk Sonnenwald*

This aureus, known as *De Quelen Aureus,* marks the beginning of the coinage of Mark Antony and Octavia. Like the next coins, this object symbolised the couple's union, more specifically the harmony of Octavian and Antony. The object features Antony on the obverse, with a caption indicating a political aspect, which would be the Triumvirate; on the reverse is Octavia, with the *nodus-type* hair common among Roman matrons of that period. She has a short, slender neck, delicate bone structure, prominent cheek bones, a small, pointed chin, and a hairstyle similar but not identical to the examples in which Fulvia appears as Victoria. Octavia wears her bun at the back of her head, just above the nape of her neck. The hair around her face forms a wide roll of waves swept out and back and a small lock of hair escapes from the hairstyle at the nape of the neck (Wood, 2001, p. 45). The reverse, with a print of a living woman, could be seen as part of the growth in the number of portraits of women on

---

[51] ID Number: 18202297. Available at: http://www.smb-digital.de/eMuseumPlus?service=direct/1/ResultLightbox-View/result.t1.collection_lightbox.$TspTitleImageLink.link&sp=10&sp=Scollection&sp=SfieldValue&sp=0&sp=1&sp=3&sp=Slightbox_3x4&sp=12&sp=Sdetail&sp=0&sp=F&sp=T&sp=13; http://www.smb-digital.de/eMuseumPlus?-service=ExternalInterface&module=collection&objectId=2355002&viewType=detailView; http://www.smb-digital.de/eMuseumPlus?service=ExternalInterface&module=collection&objectId=2355002&viewType=detailView; https://id.smb.museum/object/2355002/r%C3%B6m--republik-m--antonius. Crawford No. 527.1 (this piece); Schultz (1997) No. 326 (this piece). For the 1883 treasure, see M. H. Crawford, *Roman Republican Coin Hoards* (1969) 138 No. 527.

[52] Translation made by the author.

coins, the increase in women's public roles and some of the legal freedoms they gained in this period (Wood, 2001, p. 13 apud Rowan, 2019, p. 81).

According to Pollini, although issued under Antony's authority as triumvir, the *De Quelen Aureus* is undoubtedly based on a private portrait of Octavia, which was probably intended to commemorate her marriage to Antony in 40 BC because of the treaty of Brundisium between Octavian and Antony later that year. All the characteristics of this unique surviving aureus from its facial features and numismatic likenesses agree with those of Velletri's portrait. In both of the images, her *nodus* hairstyle, shown with a long braid of hair escaping from the side of her neck, is virtually the same. There are only minor differences: in Velletri's portrait, two small locks of hair escape in front of the ears and the hair at the back of the head is pulled back under the bun, which is placed lower in the coin image than in the sculptural portrait (Pollini, 2002, p. 32).

Figure 11 – Aureus[53], dated 38 BC, from the Roman Republic, with the face of Mark Antony turned to the right on the obverse, with the caption: M-ANTONIVS-M-F-M-N-AVGVR-IMP-TER (*Marcus Antonius Marcus Filius Marcus Nepos Augur*[54] *Imperator Tertium* = Mark Antony, son of Mark, grandson of Mark, augure[55], Commander for the Third Time). And on the reverse is the face of Octavia, turned to the right, with the caption: COS-DESIGN-ITER-ET-TER-III-VIR-R-P-C (*Consul Designatus Iterum Tertium Triumviri Rei Publicae Constituandae* = Consul Designated Again, for the Third Time as Triumvir for the Maintenance of the Constitutional Republic[56])

Source: The Trustees of the British Museum

This last coin, with Mark Antony on the obverse and Octavia on the reverse, also marks the union of the couple. However, the coin especially demonstrates the harmony between Antony and Octavian due to the Pact of Brundisium in 40 BC, an alliance that marked the Second Triumvirate, since a political agreement was established by this bond through a marriage agreement. Moreover, the coin's captions concern Antony's political life and nothing about Octavia, evidencing the expected ideal of female passivity in the face of the political ties established there.

On this coin Octavia has *nodus-type* hair, symbolising the status of the Roman matron, without any divine attribute, very close to the figures of Hellenistic women, which aimed to demonstrate the promotion of family

---

[53] Bibliography: RRC / Roman Republican Coinage (533/3a) RR2 / Coins of the Roman Republic in the British Museum, vol. 2. Coinages of Rome (continued), Roman Campania, Italy, the social war, and the provinces. (144, p. 507) PCR / Principal coins of the Romans: Volume I: The Republic c. 290 - 31 BC; Volume II: The Principate 31 BC - AD 296; Volume III: The Dominate AD 294 - 498. (302) Ghey, Leins & Crawford 2010 / A catalogue of the Roman Republican Coins in the British Museum, with descriptions and chronology based on M.H. Crawford, Roman Republican Coinage (1974) (533.3.1). Available at: https://www.britishmuseum.org/collection/object/C_1842-0523-1. Accessed: 29 Oct. 2020.

[54] Augurs was the one who carried the *lituus* (Elkins, 2017, p. 106), which was a type of staff.

[55] Mark Antony is *imperator*, *augur*, and *triumvir*. *Augur* is the one who foresees, who recognises the omens. Augur is he who makes the omen. The adjective is derived from Augustus, consecrated by augur or under favourable omens (Martins, 2011, p. 66 and 75).

[56] Translation made by the author, with consultation at https://en.numista.com/catalogue/pieces66597.html. Accessed: 9 Nov. 2019.

relationships. According to the style of Hellenistic women, the figures of Antony's wives, Octavia and Cleopatra, could appear with some of their husband's physical characteristics (Hekster, 2015; Harvey, 2020, p. 41). On this aureus and on small bronze coins from Tarentum, dated 37/36 BC, there is a slight difference in Octavia's appearance, revealing a more fleshy face with a prominent chin, features that seem to have emerged from images of Antony. In all of her images, she appears with *nodus-like* hair, possessing a roll of hair above her forehead and a bun at the back, which could change over time (Erhart, 1980, p. 125).

Deviations in hair styles and even facial features are hardly unknown in Roman coinage. In this aureus, the bun is less prominent and worn on the top of the head, while Octavia's facial features have somehow been assimilated to those of her husband. Such assimilation is found in other numismatic and sculptural portraits. Although it is not generally observed, perhaps one of the most extreme cases is seen in Cleopatra's physiognomic features, which were assimilated to Antony's on coins issued under Antony's authority in the East. Octavia's *nodus-like* hairstyle also appears to be somewhat different from that of *De Quelen Aureus*, not only in the bun placed higher, but also in the hair patterns at the temples and on the side of the head, in which the hair does not form waves, but seems to be continuously pulled back towards the bun (Pollini, 2002, p. 32-33).

According to Wood (2001), the image of Octavia has undergone a metamorphosis. The hair arrangement is now pulled straight back rather than forming a full wave roll around the face, and the bun is worn slightly higher at the back. Octavia may indeed have altered her hairstyle or the artists may have simplified it for their own convenience. Her face and neck appear more plump, her chin larger and more prominent and her head is more upright over a thicker neck. The change in her appearance from the earlier to the later coin probably reflects the assimilation of one person's appearance to another, revealing the harmony of the couple, visually reinforced by the resemblance. Thus, Octavia acquires a thick neck and protruding jaw like those of her husband.

The remarkable resemblance of Octavia's image in *De Quelen Aureus* to that of her brother is also attested in depictions of Octavia on cistophoric coins, issued between 40 and 35 BC, which may evidence her submission to her husband and brother or that she was seen as submissive to them. Silver coins featuring Octavia were minted in Asia, in Ephesus and Pergamum, with the cistophorus format, which was a type of coin issued by several cities of the kingdom of Pergamum since II BC. The name derives from the objects depicted on the coin, such as the mystical cista, which was a cylindrical basket containing items sacred to the cult of Dionysus and other elements orientated towards the god. Earlier issues from the time of the independence of the kingdom of Pergamum usually displayed the cista, with a serpent emerging from its lid on the obverse, framed by an ivy wreath, and a pair of intertwined serpents with raised heads on the reverse. However, after Pergamum and its territories became part of the Roman province of Asia, coins also incorporated references of the new authority (Mørkholm, 1991, p. 36-37 and 171-173 apud Head, 1910, p. 534-537). Thus, during Antony's hegemony over this region, his portrait, which appeared with an ivy wreath of Dionysus, was replaced by the cista within the ivy garland and grape clusters on the obverse, while the sacred basket moved to the reverse, between the two prancing serpents (Wood, 2001, p. 46-47).

The denomination of cistophorus was introduced to the region of Ephesus by the Hellenistic kings of Pergamum. The reverse of the next coin has a mystical cista or sacred basket from which snakes emerge, which is what gives the coins their name (Rowan, 2019, p. 83). During the period of Augustus and some of his successors, these types of coins continued to be struck in large pieces of silver, with a value of three denarii. In the Imperial period, cistophoric types were more in keeping with the style of Rome and were recognised by the people of the province (Sear, 2000, p. 20).

Figure 12 – Silver cistophorus Tridrachm[57], from 39 BC, Ephesus (?), Turkey, 12.24 g. On the reverse there is the bust of Antony, facing right, with ivy wreath, *lituus*[58] below, surrounded by ivy wreath and flowers, with caption: M ANTONIVS IMP COS DESIG ITER ET TERT (*Marcus Antonius Imperator Consul*[59] *Designatus Iterum Tertium* = Commander Mark Antony appointed as Consul again, for the third time). On the reverse there is the draped bust of Octavia, facing right, on a *cista*, flanked by snakes, with caption: III VIR R P C (*Triumvir Republicae Constituendae* = Triumvir of the Constitutional Republic[60])

Source: © The Trustees of the British Museum

This last example is a cistophorus coin from Ephesus, dated 39 BC, which was also minted in Pergamum between 40 and/or 35 BC, as well as others similar to it. In it, the couple appears with divine elements together with mythological categories. Antony is sometimes depicted associated

---

[57] Reference number: G.2204. RPC 1 2201. C&M catalogue number: RR2 (502) (133) (502). Bibliography: RR2 / Coins of the Roman Republic in the British Museum, vol. 2. Coinages of Rome (continued), Roman Campania, Italy, the social war, and the provinces. (p502.133) PCR / Principal coins of the Romans: Volume I: The Republic c. 290 - 31 BC; Volume II: The Principate 31 BC - AD 296; Volume III: The Dominate AD 294 - 498. (301) RPC1 / Roman provincial coinage. Vol.1, From the death of Caesar to the death of Vitellius (44 BC-AD 69) (2201/1).
Available at: https://www.britishmuseum.org/collection/object/C_G-2204. Accessed: 28 Oct. 2020.

[58] It would be a crooked staff carried by augur, augur staff, crosier, inaugural wand, available at: http://www.perseus.tufts.edu/hopper/resolveform?type=exact&lookup=lituus&lang=la, accessed 05 May 2022. The symbolism of the element *lituus* was related to the implementation of the *pontifices* and of the *augures* respectively (Elkins, 2017, p. 107).

[59] Consul usually appears as COS in coin captions. The annual activities of the consul were established soon after the abolition of the Monarchy in Rome in 510 BC. Generally, there were two consuls during the year, and they were the highest-ranking magistrates. However, their powers were diminished considerably by the presence of the tribunes of the plebs, who were not under their power. Their authority was also diminished in the last century of the Republic due to the power of the military commanders, the *emperors*. However, their powers were considerable as long as the Republic persisted. Even during the empire, consuls continued to be chosen, but with reduced powers. Sometimes the emperor was the one who carried the consulship, which caused the title to appear on his coins. In the captions of the coins, it can also appear how many times the person was consul, like COS III, which indicates that the person was three times consul (Sear, 2000, p. 73).

[60] Translation made by the author.

with Neptune, but the affinity with Dionysus is greater and better attested in art and literature. This silver tridrachm shows Antony and Octavia's connection to Dionysus, with the representation of religious symbols for the cult of the god. The bust of Antony is on the obverse, with a crown of ivy, and on the reverse is the bust of Octavia, in a smaller figure, on a mystical cista, and the serpents are sacred symbols representing Dionysus. It could be an association of the god Dionysus with his companion, Ariadne, represented by Antony and Octavia, who is recognisable by her coif (Harvey, 2020, p. 45-46).

The presence of Antony's name on coins marks him as a legal authority and with the absence of Octavia's name, it shows that there would be no type of homage to her. However, his image does not fail to represent that his figure had a sociopolitical importance, also evidencing that the Senate's concession was restricted to promoting these women (Harvey, 2020, p. 45-46). This was a common type of figure for the East and the Hellenistic period, in which Octavia's portrait appears on the cista (Barrett, 2002, p. 140). She appears once again in the background of the coin, since the reverse would be reserved for figures of lesser importance, and the captions do not even mention her, contributing only to celebrate and characterise Antony.

Octavia appears on the next example of this coin type, slightly behind Antony. The side and back of her hairstyle are not visible. However, in all other respects, her facial features and the front part of her *nodus hairstyle* agree with her image, when compared to *De Quelen Aureus* (Pollini, 2002, p. 34). What seems plausible to observe is that, in this series minted in Ephesus and Miletus, Octavia appears with a more prominent *status*, since she stands out on the obverse, even though she is behind Mark Antony (Wood, 2001, p. 48), which does not take her out of a secondary position in relation to her husband. The reverse again shows the basket of sacred utensils between a pair of intertwined serpents, but this time the object above the cista is a small full-body figure of Dionysus. Antony, on the obverse, again wears the ivy crown of Dionysus (Wood, 2001, p. 48), demonstrating his connection to the god.

Figure 13 – Silver cistophorus tridrachm[61], from 39 BC, minted in Ephesus (?), Turkey. On the obverse there is the bust of Mark Antony next to the bust of Octavia, with the caption: M ANTONIVS IMP COS DESIG ITER ET TERT (*Marcus Antonius Imperator Consul Designatus Iterum et Tertium*[62] = Commander Mark Antony, Consul appointed again, for the third time). On the reverse there is Dionysus on a mystic *cista*, holding a cup and with a *tirso* in the other hand and caption: III VIR R P C (Triumvir Republicae Constituendae = Triumvir of the Constitutional Republic[63])

Source: © The Trustees of the British Museum

On this cistophoric tridrachm, minted in Ephesus in 39 BC and in Miletus between 40 and/or 35 BC, the figure of Antony is superimposed on that of Octavia. He is wearing a crown of ivy, which associates him with his patron, the god Dionysus, who appears on the reverse standing on a mystical cista, with a thyrsus in his left hand, flanked by two intertwined snakes with their heads erect. Antony was proclaimed as "the new Dionysus" in Ephesus (Rowan, 2019, p. 84). This type of coin could have been utilised by the cult itself of objects from the mystical cista of Dionysus. Octavia appears on the object next to Antony, with part of her hair visible, and her position is secondary to her husband, in a portrayal of positive Roman values (Harvey, 2020, p. 43). In addition, the figure of the couple on the obverse presents the importance of the union, since this marriage would have reunited the relationship of Octavian and Mark Antony. Another element to take into account is the obverse caption, M ANTONIVS IMP COS DESIG ITER ET TERT, which attributes values to Mark Antony and none to Octavia, as well as the reverse caption, III VIR R P C. Moreover, Octavia is not shown

---

[61] Reference number: G.2206. C&M catalogue: RR2 (503) (136) (503). Bibliography: RR2 / Coins of the Roman Republic in the British Museum, vol. 2. Coinages of Rome (continued), Roman Campania, Italy, the social war, and the provinces (p503.136) RPC1 / Roman provincial coinage. Vol.1, From the death of Caesar to the death of Vitellius (44 BC-AD 69) (2202/1). Available at: https://www.britishmuseum.org/collection/object/C_G-2206. Accessed: 28 Oct. 2020.

[62] Available at: https://en.numista.com/catalogue/pieces66597.html. Accessed: 27 Oct. 2020.

[63] Translation made by the author.

with characteristics linked to the goddesses, as earlier depictions of Fulvia distinguished her, just as figures on coins of Livia also did later.

Coins made locally at provincial mints, such as the cistophori, produced in Ephesus, were made for regional use and did not have a caption that referred to the city. Bronze coins were struck for local use and were called the city coins (Butcher, 2005 apud Rowan, 2019, p. 88).

Returning to Octavia's historical context, when she married Antony, he did not deny his connection with Cleopatra, but he never admitted that she was his wife. Cleopatra was the most notable of Alexander's successors and Mark Antony's relationship with her would certainly have involved interests linked to the conquest of new territories. She endeavoured to maintain Egypt's independence and restore the greatness of previous centuries. However, her history was rarely told as such. Her image was always of a woman trying to act like a man, consumed by ambition, using her sexuality to manipulate first Caesar and then Mark Antony (Burstein, 2004, p. 88).

She was tied to Caesar because she had no other way to survive, since she was deposed by the court and fled Egypt into the desert to avoid being murdered. However, she saw an opportunity to ally herself with Caesar against her brother. Plutarch and Cassius Dio report that the two immediately became lovers (Vieira, 2012, p. 21). According to Bradford (2002), Cleopatra's seduction would never have been the only reason for such involvement between the leaders, considering the potential of Egyptian lands. Caesar needed Egypt's help to pay for the expenses generated by the war, and nothing was more opportune than to join his army with Cleopatra's. Consequently, the son of Cleopatra was born, Ptolemy Caesar, better known as Caesarion, in 47 BC. In 46 BC, Cleopatra settled in Rome causing controversy, as it was feared that she could influence Caesar and the government (Vieira, 2012, p. 22).

Although Caesar recognised his son with Cleopatra, the Romans did not view positively the idea of Caesarion being the heir of the empires of Rome and the East, which would benefit Egypt more than Rome. This led to Caesar's assassination by the Republicans in 44 BC (Vieira, 2012, p. 22).

At the juncture of Octavia's marriage to Mark Antony, Plutarch made it clear that he was not in favour of Cleopatra's relationship with him and hoped for the union of Octavia and Antony, for the restoration of harmony in the Roman world. The widow would have to wait ten months before remarrying, but in this case this law was transposed to the occurrence of this marriage (Plut. *Ant.* 31.1). This time interval was intended to protect the legitimacy of any children with a widow's dead husband. However, Octavia was possibly given this permission due to the fact that she was pregnant (Cass. Dio, *Roman History* 48.31.3). This marriage was symbolically the guarantee of *concordia* between Octavian and Antony, as well as *pax* for the people (DuQúesnay, 1976, p. 24). The Senate granted *ovationes*[64] to Octavian and Antony, making the two enter Rome as victors (Cass. Dio, *Roman History* 48.31.2; Suet. *Aug.* 22). The Senate awarded this prize to celebrate a victory of peace, without the need for a battle, but it seems to have been something unusual. In this way, it was expected that Octavia's beauty, intelligence, and dignity would be enough to keep Antony's attention and the peace between him and his brother, Octavian (Plut. *Ant.* 31.2-3 apud Moore, 2017, p. 88-92).

When Plutarch referred to Octavia, he said that she continued to act as an exemplary woman, staying in Rome and working for the benefits of her husband, while he was doing business with Cleopatra. In his writings, Plutarch always mentioned jealousy among Mark Antony's wives (Plut. *Ant.* 30.1 and 53.2). When the author mentioned the city of Athens, he pointed out that such a place was enamoured of the wonderful Octavia, where she won honours, which is supposed to have caused Cleopatra jealousy years later, when she went with Antony to the city (Plut. *Ant.* 57.1). Octavia's virtues exemplified the ideal Roman matron, in contrast to the decadent kind of image created by ancient writers about Cleopatra's East, secured by the Roman point of view (Fischler, 1994, p. 118).

In any case, Octavia's relationship with her husband depended on the relationship between her brother and Antony. For the Treaty of Tarentum, Antony left Athens in 37 BC to go to Italy. At the request of Octavia herself, who was pregnant, she went ahead of her husband to meet her brother in Tarentum (App. *B. Civ.* 5.93; Plut. *Ant.* 35.1). She met with Octavian and with his friends Agrippa and Mecenas. Only after winning his friends over, she was able to discuss the divisive issues that persisted between her brother and Antony (App. *B. Civ.* 5.93; Plut. *Ant.* 35.2). Octavian had felt abandoned by Antony when he needed help, as well as betrayed when Antony had sent a freedman to Lepidus. Octavia knew that the freedman had been sent to Lepidus to arrange a marriage between Antonia Major and Lepidus' son, not to plot against Octavian. To support this claim, Antony offered to send the freedman to Octavian, with permission to torture him until the truth came out (App. *B. Civ.* 5.93).

Octavia begged her brother not to make her the most miserable woman, because all eyes were upon her, since if there was an obstacle between both, being the wife of one and the sister of another, only one would prevail (Plut. *Ant.* 35.3).

---

[64] *Ovatio* was a smaller version of triumph, which was given as a prize for great military victories (Moore, 2017, p. 89).

Octavia's pleas softened her brother's anger and he agreed to meet Antony peacefully (App. *B. Civ.* 5. 93; Cass. Dio, *Roman History* 48.54.3; Plut. *Ant.* 35.3-4). The two men arrived at the agreed meeting from opposite sides of the river at the same time. Antony leapt from his chariot and, unescorted, boarded a small skiff, rowing towards Octavian. Seeing Antony's confidence and believing him to be a friend, Octavian did the same. The two triumvirs met in the middle of the river. They argued among themselves about which bank of the river they should return to. Octavian prevailed, accompanying Antony to his side of the river, saying he wished to see his sister. Placing his trust in Antony, Octavian rode with his companion in his unprotected chariot, even passing the night in Antony's camp without a guard. To return the favour, Antony similarly spent the following night in Octavian's camp (App. *B. Civ.* 5.94).

Consequently, Octavia's intervention brought about a treaty that saw Octavian and Antony join military endeavours to help each other. Within the agreement, Antony would give ships to Octavian to be used against Sextus Pompey (App. *B. Civ.* 5.95; Cass. Dio, *Roman History* 48.54.2; Plut. *Ant.* 35.4). Octavian provided Antony with more troops for his endeavour in Parthia (App. *B. Civ.* 5.95; Cass. Dio 48.54.2; Plut. *Ant.* 35.4), as well as providing Antony with 1000 additional men, to be selected by the latter (App. *B. Civ.* 5.95; Plut. *Ant.* 35.4). Antony, in return, would provide Octavian with additional ships (App. B. Civ. 5.95; Plut. Ant. 35.4). Moreover, the agreement originally made in 42 BC had expired in early 37 BC, but was consequently renewed for another five years (App. *B. Civ.* 5.95; Cass. Dio 48.54.6). To further strengthen the bonds between Octavian and Antony, he set his daughter Julia to marry Antony and Fulvia's eldest son, Antyllus. Similarly, Antony promised to betroth the daughter he had with Octavia, Antonia Major, to Lucius Domitius Ahenobarbus, son of Domitius Enobarbus (Cass. Dio, *Roman History* 48.54.4).

In accordance with the Treaty of Tarentum, there were coins such as sestertii, dupondii, aces and tremissis that featured nautical images on the reverse, with a varying number of ships, which are often referred to as "fleet coins". This choice of the maritime theme recalls the fact that ships were part of the Tarentum agreement of 37 BC, as well as that Octavia had to trade extra ships to Octavian in exchange for troops for Antony. These coins were struck by Lucius Calpurnius Bibulus, Lucius Sempronius Atratinus and Marcus Oppius Capito. Some Greek letters appear on the coins, indicating their value, such as the *delta* representing four, the *gamma*, three, the *beta*, two and the *alpha*, one. The sestertius (4 asses) bears a quadriga (a chariot with four horses) on the reverse; the tremissis (3 asses), three ships and *triskeles*; the dupondius (2 asses), two ships and two covers of *Dioscuri*[65], the "as" holding only one ship; the semi (1/2 as), the bow of the ship; and the quadrans (1/4 as), the stem of the ship's bow. The system could have been intended to communicate the values of these coins to new users (Amandry, 1990, p. 84) and was an innovation. The sestertius, which had previously only been struck in silver, was now struck in bronze; and the tremissis and the dupondius have not been struck since the 3rd century BC (Amandry, 1986). However, the fleet coinage system was abandoned after the defeat of Antony and other innovations of the Late Republic, but it could have served as an inspiration for Augustus in his reform of the monetary system (Amandry; Barrandon, 2008 apud Rowan, 2019, p. 86-87).

The obverses of these coins show Octavia, Octavian, and Antony in various configurations. On the obverse of the quadrans, Antony and Octavian are evident, and there may be a direct response to Pompey-Janus from the issue of Sextus. The captions name three fleet *prefects* and Antony as *triumvir*. In the sestertius, there are two figures: the hippocampus quadriga, commonly believed to represent Antony and Octavia as Poseidon and Amphitrite (Bahrfeldt, 1905, p. 35 apud Rowan, 2019, p. 87).

---

[65] It would be the Greek name of Castor and Pollux when they appear together (Available at: https://www.collinsdictionary.com/dictionary/english/dioscuri, accessed 21/04/2023).

Figure 14 – Copper alloy as [66], from 36 - 35 BC, from the Roman Republic, minted in Achaia, Peloponnese, Greece. On the obverse there is the bust of Antony next to the bust of Octavia with captions surrounding: M-ANT-IMP-TERT-COS-DESIG-ITER-ET.TER-III-VIR-R-P--C (*Marcus Antonius Imperator Tertium Consul Designatus Iterum Tertium Triumvir Reipublicae Constituendae* = Commander Mark Antony, appointed Consul for the third time and again triumvir, for the third time, for the maintenance of the Constitutional Republic[67]). On the reverse there is a Sailing Ship on the right; below, denominational mark[68] and Medusa's head; and the surrounding, M-OPPIVS-CA[PITO-PRO-PR-PRAEF]-CLASS-F-C[69] (*Marcus Oppius Capito Pro Prætore Præfectus Classis* = Marcus Oppius Capito, propretor and commander of the fleet[70])

Source: © The Trustees of the British Museum

---

[66] Reference number: R.9591; catalogue number: RR2 (519) (169). Bibliographical references: RPC1 / Roman provincial coinage. Vol.1, From the death of Caesar to the death of Vitellius (44 BC-AD 69) (1470), RR2 / Coins of the Roman Republic in the British Museum, vol. 2. Coinages of Rome (continued), Roman Campania, Italy, the social war, and the provinces. (169, p. 519). Available at: https://www.britishmuseum.org/collection/object/C_R-9591. Accessed: 28 Oct. 2020.
[67] Translation made by the author with verification at: https://www.davidrsear.com/academy/roman_legends.html. Accessed: 27 Oct. 2020.
[68] A, Greek letter and numeral inscription one.
[69] Mint.
[70] Translation made by the author.

Figure 15 – Copper alloy dupodius[71], from 38 - 37 BC, from Achaia. On the obverse are the busts of Antony and Octavia facing each other, with caption: [M-ANT-IMP-TERT--COS-DESIG-ITER-ET-TER-III-VIR-R-P-C] (*Marcus Antonius Imperator tertium Consul Designatus Iterum Tertium Triumvir Reipublicae Constituendae* = Commander Mark Antony, appointed Consul for the third time and triumvir for the maintenance of the Constitutional Republic again, for the third time[72]). On the reverse are two ships sailing on the right; below, denominational mark[73] above, two caps of *Dioscur* and caption: M-OPPIVS-CAPITO-PRO-PR-PRAEF-CLASS-F-C[74] (*Marcus Oppius Capito Pro Prætore Præfectus Classis* = Marcus Oppius Capito, propretor and commander of the fleet[75])

Source: © The Trustees of the British Museum

This dupondius[76] has two galleys ship on its reverse, whereas, presumably, the *asses* would have only one galley. Ships played a key role in the agreement between Antony and Octavian at Tarentum, as Antony had made a threatening show of force by sailing to Italy with three hundred ships, but in the end exchanged one hundred of his ships for two legions of men for his campaign in Parthia. In addition, Octavia secured an additional gift of twenty ships from Antony for her brother and a promise of another thousand soldiers from Antony to Octavian (Plut. *Ant.* 35.1-4).

---

[71] Reference number: R.9565; catalogue number: RR2 (518) (159). A *dupondii* was worth 2 asses (Wood, 2001, p. 49). Bibliography: RR2 / Coins of the Roman Republic in the British Museum, vol. 2. Coinages of Rome (continued), Roman Campania, Italy, the social war, and the provinces. (159, p. 518) RPC1 / Roman provincial coinage. Vol.1, From the death of Caesar to the death of Vitellius (44 BC-AD 69) (1464). Available at: https://www.britishmuseum.org/collection/object/C_R-9565, accessed 28 October 2020.

[72] Translation made by the author with verification at: https://www.davidrsear.com/academy/roman_legends.html. Accessed: 27 Oct. 2020.

[73] Inscription in Greek [B] and a numeral, two.

[74] Indicates the mint at which it was minted.

[75] Translation made by the author.

[76] The dupondius and the as, despite their similar size, could be distinguished by the colour of the metal: one would be yellow brass and the other red copper (Sear, 2000, p. 20).

Figure 16 – Copper alloy Sestertius[77], from 36 - 35 BC, 12.40 g, *Achaia*, Greece, Peloponnese, from the mint *L. Sempronius Atratinus*. On the obverse there are the bust of Antony and the bust of Octavia facing each other, with caption: M-ANT-IMP-TER-[COS-DES-ITER-ET-TER-III--VIR-R-P-C] (*Marcus Antonius Imperator Consul Designatus Iterum Tertium Triumvir Reipublicae Constituendae* = Commander Mark Antony, appointed Consul and Triumvir again for the third time for the maintenance of the Constitutional Republic[78]). On the reverse there are two figures facing each other in a *hippocampus* quadriga on the right; on the left, the captions; below, a denomination mark[79] and a square object; around, L-ATRATINVS-AVGVR-COS-DESIG[80] (*Lucius Atratinus augur consul designatus*[81] = Lucius [Sempronio] Atratinus *augur* and appointed consul[82])

Source: © The Trustees of the British Museum

In the last two examples, Octavia does not stand behind Antony, but in front of him, demonstrating a status almost equal to that of the male members of the family, which suggests that the couple were partners in marriage and politics. The coin was minted by an uncertain mint in Achaia. This type of figure, in which the couples are facing each other, implies conveying an ideology linked to the divine royal couple, as had already occurred in images of Hellenistic kings and their wives, such as those of the Ptolemies and Seleucids. This figure is not only linked to Hellenistic traditions, but is also politically significant for Antony (Harvey, 2020, p. 44).

The reverse of the sestertius deserves special attention. The nautical image illustrated on the coin is a divine couple, Poseidon and Amphitrite again, embracing in a chariot pulled by four hippocampi. This is a surprisingly

---

[77] Reference number: 1860.0328.251. Catalogue number: RR2 (515) (151). RPC 1 1453. Bibliography: RR2 / Coins of the Roman Republic in the British Museum, vol. 2. Coinages of Rome (continued), Roman Campania, Italy, the social war, and the provinces (151, p. 515), RPC1 / Roman provincial coinage. Vol.1, From the death of Caesar to the death of Vitellius (44 BC-AD 69) (1459). Available at: https://www.britishmuseum.org/collection/object/C_1860-0328-251, accessed 28 October 2020.

[78] Translation made by the author with verification at: https://www.davidrsear.com/academy/roman_legends.html. Accessed: 27 Oct. 2020.

[79] HS, Δ, and numeral indicating four asses.

[80] Indicates the mint.

[81] Available at: https://www.cngcoins.com/Coin.aspx?CoinID=232808. Accessed: 3 Oct. 2022.

[82] Translation made by the author.

romantic image, and because it was minted after the Treaty of Tarentum, the coin series should perhaps be seen as another indication that Antony did not send Octavia back to Rome after the negotiations due to a lack of regard for his wife (Moore, 2017, p. 158 apud Wood, 2001, p. 50).

For Manders, the figure of a quadriga can be ambiguous, as it is sometimes unclear whether a particular coin type with a chariot carries military connotations. When the emperor is on the quadriga, it is plausible that there are military connotations and refer to imperial victories (Manders, 2008, p. 91). However, when the quadriga is made up of gods, as is the case with the last coin, it can be interpreted as a divine tribute to the victory achieved.

The figure of Octavia on the next coin looks like she is wearing a necklace, which contrasts with the earliest figures of women on coins that appeared without jewellery in Rome. However, the fact that it was struck at an unknown mint in Achaia may go against the rule that it was common on coins of royal figures of Hellenistic women for them to appear without jewellery, which could link them to a divine character, as goddess figures on coins always appeared with jewellery (Harvey, 2020, p. 49).

Figure 17 – Tressis (three asses[83]) from 38 BC - 32 BC, 22.35g, minted in an uncertain place in Greece, possibly at a naval base in Piraeus. Obverse: Mark Antony standing next to Octavian and facing Octavia; M ANT IMP TERT COS DESIG ITER ET TER III VIR RPC (*Marcus Antonius Imperator Tertium Consul Designatus Iterum Tertium Triumvir Republicae Constituendae* = Commander Mark Antony, appointed Consul and Triumvir again for the third time for the maintenance of the Constitutional Republic)[84] Reverse: M OPPIVS CAPITO[85] PRO PR PRAEF CLASS FC (*Marcus Oppius Capito Pro Prætore Præfectus Classis* = Opium Capito pro *praetor* and commander of the fleet[86]) and 3 galleys sailing to the right

Source: Courtesy of WildWinds

This last coin with Mark Antony and Octavian facing Octavia is the great proof of a political mark identified in this type of material culture. Thus, it can be interpreted that the joining of the three of them would be the proof of imperial peace and that the image of Octavia, once again, would be used in favour of her brother. For Barrett, this type of coin was an innovation due to the appearance of the three figures (Barrett, 2002, p. 140). According to Erhart, the figure reveals the similarity between the brother and the sister, in other words, they have broad, smooth foreheads, long, straight noses and small round chins (Erhart, 1980, p. 124). In this regard, Wood mentions that their faces show the same tendency to assimilate their appearance to that of Antony, as in the aureus and cistophorus. The high, thick, columnar neck is particularly noticeable on the sestertius and dupondius, on which the image is larger and not obscured by another image in foreground (Wood, 2001, p. 51), as well as *nodus-like* hair. This demonstrates that many interpretations can be hasty

---

[83] Reference: RPC 1 1463; CRI 286; AE 32. One denarius would equal ten asses (available at: https://www.dictionary.com/browse/denarius#:~:text=Word%20Origin%20for%20denarius,WORD%20OF%20THE%20DAY. Accessed: 6 Oct. 2020). Object Available at: http://www.wildwinds.com/coins/imp/marc_antony/i.html; http://www.wildwinds.com/coins/imp/marc_antony/RPC_1463.jpg; and http://www.wildwinds.com/coins/imp/marc_antony/RPC_1463.txt. Accessed: 16 Aug. 2019.

[84] Translation made by the author.

[85] Mint master M OPPIVS CAPITO (Von Hahn, 2008, p. 43 and 96).

[86] Translation made by the author.

when following past explanations, however, it is interesting to observe the various points of view on a material culture.

Antony and Octavian, present on the obverse of this coin, represent the agreement made by them in Tarentum, adding the figure of Octavia as inevitable for this agreement to take place. On the reverse there are three galleys, indicating that it is a tremissis. Fleet and cistophorus coins were exclusively used in the East of the Empire. People from this region probably saw Octavia's portrait on coins more often than people from the West. This fact shows that each region must have had different experiences regarding the triumvirate and its ideologies. Thus, these people also had different experiences during the Principality (Rowan, 2019, p. 88).

Following the documentary sources, Antony gave up taking Octavia to Parthia when he was in Corcyra, on the western coast of Greece. He sent her pregnant back to Rome with all her children, so that she would not be exposed to the danger of his campaign (App. *B. Civ.* 5.95; Cass. Dio, *Roman History* 48.54.5; Plut. *Ant.* 35.5). However, in 37 BC, Antony rejoined Cleopatra in Antioch and impregnated her once again, giving birth to Ptolemy Philadelphus in 36 BC (Plut. *Ant.* 36.2-3).

Figure 18 – Silver tetradrachm[87], circa 36 BC, 14.36 g, 27 mm diameter, Syria, with the draped bust of Cleopatra on the right on the obverse, with diadem on her head and with the bust of Mark Antony on the right on the reverse. With obverse caption: ΒΑCΙΛΙC-CA ΚΛΕΟΠΑΤΡΑ ΘΕΑ ΝΕWΤΕΡΑ, and transliteration BASILISSA KLEPATRA THEA NEOTERA (The newest divine queen, Cleopatra[88]); and reverse caption: ΑΝΤWΝΙΟC ΑΥΤΟΚΡΑΤWΡ ΤΡΙΤΟΝ ΤΡΙWΝ ΑΝΔΡWΝ and transliteration: ANTONIOS AUTOKRATOR TRITON TRION ANDRON (Antony commander, triumvir for the third time [89])

Source: © The Trustees of the British Museum

This tetradrachm presents the transformations in Cleopatra's figure, which would be the thicker neck, the modification in the nose and the more prominent chin, as it happened in the golden age of Octavia and Antony, evidencing that after a certain time the artists put characteristics of the husband in these women (Wood, 2001, p. 46). This series of tetradrachms shows the bust of Cleopatra on the right, her head with diadem and pearl necklace. The bust of Mark Antony also faces to the right[90]. This type of tetradrachm was made after the separation of Antony and Octavia, announcing the political alliance between the triumvir and the Egyptian queen. During this period, Antony was already in the East at the battle of Parthia. Consequently, these coins could have been designed to facilitate payment for his soldiers[91]. The obverse caption reads: BACILICCA KLEOPATRA QEA NEWTERA = "The newest divine queen, Cleopatra", demonstrating her connection with the goddess Isis; on the reverse: ΑΝΤWΝΙΟC ΑΥΤΟΚΡΑΤWΡ ΤΡΙΤΟΝ ΤΡΙWΝ ΑΝDΡWΝ = "Commander Antony, triumvir for the third time". Cleopatra

---

[87] Reference number: TC, p 237.1.CleMA. Catalogue number: GC20 (BMC Greek (Galatia) (158) (56). Bibliography: RPC1 / Roman provincial coinage. Vol.1, From the death of Caesar to the death of Vitellius (44 BC-AD 69) (4094/1) BMC Greek (Galatia) / Catalogue of the Greek coins of Galatia, Cappadocia and Syria (56, p. 158) Taylor Combe 1814 / Veterum Populorum et Regum Numi qui in Museo Britannico Adversantur (The Coins of Ancient Peoples and Kings Preserved in the British Museum). Available at: https://www.britishmuseum.org/collection/object/C_TC-p237-1-CleMA. Accessed: 29 Oct. 2020.

[88] Translated by Juarez Oliveira.

[89] Translation made by the author.

[90] Available at: http://www.wildwinds.com/coins/imp/cleopatra/i.html. Accessed: 26 July 2019.

[91] Available at: https://www.acsearch.info/search.html?term=cleopatra+antony&category=1-2&en=1&de=1&fr=1&it=1&es=1&ot=1&images=1&thesaurus=1&order=0&currency=usd&company=. Accessed: 26 July 2019.

VII may have assumed the title of the Seleucid queen, Cleopatra Thea, who ruled Syria from 125 to 121/120 BC. However, the interpretation may lie in the view of Cleopatra as a "new goddess", *thea neotera* also being used outside Syria (Rowan, 2019, p. 95).

This coin breaks with the parameters of other coins minted with women, as it is the first time that coins with Mark Antony indicate the name of his wife, but in this case, it is Cleopatra (Barrett, 2002, p. 141). Coins minted in the East, with Cleopatra's bust on the obverse and Mark Antony on the reverse, evidence the agreement between the couple to conquer the East, as a celebration of their union. It could also denote something that is within the concept of the ideal matron for the Romans, in other words, it could immediately show Cleopatra as the wife of Mark Antony, who would always be by his side and support him, which would mean loyalty and fidelity to her husband. On the one hand, the obverse, the most important position of the object, is of Cleopatra, and not of Mark Antony, presenting a surrender of him to the queen of Egypt, as opposed to the demonstration of a subordinate woman. On the other hand, she would never be considered a matron in the Roman mould, because she was a foreigner, in other words, a "barbarian", possessing great political and governmental power, which led the Romans to consider her as abnormal. Thus, the coin celebrates Cleopatra as the youngest Seleucid queen and Antony as a Roman magistrate and general (Buttrey, 1954, p. 109).

Material culture, through Cleopatra, has always projected her power and sovereignty and, through her symbols and emblems, triggered a political-ideological communication and propaganda to help her stay in power, thus denoting the importance of currency as a political-institutional means. The propaganda value of coins tended to anchor royalty in the institutional frameworks of the Mediterranean (Sales, 2017, p. 10). The face of the Egyptian sovereign on the coin not only praised her authority, but also made her real, permanently present, alive, and visible, with propagandistic effectiveness. According to Plutarch, Cleopatra was like a fatal influence (Plut. *Mark Antony* 36.1), who tried to maintain her power in the Mediterranean by advertising her image, including on coins, but later Roman writers characterised her to defame her.

The introduction of portraiture into monetary typology probably came from Alexander the Great or Philip II of Macedonia. In this sense, the coins of the Ptolemies generally had a pattern of figure types similar to those of Hellenistic sovereignty: the obverse was intended for images of rulers, with attributes of royalty or their divinisation, and the reverse presented other symbols, for example, royal name, titles and protective deities (Sales, 2017, p. 11) focused on religion. These attributes can also be seen on Cleopatra's coins.

Figure 19 – Copper alloy coin,[92] minted in Alexandria, Egypt, 51 - 30 BC, c. 19.14 g. Obverse: bust of Cleopatra VII; Reverse: eagle with cornucopia and value mark (80) and caption: ΒΑCΙΛ ΙCCHC ΚΛ ΕΟΠ ΑΤΡΑC ([From] Queen Cleopatra[93])

Source: © The Trustees of the British Museum

On the obverse of the coin is the face of Cleopatra VII and on its reverse an eagle with a cornucopia, a mark of value and an inscription in Greek: the eagle perched on a beam of lightning was the bird of Zeus, on the weapon of the great Greek god. Like her Ptolemaic ancestors, Cleopatra included Zeus in her monetary issues as a proclamation and bestowal of power coming directly from the lord of Olympus, a symbol standardised by her predecessors and which became a sign of the Lagid royalty itself[94]. By becoming a recurring motif in Ptolomaic numismatics, the bird of Zeus ended up becoming a symbol of Egypt itself, even after the disappearance of the Ptolemies (Sales, 2017, p. 14).

Cleopatra was distinguished from Octavia by her relationship with power and was viewed with suspicion by Roman society. In this sense, women who distinguished themselves by having access to power seem to have been seen as those who failed to conform and accept the social construction given to them in that society, being represented as problematic women and causing

---

[92] Reference number: G.1117; catalogue number C&M: GC7 (BMC Greek (Ptolemies)) (123) (5) (123). Svoronos 1904 or 1871. Available at: https://www.britishmuseum.org/collection/object/C_G-1117. Accessed: 25 Aug. 2022.
[93] Translation by Juarez Oliveira, who says [from] shows the genitive used both in the title of *basilissa* and in the proper name.
[94] Indicates the Greek dynasty that reigned in Egypt from 306 to 30 BC.

great tensions. This view was produced by ancient authors, linked to the elite of the time, who felt threatened by these women (Fischler, 1994, p. 115-116).

However, since her relationship with Caesar, her representation was imposing. After all, Caesar recognised his son with Cleopatra and even asked for a statue of the two to be built in the temple of *Venus Genetrix*. In this way, the next case seems to allude to Caesarion's father, Julius Caesar, and his connection with Aphrodite/Venus. Appian mentions that when Caesar built the temple of *Venus Genetrix* in Rome, he placed a beautiful image of Cleopatra next to the goddess, which Appian notes was still in existence during his lifetime (App. 2.102; Cass. Dio, *Roman History* 51.22.3). The connection of Aphrodite/Venus with Cleopatra existed both in Rome and in her own territory (Rowan, 2019, p. 91-92). However, the Romans did not take kindly to the idea of Caesarion being the heir to the empires of Rome and the East, which would benefit Egypt more than Rome. This led to Caesar's assassination by the Republicans in 44 BC (Vieira, 2012, p. 22).

Figure 20 – Coin[95] of copper alloy, with Cleopatra VII on the reverse, 51 - 30, Cyprus, 47 BC. The bust with a Diadem on the head of Cleopatra, as Aphrodite, with Caesarion, as Eros, in her arms; sceptre on her shoulder. Rev. ΒΑΣΙΛΙΣΣΗΣ ΚΛΕΟΠΑΤΡΑΣ ([From] Queen Cleopatra[96]), with two filleted cornucopias. It was common to associate Cleopatra with Aphrodite/Venus, and the island of Cyprus, where there was a temple of Aphrodite/Venus, was the one given by Caesar to Cleopatra in 48 BC. The production of this coinage in Cyprus in 47 BC in commemoration of Caesarion's birth seems correct

Source: © The Trustees of the British Museum

Cleopatra appears on coins minted in Cyprus around 47 BC, which show her bust with little Caesarion on her lap, demonstrating the greatness

---

[95] Reference number: Svoronos 1874 and pl. LXII, 26. RPC 3901.9. Available at: https://www.acsearch.info/search.html?similar=1286255. Accessed: 26 July 2019 and https://www.britishmuseum.org/collection/object/C_GC7p122-2. Accessed: 28 Oct. 2020.
[96] Translated by Juarez Oliveira.

of Caesar's son with the Egyptian queen. In addition, it indicated her motherhood and devotion to her successor, with the intention of making Cleopatra an ideal woman, with her beauty, wealth, fertility, fidelity to her husband and ability to run the household being glimpsed. On the reverse of the coin are two cornucopias, a Greek symbol linked to prosperity, emphasising Cleopatra's fertility, wealth and opulence, and effectively exploiting motherhood. The coin shows both Greek and Egyptian attributes, such as a round face and prominent nose, characteristic of the Ptolemies, as well as a diadem on the head, seeming to advertise royal (Delaney, 2014, p. 3) and family dignity.

The stance of showing some examples of Cleopatra coins is interesting in order to present the difference in the minting of coins of her and Octavia. In contrast to the representations of the queen of Egypt, the figure of Octavia was clearly used on coins in a secondary way, showing her as a mere element of a political agreement involving male political parties. Her image and her marriage, confirmed by written sources, were not used for a private honour of her own, but were inserted in a hierarchy of power marked by the vaunting of a male government. Coins featuring Antony and Cleopatra began to be struck in 36 BC, however, Antony had not divorced Octavia until 32 BC (Rowan, 2019, p. 94).

In opposition was Octavian, who had returned triumphant from Sextus Pompey I, celebrated an *ovatio* and had the concession for his sister, Octavia, and for his wife, Livia, the *sacrosanctitas* from the Senate, in 35 BC, which empowered them to administer their own businesses without the presence of a guardian, the right to statues, and the same inviolability given to the tribunes of the plebs (Cass. Dio, *Roman History* 49.38.1). It should be added that the *sacrosanctitas* ensured their protection against insults, as was the case with the tribunes, as if they were in public office and as if an offence against them was an offence against the state. Octavian was also granted a similar concession, the *tribunicia potestas*, in 36 BC, which had also been granted to his adoptive father and to Octavia's great-uncle Julius Caesar in 44 BC (Moore, 2017, p. 102-103).

The *tribunicia potestas*, which may be exemplified in coin captions as TR P or TR POT, relates to the power of the tribunes of the people, who were appointed at the beginning of the Republic to protect the rights of the plebeians against the power of the aristocrats. The power of these tribunes gradually increased until they could do what they wanted. This almost unlimited power was drastically reduced at the end of the Republic by Sulla, but several privileges were restored after his death. Years later, their powers were reduced again by Julius Caesar. In 23 BC, Augustus had this power conferred on him for life. He now had the power to convene and dismiss the Senate and the Assembly of the people and to veto any order of the Senate. Moreover, the tribunitial power gave him a sacred and inviolable personality, which became a common practice for Augustus' successors (Sear, 2000, p. 72).

Octavia's *sacrosanctitas* meant that Antony could not insult her, which made it easier for Octavian to let his sister go to visit Antony when she learnt of the difficulties he was experiencing in Parthia. Octavian agreed to let his sister go, but if Antony mistreated her, it would be the trigger for a war. However, on arriving in Athens, Octavia received letters from Antony telling her to stay there. She wrote to him stating that she was bringing supplies such as clothing, pack animals, money, and officers, as well as two thousand soldiers (Plut. *Ant.* 53.1-2). Antony accepted the troops but asked Octavia to return (Cass. Dio, *Roman History* 49.33.4).

After all this attempt by Octavia to meet Antony, Plutarch mentions another case of jealousy between his wives. This time, it would be Cleopatra's towards Octavia, as if the queen of Egypt was afraid of her wife's worthy character, her pleasant company, as well as the attention she had for her husband, believing that her brother's power could make Mark Antony subjugate himself to Octavia. With this, the author reports that Cleopatra acted as if she was sick with love for Antony and was incapable of living without him, so he went after her in Alexandria (Plut. *Ant.* 53.3).

Any position taken by Fulvia or Octavia towards Mark Antony was placed by Plutarch as if it were something to shake Cleopatra, making her also act in some way to seduce Antony to go against them. The rhetoric used by these ancient authors in relation to the jealousy of these women seems to be something repetitive in their narratives, since it was common for them to place in the first instance the female characters in a role that cancelled them out to claim their undue intervention in the political context.

Differently, Plutarch characterises Octavia as the ideal Roman matron, mentioning that if she could once add the charm she had in front of society on a daily basis and her affectionate attention, she could completely gain control over her husband and make her position unattainable (Plut. *Mark Antony*, 53.2). Plutarch states that Octavia married Antony only for political reasons, for her brother's interests, but Cleopatra, being sovereign of several nations, was content to be his mistress (Plut, *Mark Antony*, 53.3).

Consequently, Octavian took away Antony's political office in Rome to justify the war and demonstrated that he delegated the eastern territories to Cleopatra's children, leaving nothing to his wife Octavia and their Roman children (Vieira, 2012, p. 29). According to Suetonius, the alliance between Mark Antony and Octavian had always been doubtful and the reconciliations only served to re-establish it and to prove that Antony had degenerated customs. Octavian made him read in assembly the will he had left in Rome, in which his heirs were to be the children he had had with Cleopatra, which led Octavian to declare him a public enemy and to dismiss his relatives and friends (Suet. *Augustus,* 17.1). Plutarch even commented that the greatest shame for Antony's countrymen was that he bestowed all his honour on Cleopatra (Plut. *Mark Antony,* 36.1). Octavian uses Octavia against Antony, for he allowed her to meet her husband in Athens, not to give his sister pleasure, but to give himself a plausible reason to declare war if she was neglected by Antony (Plut. *Mark Antony*, 53.1).

Even though Antony refused to go to meet Octavia in Athens, she continued to live in his house, taking care of her and Fulvia's children. At this point, Octavian considered Antony's attitude outrageous and wanted Octavia to leave his house. However, this was denied by her (Plut. *Mark Antony*, 54.1), suggesting an attitude over her brother's imposition.

Antony proclaimed Cleopatra queen of Egypt, Cyprus, Libya, and Syria, and declared Caesarion his consort. He left Armenia, Media and Parthia to his son Alexander, and Syria and Cilicia to his son Ptolemy. Plutarch does not mention the couple's daughter Cleopatra Selene. Antony divorced Octavia in 32 BC and sent word for her to leave his house and she left with all his children except the one he had with Fulvia, Antyllus (Plut. *Mark Antony*, 57.1). Octavian declared war on Cleopatra and took away Antony's powers, since he had given them to a woman (Plut. *Mark Antony*, 60.1). Finally, Octavia moved in with Augustus after her divorce from Antony (Hemelrijk, 1999, p. 102-103).

Octavian won the battle of Actium, Antony went to Libya and Cleopatra returned to Egypt. Later, Octavian took Alexandria without resistance, marking the end of the Ptolemaic dynasty. Octavian assumed power in Egypt and established the Principality in Rome, maintaining a republican appearance in which the Senate existed, but the final decision was given by him (Vieira, 2012, p. 31-34). To justify his power, he always used personal propaganda, through the minting of coins.

Figure 21 – Copper alloy dupondius[97], from 9 - 3 BC, from *Neumausus*, present-day Nimes, France. It has on the obverse the laureate bust of Augustus and Agrippa, facing opposite sides, with caption: IMP DIVI F (*Imperator Divi Filius* = Commander, son of god[98]). And on the reverse, there is a crocodile chained to a palm tree with the caption: COL NEM (*Colonia Neumausus*)

Source: © The Trustees of the British Museum

Octavian's mark was modified after the victory of Actium, since before his coins represented him as a figure similar to the god Apollo, god of the bow and lyre, of arts and war, and now his coins bore the crocodile in chains, marking his domination over Egypt and the end of the alliance with Mark Antony (Martins, 2011, p. 184). On this coin, Augustus and Agrippa are shown on the obverse and a crocodile on the reverse, symbol of Egypt, chained to a palm tree, which suggests the idea of Egypt subjugated by the Roman Empire after becoming a Roman province.

The crocodile represented the Egyptian god Seth, who evoked evil, for having been the murderer of Osiris, and was appropriated by Roman propaganda (Vieira, 2012, p. 35-36). However, Cleopatra and Antony also used the crocodile and placed it as a mark of the couple's daughter, Cleopatra Senele, in the provinces they left to her, Crete and Cyrenaica. The crocodile was used by the Ptolemies from the beginning of the dynasty, but other Greek symbols were favoured, such as the eagle and the cornucopia. The crocodile is important to the Ptolemies because when Alexander the Great died in 323 BC, Ptolemy Soter, who retained the lands of Egypt, captured Alexander's body and took it to Egypt for burial in Alexandria, which led to Perdicas invading Egypt and crossing the Nile to reach Memphis, where

---

[97] Reference number: 1935, 1102.9 Bibliographic references: RIC1 / The Roman Imperial Coinage, vol. 1 (158) RPC1 / Roman provincial coinage. Vol.1, From the death of Caesar to the death of Vitellius (44 BC-AD 69) (524) Walker & Higgs 2001 / Cleopatra of Egypt: from History to Myth (306). RPC 1 523, RIC 155. Available at: https://www.britishmuseum.org/collection/object/C_1935-1102-9. Accessed: 29 Oct. 2020.

[98] Translation made by the author.

the body was. The result was that half of his troops were eaten by crocodiles (Draycott, 2012, p. 43 and 53-54).

This series of coins produced by Augustus is called AEGVPTO CAPTA and was used by Roman veterans who were part of the war campaign against Egypt, minted where these former combatants lived, that was in Colonia Neumausus in Gaul (Draycott, 2012, p. 46). The elements of this coin are provincial and the largest quantity of this coin type was minted between 16/15 and 10 BC, demonstrating that it was made with imperial intent (Sutherland, 1976). This type of coin has been found in all three Gauls, along the Rhine and in Roman military camps, indicating that the material had a wider circulation than regional and was probably used to pay soldiers. By 10 BC, the production of coins from Nemausus had greatly diminished because of the Lugdunum mint. Augustus established an imperial mint there in 15 BC, which began to strike coins with elements of the emperor cult (Fishwick, 1999, p. 96-98). The coinage of the latter house may have been considered both imperial and local. The examples did not bear the name of the city, but regional elements (Rowan, 2019, p. 152-153).

Later authors, when writing about the end of Antony, attacked Cleopatra, following the traditional Roman idea regarding the dangerousness of women in power, showing that this was not an ideal model to be followed, which led to the creation of the image of a dangerous and seductive East. The figure of Cleopatra was constructed as a fatal, perverse, and corrupt woman, by writers such as Plutarch, Cassius Dio, Suetonius, Virgil, Apian, Flavius Josephus and Horace (Vieira, 2012, p. 38).

In the same way as the images of Cleopatra, which were used against Egypt, Octavian used his sister to play a key role in his own propaganda, capitalising on Antony's rejection, and then, the divorce between him and Octavia in 32 BC for his own political advantage. After Antony's death in 30 BC and the foundation of the Principality of Augustus in 27 BC, Octavia became even more important in her brother's dynastic politics because of her son Marcellus, who was promoted as Augustus' successor. To assert his position, Marcellus married his cousin Julia, Augustus' only daughter. After Marcellus' untimely death in 23 BC, attention shifted away from Octavia, although she was certainly not forgotten. However, no other portraits of her appeared on coins after Antony sent her back to Rome in 35 BC, but her sculptural images continued to be featured throughout the Empire. Portraits of her were certainly reproduced in the Late Republic (Pollini, 2002, p. 34-35).

The foundation of the Principality marked the beginning of an "apparent" period of peace, stability, and general prosperity, consequently initiating a veritable industry of replicated portraits. Most of the surviving sculptural images have been dated to this period. The effect of this portrait industry under the Principality would have been even more apparent in the case of female members of the imperial household, since honouring women in the Republic with replicated images would have been extremely rare. Octavia would undoubtedly have been honoured in Rome with an image on the Portico of Octavia, which she built at some point after the death of her son Marcellus in 23 BC (there are doubts whether it was Octavia or Octavian who built it). After her death in 11 BC, and even more so after the death of Augustus in 14 AD, Octavia's importance in the development of the dynastic plans of the Julio-Claudian house continued to diminish (Pollini, 2002, p. 35).

However, the coins with Octavia's image ended their minting when her role before the Second Triumvirate had ended, in 35 BC. Her last action was to have taken money and troops to Greece to be delivered to Antony, who did not dismiss the help, but ended up rejecting Octavia herself (Erhart, 1980, p. 125). It should be noted that the coins with the figures of Octavia did not even reach the minting period of ten years, since the examples seem to have started in 40 BC and ended in 35 and/or 32 BC. Her honour was no greater than her brother's dealings with Antony, as her coins presented her as a manipulated member of the male parties.

For this reason, it is important to emphasise that on no coin is Octavia's name mentioned and she has no divine attributes (Barrett, 2002, p. 140). The fact that there is no caption with her name shows a mark of the gender relationship constituted with regard to her position in society, composing her as the one who only lent herself to this position through her brother and her husband, proving the social irrelevance of this character, who was used to fulfil an alliance between Octavian and Antony.

The coins on which Octavia appears confirm a force of masculine order, which dismissed any kind of justification for her existence. At this moment in the Roman social elite, the male view was imposed as "neutral", "natural" or the one that is the basis of such a society. This force is recognised as a symbolic machine that tends to ratify masculine domination, on which its parts are based and divided in relation to the activities attributed to each gender and their place of action, in which the market or war would be for men and the home for women. This division is put here in a simplified way, but in reality it could have been more complex within such a social order. The social differences in question could have been applied according to the distinctions of male and female bodies, justifying the cultural and social variation constructed between the genders. It was the previously constructed social standpoint that underpinned such differentiations. Consequently, domination relations were inserted into subjectivity as objective relations to cognitive schemes, which organised divisions between genders (Bourdieu, 1998, p. 18 and 20).

Mark Antony's eldest son with Fulvia took refuge and, after many futile supplications at the foot of Caesar's statue, was killed by Octavian. Caesarion, whom, according to Suetonius, Cleopatra boasted of having had with Caesar, was arrested and condemned to torture. As for the other children Antony had with Cleopatra, Octavian spared them and dismissed them (Suet. *Aug.* 97-99). Octavian treated Antony and Cleopatra's children kindly and spared them the same fate as their mother. Octavian's idea would have been to keep the couple's children alive for use in his triumph, but only Cleopatra Selene would have lived out her entire adult life. Antony's eldest son, Antyllus, was quickly killed, betrayed by his tutor and beheaded (Plut. *Ant.* 81.1). Cleopatra had sent Caesarion away from Egypt, but in the end this strategy did not save him. This young man was also betrayed by his tutor and killed (Plut. *Ant.* 81.2-82.1).

Octavian returned to Rome in 29 BC to celebrate triumph for his victory over Illyricum in 33 BC; his victory at the battle of Actium in 31 BC; and his victory over Cleopatra in 30 BC. He took Antony and Cleopatra's children and had Cleopatra Selene and Alexander Helios paraded through the streets with him (Cass. Dio, *Roman History* 51.21.8). Them and their brother Ptolemy Philadelphus were placed in the care of Octavia, who eventually raised all of Antony's children except Antyllus, who was already dead (Plut. *Ant.* 87). Octavia did not and could not publicly mourn Antony's death, as he had divorced her a year before his death. After this episode, she was left responsible for nine children, Iullus being the eldest, aged about fifteen (Fischler, 1994, p. 123-124 apud Moore, 2017, p. 118-119).

At this time, in 29 BC, Octavia was probably about thirty-four years old, divorced from Antony, with nine children to raise and a brother who went on to lead Rome alone. She continued to assist her brother while he remodelled Rome, but without much public prominence, mainly for government propaganda (Moore, 2017, p. 128). Her son Marcellus was promising as Augustus' heir, but eventually died in 23 BC, which was an immense loss for her and made her no longer the heir's mother.

4.2. Octavia and Cleopatra: between rivals

From learning about Octavia's history, it emerges that she was recognised as Mark Antony's faithful and most tragic wife, due to the humiliating treatment by her husband and the exploitation of her brother, Octavian, in using her to propagandise a civil war. She is also remembered as the mother of Marcellus, who died prematurely. However, it can be said that Octavia was an appropriate moral model of the Roman matron. She never tried to obtain a public position of power; on the contrary, she obediently did what was expected of a woman of the imperial family: she was an excellent mother and brought up ten or more children under her care, even if only five were her own, the others being children of close relatives who could be successors to Octavian and others like Antony's son, Iullus; she was faithful throughout her traditional role of wife; as well as helping her brother to strengthen a political alliance with her marriage to Antony (Hemelrijk, 1999, p. 102-103). Her death occurred around 11 BC, according to Cassius Dio (Cass. Dio, *Roman History* 54.35.4) and Titus Livius (Livy, *Per.* 140), but according to Suetonius, she died in 9 BC (Suet. Aug. 61.2), aged about fifty-five or fifty-eight.

Regarding Cleopatra, Octavian already felt the rivalry against her after Caesar's death, when he claimed the will, which declared him as his adopted son. Caesar was proclaimed a god in Rome, which gave Octavian the powerful status of *divi filius*, but the divinisation of Caesar conferred a divine aura on Caesarion as well (Kleiner, 2005). Faced with the triumvirs' agreements, which divided the Roman government, with Mark Antony taking the eastern provinces, Octavian the western ones and Lepidus a small piece of North Africa, Cleopatra entered the dispute between Octavian and Mark Antony by proposing financial aid for Antony to conquer Parthia in exchange for Cyprus (Vieira, 2012, p. 23).

With the end of the triumvirate in 33 BC, Octavian attacked Mark Antony and declared an action against Cleopatra, starting a war against the East. Mark Antony wanted to control the East, so he sided with Cleopatra was skilful and used strategies that favoured his position. He was not a naïve subject, seduced and bewitched by a foreign queen, as Plutarch, Cassius Dio, Apian and Josephus explained (Vieira, 2012, p. 27-28).

Cleopatra was described as a beautiful, ingenious, and seductive woman, whom even a great man like Mark Antony would fall in love with. However, this image of a seductive and powerful woman was used as propaganda to mask a civil war (Vieira, 2012, p. 40) initiated by the setbacks between Octavian and Antony. She was called a "prostitute queen" by Propertius (Poems, III.11.39), a "fatal monster" by Horace (Odes, I.37.21) and "the shame of Egypt" by Lucan (Pharsalia, X.59).

Cleopatra was characterised by Cassius Dio as a woman of astonishing beauty and her voice possessed an incomparable charm, as she knew how to please everyone. The author comments that she was brilliant to be seen and heard, with the power to subdue. He mentions that Cleopatra was insatiable passion and greed, with a celebrated ambition but excessive conceit. She earned the title of queen of the Egyptians and desired to be queen of the Romans (Cass. Dio, *Roman History,* 42.34.4-6). According to Plutarch, she utilised a bold flirtation, which captivated Caesar in the first instance (Plut. *Caesar,* 49.3). Moreover, he added that since she had already won Caesar over, she had hopes of winning Antony over easily. Caesar had met her when she was young and had little experience, but during her flirtation with Antony she already possessed the brightest beauty (Plut. *Mark Antony,* 25.1).

Even when Antony was preparing for the conquest of Parthia and asked Cassius to tell Cleopatra to meet him in Cilicia to collect the money she was to raise, Plutarch reports that Dellio, who was in charge of this mission, was seduced by Cleopatra's talk as soon as he laid eyes on her and that she probably gained great influence over him (Plut. *Mark Antony,* 25.1). Moreover, when saying that Plato knew four kinds of flattery, the author adds that Cleopatra knew thousands of them (Plut. *Mark Antony,* 29.1).

Ancient authors took the rejection against Cleopatra to construct a negative image of her, using her place of power, ethnicity, and gender, as well as her political position in favour of Mark Antony, to demoralise her in their works, enhancing the figure of Augustus and demonstrating the reception of Roman society towards a foreign woman with power. Cleopatra's position seized an identity complexity that resulted in the reproduction of a woman stigmatised by the Romans. That said, the efficacy of the manipulation of Cleopatra's image had an intersectional consequence in its reproductions, which disseminated over time and spread to the present day.

That said, intersectionality[99] refers to a transdisciplinary theory that understands a complexity of identity and social inequalities through an integrated approach. It refutes the confinement and hierarchy of the main focus of social differentiation, which are the categories of sex, gender, class, race, ethnicity, age, disability, sexual orientation (Bilge, 2009, p. 70; Hirata, 2014, p. 62-63), among other conditions of inequalities. It should be borne in mind that the survey of categories is not fixed, but it is important in an intersectional analysis to raise which of them are oppressive and which may vary and be diverse.

From this perspective, norms and values that may have been of considerable significance for the formation of social identities may be based on gender, age, *status* and so on (Sjöberg, 2014, p. 320). The intersectional approach goes beyond simply recognising the multiplicity of systems of oppression that operate from these categories and postulates their interaction in the production and reproduction of social inequalities (Bilge, 2009, p. 70 apud Hirata, 2014, p. 62-63). Intersectionality as a means of understanding multiple oppressions has been applied by scholars such as Sjöberg, focusing primarily on textual evidence within the Ancient World (Sjöberg, 2014, p. 316). It is important to emphasise that intersectionality is active, not static, comprising agency.

---

[99] The problem of "intersectionality" was first raised in Anglo-Saxon countries from the heritage of black feminism, since the early 1990s, within an interdisciplinary framework, by Kimberlé Crenshaw (1989, 1994, 2002, 2010) and other British, American, Canadian, and German researchers (Hirata, 2014, p. 62).

Flowchart 1 – Intersectional system between Octavian, Cleopatra and Mark Antony.

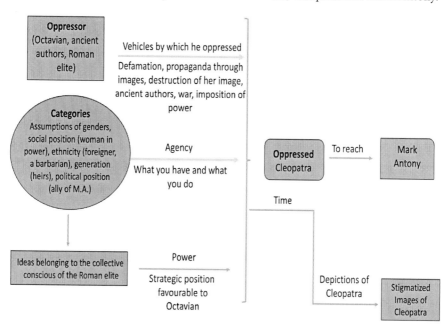

Source: © author's flowchart, 2024.

Following this intersectional theory, the oppressors at the time of the event were probably Octavian and the very elite of Roman society, which already had the construction of a gender assumption linked to women in power. In addition to Cleopatra being a foreigner, the aristocratic elite did not welcome the conquest of Roman territories being divided among their children. The disparity between Octavian and Antony fell on Cleopatra, since it was common among Roman disputes to defame the opponent's wife and not the opponent directly, as Cicero did with Fulvia, to avoid directly defaming the other man with whom he had hostility. This strategy was to ensure future agreements between the parties, since women were irrelevant on these occasions or only served to seal deals, as in the case of Octavia.

To add, the stance against Cleopatra, once seen as a powerful foreigner, was arraigned by the elite Roman social group linked to power, because if society held a kind of social assumption towards someone or a smaller group, it would strengthen the oppressor. Consequently, Octavian was empowered by a group of powerful Roman aristocrats, who would also have been against Antony, because the main target was Antony, not Cleopatra.

Ancient authors, even if they wrote about Cleopatra after the events that took place, tended to overvalue Octavian, since, by writing about her, they immortalised, beyond two thousand years, the image of a woman who used sex and manipulation to obtain power. In order to achieve his goals, Augustus took a stance that discredited the Ptolemaic queen's ability to govern and her politics. He used propaganda defaming her as a barbarian seductress, to mask his competition with Mark Antony and to favour an ideal model of Roman virtue and morality, and he destroyed images of Cleopatra, imposing his own image as the all-powerful one who subjected Egypt to his prestige. And his sister, Octavia, seems to have been dismissed soon after her role between the triumvirs' agreement ended.

Chapter 5

Livia: power, agency, and representations of prosperity

Livia (59/58 BC - 29 AD), who was the wife of Augustus (27 BC - 14 AD), had previously been married to Tiberius Claudius Nero, with whom she had Tiberius (42 BC - 37 AD) and Drusus (38 BC - 9 AD) as children (Tac. *Ann.* 5.1). Octavian arranged for her to get divorce, who was married to Scribonia, the daughter of two consular personages. In this union, although Octavian had Julia as a daughter, that was characterised as a marriage of political strategy and considered a disgust, seen that it lasted only one year (Barrett, 2002, p. 20). Consequently, Octavian divorced her for the depravity of his wife's customs. In addition, Julia suffered from the *lex Iulia de adulteriis* and was banished into exile, with her mother, Scribonia, who decided to accompany her. In this context, we must add the fact that Augustus, even before his death, did not restore his daughter from exile, but let her receive gifts and refused to accept the deposit of the ashes of Scribonia and Julia in his mausoleum (Cass. Dio, *Roman History* 56.32.4; Barrett, 2002, p. 20 and 60). Augustus' daughter died in 28 AD, after twenty years in exile, when she was supported throughout this period by charities from Livia (Barrett, 2002, p. 129).

Previously, Octavian had been betrothed to Servilia, daughter of Publius Servilius Isauricus, and then, upon his reconciliation with Antony, he betrothed his goddaughter, Clodia, daughter of Fulvia and Publius Clodius, but it only reached nubility. After Scribonia, he abducted Livia, pregnant by her husband Tiberius Nero (Tac. *Ann.* 5.1), loving and cherishing her in a singular and constant way. Livia, with whom he had no children (Suet. *Aug.* 62.1), belonged to a distinct family, of the *gens Claudii*, and her father was Marcus Livius Drusus Claudianus, who was adopted by the *gens Livii*, which suggests that he had Drusus as his adoptive father, who was a tribune of the plebs (Tac. *Ann.* 5.1). For this reason, Livia acquired the cognomen Drusilla, and her ancestry helped Octavian to strengthen his ties with distinguished families in Rome. Before the death of Tiberius Nero in 32 or 33 BC, Livia's first husband, he had appointed Augustus as guardian of his two children with Livia (Barrett, 2002, p. 8, 22 and 27).

The founder of Livia's family would have been Clausus, who supposedly helped Aeneas when the Trojan hero sought to settle in Italy. It seems that the *Claudii* were immigrants who did well and their connection with Rome would be at the beginning of the migration of the Sabine Attus Clausus, who clamoured for a position of consul in 495 BC, and of his dependents, around 503 BC; so that this political position would pass from generation to generation. Appius Claudius was also connected with the first legal code. Appius Claudius Caecus, consul in 307 and 296, was also a distinguished figure in the ancient Republic, among others. However, the Roman family tended to be formed by more than one family line, as were Tiberius Claudius Nero and Publius Claudius Pulcher, who were founders of two subdivisions of the *Claudii,* namely the *Claudii Nerones* and the *Claudii Pulchri* (Barrett, 2002, p. 4). Livia's mother was from a prosperous but less distinguished family from the town of Fundi (Harvey, 2020, p. 1). The importance of family ancestry was a fundamental prerequisite for success in Roman society. In this way, Livia's family would have conferred great status on her (Barrett, 2002, p. 4-6) and later, on Augustus.

Livia's great prosperity due to her eminent position as an emperor's wife and mother resulted in a wide power, both for political matters and for her to exercise the activity of Patronage, since she became known for her public constructions and philanthropic acts (Hemelrijk, 1999, p. 108). Consequently, she was the best represented woman of the Julio-Claudian family and her name appeared in harbours, markets and even shrines, as well as her image on coins. The presence of Livia's image in these commemorations is unprecedented. All this demonstrates that Livia had a "career" as Augustus' wife and suggests that she had an accurate political sense, leading her to considerable power and influence (Zager, 2014, p. 54-57).

Livia, like Octavia, Octavian's sister, was a model Roman matron to be followed, evidenced through motherhood, fidelity, *pudicitia* and prosperity, and became a symbol and social figure of political influence. According to Harvey's reading, Cassius Dio and Tacitus indicate Livia as the "first lady of the Roman Empire", being promoted through visual media as the most important female member of the imperial family (Harvey, 2020, p. 2 and 8).

Augustus was able to unite Livia's need to show herself with traditional gifts and power within the *domus* by having her role linked to things of the State. This must have been difficult to do, as women of this period could only influence their husbands in matters concerning the family, but with the emergence of the *domus Augusta* the affairs of family and State were inextricably linked (Barrett, 2002, p. 130).

For such tasks, Livia must have received an excellent education, which may have given "virility" to her rational power. Such types of women were praised for having a mind or character similar to that of their fathers, in other words, they were appreciated for the qualities of a masculine mind. In this way, the ability to have a masculine mind was a compliment to their fathers. However, within male dominance, these women were criticised for having rational thoughts; thus, instead of being characterised as "honourable men", they were seen as "failed men". Given this social thinking about gender roles, Livia was a case of ambiguous sexual identity, since she was perceived as having a male mind in a female body. That said, for such women, there was an impediment to their full participation in intellectual and political life (Hemelrijk, 1999, p. 87-88).

5.1. Livia's life and coins

Even so, Livia's position gained relevance and was probably earned through her circle of contacts established by Patronage in Rome and in the eastern and western provinces, which she had the opportunity to execute during the visits she made together with Augustus around 21-19 BC in these other localities. Her representations of the imperial family and as a divine figure were also influenced by local ideologies towards her in the provinces. The large number of mints that made this material with the image of Livia was in the East, accounting for 70% of production, and their coins were made in these localities from the government of Augustus to that of Antoninus. In this sense, most of these provincial coins were for local use, with freedom of choice of mintage, which meant that Livia appeared on them more intensely during the government of Tiberius than in that of Augustus (Harvey, 2020, p. 108-112), although Livia had been directly linked to Augustus after his death, and it was only at this time that it began to be coined in Rome.

Only the mints of Eumeneia, Magnesia ad Sipylum, Pergamum and Smyrna struck coins of Livia during both governments. In Eumeneia, she was referred to as HPA Λ(E)IBIA and in Thessaly as HPA ΛEIOYIA (Harvey, 2020, p. 113 and 136). The first example of Livia with a male figure was found at the mint of Ephesus. Other eastern mints, such as Bithynia, Mesia, Thrace and Achaia, depicted Augustus and Livia. They were referred to by ΣΕΒΑΣΤΟΙ (Harvey, 2020, p. 113, 126 and 136).

Figure 22 – Coin[100] with bust of Augustus and Livia on the right on the obverse, dated 27 BC - AD 14, Ephesus, Ionia. On the reverse is a stag standing on the right, above the bow case; caption: ΑΡΧΙΕΡΕΥΣ / ΑΣΚΛΑΣ / ΕΦΕ / ΝΙΚΟΣΡ / ΑΤΟΣ (Nicostratus, Archiereus of Asclas, Ephesus[101])

Source: Courtesy of Pavlos S. Pavlou

This coin minted in Ephesus bears on the obverse the bust of Augustus paired with the bust of Livia. Livia's position is secondary to that of Augustus. However, the fact that she is next to her husband shows an aspect of equal power between them. On the reverse is a deer, which could be linked to one of the elements of the goddess Diana/Artemis, representing hunting, abundance, food, sustenance, and wealth in every sense. In Ephesus, Diana and her elements are later associated with coins of Agrippina Minor, which, like Livia, is very similar to symbols linked to fertility, agricultural production, food, abundance, as well as to goddesses who are orientated towards the same virtues, such as Ceres.

---

[100] Reference: RPC I 2585. Available at: https://www.vcoins.com/en/stores/pavlos_s_pavlou_numismatist/131/product/ioniaephesusaugustus_with_livia_27_bcad_14ae1_unitjugate_bust_of_augustus_and_liviastag_bow_naming_magistrate_archiereus_asklas/224640/Default.aspx. Accessed: 5 Sept. 2020.

[101] Translation by Juarez Oliveira, who says that Archiereus is synonymous of Supreme Pontiff; and that the translation of this inscription is complicated, since the form *efe*, with *epsilon* instead of *eta*, seems an abbreviation for the place of origin or exercise of Asclas. If it were a corruption of the verb *femi*, it would have the problem that both names (of Asclas and of Nicostratus) are in the nominative, escaping the traditional regency of the verb. Therefore, perhaps in context, it could be translated as related to both figures, that is, Asclas and Nicostratus.

Figure 23 – Coin[102] from Alabanda, Asia, dated 27 BC - AD 14, 17 mm diameter, 3.75 g, with the face of Augustus on the obverse and with caption: EPAFRODITOU AMN[...] (The fortunate of Amniso[103]); Reverse with the face of Livia on the right and draped bust, with the *nodus* type of hair from the early Augustan period, with caption: ALABAND[E...] TOUTHLE(?) (Alabanda[ ](?)[104])

Source: Courtesy of the Classical Numismatic Group

The province of Asia, in 29 BC, built the temple of Pergamum for Rome and Augustus. It seems that Livia was included in the cults, since her statue was placed next to that of Augustus and a caption indicates the celebration of her birthday, as well as that of her husband (Grether, 1946, p. 230). Thus, the previous example indicates that the city of Alabanda, in the same province, had already been coining Augustus on its obverse and Livia on the reverse, as a show of respect to the imperial couple. The city of Mysia, in the same province, also struck Livia on the obverse and Augustus' daughter Julia on the reverse to honour the women of the imperial family, as can be seen on the next coin.

---

[102] Reference: RPC I 2809.1 = Imhoof-Blumer, *KM*, p. 105, 7; FITA 373; SNG München -; SNG von Aulock -; SNG Copenhagen. Available at: https://www.cngcoins.com/Coin.aspx?CoinID=114913. Accessed: 29 May 2020.

[103] Translation by Juarez Oliveira, who says that the text set at https://rpc.ashmus.ox.ac.uk/coins/1/2809 is [ΕΠΙ ΑΦ]ΡΟΔΙΤΟΥ Α[ΜΝ?]ΣΣΟ[Υ], while data 16 is EPAFRODITOU AMN[...]. The former supplements the gaps, but the latter does not. *Epafrotidos* is a Greek adjective for the Latin *Felix*, according to the LSJ (Greek-English Lexicon), thus meaning "Fortunate", "Favoured by Aphrodite/Venus". The translation could stand in the first case, "[From] Fortunate of Amn[]sso" or, in the second "[From] Fortunate of Amn[] (?)". Considering the supplementation of the first, the reference seems to point to Amniso, a region north of Crete. In both cases [From] evidences the genitive case used in the inscription.

[104] Translation by Juarez Oliveira.

Figure 24 – Coin[105] of *Mysia*, *Pergamum*, dated 10 BC - AD 2, with the draped bust of Livia, as Hera, on the obverse and caption ΛΙΒΙΑΝ ΗΡΑΝ ΧΑΡΙΝΟΣ (Livia Hera, daughter of Carino[106]). On the reverse is Julia, daughter of Augustus, as Aphrodite, with caption ΙΟΥΛΙΑΝ ΑΦΡΟΔΙΤΗΝ (Julia Afrodite[107])

Source: Courtesy of Praefectus Coins

In the time of Augustus, provincial cities could adapt the image of the emperor by connecting the imperial family to local cults. The empress, in particular, Livia, was aligned with the local goddess and was more demonstrated in eastern provinces than on imperial coinage, at least until before Hadrian. A great example is from a sample from Smyrna in Asia. The city always showed Augustus and Livia together, even when she did not yet appear on Roman coins at that time. That said, Smyrna developed its own depictions of the emperor and his family (Rowan, 2019, p. 158-159).

---

[105] RPC I 2359. Available at: https://www.vcoins.com/en/stores/praefectus_coins/130/product/mysia_pergamum_livia__julia_wife_and_daughter_of_augustus_ae_19/638966/Default.aspx. Accessed: 6 Sept. 2020.
[106] Translation by Juarez Oliveira.
[107] Translation by Juarez Oliveira.

Figure 25 – Bronze coin with lead[108], Smyrna, 10 BC (?). Obverse: laureate face of Augustus and draped bust of Livia, ΣΕΒΑΣΤΩΙ ΖΜΥΡΝΑΙΟΙ ([From] the people of Smyrna to Augusto[109]). Reverse: Aphrodite Stratonikis leaning against a column, holding a sceptre and Nike, dipping to the right, ΔΙΟΝΥΣΙΟΣ ΚΟΛΛΥΒΑΣ[110] (Dionisio Colibas[111])

Source: Courtesy of the Aegean Numismatics

Figure 26 – Bronze coin with lead[112], Smyrna, AD 4 - 14. Obverse: faces of Augustus and Tiberius facing each other, CEBACTON TIBEPION KAICAPA (Tiberius Caesar Augustus[113]). Reverse: Livia as Aphrodite Stratonikis, leaning against a column, holding a sceptre and Nike on her right side, ΛΙΒΙΑΝ ΖΜΥΡΝΑΙΩΝΟC (From the inhabitants of Smyrna to Livia[114])

Source: Courtesy of the Classical Numismatic Group, LLC

Another example minted in the same city between AD 4 and 14 is a coin on which, on its obverse, Augustus is looking at Tiberius, while on its reverse it could be Livia as the personification of the local goddess, *Aphrodite Stratonikis*. She appears leaning on a column, holding a sceptre, and Nike

---

[108] RPC 1 2466, available at: https://www.vcoins.com/en/stores/aegean_numismatics/1/product/ionia_smyrna_augustus__livia_27bc14ad_ae20/1349844/Default.aspx. Accessed: 19 May 2022.
[109] Translation by Juarez Oliveira.
[110] Rowan, 2019, p. 159.
[111] Translation by Juarez Oliveira.
[112] RPC 1 2467, available at: https://www.cngcoins.com/Coin.aspx?CoinID=348231. Accessed: 19 May 2022.
[113] Translation by Juarez de Oliveira.
[114] Translation made by the author.

is at her right side. The coin names Livia as ΛIBIAN. This connection of the empress with local goddesses can also be found in other cities, in other ways than just through coins (Matheson, 1996 apud Bartman, 2012, p. 416). Caligula's sister was associated with Persephone (RPC 1 2472) and Nero's wife, Poppaea, with Nike (RPC 1 2486). What is suggested is that coinage in the East at this time was more daring than the official Roman one, with a freer interpretation of these women (Rowan, 2019, p. 159).

In Greece, the imperial couple was usually associated with Euthenia, the equivalent of *Abundantia* or Demeter, who appears holding a cornucopia and ears of corn (Sear, 2000, p. 37). Also, coins from Alexandria of Augustus and Livia present on their reverse the figure of *Euthenia, calatos* (basket with fruits) between torches or the double cornucopia (Grether, 1946, p. 232-233). Later, Alexandria minted coins associating Agrippina Minor with Euthenia as well.

The seated Demeter on the reverse of the Pergamon coins was probably intended to represent Livia, proving to be very similar to the Livia of the Roman coins. A calendar from the island of Cyprus from 15 BC showed the months honouring each member of the imperial family, as well as Livia and Octavia. In general, the cult of Livia grew in importance, honour, and quantity (Grether, 1946, p. 232-233). In Lampsacus, Livia is given the cult of Hestia, and inscriptions from this place name her as Ioulia Sebaste, at the beginning of Tiberius' rule. The term *Sebaste* had been used since before Augustus' death, but it was also used in representations of his daughter, Julia (Barrett, 2002, p. 152). It should be added that in the same inscription Livia has the name of *nean Demetera*, referring her to Demeter/Ceres (Hahn, 1994, p. 322-332 apud Barrett, 2002, p. 145).

In the 1st and 2nd century AD, Ceres often appears as a type of coin, and she is usually holding ears of corn to symbolise her function as the goddess of agriculture. Sometimes she holds a torch to signify the search for her daughter, Proserpina, lost in darkness, who was abducted to Hades by Pluto. The epithet most commonly applied to her is *Frugifera*, meaning fruiting. On provincial coins, she appears as Demeter and sometimes with her daughter Persephone (Greek name for Proserpina) (Sear, 2000, p. 27). In a catalogue made by Hahn about the eastern provinces, it is shown that Livia was associated with nine goddesses, besides Hestia (Hahn, 1994, p. 322-332; Barrett, 2002, p. 145).

Livia was still connected to many building projects in Rome, some of which she helped finance, including *Aedes Concordiae* and *Porticus Liviae* (7

BC), which were restored during the Tiberius period (Barrett, 2002, p. 315). In addition to these, *Macellum Liviae* stands out, as well as the restoration of some temples, such as the Temple of *Bona Dea Subsaxana*, the Temple of *Muliebris Fortuna*, and the Temple of *Divus Augustus* (Barrett, 2002, p. 126). These constructions were a new way of celebrating a domestic model, with benefits to both the public and the emperor, demonstrating a harmonious marriage. Livia and Octavia, who were patrons of these types of constructions, always appeared in political power in a tangential way (Milnor, 2005, p. 62-63).

Regarding the goddess Bona Dea, the euphemistic name of Fauna or Fatua (Takács, 2008, p. 111), she was identified as the daughter, sister and/or wife of Faunus, a legendary king of Latium. There are myths about Fauna's death, such as one that a Faun beat her to death when he caught her drinking wine; and another in which he becomes a snake, who could copulate with her, since, as a daughter, she had already rejected incest. They were considered prophetic deities, but also had healing powers. The snakes were housed in the shrines of Bona Dea. This goddess could be worshipped by both men and women, but the rites conducted by the Vestals had gender restrictions (Brouwer, 1989 apud Holland, 2012, p. 207). There were festivals for the goddess, one taking place on the first day of May and the other in December. The May festival was in memory of the foundation of the Aventine temple of the goddess *ad saxum*, which Livia restored and only women could enter. However, this information is dubious, since what it seems is that, with the reform, people who were not of the elite, free women, men and even slaves, had the possibility to connect with the goddess.

The epigraphic and literary evidence that has survived presents two types of cults. On the one hand, there was the Augustan and the post-Augustan, whose worshippers were men and women, in particular those of the freed class attached to the imperial house. *Bona Dea ad saxum* was a healing deity and her temple was where serpents were restricted. Like the cornucopia, the snake appears in her iconography. On the other hand, there were other shrines of Bona Dea that men were allowed to enter. Out of thirty-one dedications made to Bona Dea in Rome, only nine were by women. The healer and fertility goddess did not have to be the same everywhere, as Bona Dea was a vague appellative name, since she was easily connected to other deities, such as the "Mother of the gods", since both goddesses could be characterised as creators of all things and generators of life. Moreover, the fertility aspect of the *mysterion* could connect them with Dionysus (Takács, 2008, p. 101-102, 106-107, 109 and 111).

Livia was also active in a key monument commissioned by the Senate, voted in 13 BC, and by the people of Rome in honour of Augustus and his imperial family, for the emperor's safe return from Spain, and for the pacification of Gaul, the *suplicatio* (Barrett, 2002, p. 42): the *Ara Pacis Augustae*, built in 9 BC, showing Augustus together with Livia, who are represented as father and mother of the Roman state (Harvey, 2020, p. 4 and 160). This monument was a public statement of the place of celebration of the Augustan family, demonstrating Augustus' ideology. The altar was decorated, but its reliefs were obscured. This altar was dedicated to Pax and nowhere was it directly stated that Livia was associated with her (Barrett, 2002, p. 126). Pax appeared holding an olive branch, a cornucopia, or a caduceus (Sear, 2000, p. 40).

In literary sources such as of Cassius Dio, Suetonius and Ovid, Livia was described as a powerful and influential woman, power-hungry, sinister, and murderous, a devoted wife and mother, as well as a divine figure, but she is referred to as having problematic power and influence by Tacitus, Cassius Dio, and Suetonius. Cassius Dio mentions that Livia performed political and public roles that exceeded female limits, as if she shared powers with Tiberius (Cass. Dio, *Roman History* 57.12.1-6), so much so that Suetonius states that she clamoured for equality alongside the role of ruler of her son (Suet. *Tib.* 50.1) and Tacitus said that she lacked self-restraint (Tac. *Ann.* 1.4.5).

Authors such as Tacitus point to her as responsible for several crimes (Tac. *Ann.* 6.2). Cassius Dio claimed that she cleared the way for her children, citing an example of when she appealed a charge of murdering Marcellus, son of Octavia, because Augustus had prioritised him (Cass. Dio, *Roman History* 60.5.I). Such accusations made towards her were common to happen. She was even accused of being involved in the death of Augustus himself. The death of Germanicus, a highly respected man in Rome, and the rumours that Livia was behind his murder threatened her popularity (Barrett, 2002, p. 36, 66 and 41).

She knew how to live according to the Roman constitutional system, without clearly creating identifiable enemies, as well as showing what was expected of Augustus' wife, namely dignity with majesty, as well as modesty and domestic virtues. Her position turned out to be dubious, as she was someone who had a public role but no public position. She was a person who was expected to dominate the private sphere, hoping to represent domestic values and the morals of a citizen. During the rule of her son Tiberius (Barrett, 2002, p. x), her position became more ambiguous, due to the titles she gained and her acquiring some privileges granted only to the Vestal

Virgins. This ambiguity may be in line with a social polarisation established in the interpretation of the Vestal and the married woman, which was created according to the structuring of society, generating a whole repertoire of female religious conducts and experiences (Chartier, 1995, p. 41).

Ovid, exiled in 8 BC, praised and consoled Livia in the hope of being brought back to Rome. During his exile, he referred to her as *femina princeps*, writing the 474- line *Consolatio ad Liviam* in 9 BC, trying to comfort her after the death of her son, Drusus. He considered her equal to Augustus (Ovid, *Pontic Letters*, 3.1.125-128; Ovid, *Tristes*, 1.6.25-27), since *princeps* was used first by Augustus and then by his heirs (Harvey, 2020, p. 162). The expression *femina princeps*, used by Ovid to refer to Livia, appeared in a poem addressed to his wife, who had Livia as a role model and teacher. The *Consolatio* refers to her as *princeps* and *Romana princeps,* but also uses the term for Drusus, Livia's son. The word *princeps* would be connoting a "prominent person", without necessarily implying any constitutional status (Ovid, *Tristes*, I.6.25; Ovid, *Pontic Letters*, 3.I.I25; Ovid, *Consulatio ad Liviam*, Livia: 353, 365; Drusus: 285, 344; Antonia: 303 apud Barrett, 2002, p. 133). The death of her son Drusus promoted Livia, for, with her desolation, she caused the Senate to vote to release her from the right, *ius trium liberorum*, allotted to women with more than three children, to have property without a guardian; in addition to the Senate calling for the erection of several statues of her (Barrett, 2002, p. 46).

Later, Tacitus characterised Livia as hostile, mentioning that she was linked to ambitious imperial women, to gain power and use it for political purposes. The author states that she lacked control and suggested that she was linked to the death of Gaius, Lucius Caesar, Agrippa Postumus and even Augustus (Harvey, 2020, p. 3-6 and 162), adding the fact that the author suggests that she was part of secret intrigues (Tac. *Ann.* 1.3). Suetonius knew of her wifely devotion to making clothes for Augustus, but also that she made Tiberius angry with her demand to share power, mentioning that Tiberius called her *Ulixes stolatus* (Ulysses in a stole) (Suet. *Calig.* 23.2). However, Anthony. A. Barrett (2002) points out that this is an allusion that appeared when Caligula was disdaining his relatives (Barrett, 2002, p. 121). Cassius Dio also considered her powerful, influential, murderous, and influential on Augustus (Cass. Dio, *Roman History* 53.33.4, 55.10a.10, 56.30.1-2 and 58.2.5-6). Tacitus even mentions that she was a terrible mother both to the State and to the house of Caesars as a stepmother (Tac. *Ann.* 1.10).

5.1.1. Livia and Augustus

Augustus himself never depicted Livia on any of his official coinage of Rome, and there is only one seated female figure associated with her on coins of his government. This figure continues to appear in the government of Tiberius (Barrett, 2002, p. 141) and others. Add the fact that Livia received no mention in his work, *Res Gestae,* and was not cited in any existing calendar until eight years after Augustus' death, but the *Ara Pacis* was held on the day of her birth, as if Augustus wanted to honour her during the celebration of her fiftieth birthday, and it was common to celebrate her birthday every year (Barrett, 2002, p. 138-139). She was the silent obedient wife behind the scenes, never in the forefront (Zager, 2014, p. 54-57), as Augustus did not promote her, giving prominence to his sister, Octavia, due to her rivalry with Mark Antony during the Second Triumvirate (Harvey, 2020, p. 1). However, he ended up depicting their children, Gaius Caesar, Julia, and Lucius Caesar, showing family harmony and prosperity through their future heirs.

Figure 27 – Silver denarius[115], dated 13 BC, from the Roman Empire, minted in Rome, weighing 3,48g, with Augustus' face turned to the right on the obverse, and the caption: AUGUSTUS; on the reverse there are the three children of Augustus, Gaius Caesar, Julia, and Lucius Caesar, with the caption: C.MARIVS.TRO III VIR (*Gaius Marius. Triumvir*[116] *Tromentina tribu* = Gaius Mario. Triumvir of the Tromentine tribe[117])

Source: © The Trustees of the British Museum

---

[115] Museum reference number: 1921.0612.1. Bibliography: RE1 106, p. 21, RIC 1 404, p. 72 or RIC 1² 405. C&M catalogue: RE1 p21. 106. Available at: https://www.britishmuseum.org/research/collection_online/collection_object_details.aspx?objectId=1214000&partId=1&images=true. Accessed: 10 Nov. 2019.

[116] III VIR is a reference to an office, a magistracy responsible for the minting of coins, which was also spelled VIR A A A FF [*Tresvirem (triumviri) aere argento auro flando feriundo* = Triúnviro (triúnviros) for the casting and minting of bronze, silver and gold. *Triumvir(i)* was the "council", "joint" of three magistrates *monetalis*, for matters concerning the minting of coins. Available at: https://www.britishmuseum.org/collection/object/C_R-6251; https://academic.sun.ac.za/antieke/coins/muntwerf/augquads.html. Accessed: 12 Oct. 2022.

[117] Translation made by the author.

On this denarius from 13 BC, Augustus appears on the obverse, keeping the most important side of the coin for himself. However, the reverse is a tribute to the royal family, with the images of his adopted sons, Gaius Caesar (who died in AD 4) and Lucius Caesar (who died in AD 2), as well as the daughter he had with Scribonia, Julia. In fact, both Gaius and Lucius were his grandchildren, sons of Julia, who were adopted as his sons. However, Harvey raises the possibility that the woman represented in this photo could be Livia (Harvey, 2020, p. 110), which is difficult to justify, since Gaius Caesar and Lucius Caesar are directly linked to Julia and she would be the most important link between Augustus and his grandchildren. The coin displays a propaganda of the royal family, demonstrating the harmony and prosperity of its members.

However, this would be the first time that his sons were represented on coins, as no other relatives of him would have been minted on them. Therefore, this could also be the beginning of an iconography that would be linked to dynastic succession. The very adoption of grandchildren would be a way to ensure the continuation of imperial power within the family. However, with the death of his grandchildren, Augustus soon adopted Tiberius and Agrippa Postumus, the younger brother of Gaius and Lucius (Claes, 2013, p. 135).

Julia had three sons in her second marriage to Marcus Agrippa, and for a long time they were the great hope of succession for Augustus. Her statues stood in public places in the East, where the Greek language was present and where groups of dynastic statues formed a familiar and acceptable sight, before the advent of Roman hegemony. In some places, she appeared as the wife of Agrippa, and in others, with her last husband, Tiberius. In several dedications, she was depicted with children, who should have been illustrated as babies in her arms. Local donors evidently appreciated the importance of births in the imperial family, celebrating them. Julia, however, fell drastically out of favour after her conviction for adultery in 2 BC. However, she never officially suffered a *damnatio memoriae*, with the result that her portraits were not destroyed (Wood, 2001, p. 29-30). After Agrippa's death in 12 BC, the Roman mint stopped striking this type of coin, which may explain why Julia never appeared minted again before her banishment to the island of Pandataria in AD 2 (Claes, 2013, p. 223).

Livia's importance in publicising imperial identity is indicated by the fact that she was also the first to appear on eastern provincial coins, around 16 BC (Zager, 2014, p. 54-57). However, the East had already been honouring Roman women since the time of Mark Antony's wife Fulvia, winged as the personification of the goddess Victoria/Nike. It was common for them to honour the wives and daughters of Hellenistic monarchs as well, showing a tendency to include those from the families of great Romans in order to bestow the proper honours on them. Egypt followed this trend for its Ptolemaic lineage and ended up minting coins of Livia in Alexandria.

Figure 28 – Coin[118] of a type of metal fusion, from about 27 BC to AD 14 of the Augustan period, minted in Alexandria, Egypt. Livia is on the obverse. Reverse: jug or *modius* with wheat branches, between two calla lily flowers on a table or altar, ΛΘ (39[119])

Source: © The Trustees of the British Museum

On this Egyptian coin, Livia is predominant on the obverse, with *nodus*-like hair, and on its reverse, there are two calla lily flowers (*Zantedeschia aethiopica*, of African origin). Surrounding the flowers are branches of caduceus plants or snakes, which often appear with cornucopias, which are related to prosperity, but it is not possible to say precisely what they are. Amongst the calla lily flowers, there is a container with sprigs of grain, which is similar to a *modius*[120], with five ears of wheat. The *modius* was related to the receipt of the *frumentum*[121], which was the imperial distribution of grain, in addition to the *congiarium*[122], for the *plebs frumentaria*. Food distribution was regularised in 123 BC, when Gaius Gracchus implemented the *lex*

---

[118] Registration number: 1864,1118,262. Bibliographic references: BMC Greek (Alexandria) / Catalogue of the coins of Alexandria and the Nomes (31, p. 4); C&M catalogue number: GC15 (BMC Greek (Alexandria)) (4) (31) (4). Available at: https://www.britishmuseum.org/collection/object/C_1864-1118-262. Acessed: 3 Sept. 2020.

[119] Translation made by the author with consultation of the site: http://www.saxa-loquuntur.nl/tools/greek-numerals.html. Accessed: 5 Dec. 2022.

[120] *Modius* was a container for measuring grain. Available at: http://www.perseus.tufts.edu/hopper/resolveform?type=exact&lookup=modius&lang=la. Accessed: 10 May 2022.

[121] *Frumentum* were grains from the harvest. Available at: http://www.perseus.tufts.edu/hopper/resolveform?type=exact&lookup=frumentum&lang=la. Accessed: 10 May 2022.

[122] *Congiarium* was a generosity to the poor of one *congius* for each man. Available at: http://www.perseus.tufts.edu/hopper/resolveform?type=exact&lookup=congiarium&lang=la. Accessed: 10 May 2022. *Congius* would be a measure of liquids. Available at: http://www.perseus.tufts.edu/hopper/resolveform?type=exact&lookup=congius&lang=la. Accessed: 10 June 2022.

frumentaria (Plut. *Caius Gracchus* 6). This activity became more organised and politicised in the Late Republic and Early Empire and was an expectation to be received from the emperor (Elkins, 2017, p. 57-58). However, the vessel cannot be characterised as a *modius*, as it always appears on coins, such as some from the period of Claudius and Nerva, with three supporting bases. Even so, the elements of the coin may suggest a celebration of the agricultural harvest season and that Livia herself could be linked to this celebration or even to the distribution of grains.

In the Roman calendar, there were two days known as *Consualia*, which could have been used by the province for the same purpose - 21st August and 15th December. These days commemorated the god Consus, linked to food storage. The *Consualia* celebrated in August was directly associated with the storage of grains, but the one in December is not known for sure. However, it could be a period of inspection of the condition of the corn stock during the winter or a harvest of a product that could be done later, such as that of the olive[123].

The distribution of grains to the people of this region could be linked to the activities of *pietas*, common among the women of the elite involved with the emperor, since the same vessel appears again on coins of Agrippina Minor, minted in the same place. Such symbolism could probably enrich her and the emperor's propaganda as philanthropic people. This type of coin could be related to the humanitarianism done by the *alimenta* system and to charitable acts and government propaganda by giving substantial gifts to communities, both in Rome and in the provinces. The purpose was to provide the necessary sustenance for children through agricultural investments to gain popularity (Sear, 2000, p. 57).

The coin container could also be linked to a Demeter/Ceres symbol, which indicated prosperity and fertility, which may demonstrate that Livia was central to dynastic succession. Ceres was related to agricultural success (Elkins, 2017, p. 57-58). The celebration of this goddess may be indicated by the reason that the vessel appears to be on an altar. The differentiation, whether it is a *modius* or not, comes with the comparison of the container interpreted by Elkins (2017) on a coin of Nerva. However, for the container of Livia's coin, it is more appropriate to consider the religious interpretation, which does not rule out food symbolism, abundance, and agricultural fertility.

---

[123] Available at: https://www.journals.uchicago.edu/doi/epdf/10.1086/362768. Accessed: 19 Sept. 2022.

Figure 29 – Bronze sestertius[124] from Rome, AD 97, 23.22 g, 34 mm diameter. Obverse: laureate head of Nerva, IMP NERVA CAES AVG P M TR P II COS III P P (*Imperator Nerva Caesar Augustus Pontifex Maximus Tribunicia Postestate secundum Consul tertium Pater Patriae* = Commander Nerva Caesar Augustus, Supreme Pontiff with Tribune power for the second time, consul for the third time and father of the homeland[125]). Reverse: *modius* with three feet, containing poppy among six ears of wheat, three to the right, three to the left, with PLEBEI VRBANAE FRVMENTO CONSTITVTO S C (*Plebei Urbanae Frumento [ex] Constituto Senatus Consulto* = Grains for the plebs of the city defined by the consent of the Senate[126])

Source: Courtesy of the American Numismatic Society

Compared to the vessel of Livia's coin, a distinction is observed in the shape of the *modius* of Nerva's coin, which appears with three feet, containing poppy among six ears of wheat, three to the right and three to the left. In addition, the caption with PLEBEI VRBANAE FRVMENTO CONSTITVTO S C demonstrates the coin's intention to be related to the distribution of grain, which is not found in the caption of Livia's coin.

Those who looked at the coins could connect the emperor's activity with the propaganda on the reverse of the object (Manders, 2008, p. 32). However, the coin in question does not feature the emperor, but Livia, which indicates that it could be linked to agricultural, food or religious activities, which focused on production and abundance. Livia was commonly honoured and associated with other goddesses, such as Hera and Demeter. Thus, it is not surprising to find instances honouring Livia in communities where Greek influence was great (Grether, 1946, p. 223-224 and 228).

The image of Livia was first coined in the eastern provinces of Greece in the period of Augustus, expanding its coinage as her influence grew,

---

[124] Available at: http://numismatics.org/ocre/id/ric.2.ner.103. Accessed: 21 June 2022. Identifier: 1944.100.42661. RIC II Nerva 103.

[125] Translation made by the author.

[126] Translation made by the author.

often being represented as a priestess (Harvey, 2020, p. 8). It can be said that public visibility and its customs, rules and ideologies differed in some respects between the provinces and the centre. In the East, for example, the public images of prominent people, such as Antony, Livia, and Augustus, directly incorporated associations with the divine earlier than in Rome. The inscriptions of the details of the contributions of women benefactors presented different images or perhaps women were not visualised as much in Rome as in the provinces (McCullough, 2007, p. 8). However, Livia only began to receive honours in Rome as a *diva* after she was deified in AD 42 under Claudius, with the consent of the Senate.

The quality of her image on coins varied, sometimes drastically, from one mint to another and was often reproduced in great detail, such as the bronze dupondius of her as Salus made at Koinon, Crete, which is easy to identify as it comes with a caption bearing her name. However, other coins have depicted her in a very crude manner, appearing even comical, as is the drawing of her at Knossos. However, her design is recognisable, as it has always followed the same characteristics and elements in various types of representations, as well as in statues, in which she appears with the *Zopftyp* and *nodus* hair style during the reign of Augustus, and the Salus type under the rule of Tiberius. Other hair styles have been found on Livia, such as *Marbury Hall, Albani-Bonn, Fayum* and the Salus type[127] (Harvey, 2020, p. 65-67).

The *nodus* hair and its variations are the elements that best identify Livia in her representations, ensuring her recognition, and sculptures of Livia with this type of hair already dated back to the period of Augustus, present in regions such as Gaul, Dalmatia, Greece, Asia Minor, Egypt and North Africa. The uniqueness of the *nodus* hair type lies in the fact that it was not a Hellenistic Greek style or used in representations of Roman goddesses. This traditionally Roman style was worn by their matrons and became a symbol that defined a social group in Rome according to their gender and status, worn by Octavia, Livia and Fulvia. It was common in the depictions of the Vestal Virgins and over time became more prominent. In addition, it distinguished Roman women from those like Cleopatra, who was seen as "the foreigner" but actually wore a hair style based on her Hellenistic precursors. For the Romans, Cleopatra was a symbol of immoral extravagance. Thus, the *nodus* hairstyle was intended

---

[127] For more information on the hair types of Roman women, see Appendix 4.

to demonstrate the *pudicitia*, virtue and valour of the Roman woman of Augustus' time. As the women of the Roman elite were seen as examples, this type of hair was also worn by other women, often by those of the subaltern classes, showing that hair became an identity mark of Roman women. Representations of Livia with the *nodus* and its variants began to exist from the period of Augustus, through Tiberius, to the government of Nero (Harvey, 2020, p. 68 and 71).

The elements of the images are important for recognising each figure and can be interpreted as a system of signs, which are employed alongside the image and fall into the paradigm of imagery elements, such as hair style, facial expressions, dress, type of bust (draped or nude) and adornments such as diadem and jewellery. Generally, busts on coins from the Late Republic and Early Empire were differentiated between men and women, with men appearing only with their heads and women varying their dress (Woytek, 2014 apud Harvey, 2020, p. 65-67). In Harvey's work (2020), the scholar draws attention to the hair of Livia's representations, which could indicate a gender or status mark and which indicated whether the Roman women were well-dressed. The scholar mentions that this element was the most significant for identifying women on coins, in sculptures and in other types of representations. Hair types codified socio-political roles of women's position in society, as well as the social relations in which they would be included. For Bartman, the practice that men should cut their hair short and women should leave their hair long and wear it in some kind of bun was something cultural and marked the participation of these individuals in a social circle (Bartman, 2001 apud Harvey, 2020, p. 67-68). Apuleius mentions that for him, women's hair was significant, overriding the importance of other elements of clothing (Apul. *Met.* 2.9).

5.1.2 Livia and Tiberius

Tiberius was the son of Livia with Tiberius Claudius Nero and the adopted son of Augustus, who assumed power because Augustus and Livia had no children (Harvey, 2020, p. 3-4). Augustus adopted him in AD 4, officially becoming his son, but on the same occasion he also adopted Agrippa Postumus, Julia's son. It is added that Tiberius was obligated to adopt Germanicus, son of his brother Drusus, before his own adoption (Barrett, 2002, p. 55-56). According to Suetonius, Augustus only adopted Tiberius because of the insistence of his wife, or for his own ambition, without suspecting that one day such a successor would bring him so much regret (Suet. *Tib.* 21.1). In 20 or 19 BC, Tiberius married Agrippa's daughter Vipsania, and their son Drusus was born in 14 BC (Cass. Dio, *Roman History* 43.41.3).

However, Tiberius had to separate from Vipsania, when she was pregnant for the second time, to marry Julia, daughter of Augustus with Scribonia, an event probably planned by Livia (Suet. *Tib.* 7.2). However, Julia had entered an extramarital relationship. She was thus accused of adultery and exiled in 2 BC. For Suetonius, Augustus claimed that Tiberius' wife, his own daughter, had been convicted of depravity and adultery, pronouncing her separation by Augustus' authority, but Tiberius felt duty-bound to write letters to her father to pardon his daughter and eventually returned her entire dowry (Suet. *Tib.* 11.3). However, Augustus re-established an old custom of punishment by means of an assembly made up of the relatives of inappropriate matrons (Suet. *Tib.* 35.1). According to Cassius Dio, Tiberius did not remove Julia from her banishment, but eventually locked her up until she died of general weakness and starvation (Cass. Dio, *Roman History* 57. 18. 1^a).

Tacitus claimed that she disdained her husband because they did not go well together. When he succeeded to the empire, he banished her and left her in disgrace, deprived of all hope after the murder of Postumus Agrippa, allowing her to perish slowly to death. Tacitus emphasises that Tiberius had reason to take revenge on Sempronius Gracchus, a man of noble family who seduced Julia when she was married to Marcus Agrippa. When she was handed over to Tiberius, her lover persisted and accused her of being disobedient, arousing hatred for her husband. Moreover, a letter sent by Julia to her father, reviling Tiberius, seems to have been composed by Gracchus, who was banished to Cercina, where he was exiled for 14 years and then executed (Tac. *Ann.* 1.53). Julia's exile was followed by the untimely death of Augustus' sister Octavia, which made Livia the only imperial woman in a position of power and prestige (Barrett, 2002, p. 51).

After Augustus' death, under the rule of Tiberius, much of Augustus' ceremonial dignity passed to Livia and that, as Julia Augusta, she was in charge of the *gens Iulia* and Augustus' deification cult. Furthermore, Livia came to occupy a position of paramount importance in the State, but this did not happen quickly. Before Augustus' death, during the Principate, she shared the honours with her husband, had statues erected, administered her estates, and was endowed with sacred inviolability, and she, along with Augustus, had the privilege of dining in the temple of Concordia. Her influence at court was like that of any ambassador of Augustus. The fact that she shared his image of the "ceremonial dignity" of the emperor's cult clearly shows her in a cult of honour and tributes of a divine nature, which she was offered and allowed to accept. Honours to her person began at the beginning of the Principality and continued until after her death, and the cult of her extended from the beginning of the Principality to the Antonine dynasty (Grether, 1946, p. 222-223).

As a widow and priestess of the new *divus*, Livia was in the public spotlight, especially soon after Augustus' death and consecration. She planned a new temple for Augustus and instituted the *Ludi Palatini* in honour of her husband; moreover, the date of the anniversary of their marriage became a public holiday. Coins commemorating the consecration of Augustus had on their reverse a female figure with a *patera* and sceptre, intended to demonstrate a priestess of his cult (Grether, 1946, p. 235-236).

Tiberius knew his mother's importance, but that didn't mean he got along with her. He did not tolerate her very well, as he argued that she was claiming a share of power. He avoided talking to her to show that he was not led by her advice and when he did follow it, it was at great cost. He became indignant with the Senate when the members proposed adding to his titles one calling him "son of Livia" and one calling him "son of Augustus". He did not allow the Senate to approve Livia as *"mater patriae"* or for her to receive any honours in public. The honours paid to Livia also seem to have irritated authors such as Tacitus, who mentions that there was a great deal of flattery, due to the fact that the Senate added names to her as *"mater patriae"* and wanted to make Tiberius use the name *"filius Iuliae"*, which resulted in a request from the emperor to have a limit to the honours paid to a woman. Tiberius also would not let a *lictor*[128] be assigned to her and forbade the building of an altar in memory of her adoption, as well as any other attribution of distinction to her (Tac. *Ann.* 1.13). Otherwise, Cassius Dio mentions that she gained the *lictor* by being declared a priestess of Augustus' cult (Cass. Dio, *Roman History* 56.46.2). Following precedents of Augustus, Tiberius discouraged the establishment of cults for living persons, but in some provinces, he tried to regulate his own cult (Grether, 1946, p. 233-234).

---

[128] The *lictors* were attendants to the magistrates, usually free men, and the number of *lictors* each magistrate had varied according to the status of the officer. They would go ahead of the magistrate, announcing his arrival and clearing spectators out of the way. The privilege of having a *lictor* was extended to the Vestal Virgins in 42 BC, after a Vestal returning from a dinner party, was not recognised and was insulted (Barrett, 2002, p. 161).

He warned her not to take part in business that did not suit a woman. It seemed that Tiberius had a hatred for his mother, caused by her insistence that he enrol a man who had been granted citizenship in the decurions. His reply was that he would only do so with the words on the record "that this favour had been extorted from him by his mother". Offended, Livia read Tiberius' old notes, which outraged him and caused her exile (Suet. *Tib.* 50.1-51.1).

In addition to leaving two-thirds of his inheritance to Tiberius and the remainder to Livia (Cass. Dio, *Roman History* 56. 32. 1), Augustus' will was that Livia be adopted into the *gens Iulia*, to receive the title of "Augusta" (AD 14) (Cass. Dio, *Roman History* 56. 46.1). Octavian had received his cognomen "Augustus" in 27 BC with his powerful religious association as an alternative to the name "Romulus". In AD 14, the name acquired the force of a title, like Caesar, which supported him as *princeps*. The position of *princeps* was not supported by the title of Augustus, but by specific powers, such as *imperium proconsulare* and *tribunicia postestas*, with which a woman could not be honoured (Barrett, 2002, p. 154).

The *gens Iulia* was part of the most remote times of the Roman people and its descendants would be linked to the goddess Venus, through her son Aeneas and, consequently, her son Julius, who gave the *gens* its name (Barrett, 2002, p. 150-151). This marked the religiosity linked to the status, since this title indicated its sacred nature and religious character, as well as being an investment that had been institutionalised since Julius Caesar and Octavian (Martins, 2011, p. 75). For a woman of the imperial family, the title presented a new political structure, and in the first two centuries it was used as a dynastic prop and as a title for mothers of emperors when their son prospered (Temporini, 1978, p. 23-34 and 44; Perkouning, 1995, p. 131; Flory, 1998, p. 115 apud Barrett, 2002, p. 152). As Livia and Augustus had no children, she ensured that her son was a potent example for the succession; moreover, Augustus himself wanted to have this guarantee by adopting him. However, this title could also be more linked to the fact that Augustus elevated her to equality as emperor, and it seems that this is how the Senate interpreted it, eventually granting her extraordinary privileges.

The title of Augusta could have conferred an imperial, political and power attribute, which could have made Livia a companion in Tiberius' government (Barrett, 2002, p. 153) or a rival, adding to her domestic virtues, as well as continuity, harmony, and stability to the State itself. This was the first time that a male title was transferred to a woman, which made Livia honoured and alluded to a high social status (Flory, 1988), and this title appeared on coins in the Greek and Latin languages, increasingly frequent in captions. Possibly, the title may have been Augustus' desire to strengthen Tiberius, because of the fact that Tacitus makes it clear that both Livia and Tiberius were his heirs. Augustus, in his lifetime, had twice asked the Senate to grant tribunitial powers to Tiberius (Tac. *Ann.* 1.8 and 10). It was possible that Augustus had seen in Tiberius a weak or rebellious ruler, who would have gone against his own imperial system, giving his mother public roles to help him in his power. Drusus, Livia's other son, might have been more likely to have been considered for this position, but he died in a premature death in 9 BC.

Livia's presence and actions in Tiberius' government could be linked to religious issues, since it was notable that in the event of a crisis or a weak government, such as Tiberius', the religious presence of women was requested to pacify divine wrath. In such circumstances, male leaders, religious and political leaders turned to matrons to appease the gods through gifts, spectacles. and female processions. At such times, women were relied upon to restore social and political stability (Cid López, 2011, p. 62-63).

This association of women with the extraordinary made it easier for them to be linked to superstitious practices due to female devotions. They were therefore later linked to foreign or exotic cults. Persecuting any cult was considered pernicious to the Roman State, but women were often blamed for having introduced some of them. However, in most cases, women only gathered to honour the goddesses in their own spaces. Only in times of crisis, when men recruited them, that men took part in the cult (Cid López, 2011, p. 63).

The presence of Livia and Tiberius's dislike of her as ruler were possibly felt in a dimension of his masculinity, since such masculinity had to be proven again and again. As soon as this happened, it was questioned again and had to be proved once more, in other words, constantly, tirelessly, unattainably. Finally, the journey for proof would become so meaningless that it would become a sport (Kimmel, 2016, p. 102). However, the presence of the mother would compose an impotent government and the denial of honours attributed to Livia would be an attempt to maintain dignity in the face of the game between men. Barrett points out that Tiberius refused Augustus' title but continued to have the right to use it (Barrett, 2002, p.

152), which suggests that this could have been another reason why Augustus could have passed the title to Livia: to ensure dynastic succession and that, sooner or later, Tiberius would take the title.

To mark Livia's adoption, the Senate voted for an Altar of Adoption (*Ara Adoptionis*), as a commemorative monument rather than a place of worship, since altars in honour of the imperial family were a relatively common phenomenon. Livia's titles and new position created by Augustus, were caused by tensions between son and mother (Barrett, 2002, p. xi, 150).

Arguably, the public sphere, which Livia took part in somehow, would be an arena in which masculinity was tested and proved, in other words, a space in which tensions between men, now between a woman, and between different groups of men were considered through meanings. These tensions suggest that cultural definitions of gender were exhausted on a contested terrain and were themselves defined as power relations (Kimmel, 2016, p. 104). In ancient Rome, and especially for the emperor, a hegemony of masculinity should be consciously symbolised for this role, which would be the man in power, a man with power and a man of power, to put it in other way, he was the one who would be strong, victorious, conquering, capable, reliable and in control, since he had power over other men, women and children. However, the Roman man should accumulate cultural symbols that denote masculinity, signs that should have been acquired, which would also frame the standards used against women, to prevent their inclusion in public life and their maintenance in the devalued private sphere (Kimmel, 2016, p. 105).

According to Suetonius, formal consultations were held between Livia and Augustus, where he considered it important enough to secure carefully prepared statements from her in response to her petitions. The author also cites that archives indicated Livia's acting in roles concerning the development of family members (Suet. *Aug.* 84.2; Suet. *Claud.* 4.1-6). Thus, Rome's aristocratic and dynastic form of government gave the family a centralised structure in the political system, which tended to blur the distinction between the public and the private (Hallett, 1984 apud Wood, 1988, p. 409), a distinction which might have been in reality much more complex than it is known.

According to Cassius Dio, Tiberius would have charged his mother to behave in a way that suited him, to prevent her from being too proud, because she occupied a very high position, far above all women, and she could receive the Senate at any time and people who wished to greet her. Moreover, the letters were as much addressed to Tiberius as to her mother. However, she never ventured into the Senate Chamber, fields, and public assemblies, but undertook to administer everything as if she were the sole ruler, an attitude carried over from the time of Augustus, when she had greater influence. She did not fail to declare that it was she who had made Tiberius emperor. Cassius Dio accused Livia of not being satisfied with ruling on equal terms with her son Tiberius and that she wished to be first in line with him. Many wanted her to take the title *"mater patriae"*, and others proposed that Tiberius be named after her, like the Greeks, who were called by their father's name. In this way, Tiberius would be called by his mother's name, which would upset him. In this sense, he did not approve of honours granted to his mother, with few exceptions, nor did he allow extravagance of conduct, eventually removing her entirely from public affairs and allowing her to run the affairs of the house. Cassius Dio cites that even then she was troublesome to Tiberius and in response he began to absent himself from public engagements and avoid her in every way (Cass. Dio, *Roman History* 57.12.1-6).

Livia's public image influenced her *status*, which did not wane after Augustus' death (14 BC), but increased significantly. By being adopted by the *gens Iulia*, acquiring the name Iulia Augusta, shortly before her husband's death, she consolidated Tiberius' position as imperial successor. In addition, she inherited a third of Augustus' state, which was more than what was allowed by law. However, Tiberius did not allow to be called *"filius Iuliae"* or to give the title of *"mater patriae"* to her, proposed by the Senate (Harvey, 2020). The name *"mater patriae"* would be directly linked to the fact that Livia would have helped many girls find a husband with gifts (Grether, 1946, p. 246).

According to Grether, Tiberius would not have vetoed honouring his mother, but refused to accept it himself (Grether, 1946, p. 238), as well as the fact that Tiberius approved the cult of Augustus, but refused a cult to himself, as well as leaving the decision of the cult of Julia Augusta to his own mother (Tac. *Ann.* 4, 55); and finally, he ended up rejecting the celebration of his own birthday (Grether, 1946, p. 240). According to Cassius Dio, Tiberius absolutely rejected the title of *"pater patriae"* (Cass. Dio, *Roman History* 57.8.1). To add to this, the Senate wanted the month of November to be called Tiberius, who asked the Senate itself what they were going to do when they had thirteen Caesars (Cass. Dio, *Roman History* 57.18.2).

With regard to the titles and cults of these people, it can be said that the rites of institution occupied a special place according to their solemn and extraordinary character. The function of these rites was linked to the establishment of a sacralisation and in the name of an entire mobilised community. Moreover, the rites of institution were a rite of passage for both young people and those who were socially worthy of receiving them. In many societies, which divided activities by sex, these rites were definitely excluded from women. The rites of manhood, par excellence, consecrated such virility by symbolically preparing men to exercise it. In some groups, such rituals signify the breaking of the original quasi-symbiosis with the mother and affirm a sexual identity of their own, something organised in advance by the group, which, faced with a series of sexual institution rites, oriented by virility, demonstrate, in all the differentiated and differentiating practices of daily existence, such as games and hunting, the encouragement of the break with the maternal world (Bourdieu, 1998, p. 35).

From this perspective, Livia, a woman and a mother, by receiving consecrations, tributes, rites and other celebrations, was enacting a denial on the part of Tiberius for her tributes. Consequently, such tributes could have represented a weak government, without a strong base to support itself and which would have had to face the help of a woman in power, who would still be her mother. The political partnership that worked well between Livia and Augustus was not as successful with Tiberius, since he seemed to have no interest in continuing Augustus' ideal.

However, Tiberius was also aware of the esteem in which Livia was held by the people and decided to allow her image to be coined or was forced by the Senate to accept it. He must have been bothered by the fact that, in a society like the Roman one, the male personality is constructed in the absence of virility, to rephrase it, of the break with the world of the mother, of womanhood and femininity, and the male *habitus* is the product of this break. All this is socially constructed, and even in Rome there was an explicit work of separation, which was linked to the family, education, religiosity, and the State. Through these means, social constructions are incorporated and inscribed in the body, making systems of dispositions principles that generate practices and appreciate practices (*habitus*) (Bourdieu, 1996a, p. 36).

However, one of the purposes of minting coins was to demonstrate, through these objects, how emperors had come to power, as well as the virtues of their ancestry and family, recording and reinforcing the legitimacy of their authority (Florenzano, 2015, p. 18). In view of this, Tiberius allowed the Senate to proclaim her a priestess of the deified Augustus, but did not agree to the construction of an arch, voted by the Senate, as well as divine fees in her honour (Harvey, 2020, p. 4-5).

At the age of 80, in AD 22, Livia became very ill and, for her recovery, the Senate decreed offerings and games, which simultaneously led to her being represented on coins as Salus Augusta, who was the personification of well-being. For Barrett, the allusion of Salus to the well-being of Livia is indirect, since the scholar points out that feminine abstractions, such as Salus or Pietas, modified by Augusta, did not refer to Livia, but to an association of the abstract personification with the house of Augustus. The connection with Salus has a long history, with coins of Augustus in 16 BC celebrating vows taken from the Emperor's Salus, which was identified as the Salus of the Republic, and oaths were taken by Salus Augusti. There was also a cult of Augustus' Salus during his lifetime (Barrett, 2002, p. 93).

Otherwise, the personification of Livia as Salus Augusta could be linked not only to her health but also to her religious activities, since Salus could be connected to the goddess Bona Dea, with whom Livia was often associated, and she restored her temple. Several statues of Livia with the cornucopia resemble statues of Bona Dea, and according to Takács, the base of a small statuette of a seated woman connects Bona Dea with Hygiea, goddess of health, who often appears as consort of Asclepius. In this way, Salus, who was tied to the meaning of bodily health, is the Latin equivalent of the Greek goddess, Hygiea (Takács, 2008, p. 102). Salus alone could be related to health and social prosperity. She could also appear with attributes of Ceres, such as the sceptre and branches of wheat, revealing the importance of grain distribution (Elkins, 2017, p. 73-75). Salus was also associated with safety and could appear holding a *patera*, from which she fed a snake that had been left coiled on an altar or could appear holding the snake in her arms (Sear, 2000, p. 40).

The series of coins called Salus was one of the first to be minted by Rome with her face. In several other provinces, it was made in a similar way, copying the style and pattern not only of Livia as Salus, but also as Pietas and Iustitia, as did the mints of Thessalonica and Amphipolis (Harvey, 2020, p. 4-8 and 114).

Figure 30 – Bronze dupondius[129], AD 22 - 23, 14.6 g, 32.2 mm diameter. Obverse: draped bust to the right of Livia, SALUS AUGUSTA. Reverse: S-C S(enatus) C(onsultum) (minted by consent of the Senate[130]), TI CAESAR DIVI AVG F AVG P M TR POT XXII (*Tiberius Caesar Divi Augustus Fili Augur Pontifex Maximus Tribunicia Potestate Vicesimum Quartum* = Tiberius Caesar Augustus, Son of the Divine Augustus, augur, Supreme Pontiff in charge of the Twenty-Fourth Tribune Power[131])

Source: © KBR *cabinet des monnais et médailles*

This dupondius of Livia as Salus Augusta is also interpreted as a tribute to her, for her recovery, according to her illness, which coincided with the games of thanksgiving to the gods for their blessing. Her image appears only on the obverse of the coin, the most important side of the object, with no indication of the emperor. However, the correlation with him is seen only in the reverse caption, letting Livia show herself as the most important at that moment. According to Harvey, this is one of the few coins of Livia minted in Rome, but there is a seated female figure that was minted earlier and seems to be Livia (Harvey, 2020, p. 121).

During this period when she was ill, an altar was promised to her in the name of her health, but it was not built until the time of Claudius, after her death and consecration. In the same year as the coinage of Livia as Salus Augusta, the dedication of *Pietati Augustae* was made on coins from AD 22, which bore the caption Pietas, together with her idealised image, which sometimes also appeared as Iustitia (Grether, 1946, p. 236-237). Pietas was associated with piousness or religiosity and obedience. She usually appeared veiled, with a *patera* and a sceptre; sometimes she was shown making a sacrifice on an altar and holding a box of incense (Sear, 2000, p. 40).

---

[129] Bibliography: RIC I² 47; BMC 81. Available at: https://opac.kbr.be/LIBRARY/doc/SYRACUSE/20734511. Accessed: 14 July 2022.
[130] Translation made by the author.
[131] Translation made by the author.

In Rome, when women wanted to intervene in politics, they did so within religious activities, as they could leave their homes to attend religious ceremonies, honour deities on certain dates of the year, and in times of crisis, men turned to women to honour deities with more effort, which gave political importance to religious activities, to female deities, thus constituting "pious" women, in which idealisation served to shape legal norms (Cid López, 2011, p. 61). With this feminine ideal, it was understandable that the public activities chosen for Livia were linked to the religious space.

It seems that the Senate made an additional gesture in honouring Livia during the year she was ill by granting attention to the children of her *pietas*, a Roman concept that involved a responsibility to both the gods and the family. As mentioned, the members of the Senate voted to build the Pietati Augustae, also referred to as the altar of Pietas Augusta. This construction was not completed throughout its 20 years, when its finalisation was reproduced in the inscriptions of Claudius. For Barrett, the original stone is lost, but the text is preserved and its transcription was made by itinerant and anonymous monks from Einsiedeln during the Middle Ages (Barrett, 2002, p. 94).

Figure 31 – Bronze dupondius[132] with the veiled bust, with a diadem on the head of Livia as Pietas, looking to the right, dated AD 22 - 23, 30.2 mm, 15.17 g, minted during the rule of Tiberius, with the consent of the Senate. Reverse: DRVSVS CAESAR TI AVGVSTI F TR POT ITER (*Drusus Caesar Tiberii Augusti Filius Tribunicia Potestate Iterum* = Drusus Caesar, son of Tiberius Augustus, with tribunitial power for the second time[133]) S C (*Senatus Consultum*)

Source: © KBR *cabinet des monnais et médailles*

---

[132] Bibliography: RIC I² 43; BMC 98. Coll. du Chastel, B 36/36; Acq. 1899. Available at: https://opac.kbr.be/LIBRARY/doc/SYRACUSE/20734513. Accessed: 14 July 2022.

[133] Available at: https://en.numista.com/catalogue/pieces247290.html. Accessed: 13 Oct. 2022.

In this dupondius in which Livia is represented as Pietas, she appears with her head veiled, with a diadem, and draped bust, demonstrating aspects linked to *pudicitia* and to Vesta, honouring her role as Roman matron, without the presence of a male, but with reference to Tiberius' son, Drusus, in the reverse caption, while the reverse of the Salus and Iustitia bears the title of Tiberius (Harvey, 2020, p. 165). It is also added that in this series of coins of Livia as Pietas, she is associated with her role as priestess of the cult of Augustus (Harvey, 2020, p. 187). Otherwise, Elkins interprets that Pietas was important to Tiberius' government, showing devotion to the memory of the deified Augustus. According to Suetonius, in Augustus' time, the surname *"Pius"* was recommended to Tiberius, but it seems that Augustus denied it to him and let him choose his own cognomen (Suet. *Aug.* 17.2), since Tiberius always refused any kind of title. Therefore, this coin is seen by Elkins as honouring an imperial quality of Tiberius by having Pietas (Elkins, 2017, p. 143-144). Pietas and Iustitia were linked to imperial virtue (Noreña, 2001, p. 155 apud Manders, 2008, p. 103).

Figure 32 – Bronze dupondius[134], AD 22 - 23, Rome, 14.26 g, 32.5 mm diameter. Obverse: bust of Livia as Iustitia, with a tiara (*stephane*, is a divine attribute[135]); and on the reverse is the smaller caption: TI CAESAR DIVI AVG F AVG P M TR POT XXIIII (*Tiberius Caesar Divi Augustus Fili Augur Pontifex Maximus Tribunicia Potestate Vicesimum Quartum*[136] = Tiberius Caesar, son of the divine Augustus, augur, Supreme Pontiff with the twenty-fourth tribune power[137]) larger caption: S C (*Senatus Consultum* = coined by consent of the Senate[138])

Source: © KBR *cabinet des monnais et médailles*

---

[134] Bibliography: RIC I² 46; BMC 79; du Chastel 370 (*Collection du Chastel Collectie du Chastel*). Available at: https://opac.kbr.be/LIBRARY/doc/SYRACUSE/20734507. Accessed: 14 July 2022.

[135] The crown or tiara verifies Livia's distinction and is linked to goddesses such as Hera/Juno and Aphrodite/Venus (Harvey, 2020, p. 137).

[136] Consulted at: https://en.numista.com/catalogue/pieces56149.html. Accessed: 5 Sept. 2020.

[137] Translation made by the author.

[138] Translation made by the author.

In this dupondius of Tiberius' government, dated AD 21 - 22, Livia is personified as Iustitia, a way of honouring her for her acts of help, which were possibly linked to her activity as patroness. It also guarantees a link with the government of Tiberius through the reverse caption, revealing the consent of the Senate, and even of the emperor, to demonstrate family harmony, as well as dynastic inheritance related to Augustus, since coins were imperial propaganda vehicles and often covered internal crises that the Empire camouflaged.

Barrett emphasises that care should be taken in interpreting figures such as Salus, Iustitia and Pietas, which could reflect the appearance of Livia. For the scholar, the female figure of Salus, with the name Augusta, would not have a specific link to Livia, as Salus would have idiosyncratic personalised elements. Outside Rome, the coin of Salus was used as a kind of portrait of Livia, but this does not prove that it was an accurate record of her appearance. It did, however, reflect her characteristics (Barrett, 2002, p. 104). Representations of these women in Antiquity often did not accurately reflect the appearance of such women, but some elements were repeated in poor or good representations, which could characterise certain people, regardless of their quality.

On the other hand, Elkins does not see the figure of this coin as Livia, but only as Iustitia, which could have composed an imperial rhetorical idea for the government of Tiberius, since Iustitia would be linked to the law, especially in a legal way, and could also represent the administrative virtue of the emperor (Elkins, 2017, p. 114 and 142). Regarding the series of coins of Pietas, Iustitia and Salus, Claes points out that the captions of the coins do not show that it is Livia, since coins from the time of Tiberius also represented other virtues such as Clementia and Modestia, without being referred to someone. There is nothing on the coins to link Livia to Tiberius' imperial position, as Caligula did on the coins in honour of his mother, Agrippina Major (Claes, 2013, p. 95).

It is interesting that Iustitia also appeared on coins of Nerva's rule as the seated female figure already mentioned here, holding an olive branch and a sceptre. Its meaning could also be linked to the maintenance of peace, as an antidote against tyranny, so the sceptre and the branch would be attributes of Pax. Both *iustitia* and *aequitas* could reflect a contemporary political rhetoric and connote a meaning of justice and equity in their literal sense (Elkins, 2017, p. 114, 117, 119 and 141). *Aequitas* is related to equity, fair dealing, abundance, holding a scale and a cornucopia or sceptre (Sear, 2000, p. 37).

However, *iustitia* resonated better for the elite who had been subjected to political abuse during Domitian's rule. Under Tiberius, *moderatio, clementia, iustitia, pietas* and *concordia* were imperial ideals, promoted by the minting of coins for the ruler's rhetorical communication (Elkins, 2017, p. 114, 117, 119 and 141). Iustitia appeared holding an olive branch or *patera* and a sceptre (Sear, 2000, p. 37).

In eastern Greece, there was also the minting of the type Salus Augusta, Iustitia and Pietas (Harvey, 2020, p. 119). In the same year, AD 22, another coin referring to Livia, minted in Rome, showed a *carpentum*, composed of a cart with two mules, usually used by the Vestals for public activities, with the caption *S.P.Q.R. Iuliae August(ae)*, which demonstrated the *supplicatio*, and the Senate decreed Livia the Vestal right to use the *carpentum*, in addition to her winning a public celebration in Rome for her birthday (Grether, 1946, p. 236-237). The permission to wear the *carpentum* was in AD 22, when she became a priestess of the deified Augustus and, consequently, was granted to sit in the theatre of the Vestals (Tac. Ann. 4.16.4), composing her character of modesty, *pudicitia*, motherhood and with feminine virtues (Harvey, 2020, p. 186).

Figure 33 – Sestertius[139] of copper alloy, dated AD 22 - 23, 33 mm in diameter, 27.7 g, minted in Rome during the rule of Tiberius. On its obverse is a *carpentum* facing right with two mules, with caption: SPQR/IVLIAE/AVGVST(ae) (*Senatus Populusque Romanus Iuliae Augustae* = The Senate and the Roman People for Julia Augusta[140]). Reverse: TI CAESAR DIVI AVG F AVGVST P M TR POT XXIIII (*Tiberius Caesar Divi Fili Augustus Pontifex Maximus Tribunicia Potestate Vicesimum Quartum* = Tiberius Caesar, Son of the Divine Augustus, Supreme Pontiff invested with the Twenty-Fourth Tribune Power[141]), S C (*Senatus Consultum*)

Source: © The Trustees of the British Museum

---

[139] Reference number: R.6358. Bibliographical references: RE1 / Coins of the Roman Empire in the British Museum, vol. 1: Augustus to Vitellius (77, p. 130), RIC1 / The Roman Imperial Coinage, vol. 1 (51, p. 97). RIC Tiberius 51. BMCRE *Tiberius* 76. CBN *Tiberius* 55. C 6. *[Rome, AD 22-3]*. Available at: https://www.britishmuseum.org/collection/object/C_R-6358. Accessed: 21Aug. 2020.

[140] Translation made by the author.

[141] Available at: https://en.numista.com/catalogue/pieces66003.html. Accessed: 18 Aug. 2020.

This sestertius with the *carpentum* on the obverse together with the name IVLIAE AVGVST(ae) shows a Vestal respect for the character, since this type of chariot was only used by the Vestal Virgins, showing a religious aspect to the image of Livia. The other images of her that present her as some kind of goddess also pass on this religious aspect linked to a kind of divine respect, adding a characteristic linked to *pudicitia*. According to Harvey, this coin is one of the few minted in Rome, like the one in which she is represented as Salus Augusta and which also had the function of honouring her, highlighting her privilege in walking in a *carpentum* (Harvey, 2020, p. 160). Harvey states that she would be crossing gender norms by using the *carpentum*, facing a status that had no antecedents (Harvey, 2020, p. 121), placing the *carpentum* as something masculine. However, the *carpentum* was something used by the Vestal Virgins, very feminine, but for a special status of woman, which does not take away the exclusive characteristic of Livia, but adds honours to her. For Barrett, the coin should be linked to Livia's illness, and the scene could be related to the procession of supplications, which the Senate must have enacted (Tac. *Ann.* 12.42.2 apud Barrett, 2002, p. 95).

Livia became more tied to religious matters after the death and consequent deification of Augustus, being appointed as priestess of her husband's cult. Furthermore, adding to her status, to help in her public roles, she was assigned a *lictor*, who would be a guardian and/or an attendant of a public magistrate, a privilege that the Senate had only attributed to the Vestal Virgins since 42 BC, since Livia was linked to the goddess Vesta, who was devoted to the home, as well as Pietas, who would be a religious personification of devotion to the State and the family. In addition, having had a *lictor* added a masculine character to her, fitting her to her new public activity, and her Vestal attributes gave her a character of purity and a distinguished matron (Harvey, 2020, p. 182-183), related to her *pudicitia*.

In the 20s AD, she and Julia were associated with the cult of Hestia, the Greek goddess equivalent to the Roman Vesta (Barrett, 2002, p. 144). Elements such as the sceptre, the *patera*, the veil veiling the head, as well as their seated images, show an iconography linked to the goddess Vesta, contributing to her position as priestess and mother (Harvey, 2020, p. 184), as can be seen in the image of the coin, from the time of Tiberius, with Livia on its reverse:

Figure 34 – Silver tetradrachm[142], from AD 14 - 37, 14.43 g, from Tarsus, Turkey, from the rule of Tiberius, with his laureate bust facing right on the obverse and caption: ΣΕΒΑΣΤΟΥ ΤΙΒΕΡΙΟΥ ΚΑΙΣΑΡΟΣ, transliteration SEBASTOU TIBERIOU KAISAROS (From Tiberius Caesar Augustus[143]); on the reverse is Livia as Hera, seated on a throne facing right, holding ears of corn and poppies, with caption: ΣΕΒΑΣΤΗΣ ΙΟΥΛΙΑΣ ΗΡΑΣ ΜΗΤΡ, transliteration: SEBASTES IOULIAS ERAS METR (Julia Augusta, mother Hera[144])

Source: © The Trustees of the British Museum

This tetradrachm shows Tiberius on the most important side of the coin, the obverse, with his bust turned to the right and laureate, emphasising his glories. On the reverse, a secondary female figure appears, with characteristics of the goddess Hera and who seems to be representing Livia. According to Harvey, she also appears to be Demeter/Ceres by the grain and poppies, symbols linked to fertility, with maternal roles (Harvey, 2020, p. 137 and 174). Livia was celebrated as the "new Hera" in Assos and Pergamum, "new Isis" in Egypt, "new Aphrodite" in Cyprus and as the "new Hestia Demeter" in Lampsacus (Spaeth, 1996, p. 169-170 apud Harvey, 2020, p. 138-139).

The coin shows Tiberius' power and a tribute to his mother, Livia, in order to demonstrate family harmony and his mother's virtues, as a Roman matron, since the ears of corn she holds may be linked to fertility and abundance, often agricultural, and poppies are a symbol linked to death, common in figures of burial altars, which reveals that she could still be watching over the death of her husband, Augustus. This first coin of Livia associated with goddesses can be compared with another coin of the goddess Vesta, from the time of Caligula, which has similar elements, such

---

[142] Reference number: 1970,0909,225. Bibliography: RPC1 / Roman provincial coinage. Vol.1, From the death of Caesar to the death of Vitellius (44 BC-AD 69) (4005). Available at: https://www.britishmuseum.org/collection/object/C_1970-0909-225. Accessed: 17 Aug. 2020.
[143] Translation by Juarez Oliveira.
[144] Translation made by the author.

as her seated position, the sceptre, the veiled head and, here, instead of the branch with grains, she is with the *patera*.

Figure 35 – Copper alloy as[145], Rome, AD 40 - 41. Obverse: bust of Caligula, C.CAESAR.DIVI. AVG.PRON.AVG.P.M.TR.P.IIII.P.P (*Gaius Caesar Divi Augusti Pronepos Augustus, Pontifex Maximus, Tribunicia Potestate Quarta, Pater Patriae*[146] = Gaius Caesar, great-grandson of the divine Augustus, Supreme Pontiff, holder of the *tribunicia* power for the fourth time, father of the nation[147]). Reverse: Vesta and S C (Senatus Consultum = minted with the consent of the Senate[148]

Source: © The Trustees of the British Museum

Vesta was one of the most honoured Roman deities, being a special protector of the family hearth and worshipped by the Roman State; moreover, when worshipped individually, she was like a guardian of family life. She was minted on coins of various emperors and appears as a matron holding a *patera* and a sceptre, or a torch, a *simpulum*[149] or a *Palladium*. The caption commonly appearing with her is MATER. She was the Greek Hestia, who rarely appeared on provincial coinage, with the exception of the city of Maeonia in Lydia, where coins were minted with the goddess and her temple (Sear, 2000, p. 36).

---

[145] R.6458. Number in the C&M catalogue: RE1 (158) (73) (158). Bibliographic references: RE1 / Coins of the Roman Empire in the British Museum, vol. 1: Augustus to Vitellius (73, p. 158), BER1 / The Roman Imperial Coinage, vol. 1 (54, p. 111), NM 2003.249 (BMC 45 - 8). RIC 38. BMCRE 46. CBN 54. C 27. *[Rome, AD 37 - 8]*.

[146] *Pater Patriae*, appears as P P in coin captions. This honorable title, which means "father of the homeland", was conferred on Augustus in 2 BC, and was assumed by most of his successors, but not all, as Tiberius did, and others only accepted it when he was already ruling for some years, like Hadrian and Marcus Aurelius (Saer, 2000, p. 73).

[147] Available at: https://en.numista.com/catalogue/pieces247171.html. Accessed: 21 July 2021.

[148] The state cult of Vesta had an association with the emperor as *Pontifex Maximus*. Available at: https://www.britishmuseum.org/collection/object/C_R-6458. Accessed: 21 July 2021.

[149] A small ladle for use in sacrifices. Available at: http://www.perseus.tufts.edu/hopper/resolveform?type=exact&lookup=simpulum&lang=la. Accessed: 22 Aug. 2022.

It seems that the fact that Livia was linked to a religious environment, with attributes granted only to the Vestal Virgins, was a way of "institutionalising"[150] her activities and acts within the State. The association of Livia with Vesta seems to have been prudent, since she was the goddess of the home or hearth, her temple next to the Regia[151], in the forum, kept a sacred fire and the Vestal Virgins protected it. As the name implies, the Vestal Virgins were to be chaste during their period of service, which was usually thirty years, after which they were free to marry. During the period of service, they were not under the authority of any *paterfamilias*, but under the responsibility of the Pontiff Maximus, who could sentence them to death if they violated their chastity, but it seems that this was a rare imposition (Barrett, 2002, p. 142).

Unlike imperial women, or any other Roman women, the Vestal Virgins had some distinctive privileges, such as the fact that they were sacrosanct, which made them inviolable; they could do anything without the consent of a guardian; they had some well-established ancient rights, as well as the right not to be guardians, which was guaranteed by the *Law of the Twelve Tables*; but they also had more recent rights, such as the use of a *lictor*, which they gained, in 42 BC, from the members of the Second Triumvirate (Cass. Dio, *Roman History* 47.19.4). Augustus aggrandised the privileges of the Vestals and at the same time they performed various kinds of honours and celebrations to the emperor, such as their participation in the annual birthday sacrifices in dedication to the *Ara Pacis* (Suet. *Aug.* 31.3 and 44.3; Cass. Dio, *Roman History* 56.10.3).

Another privilege of the Vestal Virgins was the fact that they could attend events in lower seats in the theatre, which should have a privileged view; moreover, in AD 9, they were granted the same right as women who had three children, *ius trium liberorum*. It is worth adding that Augustus asked for a temple dedicated to Vesta to be built on the Palatine, demonstrating how important the cult of Vesta was to the emperor. Perhaps Augustus used Livia's association with Vesta to reinforce the image of his wife as a symbol of chastity and an appropriate representative of the household, the *princeps* and the home of a nation (Barrett, 2002, p. 143). In this way, the public presentation of these women was to be linked to a feminine morality that imposed itself on all parts of the body and exercised continuity through coercion in terms of attire and hairstyles. The antagonistic principles of masculine and feminine identity were inscribed in permanent ways of

---

[150] The word "institutionalisation" appears here in inverted commas because it was not used in Antiquity in the specific case of women. However, the use is made only for didactic purposes.

[151] *regina sacrorum*, the wife of *rex sacrorum* (Boatwright, 2011, p. 112).

using the body or maintaining a posture (Bourdieu, 1998, p. 36), so that such agencies resulted in a naturalisation of ethics.

Moreover, Augustus could have had the idea that his family was the empire, as something unique, a thought that would not fail to exalt Livia, to place her in public and benevolent activities, which demonstrated the unity of the entire imperial family with the rest of the empire. One proof of this unity would be the Palatine itself, which was not like the Forum, or simply a public space, but was the emperor's home, the space of his family and his private life. However, Milnor points out that it incorporated a certain domesticity as a public figure and encouraged representations of the women of the imperial family. The Palatine was a complex construction that, in addition to its home, was a civic space, being a place that allocated the feminine, but on the other hand, was not intended for women (Milnor, 2005, p. 53), which demonstrated that gender and space could be something complex.

However, with preconceived ideas about Roman women, this ideal did not take hold in Tiberius' government, since the tensions of power and gender were already strong in this period. This was because, in a patriarchal society, virility, in its ethical aspect, as a quiddity of *vir, virtus*, highlights a question of honour that leads men to want to experience everything related to the principle of preserving and increasing honour, which is inseparable from physical virility, related to sexual potency (Bourdieu, 1998, p. 20), which is also charged from men. In addition, in Roman society, there was a sexual differentiation that established a link between the phallus and the *logos*; to put in another way, the male body was part of the uses of the public and the active, he stood up, took the word publicly, actions that were monopolised by men. On the other hand, women were expected to stay away from public places or to renounce public activities and even the public use of their own faces, as well as their words. Antagonistic relations, such as those of the elite in Roman society, always result in relations of domination, in which the practices and representations of the two sexes are by no means symmetrical. Seeing this, social relations of domination are embodied in a clearly differentiated *habitus* (Bourdieu, 1998, p. 26-34), in which the risk of investing the difference between the sexes, driven by a universal explanatory force, is always present (Chartier, 1995, p. 39).

The restoration of the shrine of Bona Dea highlights Livia's connection with Vestal rituals, adding to the title Augustus bestowed on her of sacrosanct[152], which also was conferred on Octavia. During the Republic, women did not have political powers, but they did have social, economic and religious powers. During married life, they also had the priesthood and public rites in which men and women of the elite could participate. The religious ceremonies in which they participated in the public sphere were rites that took place in favour of Rome and the empire. Within these sacrosanct roles, women reinforced the establishment of order. Private female duties, such as childbearing and child-rearing, were projected into the public sphere by religious ceremonies performed by matrons and Vestals. In this sense, many of these rituals emphasised the cycle of agriculture, which was important for fertility and the continuation of life. In fact, women maintained Rome through religiosity, having the rituals as crucial to the maintenance of the State, and women were important to perform such cults inside and outside Rome. However, the emergence of an imperialist Republic and then the Empire changed the roles of women, especially the Roman elite (Takács, 2008, p. xix-xx). It was still customary to link these women of the Principality to the religious sphere, in order to differentiate them from a direct role in the public sphere.

Livia gained the privilege of the *ius (trium) liberorum*, which was only granted to her on the death of her son, Drusus. Three other Vestal privileges were conferred on her after Augustus' death: the *lictor*, in AD 14; the *carpentum*, in AD 22; and the right to sit in the lower seats of the theatre, in AD 23 (Barrett, 2002, p. 143-144).

After Livia, other imperial women gained Vestal rights, just as Caligula granted Vestal privileges to his grandmother, Antonia. In addition, Claudius granted Messalina the right to the Vestals' low seats in the theatre, as well

---

[152] The *flaminicae* was a type of priestess, and the *regina sacrorum* was the queen of sacred rites. Both were women of the Roman elite who shared duties with their husbands, *flamines* and *rex sacrorum*. In Rome, the *flamines* formed the college of pontiffs with the *rex sacrorum*, who was the pontiff, and six Vestals. In relation to the Senate, this college interpreted the sacred law in the service of the Senate. The *flaminate* was ancient and its beginnings dated back to the monarchy. Augustus revised the *flaminate*, as he did the Roman religion. He added a *flamen*, a priest of Augustus and the imperial household (*domus Augusta*) to the list of these priests. The reason was to offer equestrian members another opportunity to engage in religious activities, which was traditional for the components of the Senate. Most inscriptions honoured women in the position of *flaminica* in provinces where today are Portugal, Spain, and North Africa, which demonstrates a pattern of worship. Being part of the *flaminate* was a family affair, with provincial priests being children of *flamines* or *flaminicae* or wives of men who held the *flaminate* (Takács, 2008, p. 112). In the Empire the *flaminica* no longer had to be the wife of the *flamen*. However, previously, divorce was not allowed between them. The *regina sacrorum* also had public obligations, performed in the Regia. They made sacrifices to Juno on special days of the Roman month and their husbands sacrificed to Jupiter. The *flaminica dialis* wore special clothes and had to follow various prohibitions probably designed to protect their purity. These matrons and the Vestals could conduct rites together for the worship of the "great goddess", Bona Dea (Holland, 2012, p. 206-207).

as the use of the *carpentum* (Cass. Dio, *Roman History* 59.3.4 and 60.22.2). Furthermore, it can be noted that the *carpentum* appeared on coins that emphasised Agrippina Major and Agrippina Minor, suggesting that they both enjoyed this right, or, in the case of Agrippina Major, signified a posthumous tribute that her son Caligula made in her name.

With regard to religiosity, it is also observed that the first women to be represented on coins appeared with characteristics or personifications of goddesses, having been differentiated as mortal women due to some elements such as the type of hair, which can be identified on coins of Fulvia and Livia. This information was associated with the fact that the attempt to "institutionalise" imperial women, such as Livia, in order to formalise their activities before the State, occurred in such a way as to associate them with Vestal activities, in other words, religious ones. Religion was the only opportunity to better understand the social importance of women, since women were not allowed in the public sphere, and they were seen as an instrument for maintaining social stability through the sacred (Takács, 2008, p. xxi).

In this regard, there is the suggestion that, in order to hold a public position, or to raise the hypothesis of a possible "institutionalisation", women of the Roman elite had to be associated with a status that could represent and keep an aspect linked to *pudicitia,* since this fact affirms an attempt to control and even limit the State and the emperor in the face of female actions, indicating the existence of a male and controlling power, mediated by the agency of a structure of thought articulated and constructed throughout history and facts that have culturally amalgamated and helped to mould a conception restricted to the elite women of that society, resulting in the agency of conceptions, actions and cultural ideas for the maintenance of certain power and gender relations.

Furthermore, the hypothesis that Augustus intended to convey that the imperial family would be the empire could have led to Livia being linked to public services, mainly as a benefactor, during the life of the first *princeps*. This same idea could have been absorbed and realised by the Senate, which, in an attempt to continue Augustus' ideal, voted to grant several titles to Livia after the ruler's death. Thus, even if he denied some titles to Livia, Tiberius, who was resistant to Livia's institutional and public work, needed the Senate to rule, which could have made him accept the granting of some privileges to his mother that sometimes did not affect him, especially if she was linked to Vestal activities, resulting in a political strategy that could demonstrate the haughtiness of the imperial family to preserve senatorial spirits.

The appearance of Livia on the coins of the western provinces came about, during the rule of Tiberius, following patterns from the mints of Rome. The provinces of Spain and Africa are examples of places that copied the models of Rome, as well as the types of seated Livia, Salus, Pietas and Iustitia. The most interesting thing is that Livia was referred to on these provincial coins in a direct way, which was not the case of Roman coins (Harvey, 2020, p. 118), in which Livia appears associated with the emperors, Augustus or Tiberius, or as the personification of some goddess.

It should be kept in mind that the changes in the status of these women did not only occur locally but were also linked to the spatial relations in which they governed the interactions of other provincial regions and localities (Goddard, 2000, p. 1). The implication of this involved the coining of the image of these women and the softening of acceptance of them into an object that carried the reality of contemporary power. However, provincial gender identities could cover other types of limits, such as something already defined in relation to female representativeness, or transformed, which could even be seen in a way that was not the most appropriate by the central power at first, but which was gradually accepted, since these images could have brought privileged opportunities to the imperial government with the new female conduct in their participation in Patronage activities in these regions.

Livia was often identified as Pax/Ceres in the provinces. The coin representation of Pax during the rule of Tiberius was probably intended to represent her as *Arae Cereris Matris* and *Opis Augustae*, as she would have been associated with the deity of agricultural abundance (Grether, 1946, p. 226-227 and 238). The intrinsic conception related to victory in the Roman thought was peace, which was what followed military success and its conquests. In Roman art, Pax appears holding an olive branch. Sometimes she appears on other implements such as caduceus and sceptre. During the Imperial period, she was related to Concordia and Securitas, which also signified peace and governmental stability. Pax could appear seated holding an olive branch and a sceptre, attributes that also appeared with Concordia, which was tied to military stability, border campaigns, linked to the collective conscious in times of war, but was also used in times of relative peace, appearing on coins as an appeal and political aspiration (Elkins, 2017, p. 34 and 50). Securitas was associated with trust and held a *patera* and a sceptre, often appearing reclining on a column, with her legs crossed or sitting at ease (Sear, 2000, p. 40).

Coins of Augustus, from 2 BC to AD 14, had on their reverse the image of a seated figure holding ears of corn and a sceptre, which continued to appear in other later governments, as well as in that of Tiberius and Claudius, when Livia would have already been deified (Grether, 1946, p. 226-227 and 238). In Augustus, the figure does not bear Livia's name, so there is doubt as to whether she was her representative or not, but in the other governments she appeared as Julia Augusta. The symbolism of female fertility and the triumph of imperial Rome was common in monuments of the imperial family, which marked the ideology of Augustus, providing a message of the identity of women in the imperial family, their influences, and their bodies. An example is the *Ara Pacis*, which represents imperial women and children together with men, a gesture that was supposed to connect their reproductive bodies (Milnor, 2005, p. 57).

Figure 36 – Aureus[153], Roman Empire, Lugdunum, dated AD 13 - 14, 7.88 g. Obverse: Augustus laureate head to the right, CAESAR AVGVSTVS.DIVI F PATER PATRIAE (*Caesar Augustus Divi Filius Pater Patriae* = Augustus, father of the homeland, son of the divine Caesar[154]). Reverse: draped female figure seated on right, holding a sceptre in right hand and a bunch of corn cobs in left hand, PONTIF.MAXIM (*Pontifex Maximus* = Supreme Pontiff)

Source: © The Trustees of the British Museum

This aureus is the only coin to name Augustus *pontifex maximus* on the reverse, next to a seated female figure holding a sceptre and a branch of grains, reminiscent of Pax, or Livia as Pax. If it is indeed Livia, this would be the only depiction of her on coins of Augustus. However, there is no caption to identify her. Livia, in the form of Pax/Ceres, appears under her proper name on a coin of the period of Claudius, after she had been deified, identified as DIVA AVGVSTA (RIC 12 *Claudius* 101; Wood, 2001, p. 88), but

---

[153] Museum number: 1867,0101,612; RE1 / Coins of the Roman Empire in the British Museum, vol. 1: Augustus to Vitellius (544, p. 91); BER1 / The Roman Imperial Coinage, vol. 1 (219, p. 56); registration number: 1867,0101,612; C&M catalogue number: RE1 (91) (544) (91). Available at: https://www.britishmuseum.org/collection/object/C_1867-0101-612. Accessed: 16 May 2022. Can be found under RIC 1 identification² 219.
[154] Translation made by the author.

she had already begun to appear on coins in the period of Tiberius (Rowan, 2019, p. 129-130) as Salus Augusta and other denominations.

The seated figure from the time of the first *princeps* demonstrates that he had a high regard for gestures and symbolic elements, which carried over into later governments. Symbols in their basic form are a potent instrument of power, which can both evoke what it represents and subtly bring to the fore a host of other technically unrelated images and ideas. In this sense, domesticity was one such symbol that was important to Augustus, which can emphasise an idea of the *princeps*' propagandistic articulation. However, the symbolic elements also served to mask a deeper and less personal politics. In another way, it seems that the symbolic role that emerged from the imperial discourse on private life was indispensable for Augustus (Milnor, 2005, p. 47-48). The seated female figure with accompanying elements seems to have been of great importance for the legitimisation of power, as it is repeated in later governments, even after Livia's death.

Figure 37 – Aureus[155], AD 14 - 37, 19.4 mm diameter, 7.68 g, from Lungdunum, rule of Tiberius. Obverse: laureate bust of Tiberius on right, TI CAESAR DIVI AVG F AVGVSTVS (*Tiberius Caesar Divi Augustus Fili Augustus* = Tiberius Caesar Augustus, son of the divine Augustus[156]). Reverse: female figure, which could probably be Livia, seated, facing right, with a plant branch in her left hand and a sceptre in her right, caption: PONTIF MAXIM (*Pondifex Maximus* = Supreme Pontiff[157])

Source: © KBR *cabinet des monnais et médailles*

---

[155] Bibliography: RIC I² 29; BMC 46. Available at: https://opac.kbr.be/LIBRARY/doc/SYRACUSE/20734421. Accessed: 1 Aug. 2022.
[156] Translation made by the author.
[157] Translation made by the author.

Figure 38 – Denarius[158], AD 14 - 37, from Lungdunum, Tiberius' rule, 3.73g, 18.1 mm diameter. Obverse: laureate bust of Tiberius on right, TI CAESAR DI[VI] [AV]GVSTVS [F] (*Tiberius Caesar Divi Augustus fili* = Tiberius Caesar son of the divine Augustus[159]). Reverse: female figure, who could probably be Livia, seated, facing to the right, with a plant branch in her left hand and a sceptre in her right, caption: PONTIF MAXIM (*Pontifex Maximus* = Supreme Pontiff[160])

Source: © KBR *cabinet des monnaies et médailles*

On the aureus and denarius of Tiberius' rule, the emperor is honoured as *divus*, due to his predecessor, adoptive father, Augustus. On the reverse is the image of Livia, reminiscent of Pax/Ceres, again she is associated with a goddess, with a branch of grains in her left hand, which may be linked to her son's governmental prosperity, fertility and agricultural abundance, as well as productivity and success in hierarchical transmission; and a sceptre in her right hand. On the denarius, a tiara is observed that could link it to goddesses such as Vesta. Otherwise, the coin does not mention her name in its captions.

The coins show a tribute to the rule of her son Tiberius, who also celebrates that his mother was essential for him to come to power, considering the female figure as Livia. According to Harvey, Livia seated with the attribute of Pax, with an olive branch, or Ceres, with the ears of grains, demonstrates her role as mother of the imperial family and her stable presence in the imperial dynasty, and on Lepcis Magna, Colonia Romula and Tarsus she was referred to directly as mother (Harvey, 2020, p. 132-134). For Barrett, the seated female figure that appears in Tiberius' rule exchanges the sceptre for a spear and the ears are grains of wheat (Barrett, 2002, p. 141). Elkins points out that the coin of Pax could appear with the caption PAX AVGVSTI. Often, Pax appeared on the reverse of coins when a new emperor came to power, with the intention of a smooth transition from

---

[158] Bibliography: RIC I² 30; BMC 34. Available at: https://opac.kbr.be/LIBRARY/doc/SYRACUSE/20734429. Accessed: 1 Aug. 2022.
[159] Translation made by the author.
[160] Translation made by the author.

an emperor to another, as in the case of the passage from Augustus to Tiberius and even in times of peace (Elkins, 2017, p. 35-36 and 50).

Fortuna also appeared as a seated female figure, who could be shown holding a rudder, a cornucopia, or resting on a globe, sometimes with a wheel at her side, sometimes with an olive branch or a *patera* (Sear, 2000, p. 38; Elkins, 2017, p. 69-70). Its meaning would be linked to the fortune that flowed from the emperor and guided him. She could also appear seated and holding branches of wheat and a sceptre. She could denote the affluence of the Roman people. However, wheat was something linked to the symbolism of Ceres and the supply of grain. The sceptre or *pertica* could be a measuring rod, usually associated with *aequitas*, which symbolised the measurement of justice (Elkins, 2017, p. 69-70).

Figure 39 – Coin[161], 15 - 16 BC, 11.93 g, 29.1 mm diameter, Tiberius' rule, Rome. Obverse: radiated head of Augustus, a thunderbolt in front of him and a star over his head, [DI]VVS AVGVSTVVS PATER (Augustus, divine father[162]). Reverse: draped figure of Livia (?) seated with a *patera* in her right hand and a sceptre in her left hand, S C (*Senatus Consultum*)

Source: © KBR *cabinet des monnais et médailles*

On the last case, a different type of coin of Tiberius can be seen with the female figure on its reverse. Augustus appears on the obverse with his head radiating to the left, a thunderbolt in front of him and a star above his head. While the female figure, who could be Livia, is seated on the right with a *patera* in her right hand and a sceptre in her left and her head seems to be veiled with a tiara, reminiscent of Vesta. The figure of seated Livia has also been found on coins from Sinop, Pontus, Cyprus, Knossos, Keta, and Tarsus in Syria. With the exception of Sinop, all the minting sites were

---

[161] Bibliography: RIC I² 72; BMC 151. Available at: https://opac.kbr.be/LIBRARY/doc/SYRACUSE/20734397. Accessed: 1 Aug. 2022.
[162] Translation made by the author.

Roman *coloniae* (Harvey, 2020, p. 117). However, what can be noted is that there was a tendency for the provinces to identify Livia as the seated female figure (Barrett, 2002, p. 142).

The North African city of Lepcis Magna, where a colossus head (68 cm) of Livia was found, associated with the temple of Augustus and Rome in its forum (Barrett, 2002, p. 208), struck coins of her with the title Augusta. The names and titles by which Livia was referred to on coins, during the reign of Augustus and Tiberius, were standardised and reflected her status as the most prominent woman in the imperial family and her role as *materfamilias*. In other parts of the Empire, honours were made to Livia by referring to her as divine and directly associating her with goddesses such as Hera/Juno. Some silver coin captions from Syria commemorate Livia as Hera and mother, with sayings such as "Augusta Hera mother" or on a bronze dupondius, from Lepcis Magna, which referred to her as AVGVSTA MATER PATRIA(e), "Augusta mother of the homeland", following Augustus, who gained the title of *pater patriae*, "father of the homeland", in 2 BC (Harvey, 2020, p. 3-9, 121 and 130), and the title appeared on coins minted in the same year (Rowan, 2019, p. 128).

Juno was the sister and consort of Jupiter and represented as a tall matron, both seated or standing, holding a *patera* and sceptre. She was often accompanied by a peacock when it was related to posthumous matters of the empress. The animal could appear alone, standing or flying, carrying the posthumous Augusta to heaven (the same function as Jupiter in relation to the deified emperor). The temple of Juno Moneta on the Capitoline Hill is of paramount importance from a numismatic point of view, as there was a mint in Republican times. Its titles correspond to REGINA, LVCINA (referring to her role as a deity present during births), CONSERVATRIX and VICTRIX. Representations of Hera in the Roman provinces are less frequent than those of her consort Zeus, appearing in Chalcis, in Euboea and on mints of Bithynia, on a tetradrachm of Nero, from Alexandria, with the veiled bust of Argos (Hera Argeia) (Sear, 2000, p. 30).

Livia's connection with Juno concerns the fact that the goddess was qualified at the beginning of her mythical existence by various epithets, which would be linked to multiple functions. The first to be linked to her was *Juno Feretria*, or the warrior; then *Juno Sospita*, or the protector from enemy attacks; soon after, *Juno Regina*, or the one who exercises guardianship over the Roman people. Over time, such evocations lost their importance, and the cult of the so-called *Juno Lucina* was carried out, which would be the one who helped at the time of childbirth. This goddess was honoured by women on the most important women's festival of the calendar, called *Matronalia*, in which men were not allowed. Therefore, there was another family feast to honour her when women received gifts from their husbands. The first feast came about to remember the event that occurred with the Sabines, in which they managed to mediate peace between men, at the time of the mythical Romulus. This goddess came to emphasise maternal activities in the Roman imagination. The religious imaginary constructed the image of the feminine from the constitution of the image of the goddess and the feast, which exalted the traditional virtues attributed to women in their maternal roles, motherhood being the most important activity conferred on women (Cid López, 2011, p. 61).

In particular, the worship of *Juno Sospita* in Latium was done by a cult composed of women and was related to fertility. In this cult, a virgin, probably a priestess of Juno, would go down to the sacred goddess' den to make food and an offering to the ancient serpent, who would be starving after a long winter. If the virgin returned unharmed, she was recognised as the one who made the chaste offering. The farmers would consider that she had been successful and such an act would be seen as an omen for a fruitful year. What was fundamental to the cult was the virgin's purity, not her fertility (Schultz, 2006, p. 22-28). *Juno Sospita* also emphasises the military aspect and she may appear with helmet, shield, and spear. Several Roman deities had virile aspects, such as the goddess of the hunt, Diana, who was usually depicted with a spear and shield, and was associated with Agrippina Minor later; with the goddess of war Bellona; and with Minerva (Holland, 2012, p. 210).

The best reference to Livia came from Colonia Romula in Spain, which alluded to her as IVLIA AVGVSTA GENETRIX ORBIS[163], meaning "Julia Augusta, mother of the World" or "founder of the world", with a laurel wreath, which is a masculine symbol, reflecting power, stability and success, being the first woman to wear it, and may mention that it elevated her to the status of *femina princeps,* which refers to Livia's greatness, in addition to her monumental personification on a coin. In addition, there is the association with Venus Genetrix, the ancestral goddess of the *gens Iulia*, whose cult was fundamental for imperial dynastic perpetuation, with connotations with Cybele and Magna Mater. Moreover, the crescent moon below her neck

---

[163] Even Ovid does not call Livia *mater*, but *genetrix* (Barrett, 2002, p. 194).

could be linked to Dea Caelestis, a goddess linked to the stars, the sun, and the moon (Barrett, 2002, p. 275 apud Harvey, 2020, p. 130, 142 and 174), or linked with the association of Diana with the crescent moon, as was done, later, on coins of Agrippina Minor, in Balanea, Syria, Middle East.

Figure 40 – Dupondius[164] from Colonia Romula, Spain, dated AD 15 - 16, 23.44 g, on its obverse is the bust of Augustus, facing right, with a six-rayed star on its top and thunderbolts to its right, with caption: DIVI AVG COL ROM PERM (*Divi Augustus Colonia Romula Permisso*[165] = with the permission of the Divine Augustus to Colonia Romula[166]); on its reverse is the bust of Livia, facing left, with a crescent globe, with caption: IVLIA AVGVUSTA GENETRIX ORBIS (Julia Augusta, mother of the world[167])

Source: Courtesy of WildWinds

This dupondius is a celebration of the couple Augustus and Augusta, where on the obverse is shown Augustus divinised and on the reverse Livia, who is not yet a divine pair with Augustus, but is represented with high honour as the "mother of the world", not behind Augustus himself, but representing the one who added status to the divine category of her husband and emperor. What is interesting about this coin is the depiction of the round world below Livia's bust and, above it, a crescent moon. The caption DIVI AVG COL ROM PERM refers to the *colonia*'s permission to mint such a coin, as well as carrying celestial connotations linked to Cybele, or Magna Mater and Dea Caelestis (Harvey, 2020, p. 167). This permission stamped on coins could be related to Rome's control of the provinces (Weiss, 2005, p. 57), since provincial coins tended to follow Rome's models, but also added local elements.

---

[164] Reference: RPC 73; Vives pl. CLXVII, 2; Burgos 1587; SNG Copenhagen 421. Available at: https://www.wildwinds.com/coins/ric/livia/i.html; https://www.wildwinds.com/coins/ric/livia/RPC_0073.jpg; and https://www.wildwinds.com/coins/ric/livia/RPC_0073.txt. Accessed: 17 Aug. 2020.
[165] Available at: https://www.cgb.fr/tibere-drusus-et-germanicus-as-tb,bpv_268941,a.html. Accessed: 18 Aug. 2020.
[166] Translation made by the author.
[167] Translation made by the author.

Choices about how coins should be minted could be related to the local elite, their organisation, and their decisions, and how these were made, as well as how these choices should be placed in public documents. In this way, coinage should be taken as part of a city's self-government and then placed within a larger context of cities. Coins cannot be considered in isolation, but as part of a unitary living reality. Consequently, city coins present various needs to be shown and were aimed at forming a means of identity propagation on various levels, always with a stabilising effect (Weiss, 2005, p. 58).

However, central approval seemed to be essential, or the provincial coins might proceed with something that would fit the references of the central power. It was common in the provinces of Lusitania and Baetica for the captions to appear with PERMISSV CAES(ARIS) AVG(VSTI); and in *colonia* Berytus, Syria, as PERMISSV and the name of a consular *legatus Augusti*. Another example would be in the "senatorial" province of Africa, where coins appear with PERMISSV and the names of five proconsuls, in a *colonia*. During the Domitilian period, this type of coin appeared in Achaia, also a *colonia*; in Corinth, with the caption PERM(isso) IMP(eratoris); and in the *Patrae* INDVGENTIAE AVG(usti) MONETA INPETRATA; as well as two more cities in Africa, Cercina and Thaena, with PERMISSV, where both were *civitates liberae*. This demonstrates that in various parts of the empire coinage could appear with similar aspects. The differentiation could be in the continuation or not of this type of coin, as well as the reception, which could contrast in places in the East and West. Weiss states that there could be false declarations of permission and otherwise some would have special authorisation from Rome, such as tridrachms and tetradrachms in Cilician cities under Trajan, Hadrian, and Caracalla; or in coins from Amisus under Hadrian (Weiss, 2005, p. 59).

Provincial coins allow us to notice the projection and contrast with the imperial ideology, in which these examples often seem to imitate the elements of the coinages of Rome, but also end up including regional elements. Furthermore, it should be questioned how these choices should be made and what the construction of a collective identity would look like with reference to some fundamental family categories. Hence, it is necessary to take into account aspects such as religion, representations of the past, space, choice of language, degree of identity and/or connectivity with the imperial power (Howgego, 2005, p. 2).

The coins illustrate a fundamental process of mental integration in the provincial cities of the Empire, where the ruling elite composed the *cives romani*. The political gain for these cities in honouring the central government could be immense by supporting imperial intentions or simply by being involved with the aspirations of the local elite, and emperors could intervene and regulate any need (Weiss, 2005, p. 68), considering the Roman government's acts of evergetism.

In the western provinces, the pattern in which Livia was veiled, seated on a throne, holding a *patera* and a sceptre also appeared. Seated Livia is the most recurrent type in Africa. In other localities, there is a variation on her figure, as well as that of Emerita, Spain, which appears with the caption of IVLIA AVGVSTA, but with her head uncovered, holding a torch, instead of the sceptre and an ear of grains. A model from Ithaca features Livia seated, in a more relaxed manner, for its associations with Ceres and Juno. In Emerita, the Salus type also varies its caption to PERM(isso) AVGVSTI SALUS AVGVSTA and of the type that Livia appears seated the caption is C(olonia) A(ugusta) E(merita) IVLIA AVGVSTA.

Like a *colonia*, but unlike Rome, Eremita named its coins directly after Livia, as did the Pietas type, minted in Caesaraugusta, Spain, which includes the caption AUGUSTA. In addition, the veiled type is positioned to the left, as opposed to the right, and is associated with Juno, with the caption THAPSUM IVN(oni). Another model in which Livia appears veiled is that of Panormus, Sicily, like Pietas, but with a crown of grains of Ceres, with the caption AVGVS(ta) and other differentiations follow when the provinces vary. The figure of seated Livia on the aureus and denarius minted at Lugdunum, Gaul, in the time of Augustus, must have served as a model for those minted in the time of Tiberius. Her personality was always associated in a divine way on coins and in statues, because, besides Salus, she was linked to Venus and Juno, even after her death and deification (Harvey, 2020, p. 5 and 118-120).

The reception of Livia's coins and their circulation should be significant for the "propaganda of the imperial family", showing public and provincial agency in promptly manifesting and honouring her. The appearance of the representation of these women probably came to fulfil some of the imperial purposes and, in relation to Livia's image, it seems to have worked. However, it is not possible to know what kind of reception was taken by each female image, but the number of representations and the longevity of Livia's images, for example, demonstrate the extreme acceptability of her honour, both to political institutions such as the Senate, which allowed the minting of her coins, and to the public, evidenced by the minting of these objects in provinces of the East and West, as well as the existence of other types of reproductions of her, such as statues.

However, the variety in the quality of coins of Livia sometimes changed dramatically from mint to mint, with some striking her in great detail, as did the depiction of Livia as Salus made in Rome. The image of Livia on these coins can accurately be compared with her representation in sculpture, and in the latter type of art it is more favourable to find a caption with her name. Nevertheless, there are some coins that were not minted with such accuracy, even showing a comical drawing of the honoured woman, like those minted in Knossos.

Livia's images were part of an extensive visual programme, but this does not mean that her images were made as she really looked, but with elements that characterised her. Thus, these figures followed some signs that were used to compose a certain pattern, in other words, a model of image elements, such as the type of hair commonly used in her representation, for example, in addition to facial features, clothing, or those that only reveal the bust (draped or naked), adding adornments such as diadems, jewellery, among others. Draped busts commonly occurred more for women than for men (Harvey, 2020, p. 66-67).

Another coin from Byzantium, struck during the rule of Tiberius, commemorates Divus Augustus, with a crown or radiate on the obverse, as well as divinised, secured by the caption ΘΕΟΣ ΣΕΒΑΣΤΟΣ. On the reverse is the bust of Livia, who is also in a divine form, indicated by the caption ΘΕΑ ΣΕΒΑΣΤΑ. The couple appear with their divine titles in Greek, celebrating Augustus and Livia as divine parents of the empire and anticipating Livia's eventual deification, although this honour was denied by Tiberius (Harvey, 2020, p. 178).

Figure 41 – Silver[168] coin, from Byzantium, Thrace, Asia, Marmara region, Istanbul, dated ca. AD 20 - 29, 6.27 g, with bust of Divus Augustus, radiated facing left, with caption: ΘΕΟΣ ΣΕΒΑΣΤΟΣ, caption transliteration: SEBASTOS THEOS (God Augustus[169]). On the reverse is the bust of Livia also divinised, facing right, with caption: ΘΕΑ ΣΕΒΑΣΤΑ/.BYZ., caption transliteration: SEBASTA THEA/.BUZ (Goddess Augusta. Byz[antium][170])

Source: © The Trustees of the British Museum

Regarding this and other provincial coins, it is worth mentioning that the fact that the Roman Empire encompassed a large proportion of languages demonstrates that Latin and Greek were linked to an emphatic identity proportion, an idea that should be well established, since in some contexts, as in others, the choice of language to express communal identity needs did not accurately reflect the language of such a people. In relation to the Roman Empire, the incidence of captions on coins, their content and language, such as the alphabet and the style of epigraphy used, may demonstrate important evidence of Roman influences even before the conquest began, and coins minted in Rome could feature Greek captions to be sent for use in Greek-speaking provinces. The use of a language other than Greek and Roman appeared during the period of the Republic and the beginning of the Empire, as well as with Iberian coins, with Iberian or Celtiberian inscriptions, which could signal differences between groups (Woolf, 1994, p. 86-89), which agrees with the thesis that epigraphy showed the differences between groups, language being fundamental to express identity, or it could be due to the fact that the series of coins had only a local circulation. The circulation of coins is a geographical indication that

---

[168] Reference number: 1872,0709.34. C&M catalogue number: GC3 (BMC Greek (Tauric Chersonese) (99) (61) (99). Bibliography: BMC Greek (Tauric Chersonese) / Catalogue of Greek coins: the Tauric Chersonese, Sarmatia, Dacia, Moesia, Thrace, &c. (p99.61) PCR / Principal coins of the Romans: Volume I: The Republic c. 290 - 31 BC; Volume II: The Principate 31 BC - AD 296; Volume III: The Dominate AD 294 - 498. (375A) RPC1 / Roman provincial coinage. Vol.1, From the death of Caesar to the death of Vitellius (44 BC-AD 69) (1779/1). Available at: https://www.britishmuseum.org/collection/object/C_1872-0709-34. Accessed: 9 Sept. 2020.

[169] Translation by Juarez de Oliveira.

[170] Translation by Juarez de Oliveira.

the symbolism that the material contained was accessible to all and could involve the domestic context (Howgego, 2005, p. 12-13 and 17).

Coins are not a direct guide to ethnic identities of communities, but deliberately represent political choices made by those who were in control, just as their iconography should be linked to a political status, reflecting the way in which political discourse was accepted, their identity expressions. Thus, the production of coins was in accordance with the hegemonic political system (Williamson, 2005, p. 19-20 and 24) which reflected on provincial identities.

Returning to gender relations, in three years of estrangement, Tiberius only saw his mother once and for a few hours, but when she fell ill, he did not hurry to visit her and, when she died in AD 29, aged 86, he took so long to appear that her corpse was already beginning to putrefy. Furthermore, he did not allow divine honours to be paid to her, declared her testament null and brought ruin to all the friends and relatives of the deceased (Suet. *Tib.* 51.1). According to Cassius Dio, Tiberius paid her no visit while she was ill, nor did he make any preparations for her honour, except a public funeral. He absolutely forbade her deification. Yet, the Senate ordered mourning for her throughout the year by women, and voted to build an arch in her honour, a distinction that had not been made for any other woman. The author puts it that her importance came from the fact that she saved the lives of several people, raised the children of many and helped others to pay the dowries of their daughters, so they called her "mother of the land" (Cass. Dio, *Roman History* 58.2.1-3).

Her ashes were placed in Augustus' mausoleum and, according to Tacitus, Suetonius and Cassius Dio, Tiberius forbade the deification of his mother. Nevertheless, Tacitus and Suetonius say that he had his reasons for doing so, although it seems that Tiberius' reasons were false, even for the fact that being a priestess of Augustus' cult, Livia would never have implied that she did not wish to be deified, just as she had accepted the title of Augusta and the honour of a public celebration of her birthday. The Senate, on the other hand, was in favour of her deification, but could not overrule the emperor's power, so it ended up voting for any other honour in favour of Livia's memory. Moreover, Tiberius decreed official mourning for Livia, which disqualified her as a divine being, and, as in the case of Augustus, mourning was not decreed (Grether, 1946, p. 245-246). Tacitus mentions that his funeral was simple and that out of the honours voted by the Senate to be granted to Livia, Tiberius authorised few, determining that no religious worship would be enacted (Tac. *Ann.* 5.2).

Tacitus, at her funeral, characterises her as one who was old-fashioned in the purity of her domestic life and more gracious than the women of later times, an imperial mother, and a friendly woman, who, according to him, matched her husband in diplomacy and in concealing her son (Tac. *Ann.* 5.1). What can be seen is that it was common among the Romans to accentuate female gifts to the posthumous woman, since this act had always been done to cherish and to honour the male members of the family rather than the dead woman, in order to highlight proper family relationships, commonly done in epitaphs.

5.1.3. Livia and Claudius

Her popularity continued after her death in AD 29 at the age of 86, where her sculptures survived and continued to be erected during the rule of Emperor Claudius, with many plaques attesting to her honours (Harvey, 2020, p. 4-8). While Tiberius refused to allow the Senate to honour her with official titles, such as "Mother", or to deify her, Caligula was the one who accepted Livia's wish to be deified, but ultimately, he did not put her consecration into effect. Only in AD 41, with Claudius as emperor, in order to strengthen his connection with the imperial house, not only did he undertake new honours to Augustus, but he also deified his grandmother, Livia (Grether, 1946, p. 247-249), who made the minting of coins with her figure more common in Rome (Harvey, 2020, p. 121), in addition to having, in this way, a political guarantee to himself in winning the title of *divus*. Until this period, only three people had been deified, Julius Caesar, Augustus and Drusilla, Caligula's sister. It was probably only after she was deified that coins bearing Livia appeared with the caption *diva,* the cult of Livia began to appear in AD 42, and the minting of her image became more common in Rome.

Figure 42 – Dupondius,[171] dated AD 41 - 50, 16.33 g, from the rule of Claudius, Rome. Obverse: bust of Augustus facing left, caption: DIVVS AUGUSTUS (Divus Augustus) and S C (*Senatus Consultum* = minted with the consent of the Senate). Reverse: Livia seated on the left, with an ear of corn in her right hand and a sceptre in her left, caption: DIVA AUGUSTA

Source: © The Trustees of the British Museum

In this dupondius of Claudius' rule, which marks the consecration of Livia, in AD 41 (Barrett, 2002, p. 222) or AD 42 (Claes, 2013, p. 97), and consequent deification, the seated female figure appears once again, which becomes well identified, following the pattern linked to the figure of Ceres (Barrett, 2002, p. 141 and 210). In addition, there is a celebration of the divine couple, since the deification of his grandmother, Livia, guaranteed him the status of *divus*, demonstrating the past of his own family, which helped him to come to power, legitimising him within his family lineage. The coin has the image of Augustus on the obverse, presented as the main figure, in addition to the figure of Livia on the reverse as a secondary figure, with an ear of corn in her hand, evidencing the wealth, agricultural abundance, fertility and other virtues of a Roman matron, especially the guarantee of a dynastic longevity; the sceptre would be linked to respect, wisdom and the goddess Vesta. It may be added that this material culture could represent the consent of the emperor and the Senate to celebrate the divine cult of Augustus and Julia Augusta. Livia is conceived on this coin as Ceres/Demeter, a representation that also appears on some coins from the government of Tiberius, with similar forms, but with some different attributes, such as the *patera*, the sceptre and, occasionally, with ears of grains in place of the sceptre, as she also appears on coins from the government of Galba (Harvey, 2020, p. 124).

---

[171] Registration number: R.9873. Number in the C&M catalogue: RE1 (195) (224) (195). Bibliography: RE1 / Coins of the Roman Empire in the British Museum, vol. 1: Augustus to Vitellius (224, p. 195) PCR / Principal coins of the Romans: Volume I: The Republic c. 290 - 31 BC; Volume II: The Principate 31 BC - AD 296; Volume III: The Dominate AD 294 - 498. (395) RIC1 / The Roman Imperial Coinage, vol. 1 (101, p. 12). Available at: https://www.britishmuseum.org/collection/object/C_R-9873. Accessed: 17 Aug. 2020.

Figure 43 – Bronze as[172], AD 41 - 50, Rome, rule of Claudius, 9.49 g, 29.7 mm diameter. Obverse: draped bust of Claudius left, TI CLAVDIVS CAESAR [ ] TR P IMP P P (*Tiberius Claudius Caesar [ ] Tribunicia Potestate Imperator Pater Patriae* = Commander Tiberius Claudius *Caesar*, with Tribune Power, Father of the homeland[173]). Reverse: *Libertas* or Livia as Libertas (?) standing, head to the right, S C/LIBERT[A] AVGVSTA (*Senatus Consultum/ Liberta Augusta* = minted with the consent of the Senate/Liberta Augusta[174])

Source: © KBR *cabinet des monnais et médailles*

Figure 44 – Bronze sestertius[175], AD 41 - 50, Rome, rule of Claudius, 24.77 g, 34.5 mm diameter. Obverse: right-facing bust of Claudius, TI CLAVDIVS CAESAR AVG P M TR P IMP (*Tiberius Claudius Caesar Augustus Pontifex Maximus Tribunicia Potestate Pater Patriae Imperator* = Commander Tiberius Claudius Caesar Augustus, Supreme Pontiff, vested in the Tribunicia Power and Father of the homeland[176]). Reverse: Spes or Livia as Spes (?) facing left, holding the tissue of with the left hand and with flower in the right hand, S C/SPES AVGVSTA (*Senatus Consultum/Spes Augusta* = Minted with the consent of the Senate/Hope of Augusta[177])

Source: © KBR *cabinet des monnais et médailles*

---

[172] Bibliography: RIC I² 113; BMC 202. Available at: https://opac.kbr.be/LIBRARY/doc/SYRACUSE/20734709. Accessed: 3 Aug. 2022.
[173] Translation made by the author.
[174] Translation made by the author.
[175] Bibliography: RIC I² 99; BMC 124. Available at: https://opac.kbr.be/LIBRARY/doc/SYRACUSE/20734674. Accessed: 3 Aug. 2022.
[176] Translation made by the author.
[177] Translation made by the author.

Figure 45 – Bronze dupondius[178], AD 41 - 50, Rome, rule of Claudius, 12.25 g, 28.4 mm diameter. Obverse: bust of Claudius facing right, TI CLAVDIVS CAESAR AVG P M TR P IMP (*Tiberius Claudius Caesar Augustus Pontifex Maximus Tribunicia Potestate Pater Patriae Imperator* = Commander Tiberius Claudius Caesar Augustus, Supreme Pontiff, vested in the Tribunicia Power and Father of the homeland[179]). Reverse: Ceres or Livia as Ceres (?), with veiled head, seated to the left on ornate throne, right hand with ears of corn and left hand with a long torch or sceptre, S C/ CERES AV[GUSTA] (*Senatus Consultum* /Ceres Augusta = minted with the consent of the Senate/Ceres Augusta[180])

Source: © KBR *cabinet des monnais et médailles*

On the last three samples from Claudius' rule, with the emperor on the obverse, the reverses of each coin have a female figure differentiated from each other. The first coin shows the deity Libertas, but as the captions reads LIBERTAS AUGUSTA, it raises a question as to whether this image is Libertas personified as Livia. The second coin has another female figure on the reverse, which the caption shows to be Spes Augusta, raising the same doubt as the previous coin. Similarly, the third example is a coin with another female figure on its reverse, which from the captions is presumed to be Ceres or the personification of Ceres as Livia, due to the caption CERES AUGUSTA. In the three examples, it is difficult to observe a specific physical characteristic that would be linked to Livia. Otherwise, she has always been associated with various goddesses linked to fertility, especially Ceres. However, it is questionable whether these coins were really made in honour of her, with her personified as these goddesses, or whether it was something common to be minted and that the celebration was not to Livia, but to the house of Augustus.

Moreover, Livia's identification with other goddesses continued in the provinces, as did her personification as Hera, which remained on coins

---

[178] Bibliography: RIC I² 94; BMC 136. Available at: https://opac.kbr.be/LIBRARY/doc/SYRACUSE/20734684. Accessed: 3 Aug. 2022.
[179] Translation made by the author.
[180] Translation made by the author.

from Tarsus. In Athens, she gained an epithet linked to Hera's name, which suggests the Roman Providentia, revealing that where Livia was not identified divinely, she was associated with a goddess (Grether, 1946, p. 241-242). Providentia was known as the one who saw the future. She appeared holding a staff pointing to a globe at her feet and a sceptre (Sear, 2000, p. 40).

The theme of dynastic perpetuation has always been linked to representations of Livia and in several cities of the eastern and western provinces she was referred to as divine, Θεα in eastern Greece, or Θεα ΣΕΒΑΣΤΑ in Koion, Crete, an expression

that was related to the coin type of the Iustitia of Rome from the AD 20s. There is also the fact that Livia was associated with various mother goddesses, such as Hera for her tiara, Demeter for her ears of grain and her Roman equivalents Juno and Ceres. Consequently, a divine aspect was already combined with Livia since the period of Augustus, even before she was deified by Claudius in AD 42 (Harvey, 2020, p. 135-136).

Figure 46 – Coin[181] with the bust of Claudius on the left on the obverse, 5,09 g, TI KLAYDIOS KAISAR GERMAΣE BAΣ, (Tiberius Claudius Caesar Germanicus Augustus[182]). And on the reverse, there is the bust of Livia, Θεα ΣΕΒΑΣ (Goddess Augusta[183])

Source: Courtesy of WildWinds

Livia's association with Demeter was less common than with Hera in the Greek Hellenistic East, but the link with Demeter's equivalent in Rome, that would be Ceres, was well established with Livia within the imperial ideology of the Augustan period, which made her a symbol related to prosperity and fertility. Moreover, her association with Demeter/Ceres in

---

[181] Reference No: RPC I 1030, SNG Cop 574; BMC 6. Available at: https://www.wildwinds.com/coins/ric/claudius/RPC_1030.jpg; text available at: https://www.wildwinds.com/coins/ric/claudius/RPC_1030.txt. Accessed: 6 Sept. 2020.
[182] Translation made by the author.
[183] Translation made by the author.

sculptures, cameos and coins continued after she was deified, throughout the rule of Claudius (Harvey, 2020, p. 137).

The fact that Livia is associated with several goddesses in different places also presents an identity aspect on the coins. Religion operates as something that was intended to show meaning and demonstrate the human experience, as well as functioning as a natural vehicle for expressing identity. The images associated with goddesses or gods follow the local and/or Rome's reception, just as perhaps the choices of the eastern provinces may contrast with those of the western provinces. Having noted the choices, it can be considered whether the images represent continuity, renewal, or invention. The mythologies utilised may serve to claim a position in a wider world that may have as reference a shared past and with specific articulated relationships with other cities, whether Greek, Roman (Howgego, 2005, p. 2-3 and 6) or others.

Evidence of Diva Augusta in Cirta, Africa, and altars with the sayings *Pietati Augustae* in her honour appeared at this same time. In the East, the cult of the *diva* is easily traced, since she was presented as Livia until Augustus' death, Julia Augusta after his death, and Diva Augusta after her own death, more specifically after she was deified. Remnants of her cult appear in Aquinum, Ostia, Aeclanum, Suasa, Albingaunum, Brixia, Messana, Cirta, Ipsca, Nertobriga, Nemausus, Vasio, Narona and Philippi (Grether, 1946, p. 247-249).

Even before she was deified, Livia appears to be worshipped in a sacred way, as indicated by the message on coins, through Θεα, which also appears on statues in the Agora of Athens and Achaia, next to statues of her and Augustus, in addition to her association with various goddesses, including Ceres and Juno, giving her the meaning of "mother goddess" for her role as mother of the imperial family. The roles of wife and mother were seen as key elements in maintaining the emperor (Harvey, 2020, p. 160).

In Cordoba and Baetica, there seems to have had remnants of the imperial cult, with statues of Claudius, Augustus as Jupiter and Livia as Ceres or Juno (Fishwick, 1991, p. 77-78 and 195). Another important figure of Livia seated, holding a cornucopia, very similar to those on the coins of Irippo, was found in Iponuba, Baetica, during the late Augustan or early Tiberian period, which evidences the cult in honour of Livia, which can also be verified in other regions of the provinces of Spain, as well as in cities such as Emerita, in Lusitania, which established the first cult of Augustus and later coupled that of Livia (Fishwick, 1991, p. 245). There is also evidence of statues of the cult of Livia in Tarraco and Empúries (Fishwick, p. 276; Bartman, 2001, p. 168-169 apud Harvey, 2020, p. 143).

In Africa, she is associated with Juno and Ceres at Oea and Thapsus, and with Ceres at Lepcis Magna, as well as being a significant part of the imperial cult of Augustus, Rome and other family members, with a statue of Livia as Ceres in a temple to Ceres Augusta from AD 35, some years after her own death. In Gaul, vessels attest to the imperial cult, but the worship of Livia came only after her deification (Barrett, 2001, p. 209, 223) and sculptures and inscription honouring her as wife of the deified Augustus and mother of Tiberius appear in Malta (Gaulus Insula) (Harvey, 2020, p. 143).

The cult of Livia was linked to the cult of Augustus, especially in various parts of Asia, where there were greater references to her and where temples to Augustus were erected, for the worship of Augustus or Augustus and Rome, as well as Mytilene, Assos, Cyzicus, Pergamum, Ephesus, Sardis, Tralles, Alabanda, Aphrodisias and Smyrna, where there were also coins and inscriptions in honour of Livia. The Hellenistic tradition of celebrating women of royalty, such as the queens Dynamis and Pythodoris from Pontus (Bosporan), who showed their gratitude in return, led to the celebration of both Augustus and Livia (Kearsley, 2005, p. 100-101). Moreover, Pythodoris had two cities, Sebastia and Liviopolis, which clearly exchanged their names in honour of Livia. In Ersus, on Lesbos, a temple was built to Augustus, Livia, Gaius, and Lucius; a portico with statues of Augustus and Livia, as well as a sanctuary in Ephesus, also featuring a temple to Tiberius, Livia, and the Senate in Smyrna, which was commemorated on coins of the city (Harvey, 2020, p. 140) and more.

Livia was not only considered divine, but also a benefactress, worshipped with the words Θεα ενεργετις, meaning "divine benefactress", in other words, an ideal model of a Roman matron (Kearsley, 2005, p. 107) who made herself a character linked to the imperial institution (Harvey, 2020, p. 140 and 144). Hence, it should be borne in mind that Livia's actions and her honours probably came along with the memory of her actions, which were possibly linked to Patronage.

5.1.4. Livia and other rulers

Generally, the cult of Livia was not performed in Rome, but proven in other eastern provinces by numerous inscriptions showing the existence of honours to Julia Augusta. It appears that priests of the cult of Augustus were priests of the cult of his *Genius* and that priests and priestesses of Julia Augusta would be devotees of the cult of Juno, as on some coins of Tiberius. On the island of Gaulos, she was seen as Ceres, and her cult was in the name of this goddess, while in Italian cities she was found as Ceres Augusta (Grether, 1946, p. 239).

The association of Livia's cult with that of Augustus meant that this ceremony was repeated for a prolonged time, as were her honours. In relation to Galba, for example, on his coins Livia appears as Diva Augusta, recognising her as a goddess and as an important ancestor; during the rule of Titus, she appears as Iustitia and Pietas. Already during the government of Antoninus Pius, in AD 159, the temple of Divus Augustus was remodelled and received a statue of her (Grether, 1946, p. 251; Harvey, 2020, p. 121).

After Nero's death, the memory of the Julio-Claudian family, in particular of Augustus, was an important criterion that appeared on coins. The iconography, elements and captions were adapted and even restored. Vitellius represented his father on coins using Julio-Claudian iconography; and Vespasian did not use an ancestor, but elements of Julio-Claudian iconography. The Flavian family, Titus and Domitian also utilised this iconography (Claes, 2013, p. 129).

Figure 47 – Silver denarius[184] of Catalonia, province of Tarragona, town of Tarraco, Spain. Obverse: laureate bust of Galba, facing right, with caption: SER GALBA IMP CAESAR AVG TR P (*Servius Galba Imperator Caesar Augustus Tribunicia Potestate* = Serbian Commander Galba Caesar Augustus invested in the Tribune Power[185]); reverse: draped figure of Livia, facing left, with a *patera* in her right hand and a vertical sceptre in her left hand, caption: DIVA AVGVSTA

Source: © The Trustees of the British Museum

This denarius celebrates Galba's rule and honours Livia on its reverse, with an image to strengthen the emperor's power, since the representation of Livia appears with a *patera* in her hand, which can be interpreted as a symbol of fertility, agricultural abundance, and a prosperous government. The sceptre and diadem on her head would link her to wisdom, religiosity and/or *pudicitia*. It should be added that the longevity of honouring Livia would be associated with a prolonged respect for her person, as well as being the result of the expectation to keep the memory of such an important character, which suggests a high acceptance of her representation both in periods when she was alive and later.

---

[184] Museum reference number: 1928.0120.128. Bibliographical references: RIC1 / The Roman Imperial Coinage, vol. 1 (52, p. 235). Available at: https://www.britishmuseum.org/collection/object/C_1928-0120-128. Accessed: 16 Aug. 2020.

[185] Translation made by the author.

Figure 48 – Aureus[186], from AD 68 to 69, Rome, 7.19 g, 19.7 mm diameter, Rome. Obverse: draped bust of Galba facing right, SER GALBA CAESAR AVG (*Servius Galba Caesar Augustus*). Reverse: Livia with a diadem on her head, holding a *patera* and a sceptre in her left hand, DIVA AUGUSTA

Source: © KBR *cabinet des monnais et médailles*

This last example, which is an aureus, bears similarities to the previous denarius. However, on the obverse, the bust of Galba appears draped with the caption honouring him, while Livia appears on the reverse holding a *patera* and a sceptre, as well as a diadem on her head, in a symbolism based on the goddess Vesta, linking her to *pudicitia* and honouring her as his ancestor.

Figure 49 – Bronze dupondius[187], AD 68 to 69, 14.41 g, 28.9 mm diameter, Rome. Obverse: draped bust of Galba to the right, IMP SER SVLP GALBA CAES AVG TR P (*Imperator Servius Sulpicius Galba Caesar Augustus Tribunicia Potestate* = Commander Servius Sulpicius Galba Caesar Augustus with Tribune Power[188]). Obverse: Livia (?), PAX AUGUSTA

Source: © KBR *cabinet des monnais et médailles*

---

[186] Bibliography: RIC I² 142; BMC 309; du Chastel 420 (*Collection du Chastel Collectie du Chastel*). Available at: https://opac.kbr.be/LIBRARY/doc/SYRACUSE/20735172, accessed. Accessed: 25 July 2022.

[187] Bibliography: RIC I² 323; BMC 132. Available at: https://opac.kbr.be/LIBRARY/doc/SYRACUSE/20735225. Accessed: 25 July 2022.

[188] Translation made by the author.

The last dupondius, with Galba on the obverse, features a figure on the reverse that may be a personification of Livia as Pax. However, there is doubt whether it is Livia and whether it is more a tribute to her, since the caption does not name her Julia Augusta or Diva Augusta, but Pax Augusta. However, the elements of the image on the reverse have characteristics that have always been linked to Livia, such as the *patera* and the sceptre. Another sample that follows the same doubt is a sestertius from Galba's government that has Concordia Augusta on the reverse.

Figure 50 – Bronze sestertius[189], AD 68 - 69, 25.92 g, 36.9 mm diameter, Rome. Obverse: head of Galba with laurel wreath on left, SER GALBA IMP CAESAR AVG ON PON MA TR P (*Servius Galba Imperato Caesar Augustus Pontifex Maximus Tribunicia Potestate* = Commander Servius Galba Caesar Augustus Supreme Pontiff invested in the tribune power). Reverse: Livia (?) as Concordia, CONCORD AUG / S C (*Concordia Augusta/ Senatus Consultum* = Concordia Augusta/minted with the consent of the Senate[190])

Source: © KBR *cabinet des monnais et médailles*

The last exemplar has Galba on the obverse, with the bust facing left, and apparently Livia on the reverse as Concordia. The female figure in a robe, seated to the left, has elements that commonly accompany Livia and the goddesses through whom she is personified: such as the branch, which always symbolises fertility, abundance, agricultural and dynastic success; as well as the sceptre and diadem on her head, which associate her with the religiosity linked to Vesta. However, Livia was a model to be followed by other imperial women, as was Agrippina Minor, who also had the title of Augusta. This title and even the images of these women on coins were used for a political rather than an economic context.

---

[189] RIC I² 384 v.; BMC 56; du Chastel 423 (*Collection du Chastel Collectie du Chastel*). Available at: https://opac.kbr.be/LIBRARY/doc/SYRACUSE/20735208. Accessed: 25 July 2022.

[190] Translation made by the author.

Both Claudius and Galba saw Livia as their divine ancestor, since Claudius had her as a grandmother and Galba seems to have received favours from Livia early in his career, or a large amount of money, and claimed to be related to her through his adoptive mother, Livia Ocellina, who also claimed to be connected to her, or she would be a distant relative, since this was Galba's excuse to legitimise his government as that who was linked to the first *princeps*, Augustus, after the fall of Nero, marking the end of the Julio-Claudian dynasty. However, there has always been a doubt regarding Galba's connection with the Julio-Claudian family (Harvey, 2020, p. 124). At that time, it was relevant that each candidate for emperor had some connection with the Julio-Claudian family, after Nero's death. The image of Livia was minted in gold, silver, and bronze at mints in Rome and another unknown mint in Spain, which was probably Tarraco. Galba placed himself as a direct descendant by the nomenclature of his name that remained, Lucius Livius Galba Augustus, as well as assuming the title *Caesar* and continuing the cult of Augustus, Livia, and Claudius. However, on his coins, he only celebrated Livia (Claes, 2013, p. 113-114).

Figure 51 – Aureus[191], Rome, AD 75 to 79. Obverse: laureate and bearded head of Domitian, CAESAR AVG F DOMITIANVS (*Caesar Augusti Filius* Domitianus = Domitian Caesar, son of Augustus[192]). Reverse: standing Ceres, holding ears of corn with her right hand and a sceptre in her left hand, CERES AVGVST (Ceres Augusta) (Brennan, Turner & Nicholas, 2007, p. 28)

Source: © American Numismatic Society

The last exemplar is from Domitian's government in Rome, dated from AD 75 to 79, to promote the emperor as he was young and from a new

---

[191] RIC II, Part 1 (second edition) Vespasian 975. Available at: https://numismatics.org/ocre/id/ric.2_1(2).ves.975. Accessed: 7 Dec. 2022.
[192] Translation made by the author.

imperial family. He had Tiberius as an imperial role model, but was called the "bald Nero". However, imperial misdeeds, such as treachery, espionage, informers, spies, passed from Rome to the provinces (Brennan; Turner; Wright, 2007, p. 28). The coin shown here bears something relating to Galba's rule, which had a suitability to the Julio-Claudian family, honouring Augustus as his predecessor. However, the coin seems to look for something relating to Livia on its reverse, with the presence of Ceres and with the additive in the caption of AVGVST, recalling earlier personifications of the empress as the goddess.

Figure 52 – Dupondius[193], in copper alloy, AD 80 - 81, 14.39 g, from the government of Titus of Rome. Obverse: bust of Livia; caption: PIETAS. Major reverse caption: S C (*Senatus Consultum*), minor caption: IMP T CAES DIVI VESP F AVG RES[T] (*Imperator Titus Cæsar Divi Vespasiani Filius Augusti Restituit* = Commander Titus, son of the divine Augustus Vespasian, was restored[194])

Source: © The Trustees of the British Museum

Titus must have had something similar to Galba to honour Livia on the coinage of this dupondius, where she appears on the obverse as the main figure of the coin. Nevertheless, its obverse celebrates the rule of Titus and its minting is, still in this period, consented by the Senate. Thus, the image of Livia was very well received in later times of her life. The honour that describes her as *pietas* may come from a respect for her *pudicitia* as a Roman matron and her virtues. Titus intended to link the Flavian family to the Julio-Claudian one, since the minting of coins may have been an instrument for this to happen. In this sense, the Flavian emperors began to

---

[193] Reference number: 1857.0812.19. Number in C&M catalogue: RE2 (287) (291) (287). RE2 / Coins of the Roman Empire in the British Museum, vol. II: Vespasian to Domitian (291, p. 287) BER2.1 / The Roman Imperial Coinage, vol.2 part 1: From AD 69 to AD 96: Vespasian to Domitian (426, p. 227). Available at: https://www.britishmuseum.org/collection/object/C_1857-0812-19. Accessed: 18 Aug. 2020.

[194] Available at: https://www.biddr.com/auctions/cgb/browse?a=924&l=981372. Accessed: 18 Aug. 2020.

mint coins of the same type as those of the Julio-Claudian family to forge this connection (Claes, 2013, p. 100).

Figure 53 – Cooper alloy dupondius,[195] AD 80 - 81, from the government of Titus, Rome. On the obverse is the draped bust of Livia as Iustitia, caption: IVSTITIA; on the reverse is a larger caption, S C (*Senatus Consultum*) and a smaller one, IMP T CAES DIVI VESP F AVG REST (*Imperator Titus Cæsar Divi Vespasiani Filius Augusti Restituit* = Commander Titus, son of the divine Augustus Vespasian, was restored[196])

Source: © The Trustees of the British Museum

On this dupondius, also from the government of Titus, there is a celebration of honouring Livia on its obverse. On this coin, she appears as Iustitia, a representation that may also be linked to a respect for Livia and her *pudicitia* as a Roman matron, as well as other virtues, continuing with the demonstration of a prolonged homage to the same person.

---

[195] Reference number: R.11263. Number in the C&M catalogue: RE2 (287) (289) (287). Bibliography: RE2 / Coins of the Roman Empire in the British Museum, vol.II: Vespasian to Domitian (289, p. 287) BER RIC 2.1 / The Roman Imperial Coinage, vol. 2 part 1: From AD 69 to AD 96: Vespasian to Domitian (424, p. 227). Available at: https://www.britishmuseum.org/collection/object/C_R-11263. Accessed: 18 Aug. 2020.

[196] Available at: https://www.biddr.com/auctions/cgb/browse?a=924&l=981372. Accessed: 18 Aug. 2020.

Figure 54 – Bronze sestertius[197], AD 79 - 81, 10.75 g, 26 mm diameter, Rome. Obverse: radiated face of Titus on left, IMP T CAES VESP AVG P M TR P P COS VIII (*Imperator Titus Cæsar Vespasianus Augustus Pontifex Maximus Tribunicia Potestate Pater Patriae Consul Octavum* = Commander Titus Caesar Vespasian Augustus, Supreme Pontiff, invested in the Tribune Power, Father of the homeland and Consul for the eighth time[198]). Reverse: Salus seated facing left with a *patera* in his right hand, SALVS AVG S C (*Salus Augusta/Senatus Consutum* = Salus Augusta/minted with the consent of the Senate[199])

Source: © KBR *cabinet des monnais et médailles*

During Titus' government, a coin was also minted with the Salus Augusta on its obverse, which also occurred during Antoninus Pius' government. These coins are reminiscent of those minted in honour of Livia during the period of Tiberius. However, both this coin and the coins of Iustitia and Pietas raise doubts as whether they really are tributes to Livia, or whether they are simply allusions to the goddesses, since their captions do not directly mention her name. The title *Augusta* also raises doubts, since Titus also had a daughter who had the name IVLIA AUGUSTA. Though, the very name of Tito's daughter could have been a tribute to Livia. However, after Livia, other empresses also received the title of Augusta, such as Agrippina Minor and Faustina. In this period, there was also a coin struck with Titus on the obverse and Pax[200] on the reverse, as a seated female figure, which causes the same doubts, because the reverse caption reads PAX AUG. To add, there are still the same questions concerning coins minted as CONCORDIA AUG on the reverse caption, from the period of Nero[201] and Titus[202], but

---

[197] Bibliography: RIC, II, 204. Call number: 2B48 / 22. Provenance: Don Tinchant. Available at: https://opac.kbr.be/LIBRARY/doc/SYRACUSE/10043561. Accessed: 26 July 2022.
[198] Translation made by the author.
[199] Translation made by the author.
[200] Bibliography: RIC II 551; BMC 110 (Trésor de Braibant Schat van Braibant). Available at: https://opac.kbr.be/LIBRARY/doc/SYRACUSE/20735702. Accessed: 26 July 2022.
[201] Bibliography: RIC I² 48; BMC 61; Thirion 10 (Trésor de Liberchies; don BNB Liberchies hoard; gift NBB). Available at: https://opac.kbr.be/LIBRARY/doc/SYRACUSE/20734827. Accessed: 26 July 2022.
[202] Bibliography: RIC 320, BMC p. 93, RIC² 1416 (Coll. du Chastel).

such iconographies may just be allusions to the deity. It is more prudent to consider the reference to these goddesses next to the title AUGUSTA as something religious within imperial monetary iconography, without emphasising the homage to Livia or to another woman of the Roman elite who could have earned the same title.

Figure 55 – Caesarea Panias, bronze. Issuing authority: Philip I. Obverse: conjoined busts of Augustus, laureate and Livia to the right. Captions in Greek, KAICAPI CEBACTW (Augustus Caesar). Reverse: facade of a tetrastyle temple built on high platform (the *Augusteum* in *Panias*); columns with Ionian capitals, two concentric circles in centre. Small pediment. Captions: FILIPPOY TETPAPXOY (Philip the tetrarch)[203]

Source: (Porto, 2018, p. 147)

This coin from Caesarea Panias, Philip I government, mentions the imperial cult with the representation of the imperial family, since Augustus is next to Livia on the obverse. In addition, the imperial cult extended throughout the imperial family, resulting in various cults that were expanded to the entire family, so that wives and daughters were elevated to the status of *diuae*. On the reverse of the coin, a temple dedicated to Augustus can be seen, demonstrating the imperial cult promoted by Herod, the Great. Augustus worked hard to ensure that the reconstructions of old and new temples were close to his image. Herod thus promoted the cult of the emperor in the East, serving Rome in the most diverse ways (Porto, 2018, p. 148).

What it can be concluded from Livia is that the position she achieved was fundamental to the social change in the position of imperial women. The transformation of her status began when she was adopted by Augustus and granted the title of Augusta, which probably happened because of Tiberius' refusal to receive such a title and when the tensions of power and

---

[203] Reference: Meshorer TJC 100 (Porto, 2018, p. 147).

gender began, once the title was part of an imperial system put in place by Augustus. It seems that the Senate approved, so that this institution went in a direction in favour of the first *princeps*, who would be the continuation of the system by dynastic transmission, which Tiberius seemed to be against, and the Senate possibly saw in Livia his continuation. In this way, the Senate promoted Livia, who was a priestess in the cult of Augustus and also received Vestal rights.

Being tied to the Vestal Virgins or religiosity would be the only way for her to obtain an "institutionalisation" of her public role, because of the fact that religious activity was an acceptable aspect of women's lives and execution of Livia's public activities. Public rituals were taken as a benefit to the whole state, so Livia was seen as a guarantee for Rome's prosperity (Takács, 2008, p. 23). The presence of women in the Roman forum for the purpose of religious activities generally did not attract favourable or unfavourable comments. Yet, women involved in social and political issues were not well regarded (Boatwright, 2011, p. 112). Such a position of Livia would be pertinent, since Tiberius could have been considered a weak ruler, or one who had no intention of continuing the imperial system according to Augustus, and Drusus, his brother, who died prematurely, and who could have been the most considered for the position. However, Drusus left a son named Germanicus, beloved like his father, who apparently saw his end at the hands of Tiberius and, occasionally, Livia.

In this perspective, it can be remarked that Livia's position as a widow with the emperor son brought her perks never seen for an imperial woman, thus obtaining the highest point of power attained by a woman of the Roman elite, especially after the deification of Augustus. The status of these women and their authority grew in the family after they became mothers, especially if it was of a male child. Their authority grew even more when they became widows, as they could exercise great power over their children, despite the legal lack of *potestas* over them. In this context, it was more through their children than through their own husbands that such women were able to exercise political power. As widows and mothers of emperors, the women of the Roman elite in general began to take centre stage, running their own businesses, overseeing the education of their children, occupying a position of respect in their families and publicly, given that they could make public use of their wealth as matrons (Hemelrijk, 1999, p. 15).

However, Livia showed the way to be followed by other later imperial women, who did not fail to take her as an example, such as Agrippina Minor. This idealisation of power was also a device for Tacitus to write that the wife of Emperor Claudius could possibly have killed him to achieve such status.

Chapter 6

Agrippina Major and her posthumous importance

Agrippina Major (14 BC - AD 33) makes up the third generation of imperial women, born of Julia, daughter of Augustus, who was married to Claudius Marcellus, who died in 23 BC, then married Marcus Vipsanius Agrippa in 21 BC, a competent military commander and old friend of her father, Augustus, with whom Julia had five children: Gaius Caesar (20 BC); Lucius Caesar (17 BC); Agrippa Postumus (born after his father's death, AD 12); Julia (19 BC); and Vipsania Agrippina (14 BC), known as Agrippina Major, to distinguish herself from her daughter, Agrippina Minor (Burns, 2007, p. 41). Agrippina lost her father at the age of two and saw her mother banished by Augustus at the age of ten, furthermore, at the age of twenty-two, she saw her siblings, Julia and Agrippa, meet the same fate as their mother (Burns, 2007, p. 41).

Agrippa, her father, was a builder, who designed the Pantheon of Rome, remodelled by the emperor Hadrian; he built the bridge and aqueduct of Nemausus, Gaul, current *Pont du Gard,* Nîmes, France. He was known for his courage, wisdom and modest nature, as well as being a public benefactor, which included bath houses, which were freely open, without any charge to the public of Rome, continuing to function even after his death (Burns, 2007, p. 42).

Julia, her mother, had a thorny relationship with Livia, her husband's grandmother, Germanicus, born in 15 BC, son of Drusus, whom Agrippina wished to see on the throne, but Livia dissimulated Augustus from adopting him (Barrett, 2002, p. 54-55). Agrippina married Germanicus, who was her second cousin, around AD 4/5, aged 17 or 18. He was the son of Antonia and Livia's youngest son Drusus (Burns, 2007, p. 42). Germanicus was adopted by Tiberius and probably a year later married Agrippina, obtaining the same rights and relations as Tiberius' legitimate son, Drusus (Barrett, 2002, p. 56). They had nine children, of whom only six survived: Nero (AD 6); Drusus (AD 7/8); Gaius (Caligula, AD 12); Agrippina Minor (AD 15); Drusilla (AD 16); and Julia Livilla (AD 17/18) (Burns, 2007, p. 42). Consequently,

Agrippina became active within her husband's career and cared about her own public image (Zager, 2014, p. 82), as she knew that she could provide a lineage with Augustus' blood, relying on her fruitful marriage (Barrett, 2002, p. 56 and 119).

According to Tacitus' *Annals*, she was characterised at first as "determined", which was a good trait, added to her fidelity to her husband. She was praised by the author as intelligent and polite, a description that changed throughout the narrative, when the author started to characterise her as a fierce, angry, violent, and emotional woman (Tac. *Ann*. 1.33; 1.69; 4.12; 4.52; 4.51-2; 5.3 and 6.25). Tacitus portrays the performance of these imperial women, as well as Livia, Augustus' wife, who describes her as the bad mother-in-law, pointing out that there was a female jealousy there, because, according to him, Livia felt the bitterness of a mother-in-law towards Agrippina Major (Tac. *Ann*. 1.33).

Agrippina's husband, Germanicus, became beloved by the populace for many reasons, but mainly because he began to be similar to a lawyer for various people, defending them both before Augustus himself and before other judges (Cass. Dio, *Roman History* 56. 24. 7). Germanicus was involved in the conquest of the Germanic tribes, which had begun at the end of Augustus' period, which made Livia's sons, Tiberius and Drusus, important generals. However, in AD 9, this endeavour began to stagger (Burns, 2007, p. 42).

It all started when Publius Quinctilius Varus led three legions through the Teutoburg Forest in Germania and was surprised by an ambush led by a tribal chieftain, Arminius, who annihilated the Roman forces (Suet. *Aug*. 23.1; Cass. Dio, *Roman History* 56.19-23). After this event, a new general was summoned, Germanicus, to bring the situation under control (Tac. *Ann*. 1.3), but even if the problem was solved, the borders were still precarious, mainly because the Roman troops began to lose confidence in the Roman army after what happened to Arminius (Cass. Dio, *Roman History* 56.23.1-4, 57.5.4). The soldiers of the province, which is current Germany, realised that Germanicus was like a Caesar and far superior to Tiberius, but made the same demands, but was hailed as an emperor (Cass. Dio, *Roman History* 57.5.1).

In the spring of AD 14, Agrippina was pregnant and joined her husband's tour of Gaul, in which Germanicus commanded eight legions, which was stationed along the Rhine River, on the border between the Roman Empire and the so-called "barbarians" of Germania. After two months, his son Gaius was sent by Augustus (Suet. *Calig.* 8.4). As the mascot of the troops, Gaius became better known as Caligula among the soldiers (Tac. *Ann.* 1.41) since he was raised largely in the camp and wore military boots instead of sandals, commonly worn in the city (Cass. Dio, *Roman History* 57.5.6).

During this period there was the death of Augustus (AD 14), succeeded by Tiberius, whom Augustus forced to adopt Germanicus, making him the husband of Agrippina, the first in line to the throne, because he was older than Tiberius' own son Drusus (Suet. *Tib.* 15; Suet. *Calig.* 1; Cass. Dio, *Roman History* 55.13.3).

Before becoming emperor, Tiberius was respected as a soldier and feared as a commander (Burns, 2007, p. 44). Cassius Dio mentions that Germanicus was already seen as a rival to Tiberius, since he considered him to be on the prowl for sovereignty or to be excellent by nature (Cass. Dio, *Roman History* 57.13.6). Germanicus acquired a reputation mainly for his campaign against the Germanic tribes, which inflicted a crushing defeat on the "barbarians", collected and buried the bones of those who had fallen with Varus, what led him to reconquer the Roman military standards (Cass. Dio, Roman *History* 57.18.1).

After Tiberius became emperor, a mutiny broke out among the Roman soldiers, who began to demand lighter work, higher wages, and dismissal for the veterans. The reaction was great, in that they even began to attack the officers, throwing them into the Rhine (Tac. *Ann.* 1.31-32). Germanicus' reaction was to quell the mutiny by taking Agrippina and Caligula along in an attempt to embarrass them, which apparently worked, but just as Germanicus entered one of the trenches the crowd of soldiers surrounded him, mainly veterans who wished to retire (Tac. *Ann.* 1.34-35). Germanicus and his soldiers, who were still on his side, learnt that the rebel legions planned to send delegations to the rest of Germanicus' army, urging them to join the uprising. There was even talk of abandoning the Germanic frontier and sacking the cities of Roman Gaul (Tac. *Ann.* 1.35-36).

Tiberius instructed Germanicus to release the veterans and to pay the soldiers double the amount offered by Augustus (Cass. Dio, *Roman History* 57.5.3). The soldiers accepted the offer on the condition that they would have to be satisfied immediately. Germanicus did not have the funds at that time but promised to deliver as soon as the soldiers returned from their winter camps. However, only two of the legions accepted, while the other two refuted. Germanicus and his officers had to find money from the taxes collected in Gaul to pay the soldiers (Tac. *Ann.* 1.37), which apparently resulted in a controlled situation. However, the soldiers learnt that Tiberius' letter in agreement was a deception, causing the troops to rebel again. They took the senators into custody, entered Germanicus' barracks and confiscated symbols of the empire, such as the golden eagles and banners (Tac. *Ann.* 1.39). According to Cassius Dio, Germanicus was the one who drafted the letter, pretending to be Tiberius, and then gave them twice the value of the gift left by Augustus and dismissed those who were beyond military age (Cass. Dio, *Roman History* 57.5.3).

Consequently, it was decided that Agrippina and Caligula should be taken out of the camp, as it seemed that they would be safer among the local Gauls, who had more loyalty to Rome than the soldiers (Tac. *Ann.* 1.40). However, this attitude led the mutiny to a climax, with the chariot surrounded by the soldiers, who would not let them leave the camp (Tac. *Ann.* 1.41). Cassius Dio mentions that they managed to leave safely but were seized by the soldiers. They ended up releasing Agrippina, as she was pregnant, but restrained Caligula, whereupon a change of mind caused them to release the boy and turn to some of the leaders of the riot, even going so far as to execute some (Cass. Dio, *Roman History* 57.5.5-7).

Caligula's participation in this act would have had consequences for the future, since as emperor he made the attempt to massacre the soldiers who rebelled against his father (Suet. *Calig.* 48). However, it seems that Agrippina's departure from the camp intimidated the soldiers and Germanicus, so to give them a chance to redeem themselves, he summoned them to attack the Germanics, to which end they built a bridge across the Rhine (Tac. *Ann.* 1.49). In the meantime, Agrippina's mother died in exile and her brother was killed, apparently at the behest of Tiberius (Cass. Dio, *Roman History* 57.18.1 and 57.3.5-6).

After a few weeks, Agrippina received news of a battle against Arminius, which was taking place in the woods and that there had been some flooding which had destroyed Roman fortifications and some bridges. A part of the army that was returning to the Rhine bridge got stuck in a swamp and some soldiers started to desert (Tac. *Ann.* 1.64-68). Other soldiers and civilians rushed to the Rhine bridge at the Roman fortress of Castra Vetera in order to destroy the bridge before the Germanics could cross it (Barrett, 1996, p. 27; Burns, 2007, p. 56). At this point, Agrippina realised that the destruction of the bridge would condemn any returning Roman soldier to death. As such, she refused to leave the bridge until all the soldiers had returned safely. She then ordered food, bandages, and clothing for the returning troops, and thanked the troops for their courage (Tac. *Ann.* 1.69).

Tacitus points out that Agrippina assumed the duties of a general, inspecting the troops, attending to their basic needs, and she was in command until Germanicus returned, adding that it all happened when she was seven months pregnant. This story of bravery made her famous and admired by the empire. However, Tiberius did not like the leadership of a woman (Tac. *Ann.* 1.69).

Agrippina Major's attitude, corroborated by Tacitus during this Roman endeavour against the Germanics, demonstrates well a view in which the author, even for the good acts of these women, guarded them with suspicion. When the Roman army was short of supplies, Agrippina prevented the Vetera bridge from being destroyed on the Rhine and saved the Roman troops from being caught on the east side of the river. Some, with their cowardice, would not have dared this act. Tacitus describes her with a heroic spirit, who assumed the duties of a general and distributed clothing and medicines to the soldiers; according to Gaius Plinius, from the bridge, she bestowed praise and thanks on the returning legions. All this attitude made a deep impression on Tiberius, who, according to Tacitus, thought that all this zeal could not exist without guilt and that it was not against foreigners that she would be wooing the soldiers. For Tacitus, she was a woman who went to the entourages, attended to every measure, ventured into bribery, and frankly showed an ambition in displaying her son in common soldier's uniform, wishing him to be called Caesar Caligula. In this way, Agrippina managed to have more power with the armies than the officers and generals themselves. A woman who dominated a mutiny in the name of the sovereign was not a common sight, Tacitus emphasised (Tac. *Ann.* 1.69).

All this movement by Agrippina also saved her husband, Germanicus. Her contribution to the army was crucial, but it infuriated Tiberius, who was offended by a woman stepping into the role of commanders. Agrippina's gesture must have offended conservative Romans, just as it must have done with Fulvia (Barrett, 2002, p. 77 and 82). Agrippina's attitude cannot be categorised as that of a woman resisting against a society for another role that was not presumed for such women of the Roman elite, but her actions are better explained as an alternative of femininity (Weedon, 1987, p. 86 apud Moore, 2000, p. 26), within a loyalty to her husband, as she appeased a riot.

Agrippina Major, as Fulvia, was criticised for acting in male roles. Part of this criticism could be explained by the fact that they were the wives of men who were detested or envied and who showed no regard for traditional feminine virtues. Agrippina had undesirable masculine traits, as well as a difficult, obstinate, and domineering temperament. However, she was praised for her incorruptible chastity, loyalty, devotion to her husband and exemplary fertility. The female mind was thought to be different from the male mind, being characterised as irrational, hence, the male mind was associated with good judgement and good manners. Women who showed rational judgement were thought to be exceeding the expectations of their roles. However, those who were known for their "manly" courage or self-control were regarded as a "honorary men" (Hemelrijk, 1999, p. 86-87).

Agrippina's attitude could have been another reason for Livia and Tiberius to invest against Germanicus, since they used the excuse that Germanicus had republican ideas, with the intention of putting an end to the imperial system, with the desire to restore *libertas,* like his father Drusus (Tac. *Ann.* 1.33 and 2.82.2; Suet. *Calig.* 3). Germanicus ended his involvement with Germania in AD 17, when Tiberius summoned him to post in the eastern provinces. Thus, Germania was never fully conquered by Rome and the Rhine River was its border until 400 years after Germanicus' death (Burns, 2007, p. 47).

The people of the East, accustomed to treating their rulers as gods, greeted Germanicus and Agrippina with enthusiasm (Griffin, 1985, p. 214 apud Burns, 2007, p. 48), adding the fact that Agrippina gave birth to Julia Livilla during the journey to the island of Lesbos (Tac. *Ann.* 2.55). The couple stopped to rest in the province of Syria, whose Roman governor Gnaeu Calpunius Piso disliked Germanicus and resented being under his command. Piso was described as arrogant, violent, irritable, and inflexible (Tac. *Ann.* 2.43). His wife Plancina, of great wealth and high lineage, also shared his dislike of Germanicus and detested Agrippina (Tac. *Ann.* 2.57).

After a trip to Egypt, which Tiberius was furious that he went without his permission (Tac. *Ann.* 2.59; Suet. *Tib.* 52), Germanicus returns to Antioch in Syria and finds that Piso has cancelled all his orders while he was away (Tac. *Ann.* 2.69). In this setback with Piso, Germanicus feels ill and declares that he has been poisoned by Piso and Plancina (Suet. *Calig.* 3; Tac. *Ann.* 2.70).

In Germanicus' last hours, he was convinced that he had been poisoned and that Piso and Plancina were involved. Suetonius and Cassius Dio point out that Germanicus had signs of poisoning, such as dark spots on his body and foam in his mouth (Tac. *Ann.* 2.73; Suet. *Calig.* 1; Cass. Dio, *Roman History* 57.18.9). He begged Agrippina to be more diplomatic. Tacitus made the association of Plancina with Livia but left it somewhat ambiguous (Tac. *Ann.* 2.71.2-3). Germanicus died in AD 19, aged 33 (Suet. *Calig.* 5).

It is noteworthy that Tacitus states that Germanicus asked Agrippina Major to be more diplomatic. This content remains dubious in the work, but it seems that the author characterises Agrippina as an uncontrolled person, emphasising through Germanicus a caution that she did not have. This type of discourse in which the author characterises a woman as someone without balance also occurs in the text by Cassius Dio, when referring to Fulvia, Mark Antony's wife, when he mentions that Caesar could not stand his mother-in-law's difficult temperament and used this to demonstrate that he was at odds with her. He ended up sending Fulvia's daughter back, with the remark that she was still a virgin, something he confirmed by oath (Cass. Dio, *Roman History* 48.5.2-5).

Otherwise, Germanicus' final words to Agrippina could not be a demonstration that her personality was difficult, but a warning to her and her children. However, Tacitus puts this in a dubious way, but on the one hand he portrays Agrippina's weakness as responsible for her death, and on the other he cites that through her actions she proved to follow the proud tradition of her ancestors, demonstrating courage and dexterity in caring for her family. However, the author also reported that several people were disturbed to see such behaviour in a woman (McHugh, 2011, p. 90), as were Tibertius and Livia.

Insufficient to really subvert the relationship of domination, these authors use these strategies to result in a confirmation of the dominant representation of women as evil beings, whose identities, entirely negative, were essentially constituted of prohibitions, generating occasions of transgressions that would be attributed to such women, resulting in an undeclared violence, invisible at times, which is opposed to physical violence. However, it is a symbolic violence exerted on them by men that can cover various spheres to defame them, from sorcery, cunning, lying, passivity, possessive love of the maternal wife, among other themes. However, women, in these social contexts, were condemned to give proof of their malignancy, usually pointed out by the other sex. Thus, they had to justify prohibitions and prejudices attributed to them in the face of an evil essence. This is a tragic logic constructed in a social reality that produces masculine domination and confirms the representations that society itself invokes in its favour in order to exercise and justify itself. Consequently, the male view is continuously legitimised by the very practices that society determines: its dispositions result in an unfavourable prejudice against the feminine and, according to this social logic, women have no way of disengaging from it, but to confirm this prejudice over and over again (Bourdieu, 1998, p. 44).

When they reacted to prejudice, tensions were produced and, by the system itself, women lost space and defamation occurred once again. This logic would be a curse, which was underway on a daily basis in various exchanges between the sexes, being the same dispositions that led men to attribute to women the inferior tasks and ungrateful arrangements, even blaming them if they failed in the tasks that were left to them, without giving credit for any success (Bourdieu, 1998, p. 44).

Rumours of Tiberius being behind Germanicus' death increased when he failed to grant Germanicus honours such as a state funeral; moreover, Tiberius interrupted the mourning of the general as he considered it too long (Tac. *Ann.* 3.6-7). Consequently, Agrippina not only lost her beloved husband, but also the hope of becoming an empress, for which she had been preparing all her life (Burns, 2007, p. 51).

Piso was even accused by the Roman Senate of being a conspirator in the death of Germanicus (Tac. *Ann.* 3.10-18) and went through a trial, but was not supported by Tiberius. Consequently, Piso committed suicide by cutting his throat. Meanwhile, Livia intervened to protect Plancina, who must have confirmed her enmity to Agrippina (Tac. *Ann.* 3.17).

In the meantime, after the events with Agrippina and Germanicus, when attacking Gallus, because he had some reasons against him, Tiberius began to court Sejanus, because he believed that this minister could become emperor or wished to approach him in order to later build a conspiracy against him. He therefore proposed to him the largest and most important part of the honours voted (Cass. Dio, *Roman History* 58.3.1-2).

According to Suetonius, Agrippina was lamenting the death of her husband Germanicus, and the emperor asked her why she was not reigning and whether she understood that an injustice was being done to her. Once, after Germanicus' death, Sejanus warned her that she might be poisoned by some food that Tiberius would offer her, so she should avoid her father-in-law's table. Accordingly, she sat at the table and did not touch the food. Noticing her attitude, Tiberius offered her fruit, as a test, and she did not accept, passing it on to the slaves (Tac. *Ann.* 4.54). Tiberius believed that she knew he intended to poison her, but this scene was arranged to put her to the test. He falsely accused her of wanting to take refuge either by the statue of Augustus or by the army, and eventually banished her to the island of Pandataria. Feeling insulted by her, Tiberius gouged out one of her eyes with blows of a scourge (*flagrum*) by one of his centurions. She decided to starve, but Tiberius tried to make her swallow her food, and finally she could not resist and died. After this episode, Tiberius covered her with all the slanders and proposed to include her birthday in the list of the evil days (Suet. *Tib.* 53).

Agrippina's death can also be understood from another point of view: only four years after Germanicus' death, Tiberius' son Drusus died, leaving no direct heirs from the emperor. Consequently, Drusus and Nero, Agrippina's sons, were the candidates to succeed Tiberius, who, by his mid-sixties, was semi-retired and left everything in the hands of his lieutenant Lucius Aelius Sejanus (Burns, 2007, p. 51), who seemed to have an interest in the position of emperor, since he was suspected of the death of Tiberius' son and seemed to want to wipe out Agrippina's family (Tac. *Ann.* 4.12) and people close to her. In AD 29, Sejanus succeeded in persuading Drusus, Agrippina's second son, to go against her and her eldest son Nero. Sejanus convinced him that if Nero was eliminated, he would be the one to succeed Tiberius. Thus Drusus, together with Sejanus, conspired against Nero (Tac. *Ann.* 4.60.5-6). Nero was accused of perversity and Agrippina was attacked by Tiberius, who accused her of insolence and disobedience (Tac. *Ann.* 5.3). There was protest in favour of Agrippina's family (Tac. *Ann.* 5.4), but Tiberius scorned the act and ordered Agrippina and Nero to be exiled. When Agrippina objected, she was flogged so severely by the soldier that she lost an eye (Suet. *Tib.* 53). Mother and child were exiled to separate islands off the coast of Italy. She went to Pandataria, the place where her mother was banished 30 years before (Suet. *Tib.* 64). Suetonius mentions that she intended to kill herself by going without food, but her guards forced her to eat (Suet. *Tib.* 53). In AD 33, after four years of exile, Agrippina died of starvation, aged 46 (Burns, 2007, p. 53).

Tacitus describes her as a woman who longed for revenge for her husband's death, and for this reason he characterises her as a woman of high nobility (Tac. *Ann.* 2.75). However, later in his narrative, Tacitus presents her as a stubborn and angry woman who insistently asked Tiberius to grant her a new marriage. Once, when Agrippina was ill, Tiberius went to visit her and she asked him to allow her to remarry, but perhaps he was wary of the fact that a new husband could be a potential rival (Tac. *Ann.* 4.53).

Tacitus describes Agrippina with the word *ferocia*, which was usually used to demonstrate a fierce, angry, and even savage behaviour, being employed more for a man, like other adjectives - *ferox, atrox, contumax* -, indicating a person who was fight-oriented (Tac. *Ann.* 1.69, 4.12, 4.52, 5.3 and 6.25). However, this would be a pejorative word when applied to a woman (McHugh, 2011, p. 73). Tacitus characterises her as courageous, not describing her negatively as *dux femina*, while she was on the Vetera bridge (Tac. *Ann.* 1.69), in the same way the author does with Boudica, for example.

In Sejanus' time, Tacitus mentions that Tiberius criticises Agrippina for her insolent tongue and her arrogance. Furthermore, Tacitus uses the adjective *atrox* to describe Agrippina, which was used to narrate a conflict between soldiers. Agrippina's behaviour was pertinent to the traditional virtues of a woman, as well as some acts of heroic virtues, which were typically considered masculine, but sometimes exhibited by women in exceptional circumstances. However, in general, these women were criticised for political motivations (McHugh, 2011, p. 84-87).

Agrippina acted in accordance with the quality of her father's service to the *princeps*, demonstrating a paternal inheritance of leadership in battle. She never took on the duties of generals and male leaders, although she has been described as taking on the responsibilities of a general. However, as a widow, she was able to fulfil her responsibility as a matron, looking after her safety and that of her children. Agrippina nevertheless acquired a public status befitting a male lineage (Hallett, 1984, p. 339; Hallett, 1989, p. 62-63 apud McHugh, 2011, p. 90).

The division of labour consists of the relationship that women get pregnant and have to take care of the house. Thus, the body is the one that announces these separations, a thought that does not escape reality and that can be used to think of such a division in the society of the Roman elite. However, there was a masculine order that was inscribed on bodies through tacit injunctions, implicit in the routines of the division of labour or collective or private rituals, an example would be the marginalisation imposed on women with their exclusion from male places. From this point of view, it can be concluded that the physical and social regularities imposed and inculcated measures that excluded women from the noblest tasks, signalling inferior places for them, with specific body postures, such as childcare (Bourdieu, 1998, p. 34), while men ruled, fought wars and built strategies of conquest. The focus on the body immediately raises the question about how to distinguish between practical and discursive knowledge (Moore, 2000, p. 19).

When Agrippina died, Tiberius announced that he should have been stricter with her, as the punishment for treason was strangulation or being thrown down a flight of stairs to die. Tiberius made grave insults against her, accusing her of committing adultery with a senator named Gaius Asinius Gallus, who had also died of starvation in exile (Tac. *Ann.* 6.23). Tacitus rejects this accusation (Tac. *Ann.* 6.25) and criticises Tiberius, pointing him out as cunning and cruel, a wicked criminal and a tyrant of the worst kind (Tac. *Ann.* 1-6). Suetonius describes him as a savage, a sadist, who clearly suffered from severe depression and self-loathing (Suet. *Tib.* 56-68). Cassius Dio describes him as peculiar, false, and malicious (Cass. Dio, *Roman History* 57.1.1-4).

Agrippina saw three brothers, a husband and two sons cheated out of their rights to be rulers. Two of her sons died in prison before her. However, four years after her death in AD 37, her son Caligula became emperor (Burns, 2007, p. 54). Before that, Caligula had entered Tiberius' room with a dagger in his hand while he was sleeping, with the purpose of avenging the death of his mother and brothers. However, he was unable to carry out the deed, throwing his weapon to the ground and leaving without Tiberius realising (Suet. *Calig.* 12).

On becoming emperor, Caligula eventually went to Pandataria to collect the ashes of his mother and brother for a better demonstration of filial love and named the month of September "Germanicus". He appointed his uncle, Claudius, a fellow consul, who was only a Roman knight, adopted his brother Tiberius on the day he took the virile robe and named him "Prince of Youth" (Suet. *Calig.* 15).

The annual day of funeral sacrifices was instituted in honour of Agrippina, as were the circus games, when her image was carried in a chariot, called a *carpentum,* which was shown on coins of Caligula in honour of his mother. However, the young emperor, only twenty-four years old, cancelled all measures against her and his brothers, punished his persecutors and called back his friends, who were still alive in exile (Cass. Dio, *Roman History* 59.3.6 and 4.3).

Figure 56 – Bronze sestertius[204], 37 - 41 BC, Rome, Caligula's rule, 28.19g, 36.1 mm diameter. Obverse: draped bust of Agrippina on right and hair on tail along neck, AGRIPPINA M F MAT C CAESARIS AVGVSTI (*Agrippina Marci Filia Mater Caii Caesaris Augusti* = Agrippina, daughter of Marcus [Vipsanio Agrippa], mother of Gaius Caesar Augustus). Reverse: *carpentum*, S· P· Q· R / MEMORIAE AGRIPPINAE (*Senatus Populusq Romanus / Memoriae Agrippinae* = The Senate and the people of Rome / In memory of Agrippina[205])

Source: © KBR *cabinet des monnais et médailles*

    This coin is a great tribute from Caligula to his mother Agrippina, who is on the obverse, the most important side of the coin, where emperors usually appear, and without male accompaniment, demonstrating her importance and ensuring his descent by caption, as well as having been a special person for Caligula, who helped him reach his position. Agrippina Major provided her son with a direct lineage to the *Divus Augustus*, which was important to legitimise his imperial power. His father, Germanicus, was also important for his legitimation (Claes, 2013, p. 95), having been honoured on coins like his mother.

    On the reverse of the coin is a chariot, known as a *carpentum*, which was commonly used by the Vestal Virgins. However, the *carpentum has* also appeared on coin depictions of Livia, demonstrating a virtuous dignity for her. It was considered an honour and a reward for the privilege of her status, since even Messalina and Agrippina Minor used it in the city only on special occasions (Zager, 2014). However, Livia's coin with the *carpentum* elevated Agrippina's status, which may have been Caligula's strategy to institutionalise and legitimise himself as emperor (Claes, 2013, p. 96). The obverse caption, AGRIPPINA M F MAT C CAESARIS AVGVTI, highlights Agrippina's relevance as the emperor's mother, and the reverse caption, S P

---

[204] Bibliography: RIC I² 55; BMC 86; du Chastel 387 (*Collection du Chastel Collectie du Chastel*). Available at: https://opac.kbr.be/LIBRARY/doc/SYRACUSE/20734623. Accessed: 7 Sept. 2022.

[205] Translation made by the author.

Q R / MEMORIAE / AGRIPPINAE, pays posthumous tribute to her, with the consent of the Senate.

This series of sestertius was dedicated to the memory of Agrippina, which on its reverse showed honours after her death; for this reason, this example is part of a series of posthumous type coins, with the demonstration of the *carpentum* carrying her ashes. Emperors and empresses were commonly honoured on coins after their deaths. This coin with a *carpentum* on the reverse suggests that this vehicle carried her image in games of *Circus Maximus*, being the first to have a full devotion after passing away. The coin bears no image or caption of the emperor, as other coin issues appeared with the emperor on the obverse and his mother on the reverse, demonstrating the physical resemblance between them (Wood, 1988, p. 410).

Figure 57 – Aureus[206], Rome, AD 40, 7.71g, 18.6 in diameter. Obverse: head of Caligula with laurel wreath on right, C CAESAR AVG PON M TR POT III COS III (*Gaius Caesar Augustus Pontifex Maximus Tribunicia Potestate tertium consul tertium* = Gaius Caesar Augustus, Supreme Pontiff, invested in the tribune power for the third time and consul for the third time). Reverse: Draped bust of Agrippina to the right, hair in tail along neck, AGRIPPINA MAT C CAES AVG GERM (*Agrippina mater Gai Caesaris Augusti Germanici* = Agrippina mother of Gaius Caesar Augustus Germanicus)

Source: © KBR *cabinet des monnais et médailles*

This aureus emphasises that Caligula intended to revive the memory of his mother, whom Tiberius had banished to the island of Pandataria. Caligula even destroyed the *villa* of Herculaneum, where his mother had been a prisoner before her exile, and purified the day of her birthday, which was formally declared as *dies nefastus* (Claes, 2013, p. 96).

---

[206] Bibliography: RIC I² 21; BMC 22; du Chastel 381 (*Collection du Chastel Collectie du Chastel*). Available at: https://opac.kbr.be/LIBRARY/doc/SYRACUSE/20734615. Accessed: 14 July 2022.

During Caligula's rule, the image of his mother was also minted in provinces, following the tradition of imitating the models minted in Rome, as did the mint of Antioch, Turkey.

Figure 58 – Silver tetradrachm[207], dated AD 37 - 38, minted in Antiochia, Turkia, with the bust of Caligula laureated on the obverse and caption: ΓΑΙΟΥ ΚΑΙΣΑΡΟΣ ΣΕΒΑ ΓΕΡΜΑ, transliteration: GAIOU KAISAROS SEBA GERMA (Gaius Caesar Augustus Germanicus[208]); and the draped bust of Agrippina Major on the reverse and caption: ΑΓΡΙΠΠΕ[ΙΝΗΣ ΑΝΤΙΟ] ΜΗΤΡΟ and transliteration: AGRIPPE[INES ANTIO] METRO (Farewell to Mother Agrippina[209])

Source: © The Trustees of the British Museum

This silver tetradrachm from the Caligula period honours the emperor with a laureate bust on the obverse and Agrippina Major on the reverse. She is remembered as an important person, both for the emperor and for this province. The history and importance of Agrippina Major was key to other governments and she was eventually honoured during the period of Claudius and Titus.

---

[207] Reference number: 1867.0101.1602. Bibliography: RPC1 / Roman provincial coinage. Vol.1, From the death of Caesar to the death of Vitellius (44 BC-AD 69) (4166/1) BMC Greek (Galatia) / Catalogue of the Greek coins of Galatia, Cappadocia and Syria (165, p. 171).
Available at: https://www.britishmuseum.org/collection/object/C_1867-0101-1602. Accessed: 25 Oct. 2020.

[208] Translation by Juarez Oliveira.

[209] Translation by Juarez Oliveira.

Figure 59 – Coin[210] from the Smyrna mint, 37 - 38 BC. Obverse: laureate bust of Caligula, Γ ΑΙΟΝ ΚΑΙΣ ΑΡΑΓ ΕΡΜΑΝΙΚΟΝ ΕΠ Ι ΑΟΥΟΛ Α (Gaius Caesar Germanicus under Aviola[211]). Reverse: draped bust of Agrippina Major facing the bust of Germanicus, ΓΕΜΑ-ΝΙΚΟΝ ΑΓΡΙΠΠΕΙΝΑΝ ΖΜΥΡΝΑΙΩΝ ΜΕΝΟΦΑΝΗC (From the People of Monophanes of Smyrna to Germanicus and Agrippina[212])

Source: © The Nicholson Museum

The last example is a coin minted in Smyrna, dated 37 - 38 BC, on the obverse of which is the laureate bust of Caligula. However, what is most interesting is the reverse, on which are the busts of Germanicus and Agrippina Major facing each other. The coin is a tribute to Caligula and his family and had the power of celebrating the emperor's loved ones who were no longer alive. However, this object is characterised as a coin of a family type, but also of a posthumous type, preserving the memory of his ancestors.

Agrippina continued to be honoured by Caligula's successor, Claudius, who was Germanicus' brother, and in AD 49 he married Agrippina's daughter, who bore her same name, Agrippina Minor. Some aspects of Caligula's official propaganda were effective enough to provide models for his successor, Claudius, so that the sestertius in memory of Agrippina Major was a notable example. After Messalina, when Agrippina Minor married Claudius, the governor's coins changed dramatically, as the reverses of gold and silver coins, which had previously celebrated military and political proceedings, began to focus exclusively on his new wife's family and even his adopted son, Nero, mainly for the emperor dissociate himself from the figure of Messalina and to legitimise his remarriage to his niece, as well as securing the title of Augusta for Agrippina Minor. The reappearance of the empress's

---

[210] Collection of Walter Holt, RPC 2471. The coin figure was taken from "Faces of power: imperial portraitures on Roman coins", Nicholson Museum, by Brennan, Turner and Wright (2007).

[211] Name of a proconsul (Brennan; Turner; Wright, 2007, p. 12).

[212] Translation by Juarez Oliveira.

mother on the bronze coin from the same period could have been one of the first invocations to her mother's memory to legitimise honours conferred for her daughter's use (Wood, 1988, p. 410).

Figure 60 – Sestertius[213] of copper alloy, dated AD 50 - 54, rule of Claudius, with draped bust of Agrippina Major, facing right, with caption: AGRIPPINA M F GERMANICI CAESARIS (*Agrippina Mater Filii Germanici Caesaris*[214] = Agrippina mother of the sons of Germanicus Caesar[215]); and the reverse with major caption S C (*Senatus Consultum* = minted with the consent of the Senate), and minor caption: TI CLAVDIVS CAESAR AVG GERM P M TR P IMP P P (*Tiberius Claudius Caesar Augustus Germanicus Pontifex Maximus Tribunicia Potestate Imperator Pater Patriae*[216] = Commander Tiberius Claudius *Caesar* Augustus Germanicus, Supreme Pontiff, vested in the Tribunicia Power and father of the homeland[217])

Source: © The Trustees of the British Museum

In this sestertius of Claudius' rule, Agrippina Major appears uniquely highlighted on the obverse of the coin, demonstrating her importance and value to the emperor of that period, who indirectly also honours his father-in-law, Germanicus, as shown in the obverse caption. The larger caption, S C, shows that the tribute was consented to by the Senate and the smaller caption shows the emperor's approval.

This coin confirms that Claudius, after marrying Agrippina Minor in AD 49, commemorated his wife's parents on coins, who were linked to great ancestors, because Agrippina Major was the daughter of Agrippa; and

---

[213] Reference number: R.9871. Bibliographical references: RE1 / Coins of the Roman Empire in the British Museum, vol. 1: Augustus to Vitellius (221, p. 194); RIC1 / The Roman Imperial Coinage, vol. 1 (102, p. 128). RIC 102. BMCRE 219. C *Agrippina Senior* 3. *[Rome, AD 42]*. Available at: https://www.britishmuseum.org/collection/object/C_R-9871. Accessed: 25 Oct. 2020.

[214] Available at: https://en.numista.com/catalogue/pieces66071.html. Accessed: 25 Oct. 2020.

[215] Translation made by the author.

[216] Available at: https://en.numista.com/catalogue/pieces66071.html. Accessed: 25 Oct. 2020.

[217] Translation made by the author.

Germanicus was the adopted son of Tiberius and grandson of Augustus. This factor connected Claudius with the founders of the Julius-Claudian imperial house. From Augustus (27 BC) to Carinus (AD 285), many emperors used retrospective messages on their coinage. These messages not only promoted previous emperors, but also ancestors, *gentes*, female ascendants, imperial mothers or grandmothers, and even messages calling for a noble Roman birth of the emperor. However, the frequency with which women were minted in the Early Empire was certainly somewhat innovative (Claes, 2013, p. 125 and 127).

Almost half a century after Agrippina died, Emperor Titus also honoured her memory. She became a legendary figure, as a heroine and as a victim (Burns, 2007, p. 55).

Figure 61 – Sestertius[218] of copper alloy, Rome, dated 80 - AD 81, from the government of Titus, bust of Agrippina draped to the right, on obverse, with caption: A[GRIPPINA] M F GERMANICI CAESARIS (Agrippina Materi Fili Germanici Caesaris[219] = Agrippina mother of the sons of Germanic Caesar[220]); and larger caption on reverse, SC (*Senatus Consultum* = minted with the consent of the Senate), and smaller caption: [IMP T CAES] DIVI VESP F AVG [P M TR P P COS VIII] (*Imperator Titus Caesar Divi Vespasianus Fili Augustus Pontifex Maximus Tribunicia Potestate Pater Patriae Consul Octavum*[221] = Commander Titus Caesar, Son of the Divine Vespasian Augustus, Supreme Pontiff, vested in the Tribune Power, Father of the homeland and Consul for the Eighth Time[222])

Source: © The Trustees of the British Museum

---

[218] Reference number: 1867.0101.2032. Bibliography: RE2 / Coins of the Roman Empire in the British Museum, vol.II: Vespasian to Domitian (296, p. 289). RIC2.1 / The Roman Imperial Coinage, vol. 2 part 1: From AD 69 to AD 96: Vespasian to Domitian (419, p. 226). Available at: https://www.britishmuseum.org/collection/object/C_1867-0101-2032. Accessed: 25 Oct. 2020.

[219] Available at: https://en.numista.com/catalogue/pieces66071.html. Accessed: 25 Oct. 2020.

[220] Translation made by the author.

[221] Available at: https://en.numista.com/catalogue/pieces66071.html. Accessed: 25 Oct. 2020.

[222] Translation made by the author.

This sestertius from Titus' rule is similar to that of Claudius' rule. As he did with coins bearing the image of Livia, Titus seems to want to get closer to and boast about the characters of the Julio-Claudian family by minting their faces again during his rule. The coin, like that of Claudius, also honours the husband and children of Agrippina Major, since this is depicted in its obverse caption: A[GRIPPINA] M F GERMANICI CAESARIS. The reverse caption is geared towards honouring the ruler Titus, [IMP T CAES] DIVI VESP F AVG [P M TR P P COS VIII], and it is shown that the minting of this coin was consented to by the Senate through the S C, however the use of these letters is still questioned, as it is uncertain whether the coins would even have to go through a Senate sieve to be minted.

The variety in the typology of Agrippina's portraits reflected her role in the political propaganda of the period of her life and after her death. Her depiction, during the rule of both Caligula and Claudius, seems to have worked well with the commitment to make the representation along contemporary shapes, as does the form of her hair, but also idealised as a goddess and inspired by classical Greek models. In this sense, she is no longer represented as a martyr of the tyrannical Tiberius, but as a precedent of his daughter's ambition (Wood, 1988, p. 409), as well as of his son Caligula and of Claudius himself.

The use of Agrippina Major's image by her daughter seems to have played a key role in the propaganda of Agrippina Minor and her supporters. In this way, representations of aristocratic women offer a demonstration of gender roles in Roman society. However, the images can offer considerable evidence as to qualities and types of activities that were admired for these women, as well as those that were condemned. Older women, relatives, or ancestors of emperors, kept in public and in memory, demonstrated *pietas* and could be invoked by the emperor as a demonstration of bloodline. Living women who represented a hope for births and heirs could be praised in their family roles, as well as wives and mothers. All imperial women, living or dead, fertile or childless, could represent various virtues, so that the emperor could claim them as belonging to his family and regime, as well as being capable of considerable influence (Wood, 1988, p. 409).

Agrippina Major was honoured mainly after her death. Her memory was recalled by her youngest son, Caligula, without dissociating her memory from the hated Tiberius. She was also known as the mother of Agrippina Minor and invoked by her daughter for political ambitions and especially to have her roles recognised (Wood, 1988, p. 410) and linked to power. Thus, she was also recognised as the grandmother of the emperor Nero and the mother of Caligula, giving her a character of one who contributed to the continuation of the imperial family, which brought a positive attitude to her whole story, granting her a position of victim before an unscrupulous emperor, who was Tiberius.

Chapter 7

Agrippina Minor and the dream of being Augusta

Germanicus' daughter with Agrippina Major, who was called Agrippina Minor (14/15 - AD 59), was born into the imperial family around AD 14, with Augustus as her great-grandfather and Tiberius as her great-uncle. She was first recognised as one of Caligula's sisters, then as the wife of Claudius and the mother of Nero. In her family, she was in three sisters, Agrippina, Drusilla, and Livia, born in three consecutive years; and had three more brothers: Nero, Drusus, and Gaius Caesar. As a result of Tiberius' accusations, Nero and Drusus were indicted by the Senate as public enemies (Suet. *Calig.* 7).

According to Suetonius, Caligula proclaimed that his mother was the fruit of incest between Augustus and his daughter Julia, and called his great-grandmother, Livia Augusta, "Ulysses in a stola", having, in a letter to the Senate, accused her of coming from a humble lineage, on the pretext that her maternal grandfather was a decurion from Fundi, although public monuments attested that Aufidius Lurco had been a magistrate in Rome. To add to this, Suetonius remarks that Caligula entertained his sisters in a shameful sex trade, where at great banquets he would alternately put them under him while his wife was on top, and may have devirginated Drusilla, who married Lucius Cassius Longinus, a consular personage, publicly treating her as his legitimate wife. When she fell ill, he insisted on making her his heir, and when he saw her dead, he fled the city in the middle of the night, going to places like Campania and Syracuse. Every oath Caligula took was "by the divinity of Drusilla". He did not attribute equal love for his other sisters, and he prostituted them, often with his own favourites, being able to easily prosecute them as adulteresses and accomplices in the plots against his wife. And he ended up calling his daughter Julia Drusilla (Suet. *Calig.* 23-25).

Next to his sisters, the following coin depicts Agrippina as Securitas, Drusilla as Concordia, and Julia as Fortuna (Florenzano, 2015, p. 18), so that each of them carries a cornucopia, a symbol of fertility, abundance, and wealth. Caligula's sisters occupy a secondary position on the coin, leaving the obverse for the sampling of the emperor's figure and to notoriously make his name explicit, along with his descendants. The coin symbolised Caligula's right to rule as a member of the imperial family (Zager, 2014, p. 64).

Figure 62 – Bronze sestertius[223], 37 - 38 BC, Rome. Obverse: Head of Caligula with laurel wreath on left, C CAESAR AVG GERMANICVS PON M TR POT (*Gaius Caesar Augustus Germanicus Pontifex Maximus Tribunicia Potestate* = Gaius Caesar Augustus Germanicus, Supreme Pontiff, invested in the Tribunicial Power[224]). Reverse: Caligula's three sisters, standing: Agrippina holds cornucopias in her right hand, leaning on a column (as Securitas), with her left hand on Drusilla's shoulder, who holds a *patera* in her right hand and cornucopias in her left hand (as Concordia), and Julia holds a rudder in her right hand and cornucopias in her left hand (as Fortuna); AGRIPPINA DRVSILLA IVLIA / S C (Agrippina Drusila Julia /minted by consent of Senate[225])

Source: © KBR *cabinet des monnaies et médailles*

In the last case, Caligula's three sisters appear on the reverse standing, facing and with their bellies out, wearing a Greek *quíton* and *himation* instead of a *stola* (Wood, 1995, p. 461). They hold attributes of divine personifications forming a harmonious triad, like the male triumvirs of previous generations composed of *Horae, Parcae* and *Gratiae*[226] (Porto, 2023, p. 23): on the left,

---

[223] Bibliography: RIC I² 33; BMC 36. Available at: https://opac.kbr.be/LIBRARY/doc/SYRACUSE/20734551. Accessed: 20 July 2022.

[224] Translation made by the author.

[225] Translation made by the author.

[226] In Greek mythology, the Horae were a group of goddesses who presided over the seasons. Daughters of Zeus and Themis, they personified the order of the world and were originally three: Εúvouια, who represented legality, good order, civic laws; Ειρvn, who represented peace; and Αίn, who represented justice (MURRAY, 1997, p. 78 and 102). The Parcae were deities of fate. Three in number, Atropos, Clotho and Lachesis who were represented as spinners in Roman mythology, imbued with regulating the duration of life from birth to death. Atropos spun life, Clotho rolled it up and Lachesis cut it, when the existence of a being came to an end (SILVA, F. de S., 2008, p. 19). The Gratiae, in Greek mythology, were the goddesses of the banquet, concord, charm, gratitude, family prosperity and luck, in other words, the goddesses of graces. They were usually considered daughters of Zeus with Eurynome. However, other versions of the myth place them as daughters of Zeus with Eunomia, daughters of Dionysus, Hera, and even the sun god Helios. The name of each of them varies in the different legends. In Homer's *Iliad*, there is only one Gratiae, Aglaia. Despite the regional variations, the most frequent trio was: Thalia (Oalia or Odlera) - the one who makes flowers sprout; Euphrosina (Ειxppocn) - the sense of joy; wife of Hypnos; and Aglaia (*Aylazia*) - and clarity, who was the wife of Hephaestus (HANSEN, 2004, p. 152; Porto, 2023, p. 27).

Agrippina (as Securitas), head turned to the right, holding a cornucopia in her right hand, resting her right hand on the column and her left hand on Drusilla's shoulder; in the centre, Drusilla (as Concordia), head to the left, holding a *patera* in her right hand and a cornucopia in her left; on the right, Julia (as Fortuna) appears with the head turned to the left, holding a rudder in her right hand and a cornucopia in her left hand. The cornucopia demonstrated abundance and imperial success. Each of the sisters represented a benefit or virtue brought by Caligula, such as Securitas, Concordia, and Fortuna. This coin depicts the sisters according to age, from left to right (Claes, 2013, p. 223). Caligula could have minted his sisters to demonstrate that a descendant of any of them would be accepted as an heir (Wood, 1995, p. 459).

From this perspective, their images served as a reminder of their positions within the imperial dynasty, with the role of securing the emperor's future. Drusilla, Caligula's favourite, was deified, with the posthumous title of Panthea, as a universal goddess of Rome. With this, she was the first Roman woman to be deified, remaining with the name Diva Drusilla Panthea (Porto, 2023, p. 24). After Drusilla died, Agrippina and Livilla were banished for participating in a conspiracy against him. Thus, Caligula no longer minted the coin type with the three sisters (Claes, 2013, p. 224). This coin type was also found in Banias, which was a considerable distance away from Rome. This suggests that it was common for iconographic coin patterns to circulate around the Mediterranean, being absorbed by local leaders with haste (Porto, 2023, p. 24).

Family-type coins were common in the Early Empire, such as this example with the three sisters of Caligula; or with representations of empresses, such as coins of Tiberius, with Livia on the reverse, or even coins of Claudius, with his wife, Agrippina, on the reverse; and, in rare cases, of dead relatives, such as the coin of Caligula, with Agrippina Major on the reverse; and of some heirs of the empire, such as the coin of Augustus, with Julia on the reverse and his two grandchildren (Sear, 2000, p. 45).

In AD 49, Agrippina Minor married Claudius, but Nero's father, according to Suetonius, was the son of Antonia Major, whose life was in every respect abominable. Suetonius tells us that his father Domitius, after congratulating him on his birth, said that nothing could be born to him and Agrippina that was not detestable and disastrous, a sign of their calamitous fate. Agrippina did not name him after her uncle Claudius, because, at that time, he was a court plaything. When Nero's father died, he was three years old and was heir to the third part of his estate, but this did not come to him because Caligula confiscated all his property, his mother was banished, without resources and indigent. She sought her aunt Lepida's house, where Nero's pedagogues were a dancer and a barber. With Claudius in power, she recovered her parents' possessions and enriched herself with the inheritance of her godfather, Passienus Crispus. Agrippina, by increasing her power, made Nero a threat to Britannicus, and a rumour began to circulate that Messalina had sent agents to strangle Nero during his siesta (Suet. *Ner.* 5-6.2).

Agrippina is characterised by Tacitus as a character with a desire for power since the author describes her activity for the benefit of her son Nero and her privilege in receiving the title of Augusta (Tac. *Ann.* 12.25-26 and 12.41-43). Suetonius comments that Claudius was seduced by the charms of Agrippina, daughter of Germanicus, who was his brother, through the caresses she made to win his heart. He also comments that she was able to bribe senators to force him to marry immediately, as if this were a high interest for the State, and to grant others the power to make such unions, which were considered incestuous. This led Claudius to marry Agrippina after only one day, but he found no one to follow the example. Moreover, he adopted Nero as his son (Suet. *Claud.* 26.1-27). To add, still according to Suetonius, who considered this marriage as a contract and illegitimate, Claudius kept calling her "his daughter" or "his soul" and that "she was born and grew up on his knees". He adds that when he was about to adopt Nero, his son being already grown up, no one would ever have entered the Claudian family by adoption (Suet. *Claud.* 39).

Tacitus also mentions the marriage in AD 53 of Nero to Octavia, daughter of Claudius and Messalina, after Claudius had promised his daughter to Silanus. For Suetonius, after the episode of Messalina's death, *Claudius'* forgetfulness and lack of thoughtfulness were astonishing, as was his insensitivity when he sat down at table, shortly after having had her killed, asking why the empress was not coming (Suet. *Claud.* 39).

Suetonius mentions that, towards the end of his life, Claudius had shown signs of regret for having married Agrippina and adopted Nero, as well as for having had an adulterous wife in his past, recognising that his destiny was to have impudent but not unpunished wives. This author emphasises that, by Claudius' will, his son Britannicus was to be his successor. He wrote the will, which was opposed by all the magistrates, and was prevented by Agrippina, who already had informers accusing her of numerous crimes (Suet. *Claud.* 43-44.1).

The status that Agrippina achieved with her marriage to Claudius soon appeared on coins, along with her title of Augusta, and on several coins from the reign of Claudius and Nero (Zager, 2014, p. 69). However, at the beginning of book 11, Tacitus makes it clear that the presence of women in Claudius' life was damaging his reputation (Tac. *Ann.* 11.2).

In relation to the minting of coins, the next example, which is a golden one, gives great importance to the imperial couple, with Claudius on the obverse with a laurel wreath and a caption with his name and titles; on the reverse, Agrippina is placed in a secondary way, but with great importance because she is accompanying her husband on a gold coin. Her esteem on the coin is indicated by her name in the caption and she appears wearing a crown of ears of corn, which was a symbol linked to Ceres, fertility, abundance, heredity and dynastic success.

Figure 63 – Aureus[227], AD 50 - 54, Rome, rule of Claudius. Obverse: head of Claudius with laurel wreath on right, TI CLAVD CAESAR AVG GERM P M TRIB POT P P (*Tiberius Claudius Caesar Augustus Germanicus, Pontifex Maximus, Tribunicia Potestate, Pater Patriae* = Tiberius Claudius Caesar Augustus Germanicus, Supreme Pontiff, invested in the Tribunicial Power, father of the homeland[228]). Reverse: Bust of Agrippina on right, with crown of corn cobs, hair braided, AGRIPPINAE AVGVSTAE

Source: © KBR *cabinet des monnaies et médailles*

Provincial coins used to imitate the models of Rome, as can be seen in the next example that was minted in Ephesus, with Claudius on the obverse and Agrippina on the reverse. On many examples, Agrippina is accompanied by the crown of ears of corn and other elements symbolising fertility, agricultural production, abundance, and dynastic success.

---

[227] Bibliography: RIC I² 80; BMC 72; du Chastel 394 (*Collection du Chastel Collectie du Chastel*). Available at: https://opac.kbr.be/LIBRARY/doc/SYRACUSE/20734780. Accessed: 18 July 2022.
[228] Translation made by the author.

Figure 64 – Silver tridrachm cistophori[229], AD 50 - 51, Ephesus, Izmir province, Aegean region, Turkey. Obverse: laureate bust of Claudius facing right, TI CLAVD CAESAR AVG P M TR P X IMP XIIX (*Tiberius Claudius Caesar Augustus, Pontifex Maximus, Tribunicia Potestate Decima, Imperator Duodevicesimus* = Tiberius Claudius Caesar Augustus, Supreme Pontiff, invested in the Tribunicial Power, for the tenth time, Supreme Commander for the eighteenth time[230]). On the obverse is the draped bust of Agrippina, facing right, with hair in three rows of curls in front and in braids behind, with the caption: AGRIPPINA AVGVSTA CAESARIS AVG = Agrippina Augusta of Caesar Augustus[231])

Source: © The Trustees of the British Museum

Figure 65 – Sestertius[232], from AD 50 - 54, Rome. Obverse: draped bust of Agrippina Minor on right, hair with a long braid, AGRIPPINA AVG GERMANICI F CAESARIS AVG (*Agrippina Augusta Germanici Filii Caesaris Augusti* = Agrippina Augusta, daughter of Germanicus Caesar Augustus[233]). Reverse: *carpentum* guided by two mules, facing left

Source: Courtesy of the American Numismatic Society

---

[229] Reference number: 1844.0425.462.A; C&M catalogue number: RE1 (197) (234). Bibliography: RIC1 / The Roman Imperial Coinage, vol. 1 (p130.117) RE1 / Coins of the Roman Empire in the British Museum, vol. 1: Augustus to Vitellius (p197.234) RPC1 / Roman provincial coinage. Vol.1, From the death of Caesar to the death of Vitellius (44 BC-AD 69) (2223). Available at: https://www.britishmuseum.org/collection/object/C_1844-0425-462-A. Accessed: 1 Dec. 2020.

[230] Translation made by the author with verification at: https://en.numista.com/catalogue/pieces247002.html. Accessed: 1 Dec. 2020.

[231] In this case the caption indicates that Agrippina would be the wife of Claudius Caesar Augustus or of Caesar Augustus' family. Translation made by the author with verification at: https://en.numista.com/catalogue/pieces247002.html. Accessed: 1 Dec. 2020.

[232] RIC I² *Claudius* 103. Available at: http://numismatics.org/ocre/results?q=Agrippina+carpentum. Accessed: 6 Oct. 2022.

[233] Translation made by the author.

The preceding sestertius reflects Agrippina's power to use the *carpentum*, demonstrating great status, like her predecessors Livia and Agrippina Major. Her mother and Livia had a type of monetary coinage that was repeated later by other imperial women and the *carpentum*, such as Julia Flavia, Marciana and Faustina Major, which made it possible to honour these women within the traditional Julio-Claudian iconography, in an attempt to link the houses. The coin also denotes the linearity of Agrippina, confirming her as the daughter of Germanicus in its caption and recapitulating on its reverse the *carpentum* that her mother, Agrippina Major, received from Caligula. Thus, Agrippina's coin links her to the Julio-Claudian bloodline, which would be of great legitimacy for Claudius (Claes, 2013, p. 102 and 195).

Agrippina Minor's success in entrusting herself at the head of political activities and public consciousness was immediately evidenced upon her marriage to Claudius and was perhaps reflected in the changing content of her husband's government coins. Agrippina's profile, identified in the caption and adorned with a corn-cob crown of Ceres, appeared on the reverse of coins of Claudius and his son, marking the first time a living imperial woman was characterised in this way. Agrippina Minor was also represented in other ways, as well as in statues, such as in the Olympia group of statues, which revealed an impressive degree of propaganda. She was represented as the priestess of her deified husband, a role that gave her religious authority, while her maternal image was recognised by a different type of figure, both types being illustrated as a divine image linked to her lineage from Augustus, as a beloved and respected memory who played an active role in dynastic politics and enjoyed his factions of consideration and loyalty (Wood, 1988, p. 421).

Figure 66 – Silver tridrachm cistophori[234], Ephesus, Turkey, Izmir, from AD 51. Obverse: laureate head of Claudius, together with a draped bust of Agrippina Minor facing left, caption: TI CLAVD CAES AVG AGRIPP AVGVSTA (*Tiberius Claudius Caesar Augustus, Agrippina Augusta* = Tiberius Claudius Caesar Augustus and Agrippina Augusta). Reverse: Worship statue of Diana of Ephesus, caption: DIANA EPHESIA (Diana of Ephesus[235])

Source: © The Trustees of the British Museum

This cistophoric tridrachm, which was minted in Ephesus during the rule of Claudius, shows him on its obverse with Agrippina, who appears in a secondary position, but even so she is shown as his partner, which reveals that this is how the province saw them. On the reverse, there is a representation of a deity, Diana, goddess of the hunt, which may represent wealth, abundance when celebrating the current emperor.

Diana was the sister of Apollo, known as the Moon-goddess, and was sometimes depicted with the crescent Moon over her head. She was also given the name LVCIFERA (who brings the light) and thus appears holding a torch, symbolising the light of the Moon. She was also the protector of youth and the deity of hunting. She was equipped with a bow and arrows, and could also appear accompanied by a hunting dog or a deer. Her other titles may include: CONSERVATRIX and VICTRIX. As DIANA EPHESIA, she appears as an Asiatic cistophoric cult figure from the period of Claudius (Sear, 2000, p. 28). Apollo was a deity closely linked to Augustus and, on this coin, Diana could be indirectly linked to the first *princeps*.

---

[234] Registration number: 1867.0101.1603. Number in the C&M catalogue: RE1 (197) (231). Bibliography: RIC1 / The Roman Imperial Coinage, vol. 1 (p130.119) RE1 / Coins of the Roman Empire in the British Museum, vol. 1: Augustus to Vitellius (p197.231) PCR / Principal coins of the Romans: Volume I: The Republic c. 290 - 31 BC; Volume II: The Principate 31 BC - AD 296; Volume III: The Dominate AD 294 - 498. (409)RPC1 / Roman provincial coinage. Vol.1, From the death of Caesar to the death of Vitellius (44 BC-AD 69) (2224/1). Available at: https://www.britishmuseum.org/collection/object/C_1867-0101-1603. Accessed: 21 Feb. 2021.

[235] Translation made by the author.

Figure 67 – Copper alloy coin[236], AD 41 - 54, minted in Balanea, Syria, Middle East. Obverse: Claudius with radiused head, facing right, caption: ΛΑΥΚΑΔΙ ωΝ; transliteration: LEUKADI ON (From the people of Leukas[237]). Reverse: head of Agrippina, facing right, with a crescent moon at its top, caption: TωNKKAI KΛAVΔIAIωN; transliteration: TONKAI KLAUDIAION (And from Claudius[238])

Source: © The Trustees of the British Museum

In this last coin, which honours the imperial couple, and which was minted in *Balanea,* Syria, Middle East, Claudius appears as the main honoured on the obverse, his face is turned to the right and radiated by a type of crown. Agrippina appears in a secondary position, on the reverse, no less important, carrying at the apex of her head a half crescent moon, which could be associated with Diana, which emphasises once again the connection that the East made of Agrippina with this goddess. Other places also minted coins with Claudius and Agrippina, according to the British Museum catalogue: Crete and Smyrna.

---

[236] Registration number: G.4161. Bibliography: BMC Greek (Galatia) / Catalogue of the Greek coins of Galatia, Cappadocia and Syria (1, p. 296). Available at: https://www.britishmuseum.org/collection/object/C_G-4161. Accessed: 22 Feb. 2021.

[237] Translation by Juarez Oliveira.

[238] Translation by Juarez Oliveira.

Figure 68 – Silver drachm[239], Crete. Obverse: draped bust of Agrippina the Younger, with a corn cob of Ceres, caption: ϹΕΒΑϹ ΑΓΡΙΠΠΕΙΝΗΝ ϹΕΒΑϹ ΓΥΝΑΙΚΑ, transliteration: SEBAS AGRIPPEINEN SEBAS GUNAIKA (Agrippina Augusta, venerable woman[240]). Reverse: quiver, arrow, bow and torch

Source: © The Trustees of the British Museum

This silver coin minted in Crete, which is undated, features Agrippina alone on the obverse, giving importance to her representativeness, and the caption mentions her name and no emperor. Her bust appears draped with a crown of corn cobs, a symbol of Ceres, which can signify fertility, productivity, and dynastic success. The elements on the reverse are interesting, composed of: a quiver, an arrow, a bow, which are instruments of hunting or war; and a torch, linked to the goddess who brings light (Lucifera). Thus, it can be suggested that these objects could be related to the evocation of Diana/Artemis, demonstrating once again that in the East Agrippina could be called together with this goddess, or even with war, giving her a masculine aspect. However, what is masculine or feminine can be complex for such a society and can be part of a symbolic system in which this division is not clear, or even non-existent. In this way, it can be taken into consideration that hunting instruments can express food abundance, and those of war can classify the territory as a strong land in every sense. According to Sear, this type of coin appears in various forms throughout the imperial period and was often related to religiosity (Sear, 2000, p. 63).

---

[239] Reference number: BNK,G.1152. Bibliographic references: RPC1 / Roman provincial coinage. Vol.1, From the death of Caesar to the death of Vitellius (44 BC-AD 69) (972/1). Available at: https://www.britishmuseum.org/collection/object/C_BNK-G-1152. Accessed: 22 Feb. 2021.

[240] Translation made by the author.

Figure 69 – Æ *Diobol* (two *obols*)[241] of alloy, dated AD 41 - 54, 9,980 g, from the rule of Claudius, minted in Alexandria, Egypt. Obverse: draped bust of Agrippina Minor with grain crown, ΑΓΡΙΠΠΝΑ ϹΕΒΑϹΤΗ (Agrippina Augusta[242]). Reverse: draped bust Euthenia (Euthenia) with diadem and holding branches of grains, [E]YΘΗΝΙΑ (Euthenia or Euthenia[243] = Greek goddess of prosperity and abundance)

Source: © The Trustees of the British Museum

This Æ *diobol* minted in Alexandria is further evidence of the breadth of the celebration of Agrippina. The obverse of the coin shows the draped bust of Agrippina Minor facing right, wreathed in grains, with a caption of her name in Greek. On the reverse is the Greek/Egyptian goddess Euthenia, linked to prosperity and abundance. The goddess on the reverse shows once again Agrippina's focus on fertility, dynastic success, and abundance of grains, which may prove the empress's connection with agriculture, or grain distribution, or even with an agriculturally orientated religiosity, or simply with maternal fertility.

---

[241] Registration number: TOW.150. Number in the C&M Catalogue: GC15 (BMC Greek (Alexandria)) (14) (108). Available at: https://www.britishmuseum.org/collection/object/C_GC15p14-109. Accessed: 21 Feb. 2021. Bibliography: BMC Greek (Alexandria) / Catalogue of the coins of Alexandria and the Nomes (109, p. 14). Available at: https://www.coinarchives.com/a/lotviewer.php?LotID=2064467&AucID=4912&Lot=283&Val=98f4b22eaefe24faa18109d1379c741b. Accessed: 14 Oct. 2022. Two obols formed a "diobol", weighing about 1.41-1.43 grams of silver (Available at: https://www.collinsdictionary.com/dictionary/english/diobol, accessed 14 October 2022. RPC I 5194; Köln 110-2; Dattari (Savio) 179 (Available at: https://www.wildwinds.com/coins/greece/egypt/alexandria/i.html; https://www.wildwinds.com/coins/ric/agrippina_II/RPC_5194.txt; https://www.wildwinds.com/coins/ric/agrippina_II/RPC_5194.jpg. Accessed: 14 Oct. 2022.
[242] Translation made by the author.
[243] Translation made by the author.

Figure 70 – Coin[244] of metal alloy, from AD 41 - 54, from the rule of Claudius, minted in Alexandria, Egypt. Obverse: draped bust of Agrippina, with a diadem on her head, facing right. Reverse: jug with sprigs of wheat, poppy, or other types of grain with a candle or a calla lily flower on a table

Source: © The Trustees of the British Museum

This coin, minted in Alexandria, celebrates Agrippina Minor as an important woman for the locality, since she stands alone on the obverse of the coin and follows the same type of figure minted on the preceding example, in other words, she is shown with a draped bust, facing right, with a diadem on her head, which was related to religiosity or *pudicitia*. The constituent elements of the reverse characterise her as a Roman matron, since the container seems to have wheat, poppy and other types of grains, with a calla lily flower (*Zantedeschia aethiopica*) on the right, which could link her to fertility, agricultural abundance, productivity and prosperity, within a religious symbolism or she could be someone who ensured the distribution of grains to that region or involved with the celebration of the grain harvest season.

To add to this, this coin in comparison with an Egyptian coin of Livia[245] shows the same type of receptacle with branches of grains, very similar to a *modius*, which may be related to the receipt of *frumentum*, or imperial distribution of grains, linking Livia and Agrippina to the activity of *pietas*. However, the *modius* was characterised as a vessel with three feet. Though, it is not ruled out that this monetary iconography could suggest that women like Livia and Agrippina were fundamental within the grain distribution policy, as well as demonstrating the public expectation of food

---

[244] Registration number: 1887,0704.24. C&M catalogue number: GC15 (BMC Greek (Alexandria)) (14) (111). Bibliographic references: BMC Greek (Alexandria) / Catalogue of the coins of Alexandria and the Nomes (111, p. 14). Available at: https://www.britishmuseum.org/collection/object/C_1887-0704-24. Accessed: 21 Feb. 2021.

[245] Registration number: 1864,1118.262. Bibliographical references: BMC Greek (Alexandria) / Catalogue of the coins of Alexandria and the Nomes (31, p. 4); C&M catalogue number: GC15 (BMC Greek (Alexandria)) (4) (31) (4). Available at: https://www.britishmuseum.org/collection/object/C_1864-1118-262. Accessed: 3 Sept. 2020.

distribution. As for Livia, the container could also be linked to a symbolism linked to Demeter/Ceres, which would indicate prosperity and fertility, since these women were associated with abundance and dynastic transmission. In addition, as the object is on a table or an altar, it could be something related to religiosity, which would show abundance, prosperity, and fertility.

Coins bearing only the image of Agrippina Minor were minted in several places, according to the catalogue of the British Museum: Corinth, Halicarnassus, Cadi, Sebaste (Phrygia), Eumeneia, Loadicea ad Lycum, Docimeium, Alaşehir, Hierocaesarea, Julia Ipsus, Smyrna, Hierapolis, Acmonea, Teos and Cotiaeum.

Figure 71 – Prutah[246] of copper alloy, AD 54 - 55, minted in Jerusalem, Middle East. Obverse: caption inside a garland, tied at the bottom: ΙΟΥ ΛΙΑΑΓ [Ρ]ΙΠΠΙ[Ν]Α; transliteration: IOULIA AGRIPPINA (Julia Agrippina[247]); caption note: Ioulia Agrippina was Claudius's wife. Reverse: Two palm branches crossed, dated between the stems; caption: [ΤΙ]ΚΛΑΥΔΙΟΣΚΑΙΣΑΡΓΕΡΜ. ΛΙΔ; transliteration: TIKLAUDIOSKAISARGERM. LID (Tiberius Claudius Caesar Germanicus. Lydia (?)[248])

Source: © The Trustees of the British Museum

---

[246] Reference No: G.2638. Number in the C&M catalogue: GC27 (BMC Greek (Palestine)) (261) (4). Bibliography: BMC Greek (Palestine) / Catalogue of the Greek coins of Palestine (Galilee, Samaria and Judaea) (4, p. 261) Hendin 2001 / Guide to Biblical Coins (Fourth Edition) (243.651, p.) RPC1 / Roman provincial coinage. Vol.1, From the death of Caesar to the death of Vitellius (44 BC-AD 69) (4970). Available at: https://www.britishmuseum.org/collection/object/C_G-2638. Accessed: 22 Feb. 2021.
[247] Translation made by the author.
[248] Translation made by the author.

Figure 72 – Prutah[249] of copper alloy, AD 54 - 55, minted in Jerusalem. Reverse: caption inside the garland, tied at the bottom: ΙΟΥ ΛΙΑΑΓ ΡΙΠΠΙ ΝΑ; transliteration: IOULIA AGRIPPINA (Júlia Agrippina[250]); caption note: Ioulia Agrippina was Claudius' wife

Source: © The Trustees of the British Museum

The two prutah, minted in Jerusalem, are different, but follow similar coin styles and totally different from other regions, where coins with Claudius or/and Agrippina were minted, which points to a local initiative to mint such a coin type, often without the consent of the central government. The palm branches that appear on both samples are recurrent in the region, which indicates an element of local acceptance, in addition to the homage to Agrippina Minor in its caption.

---

[249] Registration number: 1908.0110.555. C&M catalogue number: GC27 (BMC Greek (Palestine)) (263) (20). Bibliography: BMC Greek (Palestine) / Catalogue of the Greek coins of Palestine (Galilee, Samaria and Judaea) (20, p. 263) Hendin 2001 / Guide to Biblical Coins (Fourth Edition) (243.651b, p.) RPC1 / Roman provincial coinage. Vol.1, From the death of Caesar to the death of Vitellius (44 BC-AD 69) (4970).
Available at: https://www.britishmuseum.org/collection/object/C_1908-0110-555. Accessed: 22 Feb. 2021.
[250] Translation made by the author.

Figure 73 – Silver didrachm[251], from the rule of Claudius, AD 50 - 54, minted in Antiochia ad Oronten, Turkey, Mediterranean region, Hatay province, Antakya. Observe: draped bust of Agrippina facing left, ΑΓΡΙΠΠΕΙΝΗС СΕΒΑСΤΗС, transliteration: AGRIPPEINES SEBASTES ([From] Agrippina Augusta[252]). Reverse: draped bust of Nero, facing left, [ΝΕΡΩ]ΝΟС ΚΑΙСΑΡΟС [ΓΕΡΜΑΝΙΚΟΥ], transliteration: [NERO]NOS KAISAROS [GERMANIKOU] ([From] Nero Caesar Germanicus[253])

Source: © The Trustees of the British Museum

During the rule of Claudius, the region of Antioch honoured on coins, first of all Agrippina, who appeared on the obverse where it was usually the male figures who appeared, as it was the most important side of the coin, but it is she who was leading her son to be emperor. The coin illustrates Nero well as emperor in its reverse caption, demonstrating that the region guaranteed acceptance of this new position, even if his image appears in a secondary way, as if Agrippina still had more power. However, the coin shows the reception of the future ruler, who had also been minted in Rome, as on the next coin, confirming that the provinces tended to follow the minting parameters of the central government.

---

[251] Registration number: 1860.0330.40. Bibliography: RPC1 / Roman provincial coinage. Vol.1, From the death of Caesar to the death of Vitellius (44 BC-AD 69) (4170/1). Available at: https://www.britishmuseum.org/collection/object/C_1860-0330-40. Accessed: 21 Feb. 2021.

[252] Translation by Juarez Oliveira, who says that [From] would only be used to emphasize the genitive case in onomastic forms.

[253] Translation by Juarez Oliveira.

Figure 74 – Silver denarius[254], minted in Rome, AD 50 - 54, rule of Claudius. Obverse: draped bust of Agrippina Minor, facing right, with corn cob crown and caption: AGRIPPINAE AVGVSTAE. Reverse: draped bust of Nero, without a crown, with caption: NERO CLAVD CAES DRVSVS GERM PRINC IVVENT (*Nero Claudius Caesar Drusus Germanicus Principes Juventutis* = Nero Claudius Caesar Drusus Germanicus, prince of youth[255])

Source: © The Trustees of the British Museum

This denarius, from the government of Claudius, honoured Agrippina and her son Nero. Agrippina appears on the obverse, as the most important to be paid attention to, with her bust draped and with a crown of ears of corn, following the symbolic demonstration of fertility, abundance and prosperity, as well as the guarantee of dynastic descent through her son Nero, who appears with his bust draped on the reverse and with a caption in his honour. The crown of ears of corn refers directly to the empress's fertility and Nero on the reverse is also evidence of her descent. This type of coin emphasises motherhood and the adoption of her son by Claudius. However, the emperor's biological son with Messalina, Britannicus, was never minted (Claes, 2013, p. 195).

In AD 54, there was the assassination of Claudius, of which Agrippina was a suspect, because by doing so she could secure the throne for Nero (Tac. *An.* XII, 64-69). No one doubted that Claudius had been poisoned, but rather the place and who had administered the drug. It could have been in the citadel, during a feast, and the perpetrator could have been Haloto, his taster, or during a dinner at home, or that Agrippina herself would have administered the poison in a dish of boletus of which he was very fond, besides other versions (Suet. *Claud.* 44.2).

Nero was sixteen when Claudius died. Assuming power, Suetonius recounts that he handed over the sovereign administration of all public and private affairs to his mother. He assured the tribune of the guard, on

---

[254] Registration number: 1844.0425.732. C&M catalogue number: RE1 (176) (83). Bibliography: RE1 / Coins of the Roman Empire in the British Museum, vol. 1: Augustus to Vitellius (83, p. 176) RIC1 / The Roman Imperial Coinage, vol. 1 (75, p. 125). Available at: https://www.britishmuseum.org/collection/object/C_1844-0425-732. Accessed: 22 Feb. 2021.

[255] Translation made by the author.

his first day of government, that Agrippina would be the best of mothers, walking with her in public several times (Suet. *Ner.* 8-9). In addition, the author mentions that when he rode in a litter with his mother, he satisfied his incestuous appetites, as evidenced by the stains on his clothes. The same author calls him a parricide, being an accomplice in the death of Claudius, and a murderer, for poisoning Britannicus (Suet. *Ner.* 28 and 33).

Tacitus describes the image of Nero's government, which was carried away by female influence in political affairs. Based on the common sense of his society, this author suggests that Nero's bad decisions were only possible due to the advice given by women such as Agrippina, his mother; Octavia, his first wife, from 53 to 62; and Poppaea, his second wife, from 62 to 65. Tacitus points out the perception that it would be impossible for a good government to be characterised by the presence of women. The first phase of Nero's government, for example, from 54 to 59, it is described as an administration of a good man, without female influences. However, from the year 60 to 62, his government is described as passive to female manipulation, which is why, according to the narrative, it declines. The third phase, from 63 to 66, is the period of greatest vice, in which female control over him is more emphasised (Varella, 2006).

At the beginning of the *Annals*, Tacitus, when mentioning Nero, points out that he was the only stepson of Claudius and that everything was centred on him. He was adopted as a son, as a friend of the empire, a companion of power in the courts and who boasted all the armies, no longer due to the secret intrigues of his mother (Tac. *Ann.* 1.3), Agrippina, whom the author declares to have a domineering temperament, by virtue of her sex, also proclaims her to have an extravagant ambition (Tac. *Ann.* 12.57).

Agrippina is one of the most famous imperial women who expressed her actions as follows: Claudius needed a wife he could trust, because he lacked a political ally to help him keep his distance from the forces that threatened to overthrow his Principality (Barrett, 1996, p. 95); she was to be noble by birth; with maternal experience, sharing her offspring with his descendants, Britannicus and Octavia; as well as having purity of character. Thus, he realised that Agrippina had all the characteristics he desired, and so he chose her with sagacity. Claudius also searched other noble houses and surely chose the one who was already, by descent, within two imperial houses (Barrett, 1996, p. 95, 101). According to Tacitus, Pallas selected Agrippina with special praise because she would bring along Germanicus' grandson, who was definitely worthy of an imperial position, coming from a noble family and descended from the *gens Claudia* (Tac. *Ann.* 12.2).

Agrippina was from the *gens Iulia* on her mother Agrippina's side, and of the *gens Claudia*, on her father Germanicus' side. That said, she could play an important political role in trying to amalgamate a rift that had arisen simply because Augustus and Livia had no surviving children. The marriage between Claudius and a woman descended from an imperial family could heal past wounds and lessen the threat between the couple. To add to this, Agrippina already had a grandson by Germanicus, a descendant of Augustus, who was a great option for the succession. As much as Claudius had a son to succeed him, he might have wanted a guarantee that his regime would survive. However, his interest in tying himself to the family of the *gens Iulia* was inclined to the fact that he would obtain the title of "Caesar", which was a cognomen acquired by the Octavians, when Octavian was adopted by Julius Caesar, and transmitted to Tiberius and from Germanicus to Caligula. Claudius' marriage to Agrippina was the guarantee of a perfect partnership, as long as she shared with him the union of the tradition of two dynasties, giving rise to a strength and a stability (Barrett, 1996, p. 96-98).

Agrippina certainly had the patience and skill to be prepared; a characteristic she always retained, but even after her marriage, she mustered the strength and dexterity to make way for her son, Nero. He was three years older than Claudius' son, Britannicus. She knew the threat her son was under with the presence of Claudius' son as his father's successor, so she did not wait for the facts to happen before she took action. Therefore, she had Claudius adopt him as her son and summoned Seneca to be his tutor (Barrett, 1996, p. 98 and 114). Seneca was probably one of the few intellectuals Agrippina funded, as she herself had no interest in philosophy or rhetoric. Agrippina's Patronage was mediated with her husband, Claudius, and done to please the people or for political reasons (Hemelrijk, 1999, p. 109).

To consolidate her son's future, nothing was more qualified than Nero's marriage to Claudius' daughter, Octavia, the daughter he had with his first wife, Messalina. In the *Annals* of Tacitus, the author mentions that Agrippina, before marrying Claudius, made several visits to her uncle and already possessed the "power of a wife", being certain that she would marry him. For this reason, she began to aim for great opportunities and started planning alliances, such as the marriage between her son and Octavia, who was already promised to Lucius Silanus (Tac. *Ann.* 12.3).

Tacitus and Cassius Dio insisted that Agrippina had been plotting her scheme since 48, before she was married to Claudius (Barrett, 1996, p. 98). Tacitus' description of the year 49 begins with the marriage of Agrippina and Claudius, so that the problems of this union eventually appear in later chapters, from the moment Agrippina appoints Seneca as Nero's tutor: *"quia Seneca fidus in Agrippinam... et infensus Claudius"* (Tac. *Ann.* 12, 8, 2), *"because Seneca trusted Agrippina and was opposed to Claudius"* (Funari; Garraffoni, 2016, p. 124).

Tacitus insisted on emphasising the improprieties of Agrippina's sexuality, one of them being her marriage to Claudius, who was her uncle, her father's elder brother (Barrett, 1996, p. 100-101), an act which, according to the laws of Rome, consisted of incest. Tacitus mentioned that this love was illicit, that they should not dare to celebrate the nuptials in the proper way, and that there had been no precedent for the introduction of a niece into her uncle's house. Such an act was definitely incest (Tac. *Ann.* 11.5). Vitellius, in his speech to the Senate in defence of this marriage, explained that a marriage with his brother's daughter was a novelty for them, but it was common elsewhere and that there was no law to prohibit it. He went on to say that marriages between cousins had previously been unknown, but at that time they were frequent, as custom adapted itself to convenience, so that this novelty would in future take its place among the recognised usages (Tac. *Ann.* 12.6). Thus, the senators approved the marriage of Germanicus' daughter and the union came to be seen as appeasing future conflicts over the succession. For Tacitus, this represented a profound moral degeneration, as well as Octavia's marriage to Nero, which, according to the author, was the cause of all the following calamities (Barrett, 1996, p. 101-102). Adding the fact that Nero was adopted by Claudius and became like a brother to his daughter, who married the former.

For Tacitus, Claudius' marriage signified Agrippina's effective hold on power, but in the following accounts, from AD 50 to 54, this subject was dominant, since the author describes his wife's activity for the benefit of her son Nero and her privilege in receiving the title of Augusta (Tac. *Ann.* 12, 25-26; 12, 41-43), as well as the marriage in AD 53 of his son to Octavia and, in AD 54, the assassination of Claudius, described as having been carried out by Agrippina to secure the throne for Nero (Tac. *Ann.* 12, 64-69). Thus, according to Tacitus, it was Agrippina who ruled and the emphasis given *"to personal and family relationships and the deleterious effect of the domination of one who should be subordinate"* (a woman, Agrippina) *"is evident as the engine of History for Tacitus"* (Funari; Garraffoni, 2016, p. 125). When mentioning the exhibition of gladiatorial combat, Tacitus questions how a prince, with his mere seventeen years, could fight and avoid such danger, referring to Agrippina, as well as asking how the Romans could resort to someone who was dominated by a woman (Tac. *Ann.* 13.6). One of the few moments when Tacitus states that Agrippina's influence over her son Nero was weakening was when he fell in love with a free woman, Acte (Tac. *Ann.* 13.12).

Cassius Dio stated that Agrippina had Claudius in her control and that, for Tacitus, this marriage represented a transformation in the development of the State of Rome, since relations were now in the control of a woman, but not a woman like Messalina, who used power only to consume excesses, given that her desire was not for passion, but for power. Tacitus conceived her as an austere person, totally free of promiscuous behaviour, but one who acted to contribute to her own power. Even her greed is seen by the author as a device to reinforce her dominance. Cassius Dio mentions that, after marriage, Agrippina began to have total control over her husband with a mixture of intimidation and bribery. Her tactic was to get a free man to persuade Claudius to follow her advice. Moreover, Cassius Dio expresses the passivity of Claudius, who was sure that Agrippina would bring to the marriage a keen political sense (Barrett, 1996, p. 102-103).

In AD 49, Agrippina was married to the emperor of Rome and had betrothed her son to her husband's daughter. Her success was further significantly symbolised by her receiving the title of Augusta in AD 50. She was the first wife of a living emperor to receive this title. Livia, for example, also received the same title, but she was already a widow (Barrett, 1996, p. 108).

Agrippina poisoned Claudius to put Nero in power (Tac. *Ann.* 12.66). According to Tacitus, Pallas suggested that Claudius had ruined himself through an incestuous marriage and by the fatal adoption of a son (Tac. *Ann.* 13.2). Just before Agrippina's death, Tacitus describes the attempted incest between her and her son Nero. The author mentions that, out of eagerness to maintain influence over his son, who was seduced by Acte, she presented herself attractively dressed to her son, who was not fully intoxicated by her, and offered herself to him (Tac. *Ann.* 14.2).

After this episode, Nero decided to destroy his mother (Tac. *Ann.* 14.3-4). In the last years of Agrippina's life, in AD 59 (Tac. *Ann.* 16), her tension with her son, who was ending his mother's life, grew more and more, resulting in a long-planed crime. Tacitus' narrative shows signs that the emperor was losing his self- control and was letting himself be carried away by passions, as if he were a woman. *"The tone of condemnation of the lack of moderation continues in the account of the following years"*, *"without restraint, Nero gave in more and more to desires and killed Sila, Rubelio, Octavia, Palas and Dariforo"*, following this same trend until the end of his government and his life (Funari; Garraffoni, 2016, p. 125-126). Moreover, before Agrippina's death, Tacitus states that of all human things, the most precarious and transitory one was a reputation for power, which had no strong support in itself (Tac. *Ann.* 13.19). Upon Agrippina's death, Nero attributes all the abominations that occurred to his mother, endeavouring to show that it was the good fortune of the state that destroyed her (Tac. *Ann.* 14.11).

According to Suetonius, Nero decided to kill his mother because she lurked around and criticised his every word and action, rebuking him from the beginning on repeated occasions. He made her odious by pretending to want to give up the reins of the Empire and leave for Rhodes. Consequently, he deprived her of all fortune, honours and power, removed her guard from Germanic soldiers and expelled her from the palace, sparing no effort to torment her. In Rome, he had secret agents pursue her with lawsuits and in the countryside they covered her with insults. Threatening her with violence, Nero decided to kill her. He tried to poison her three times, but she guarded herself with antidotes; he built a roof over her, which was supposed to fall down during her sleep, but it was unravelled by her confidants. He pretended a reconciliation and invited her to take a walk in the Bay. When she wished to return, he offered her the machined ship and accompanied her there, parted with her kisses and awaited the outcome. However, everything went the other way round and his mother swam away safe and sound. Learning the news, he plotted his mother's murder and was unable to quell the rumours of his crime (Suet. *Ner.* 34.1).

Moreover, disgusted with his relationship with Octavia, he tried to strangle her several times and repudiated her as sterile. Since the people disapproved of this divorce, he went so far as to expatriate her and murder her on the charge of adultery. This act was seen as a slander and there was protest about Octavia's innocence, which led him to force Anicetus, a pedagogue, to confess to the abuse (Suet. *Ner.* 35.1).

Regarding Poppaea, whom he had married twelve days after his divorce, he kicked her to death when she was pregnant, when she scolded him for being late because of a chariot race. He had a daughter with Poppaea, Claudia Augusta, who died as a child (Suet. *Ner.* 35.1). Tacitus also recounts Nero's heavy-handed and misogynistic behaviour towards Poppaea. Firstly, the author mentions that she died from a casual attack of anger by her husband, and thus he knocked her down with a kick from a ladder, while she was pregnant: "*Post finem ludicri Poppaea mortem obiit, fortuita mariti iracundia, a quo gravida ictu calcis adflicta est*" (Tac. *Ann.* 16.6).

With regard to the deaths of Poppaea, Octavia and her mother Agrippina, it can be mentioned that, like honour, violence is experienced in front of other men and thus virility is validated and attested by the recognition of being part of a group (Bourdieu, 1998, p. 65), since Nero's government was worn out and defamation by female manipulation was the tension caused by such a male group as a result of the emperor's manly acceptance. Such examples of episodes could be in accordance with the original *illusio*, constitutive of masculinity, which makes men, unlike women, socially led to let themselves be trapped, in a childish way even, in games that are socially destined for them, which may involve violence, murder, rape and, finally, war, assuming a blind attitude, as if the man were a child who plays at being a man (Bourdieu, 1998, p. 93-93) and who assumes a predilection for games of domination.

One of the prerogatives of being a man of Rome's elite was not being like women, often rejecting them, having power, success, wealth, status, being in control of their own emotions, and exuding an aura of aggressive virile boldness. This anti- femininity thinking lies at the heart of historical and present concepts of masculinity (Kimmel, 2016, p. 106). Historically, masculinity has been defined as an avoidance of women and a repudiation of femininity. The boy must develop a self-assured identity as a man. The Oedipal project is a process of the boy's renunciation of his identification and emotional attachment to his mother, whom he must replace with a father as an object of identification. A movement of the boy's sexual desire for his mother is established. The father stands in the way and he is the one who brings the son fear because he is bigger, stronger and sexually powerful. This symbolically experienced fear is like the fear of castration, making the boy renounce identification with his mother and seek to identify with his father. In this way, the boy becomes able to realise a sexual union with a woman other than his mother. The boy becomes gendered and heterosexual at the same time (Freud, [1933] 1966 apud Kimmel, 2016, p. 106-107).

This does not mean that he will respect women, but rather the group of men in which he will be inserted, because this agency is made as proof of masculinity. However, the masculine identity is born from the renunciation of the feminine, in other words, it is not directly linked to the masculine, which leaves the gender identity tenuous and fragile. Thus, the boy also learns to devalue women, since they are the living embodiments of those traits he has learnt to despise. It was from this thought that Freud spoke of the origins of sexism, in the face of the boy's desperate efforts to separate himself from his mother (Freud, [1933] 1966). It is concluded that the silence of men is what keeps the system going, so homophobia - the fear of men - and sexism go hand in hand (Kimmel, 2016, p. 108, 112 and 114). The origins of male self-identity are linked to a dense sense of insecurity and loss that haunts the individual's unconscious memory. Basic security is jeopardised as the boy is abandoned to the world of men by his own parents. The phallus, the imaginary representation of the penis, symbolises the fantasy of domination over women, separation, revolt, and freedom (Chasseguet-Smirgel, 1976 apud Giddens, 1992, p. 130).

In this type of society, such attitudes cannot be predicted in a sense that women or even their families could avoid such marriage or estrangement from the male individual, since male attitudes are part of a social structure, which has been developed historically and brought to families by older generations, education, and the communicative media of a certain time. In this way, women are condemned to participate in the effect of masculine domination, being that this social system is the right one to be lived, which traps them in a state imposed by society and which works as an affective solidarity with the player, as unconditional supporters, but misinformed of the reality of the game (Bourdieu, 1998, p. 93), because their role ends up being to facilitate the male game so that only men achieve success.

Because of this masculine aspect, Agrippina and Poppaea were described by Tacitus as women of very bad reputation. Being enemies, they also had personalities quite different and seemed to compete to influence Nero (Hemelrijk, 1999, p. 110) or the author describes them in this way, as if it were something inherent to women. This rhetorical device of jealousy between women was also used on Mark Antony's wives, Fulvia and Octavia against Cleopatra, and vice versa, in Plutarch's narratives (Plut. *Ant.* 53.2 and 5).

It was common for Agrippina and Poppaea to be characterised as ambitious and power-hungry. Otherwise, they were both prosperous, well-educated and had important connections, although Agrippina was superior to Poppaea in these requirements. They differed from characters like Octavia Minor and her daughter Antonia in that their mother and wife were not interested in cultural Patronage, for example, but seem to have focussed on political ambition for power with Nero. Agrippina has never been described as a model matron, like Octavia and Antonia, yet in the face of these standards she transgressed the gender boundaries that were imposed by interfering in politics, endeavouring to receive ambassadors and attend meetings with senators on the sly. Despite this, such actions could have been criticised for Nero's masculine behaviour (Hemelrijk, 1999, p. 110), as he would not have given limits to his own mother.

It should be noted that these feminine attitudes had already occurred since the Republic, with women like Fulvia, suggesting that these feminine characteristics were traditionally described by various authors to portray such women. However, it is not known for sure how much Agrippina would be overstepping her limits as a woman at that time with several similar cases that had occurred previously, such as that of Livia.

Regarding Agrippina's intellectuality, Tacitus mentions that she wrote her memoirs (Tac. *Ann.* 2.69.1 and 4.52.3), something unexpected for a woman, but with reason to do so, since her position interceded her directly to three emperors: as sister of Caligula; wife of Claudius; and mother of Nero. However, such a work by Agrippina has not reached the present day, which is why it is not known what her writing style was or what she wrote about. She may have written about various topics, such as: her relationship with such emperors and family members; demonstrating how much each emperor owed her the position they achieved; defending her right to power; writing about her mother, in order to use her memory to gain sympathy and thus power (Hemelrijk, 1999, p. 179); or she could have written about something peculiar, such as a work that showed the Roman society of her time from a female perspective, which could have been characterized as a scandalous and subversive work.

Tacitus placed great emphasis on the family and psychological background of the characters, placing their administrative destinies in their hands. His approach, which closely resembles that of Sallustius, sets out a vision of the degradation caused by the corruption of the exercise of power. In this way, dominates his narrative, the concept that whether people give in to pleasure, it ruins them (Funari; Garraffoni, 2016, p. 126).

Imperial women of the Julio-Claudian period were mostly characterised as transgressive and as violators of their roles in society. The Julio-Claudian period has been taken as an aberration in the history of Rome, given that emperors violated privileges and threatened the lives of senators or other leading figures. Such characteristics are common for authors of this period, mainly because they consider this a moment of transition (Fischler, 1994, p. 120).

Another occurrence to take into account concerns the fact that the literary tradition has always had a particular interest to build upon, which suggests that there was a need to comment on those women who, before Roman eyes, stepped outside the norms, revealing the abuses that were generally believed to be plausible and what was particularly objectionable. The description of these women and their behaviours were highlighted to illuminate the character of the "bad" imperial woman for the reader and to show what they expected from a woman of the ruling class. Such attitudes make us wonder how societies react to women who have access to authority or power (Fischler, 1994, p. 121). However, it is limited and obsolete to try to characterise a gender relationship in a dual, 'bad' or 'good' way, causing a simplistic analysis of a more complex whole.

As the relationship between Agrippina and her son Nero deteriorated, she was banned from public activities, a decline demonstrated in the production of coins. Some of her coins, made of gold and silver, show Agrippina and Nero facing each other and with a bunch of wheat, which represents fertility (Zager, 2014, p. 70-71), abundance and food production. However, this coin type otherwise showed that in the first two years of Nero's rule the representation of Agrippina on coinage was more notable. In AD 54, Agrippina was depicted alongside Nero on the obverse of aurei and denarii in a pair of clashing busts, which were understood to be figures of equal importance, having her title being emphasised in the caption. Nero's titles, with the *corona civica*, were relegated to the reverse. This coin signifies what Tacitus would have said about Agrippina in the early years of Nero's rule, that she would take a place alongside her son. Agrippina proved to be a woman determined to have her public authority recognised and "institutionalised". However, this series of coins had the approval of Nero (Wood, 1988, p. 421) and the Senate to be minted.

Figure 75 – Silver denarius[256] with Nero and Agrippina Minor facing each other on the obverse, Rome, dated AD 54, weighing 3.22 g. Caption: AGRIPP AVG DIVI CLAVD NERONIS CAES MATER (*Agrippina Augusta Divi Caudii Neronis Caesaris Mater* = Agrippina Augusta, [wife[257]] of the divine Claudius and mother of Nero Caesar[258]); Reverse: NERONI CLVD DIVI F CAES AVG GERM IMP TR P / EX S C (*Neroni Claudii divi filio Caesari Augusto Germanico Imperatori Tribuniciae Potestate* = Nero, son of the divine Claudius Caesar Augustus Germanicus Commander invested in the tribunicial power[259] / minted according to the consent of the Senate[260]), with an oak crown

---

[256] ID: 76001396. Reference: RIC 002 (original from Rome), WCN 36, RSC 7, *Classical Numismatic Group*. Denomination: denarius. Available at: http://www.cngcoins.com/Coin.aspx?CoinID=109071 and http://www.coinproject.com/coin_detail.php?coin=283510. Accessed: 6 Mar. 2019.

[257] Translation made for implying that the divine Claudius was Agrippina's husband.

[258] Available at: http://www.forumancientcoins.com/numiswiki/view.asp?key=AGRIPP%20AVG%20DIVI%20CLAVD%20NERONIS%20CAES%20MATER%20EX%20S%20C. Accessed: 8 Mar. 2019.

[259] Available at Schmitt and Prieur (2004, p. 208).

[260] Translation made by the author with consultation at: http://www.forumancientcoins.com/board/index.php?topic=51364.0. Accessed: 8 Mar. 2019.

Source: Courtesy of Classical Numismatic Group, LLC

Figure 76 – Aureus[261], 7.63g, AD 54, Rome, rule of Nero, AGRIPP AVG DIVI CLAVD NERONIS CAES MATER (*Agrippina Augusta, Divi Claudii Neronis Caesaris Mater*[262] = Agrippina Augusta, [wife] of the divine Claudius and mother of Nero Caesar[263]); Reverse: NERONI CLVD DIVI F CAES AVG GERM IMP TR P / EX S C (*Neroni Claudii Divi filii Caesaris Augusti Germanici* = Commander Nero Caesar Augustus Germanicus, son of the divine Claudius invested with tribune power / minted according to the consent of the Senate[264]), with an oak crown[265]

Source: © The Trustees of the British Museum

The coins with the bust of Nero and Agrippina together demonstrate Agrippina's equality with the emperor, valorising the bond between them by the materials in which they were minted, gold and silver. When the couple is in front of each other, the emperor always tends to appear on the left and the woman on the right (Brubaker; Tobler, 2000, p. 573).

The captions confirm the divine descent with the mention of Agrippina's connection as Claudius' wife and Nero as her son, as well as the Senate's consent to the coinage. The coins also testified how much Nero owed his mother Agrippina for the conferral of the position of emperor, since in several of these depictions she appears alongside Nero, in a much

---

[261] Museum reference number: R.6509. Bibliography: RE1 2, p. 200, BER1 3,p. 150. Number in the C&M catalogue: RE1p200.2. Bibliography: RE1 / Coins of the Roman Empire in the British Museum, vol. 1: Augustus to Vitellius (2, p. 200) RIC1 / The Roman Imperial Coinage, vol. 1 (3, p. 150)
Available at: https://www.britishmuseum.org/research/collection_online/collection_object_details.aspx?objectId=1216066&partId=1. Accessed: 10 Nov. 2019.
[262] Available at: https://en.numista.com/catalogue/pieces246187.html. Accessed: 23 Feb. 2021.
[263] Available at: http://www.forumancientcoins.com/numiswiki/view.asp?key=AGRIPP%20AVG%20DIVI%20CLAVD%20NERONIS%20CAES%20MATER%20EX%20S%20C. Accessed: 8 Mar. 2019.
[264] Translation made by the author with consultation at: http://www.forumancientcoins.com/board/index.php?topic=51364.0. Accessed: 8 Mar. 2019.
[265] ID: 76001396. Reference: RIC 002 (original from Rome), WCN 36, Classical Numismatic Group. Denomination: denarius. Available at: http://www.cngcoins.com/Coin.aspx?CoinID=109071 and http://www.coinproject.com/coin_detail.php?coin=283510. Accessed: 6 Mar. 2019.

more common way than Nero with Claudius (Zager, 2014, p. 71), or than Nero with his wives, Octavia or Poppaea, for example. In addition, the son and mother together draw attention due to the fact that they reinforce a dynastic continuity, but it could also be intended to show imperial unity, which would otherwise be camouflaging a crisis. The images of imperial women seemed to grant legitimacy over their husbands and sons. Thus, symbols of legitimacy were always important, especially during succession crises (Brubaker; Tobler, 2000, p. 590), which would lead to the valorisation of space on coins for positive propaganda of the State.

Figure 77 – Aureus[266], AD 55, Rome, rule of Nero. Obverse: busts of Nero next to bust of Agrippina Minor, NERO CLAV [DI] VI F CAES AVG GERM IMP TR P COS (*Nero Claudius Divi Filius Caesar Augustus Germanicus Imperator Tribunicia Potestas Consul* = Nero Claudius, son of the divine Caesar Augustus Germanicus, commander invested in the Tribunicial Power and consul[267]). Reverse: elephant quadriga with Claudius and Nero, AGRIPP AVG DIVI CLAVD NERONIS CAES MATER/EX S C (*Agrippina Augusta, Divi Claudii Neronis Caesaris Mater/ex senatus consulto* = Agrippina Augusta, [wife] of Divine Claudius and mother of Nero Caesar/ minted according to the consent of the Senate[268])

Source: © KBR *cabinet des monnais et médailles*

This series of aurei coins features Nero and Agrippina on the obverse, next to each other. She is in a secondary position to him, as Nero is in front of her. The obverse caption commemorates the current emperor, Nero, and his ancestry, as well as emphasising the divine title of Claudius and Augustus, with a demonstration of a future divinisation. The reverse brings the strength of the Roman Empire, through the elephant quadriga with Claudius, with a crown of rays and an eagle sceptre in his right hand, and Augustus with a

---

[266] Bibliography: RIC I² 6; BMC 7; *du Chastel 401 (Collection du Chastel Collectie du Chastel)*. Available at: https://opac.kbr.be/LIBRARY/doc/SYRACUSE/20734795. Accessed: 18 July 2022.
[267] Translation made by the author.
[268] Translation made by the author.

crown of rays and a *patera* in his right hand and a sceptre in his left. They are representing dynastic ascendancy and the right to rule, with symbols of power, such as the sceptre with the eagle; and symbols of prosperity, such as the *patera*. The caption marks the marriage of Agrippina to the former emperor and now mother of the current one. The pairing of Agrippina and Nero is somewhat extraordinary and may have mimicked the pairing of figures from the Hellenistic period, demonstrating the consanguinity of kings, queens, and children. This pairing reflects the position of influence she had over him (Claes, 2013, p. 97 and 100).

Figure 78 – Aureus[269] minted in Lyon, with bust of Nero and Agrippina on the obverse, NERO CLAVD DIVI F CAES AVG GERM IMP TR P COS (*Nero Claudius Divi Filius Caesar Augustus Germanicus Imperator Tribunicia Potestas Consul* = Nero Claudius, son of the divine Caesar Augustus Germanicus, commander invested in the Tribunicial Power and consul[270]). Reverse: Quadriga of elephants carrying two chairs on which are seated *Divus Claudius* (the farthest one), irradiated and holding an eagle-tipped sceptre in his right hand, as well as *Divus Augustus*, irradiated, holding a *patera* in his right hand and the sceptre in his left and with caption: AGRIPP AVG DIVI CLAVD NERONIS CAES MATER/EX S C (*Agrippina Augusta, Divi Claudii Neronis Caesaris Mater/ex senatus consulto* = Agrippina Augusta, [wife] of Divine Claudius and mother of Nero Caesar/sister-in-law according to the consent of the Senate[271])

Source: © *Bibliothèque Nationale de France*

This last example, like the previous one, is interesting for the grooves on the obverse and reverse. On the obverse, the grooves are mainly on the mouths of Nero and Agrippina, suggesting that whoever made them could

---

[269] Available at: http://ark.bnf.fr/ark:/12148/cb439284586. Accessed: 20 June 2022. BNC II Néron 12, BMC 7, RIC 6. *Description historique des monnaies frappées sous l'Empire Romain / Henri Cohen, Paris, 1880-1892, Agrippine et Néron 3. dentifiant de la notice:* ark:/12148/cb439284586. Notice n°: FRBNF43928458. mage 1. - IFN-10445265: ², Droit. Image 2. - IFN-10445265: ², Revers.

[270] Translation made by the author.

[271] Translation made by the author.

be going against what those characters were saying and, consequently, could be an act against that government. On the reverse, the grooves are repeated and are mainly on the figure of Nero, as if disapproving of such an image, and the letters S C also appear, erasing them, as if also disapproving of the acts of the Senate or because this institution was not directly linked to the minting of coins and such letters continued to be used in an unrelated way.

Figure 79 – Aureus[272], AD 64 - 65, Rome, rule of Nero. Obverse: head of Nero with laurel crown and beard on right, NERO CAESAR AVGVSTVS. Reverse: Emperor on the left and empress on the right, AVGVSTVS AVGVSTA

Source: © KBR *cabinet des monnais et médailles*

The last example contains Nero on its obverse, but the most interesting part is the reverse, where the emperor appears with a crown of rays and wearing a toga, a *patera* in his right hand and a long sceptre in his left hand; on his left side there is the empress, with her head veiled, holding a *patera* in her right hand and a cornucopia in her left hand, symbolising abundance, fertility and prosperity. The couple on the obverse may be a representation of Nero and his mother Agrippina, or a celebration of their ancestors Augustus and Livia, characterising this coin as a family and/or posthumous type.

Coins featuring Nero and Agrippina also appear in provincial mints, often copying the models minted in Rome and sometimes with very local aspects.

---

[272] Bibliography: RIC I² 44; BMC 52; du Chastel 406 (*Collection du Chastel Collectie du Chastel*). Available at: https://opac.kbr.be/LIBRARY/doc/SYRACUSE/20734809. Accessed: 18 July 2022.

Figure 80 – Silver didrachm[273], AD 58 - 59, Caesarea Mazaca. Obverse: laureate head of Nero, NERO CLAVD DIVI CLAVD F CAESAR AVG GERMANI (*Nero Claudius Divi Claudii Filius Caesar Augustus Germanicus* = Nero Claudius Caesar Augustus Germanicus, son of the divine Claudius[274]). Reverse: draped bust of Agrippina Minor, AGRIPPINA AVGVSTA MATER AVGVSTI (Agrippina Augusta, Mater Augusti = Agrippina Augusta, mother of Augustus[275])

Source: © The Trustees of the British Museum

This didrachm, minted in Caesarea, honours the emperor and his mother. Nero appears on the obverse with his laureate head, turned to the right, together with the caption with his name and ancestry, demonstrating his right to rule. Agrippina is in a secondary position on the reverse, but her importance remains strong with the emperor. Thus, the caption reinforces her position as a mother who helped her son to reach such a position.

---

[273] Registration number: 1914,1003.5. Number in the C&M catalogue: RE1 (283) (422). Bibliography: RPC1 / Roman provincial coinage. Vol.1, From the death of Caesar to the death of Vitellius (44 BC-AD 69) (3632/1) RE1 / Coins of the Roman Empire in the British Museum, vol. 1: Augustus to Vitellius (p283.422). Available at: https://www.britishmuseum.org/collection/object/C_1914-1003-5. Accessed: 24 Feb. 2021.

[274] Translation made by the author.

[275] Translation made by the author.

Figure 81 – Drachm[276] silver, AD 58 - 59, minted in Caesarea Mazaca. Obverse: laureate head of Nero, facing right, [NER]O CLAVD DIVI CLAVD F CAESAR AVG GERMANI (*Nero Claudius Divi Claudii Filius Caesar Augustus Germanicus* = Nero Claudius Caesar Augustus Germanicus, son of the divine Claudius[277]). Reverse: veiled bust of Agrippina Minor, facing left, AGRIPPINA AVGVSTA MATER AVGVSTI (*Agrippina Augusta, Mater Augusti* = Agrippina Augusta, mother of Augustus[278])

Source: The Trustees of the British Museum

This drachm was also minted in Caesarea Mazaca, which is similar to the previous didrachm, but on the obverse the difference is that Agrippina Minor appears with her head veiled, very similar to the coins minted in Rome of Livia as Pietas, in addition to the representation of Vesta herself, which appears in the same way.

---

[276] Registration number: 1886,1107.1. Number in the C&M catalogue: RE1 (284) (425). Bibliography: RPC1 / Roman provincial coinage. Vol.1, From the death of Caesar to the death of Vitellius (44 BC-AD 69) (3642/1) RE1 / Coins of the Roman Empire in the British Museum, vol. 1: Augustus to Vitellius (p284.425). Available at: https://www.britishmuseum.org/collection/object/C_1886-1107-1. Accessed: 24 Feb. 2021.
[277] Translation made by the author.
[278] Translation made by the author.

319

Figure 82 – Silver As[279], AD 58 - 59, Caesarea Mazaca, Turkey, central Anatolia region, Kayseri. Obverse: laureate head of Nero, facing right, NERO CLAVD DIVI CLAVD F CAESAR AVG GERMANI (*Nero Claudius Divi Claudii Filius Caesar Augustus Germanicus* = Nero Claudius Caesar Augustus Germanicus, son of the divine Claudius[280]). Reverse: bust of Agrippina Minor, facing right, with a wreath, AC IT IB (AC(cαρια) IT(αλικα) IB (12[281]) = 12 *italiai as*[282])

Source: © The Trustees of the British Museum

In this As, once again the model follows that of the other coins struck in Caesarea. However, it is the figure of Agrippina that undergoes the most changes in the last three examples of coins. Agrippina is on the reverse, without her veil but with a garland. Her image is more similar to that of the first Caesarea model.

---

[279] Registration number: 1846.0910.197. C&M catalogue number: RE1 (284) (427). Bibliography: RPC1 / Roman provincial coinage. Vol.1, From the death of Caesar to the death of Vitellius (44 BC-AD 69) (3643/1) RE1 / Coins of the Roman Empire in the British Museum, vol. 1: Augustus to Vitellius (p284.427). Available at: https://www.britishmuseum.org/collection/object/C_1846-0910-197. Accessed: 24 Feb. 2021.

[280] Translation made by the author.

[281] Available at: http://www.saxa-loquuntur.nl/tools/greek-numerals.html. Accessed: 6 Dec. 2022.

[282] This is a currency unit (Available at: http://regeszet.org.hu/wp-content/uploads/2020/03/R%C3%A9g%C3%A9szeti-K%C3%A9zik%C3%B6nyv-2011_3_5.pdf, p. 422. Accessed: 6 Dec. 2022.

Figure 83 – Silver tetradrachm[283], AD 56 - 57, Antiochia ad Orotem, Mediterranean region of Turkey, Antakya. Obverse: laureate head of Nero, facing right, [ΝΕΡΩΝΟΣ ΚΛΑΥΔΙΟΥ ΘΕΟΥ ΥΙ ΚΑΙΣΑΡΟΣ ΣΕΒ], transliteration: [NERONOS KLAUDIOU THEOU UI KAISAROS SEB] (From the Divine Claudius Caesar Augustus to his son Nero[284]). Reverse: draped bust of Agrippina Minor, facing right, [ΑΓΡΙΠΠΕΙΝΗΣ] ΣΕΒΑΣΤΗΣ, transliteration: [AGRIPPEINES] SEBASTES (Agrippina Augusta[285])

Source: © The Trustees of the British Museum

This tetradrachm minted in Antiochia ad Orotem is very similar to the examples from Caesarea. The coin follows Nero's sample, with the head facing right on the obverse and Agrippina on the reverse. The differentiation is emphasised by the Greek caption, which has practically the same meaning, in other words, on the obverse it names Nero and his dynastic descent, explaining his right to rule. On the reverse, there is the name of Agrippina Augusta, as his partner in power and the one who paved the way for him to reach his status. Agrippina's hair style follows the same on coins struck earlier, at the same mint, in the time of Claudius, with Agrippina on the obverse and Nero on the reverse.

---

[283] Registration number: 1956,1208.8. Bibliography: RPC1 / Roman provincial coinage. Vol.1, From the death of Caesar to the death of Vitellius (44 BC-AD 69) (4175). Available at: https://www.britishmuseum.org/collection/object/C_1956-1208-8. Accessed: 24 Feb. 2021.
[284] Translation made by the author and by Juarez Oliveira.
[285] Translation made by the author.

Figure 84 – Brass coin[286], minted in Eumeneia, Phrygia (Phrygia), during the rule of Nero, 3.09 g, 15 mm. Obverse: draped bust of Agrippina Minor, with crown of corn, long hair, ΑΓΡΙΠ ΕΙΝΑ ΣΕΒΑΣΤΗ (Agrippina Augusta[287]). Reverse: seated female figure who could be Cybele, with a *patera* in right hand, ΒΑΣΣ Α ΚΛ ΕΩ ΝΟΣ ΑΡΧΙΕΡΗΑ ΕΥΜΕΝΕΩΝ (Bassa, daughter of Kleon, High Priestess of the people of Eumeneia[288])

Source: Roman Provincial Coinage online

According to the catalogue of the British Museum, coins of Nero and Agrippina Minor were minted in other provinces such as: Apamea (Phrygia), Ilium, Synaus, Smyrna, Magnesia ad Sipylum, Myndus, Euromus, Mytilene, Cime, Samos and Orthosia (Caria).

Coins were linked to some kind of deity, like the next example, which on its reverse bears the caption, CONCORDIA AUGUSTA, and her figure. The goddess Concordia is associated with similarities with other goddesses who appeared as personified Livia, such as Ceres, Pax, Vesta. What can be interpreted is that such women of the Roman elite, related directly to the emperor, were associated with goddesses who were linked to fertility, abundance, and prosperity. However, the Concordia Augusta can be attributed to Agrippina Augusta, as a tribute to the memory of Nero's mother, characterising both a family-type and a posthumous coin.

---

[286] BMC 44. RPC I 3151. Available at: https://rpc.ashmus.ox.ac.uk/coins/1/3151. Accessed: 14 Oct. 2022.
[287] Translation made by the author.
[288] Translation by Juarez Oliveira.

Figure 85 – Aureus[289], AD 58 - 68, Rome, minted during Nero's rule. Obverse: laureate face of Nero facing right, NERO CAESAR AVGVSTVS. Reverse: female figure, Concordia or Agrippina (?) seated with a *patera* in her right hand and a sceptre in her left hand, CONCORDIA AVGVSTA

Source: Courtesy of CoinArchives

After December 55, no more coins featuring Agrippina were struck in Rome, which may demonstrate that her influence over Nero had waned. The reduction in the minting of her figure may reflect the decline of her power. In addition, after the same date, coinage of Claudius' divine descent also stopped, but it is not known for sure why (Claes, 2013, p. 98).

In general, Nero was a little negligent in showing his roots in the Julio-Claudian family, with little mention of *Divus Augustus*. His mother, Agrippina, and his adoptive father, Claudius, were mentioned a lot at the beginning of his rule, but stopped appearing after two years, when he apparently no longer felt the need to announce that he was Claudius' successor, or to propagate that he was part of the Julio-Claudian family (Claes, 2013, p. 128).

Women of the Roman elite, such as Agrippina Minor and even her mother, Agrippina Major, took to the extreme the attention to care in order to have a "career" as imperial women, taking the model of Livia as an example and, above all, the status she had achieved. These women were the privileged victims of symbolic domination and the appropriate instruments that might be able to modify its effects in relation to the dominated categories. Symbolic domination is a construction that has cognitive instruments. When it is spoken of a symbolic, it is denoted something that is in the order of knowledge. This type of domination would be something concerning the disputes of power relations that pass through knowledge and recognition,

---

[289] RIC 1 48. Available at: https://www.coinarchives.com/a/lotviewer.php?LotID=1982352&AucID=4682&Lot=590&Val=518510a3f2e71127be61360631a4b54a. Accessed: 2 June 2022.

which function through mental structuring. Therefore, these mental schemes are constructed to the point that there is the structuring of mentalities, that there is cognitive struggle in a strong system that is robustly closed in on itself. Symbolic domination exerts complicity on the part of the dominated or complicity of the structures that the dominated has acquired in prolonged confrontation with the structures of domination, since it is necessary to become aware in order to profoundly transform the acquired dispositions, through a kind of re-education, which can make a bad habit disappear, changing the symbolic order. Awareness-raising is indispensable for triggering the transformation process and ensuring its results (Bourdieu, 1996a, p. 33 and 37-38). It can also be mentioned that the use of force by the state leads to a retreat of brute violence, to a pacification of relations between individuals. However, the result can be a substitution of bodily confrontations by symbolic struggles (Chartier, 1995, p. 40).

However, they were also marked by the aspiration to identify with the dominant models and, consequently, were inclined to appropriate, at any price, to the distinctive properties, because they were the ones that distinguished the dominant, in other words, the ones whose actions were fundamental to make their own husbands, brothers and/or sons emperors. They also contributed to the imperative spread in their favour, especially in the face of circumstantial symbolic power to ensure proselytism and thus secure a position within this system. In view of this factor, they gained a better status, acted as patrons, received honours, because they worked in favour of the prevailing system, which brought an "apparent freedom" that aimed to obtain from them a diligent submission and a contribution to symbolic domination, which were exercised through social, economic and cultural mechanisms, considered symbolic goods, and which made them the submissive ones in this environment. Thus, through their "responsibilities" and their agency, they were reduced to the condition of instruments of symbolic manipulation (Bourdieu, 1998, p. 121).

The relations between men and women of the Roman elite were established in all social spaces and sub-spaces, that is, not only within the family, but throughout society, such as in religion and especially within the State, marking them within an "eternal feminine", characterised by specific stigmas, which contributed to such structural permanence of the relationship of domination. This situation was historically constructed and reproduced through learning, linked to the experiences that agents had within social spaces. In this society, the sexual unconscious was found as a "logical" extension of the social universes of that time, taking root and reproducing itself through objectified forms of the establishment between social positions, which, in this case, would be the divisions between the masculine and the feminine. This marked the structure of masculine domination as an ultimate principle of countless relations of domination/submission, which apparently brought a "familiar" air and tended to separate men and women. The break with the common or prevailing order, would not be achieved through a single blow, or once and for all, but, firstly, these women should be aware of their position and the reality of masculine domination. They would then have to invest in an incessant and insistent work (Bourdieu, 1998, p. 122-130) against this order.

In the meantime, Agrippina Minor is taken as the best example to claim that women should have different gender identity crises. It seems that their frustrations and depression were more due to the fact that they were in a society that excluded them from public power than to a statement about whether they were feminine enough (Kimmel, 2016, p. 108), in contrast to the masculine identity, which should always be on trial.

Conclusion

This work has focused on the coins minted with images of the women of Rome. Ancient written sources have almost always helped make the case that women belonged to a domestic sphere, where their major tasks were within their homes and their most laudable roles were as wives and mothers. Augustus' source, *Res Gestae,* even hinges on the separation of the "private" and the "domestic", where the political world was necessary, but which brought a domestic full of values that were important for public life. The domestic functioned as a kind of private moralisation, which functioned as an apolitical ethical truth (Milnor, 2005, p. 27).

Other written sources, such as those used in this work, and as material sources, the coins, have also shown that women of the elite achieved some prominence, building a social life that led them to a certain political openness during the Late Republic and Early Empire, when they emerged as benefactors, patrons, and property owners, contributing to be important authors in the political history of Rome. Such changes of this era may have ensured a social alteration in all female categories arising from their cultural constructions and political performances. However, the Augustan period did not turn out to be a time when this division was distinct, but Roman society was moulding itself into a tangle of circumstances in which these divisions were intertwined, which rises the question of whether this separation was even evident or more complex than the written sources present.

In relation to material culture, it can be concluded that the images reproduced on the coins had to be something acceptable to the standards of representation that the public would expect, in other words, the type of figure had to be something that demonstrated that the imperial family was well cultivated or successful and, in the specific case of women, they had to be reported highlighting their domestic virtues. Likely, these images would have been made with political, self-propaganda and control intentions.

The images of Roman women on coins clearly demonstrated that they were idealised, as were Hellenistic queens, who were depicted with a lack of individualisation in the features of the figure, as well as facial features of the men with whom they were portrayed. In some depictions in which they are less idealised, their individual characteristics are better presented, but the idealisation comes with a youthful representation of women or showing maturity, which did not reflect reality, but rather their status and socio-political roles (Harvey, 2020, p. 48).

This scenario was made possible during the time of Augustus, as domestic life continued to constitute a central place in civic life. However, with all the changes, Augustus gave a new meaning to what it meant to participate in the functions of the Roman state, giving a new definition to the *res publica,* making social and political institutions seem to subsidise the idea of a single ruler. Consequently, there was a redefinition of the public and the private, since the State focused on a single man and a single family. Imperial women came to play an important role in Roman society as representatives of what the new regime could offer, overvaluing female virtue (Milnor, 2005, p. 4).

Apparently, Augustus was concerned with the significance of religious, civic, and moral issues, which led to the restoration of several temples, the *Forum Augustum* space, Greek and Latin libraries, harbours, and art collections. The idea was not only to beautify the city, but also to ratify what it was to be Roman. However, the domestic was the means by which morality was judged, to which public discourse about Rome increasingly returned, and women were traditionally associated with it. In this way, Augustus' government is known as one that paid attention to traditional Roman values, not only through legislation, which aimed to preserve the aristocratic family through incentives for those who conformed and punishments for those who did not, but also in more personal statements (Milnor, 2005, p. 9 and 11).

The characterisation of the "good" or "bad" housewife is an obsolete principle of distinguishing these women. However, academically the interpretative analysis of how ancient authors denounced such women shows that the "good" housewife was associated with the *princeps* and his kingdom, in which the idea of virtuous domesticity circulated as part of Augustus' discourse. In this period, not only were there transformations in the Roman political system, but also in ideas, ideals, and values. Morality dominated unprecedented political, social, and artistic aspects. In this context, in addition to a revival of traditional values, there were social, political, and cultural changes, which culminated in a new state. The virtue of daughters, wives, mothers, and sisters became the focus of public attention. What it seemed was that Augustus was asking that Romans contemplated a part of their lives that was outside of politics, but concerning as something public.

The representations of female virtue in imperial ideology were merely a way back into the private lives of Roman citizens, which needed to be re-examined and refined (Milnor, 2005, p. 12 and 15-16).

In several circumstances of this work, the questioning of female power at that time has been raised, since it should be borne in mind that gender relations can be found within a "sexed *habitus*" (Bourdieu, 1998, p. 9), having been moulded within a division, which represented the reality of that moment, within a social elite, and which is sometimes demonstrated in written and material sources, as it left consequences in practice. Thus, women in coins did not fail to delimit the material and symbolic forces between the genders contemplated here, demonstrating that their public visibility did not cease masculine domination, but gave them power, which was framed in a domestic unit, insofar as fertility symbols were used, which mainly follow Livia and Agrippina Minor in the representations. It should be borne in mind that the State and private life itself were elements of elaboration and imposition of principles of domination, which could have been places of tension, since these women took on activities outside the original, which had not immediately been well defined in this division.

However, it can be seen that the agency of these women's relations improved their social status, often with the help of activities such as Patronage. Military attitudes such as those of Fulvia and Agrippina Major were consecutively honoured in the East and criticised in Rome. Likewise, political attitudes, such as Livia's actions, demonstrated the opening up of a social complexity and of perspectives of actions not yet clearly delimited in research on this type of female social establishment. In this sense, there is still a need for academic work focused on studies of women of the past, especially with a tendency to show how gender relations are constructed and negotiated, since gender provides a useful focus for analysing the complexity of social, economic, and political transformation. Following this perspective, gender analysis encourages looking at the experience and agency of characters, since gender identities are fundamental to the construction of subjectivities and the establishment of individuals in their social world, internally and externally, and even to being agents of change in their own community and beyond (Goddard, 2000, p. 2).

The gender discourse expressed in materiality, in this case in coins, manifested gender ideologies that determined positions of women's activities of the time, informing experiences and perceptions of lived situations.

Gender discourses were fundamental to the production of symbols, with meanings and signifiers spreading in ramifications and in conjunction with the exchange networks of the coins. For this reason, gender discourses are deployed by collective actors, organisations and those who instigate social change in some way (Goddard, 2000, p. 7).

Coins were often used by the central power, especially by Augustus, to emphasise and propagandise imperial family harmony, a period in which there was great adherence of these women to Patronage. Demonstrations of honour to these women in the provinces often exceeded that of the central power, opening up a great public power, beyond Rome, imbricated in the provinces. Thus, gender discourses were also produced privately and collectively outside Rome, following local traditions, usually to honour gratitude for benefits, with a mixture of native and Roman elements.

In addition, coins tended to legitimise the power of those who were minted on them, insofar as they were produced according to the consent of the Senate or by the provincial elites, when it came to a local coinage, which would often also have to receive the approval of the central power. From this perspective, the coin can be seen as a communicator and an instrument of dissemination, constituting an active way of accepting new characters of power.

However, reactions such as those expressed in textual sources of that time could have been a great cunning to emphasise gender assumptions when talking about these Roman women who gained more openness and a new social positioning at the end of the Republic and beginning of the Empire. The unfolding of gender symbols, placed in various ways to represent them on coins, which in their scope were symbols linked to fertility, were fundamental to demonstrate a construction of collective identity, in particular of government entities, which are essential for the legitimisation of state symbols. It must be taken into account that collective identities and individual subjectivities are correlated in parts, linked to exchanges and complex flows, which are part of discursive practices and power effects of gender, sexuality, race, and class, simultaneously as investments of State-building (Radcliffe; Westwood, 1996, p. 166), which are listed at different levels depending on the locality and its context (Goddard, 2000, p. 8).

The power and the position that these imperial women aspired took different levels with regard to the localities of the Roman Empire. The coins corresponded to a cognitive entanglement in which individuals and groups engaged in a creative and interpretive process that could vary from what was produced as "official" (Goddard, 2000, p. 8) for the central power and its provinces, since the symbolic interpretation could vary from one province to another, considering that the honour for such women was possibly also collated in a multiple way, taking into account local cultural elements, but which were not delimiting for central Roman interests, so that they had no reason to be banned.

In this regard, it cannot be denied that the Roman women of the elite minted on coins, as well as in other arts, were fortifying for the change in their public positioning and power. The coin would come to delimit a mark of the relationship of power, gender and the family system and its values, as well as an object that would be the corollary of political changes, since the private and domestic demand listed for women was on the agenda in order to a public visibility still based on morality and values close to the most traditional ones, and their images were mostly attributed to the personifications of goddesses and together with symbols representing fertility, religiosity and *pudicitia*. The religious boundary has the capacity to strictly define the patterns of men and women linked to a studied society, their activities, ritual forms, and devotional practices that suit each of the sexes (Chartier, 1995, p. 41).

However, women's representations were still symbolically oriented towards resignation and discretion, which resulted in an agency in which they could exercise some power by accepting their own limits of strength, often accepting to erase or deny a power that they could only exercise by proxy, through a procurator or a representative (Bourdieu, 1998, p. 43).

As a result of the symbolic elements relating to fertility, it is thus interpreted that there was a sexual topology of the socialised body, with the female body being the one recognised for procreating. The bodies, in view of their displacements and movements, are coated with social meanings. The differences between the male and female body could have led to the use of different practices and metaphorical elements to elucidate them, which were used for each sex and differentiated equally in their appearances, being linked to the agents' *habitus,* which functioned as schemes of perceptions, thinking and actions. This experience apprehended the social world and its arbitrary divisions, starting with the social division between men and women, seen as "natural", a thought that legitimised such separations. Given this "naturalisation", the patriarchal view was imposed as neutral, causing masculine domination to be symbolically grounded, creating a sexual division of labour, its instruments, and places (Bourdieu, 1998, p. 16-18).

The "naturalisation" of female subordination has already received several feminist criticisms, since it is argued that women's subordination is caused from the ways in which women are socially constructed, because it is believed in the underlying idea that what is constructed can be changed. From this perspective, by changing the ways in which they are perceived, it would be possible to change the social space they occupy (Piscitelli, 2002, p. 10). However, for other social changes, women would have to become aware of their subordination. In this regard, Bourdieu (1998) comments that this "naturalisation" occurs when awareness is not recurrent, so that such female performances are seen as "right" to be performed in a given social group.

However, State decisions on how these women should have been represented must have had an impact on provincial reproductions, since it must have also been in the provincial interest to reproduce images within certain standards in order to have a good relationship with the centre. However, in some cases, these images, as much as those expressed in other types of material culture, would have to be in accordance with the locality, since they should directly imply a sense of significance for the group in that provincial area.

In relation to the place where these women acted, it is customary to relativise an exact division of spaces, demonstrating male privilege over female privilege and not listing a "subjectivity of places". Certainly, both in the public and private arenas, they had limits to their activities. That said, the interpretation of the places of action can define and make such places objects of reflection and definition of what the political performance would be, taking into account that the coin could be listed as a public place to carry out a discourse. However, the local place and, in particular, the way the public arena and the private arena were delimited could define a certain value (Scott; Kaplan; Keates, 1997), leading to an elucidative complexity and a range of interpretation, within concrete limits. As well as the redefinition of what is "political action" (Goddard, 2000, p. 10), since the "institutionalisation" of Roman women, observed by the example of Livia, seems to have been totally linked to religion, camouflaging the political into the religious, making way for the agency of these women, guaranteeing them a place, which they did not have before. Even so, women tended not to be so well accepted, but it was possible to count on a new establishment of them between the public and the private, especially after Livia.

The lack of a place or position for them to act demonstrates the difficulty of fitting into a social position. Thus, the problematisation is not only spatial, but also linked to a gender subjectivity. When thinking about the women of the present, the same problem of framing women in a social position is observed in another reality. According to *Pesquisa Fapesp*[290] magazine, even though women academics are already making up a large part of the scientific community, surpassing men in the number of PhDs defended per year in Brazil, they are still at a disadvantage when it comes to occupying positions of greater power at universities, research institutions and funding agencies. For this reason, they constantly need to prove that they are as or more capable than men, facing moral and sometimes sexual harassment; solve the professional costs involved in motherhood; and strive to conquer a scientific place within their "feminine condition", presenting problems and perspectives that enrich science as a whole (Almeida, 2020, p. 7). This digression is elucidating, since the problematisations of women of the past can be enlightening and conscientious for nowadays.

And this means that masculine domination is in its full exercise. It should be borne in mind that such social compositions are not so easy to modify and the condition of men is affirmed by the objectivity of the same social compositions, productive and reproductive activities, which consequently divide activities between men and women, giving men the better part, directly linked to the *habitus* moulded by conditions that function as matrices of the perceptions of the thoughts and actions of all members of society, something that is historically instilled and universally shared. However, male dominance is invested by common sense, which women themselves apply to their own reality, and even in power relations, in which they find themselves involved in thought schemes that are products of the incorporation of these relations and that express foundational oppositions of a symbolic order (Bourdieu, 1998, p. 45).

The greatest example of female complacency in the past was Octavia. The position of women in the Roman elite could have changed after the actions of Fulvia, Livia and even Agrippina Major. However, male opposition existed in objectivity and mentalities, causing a continuation of the *habitus* already established. In this way, the performances of women like Octavia were still organised in such a way as to be rooted in a masculine order, which was both material and mental.

---

[290] Fapesp (Foundation for Research Support of the State of São Paulo) funding agency magazine, which communicates the research carried out under its endorsement.

Hence, a rupture of the complicity of violence in the relationship of symbolic domination can only be reached with a radical transformation of the social conditions of production of the tendencies that lead the dominated to take the dominant's point of view over the dominant and the dominated. Symbolic violence is only processed through an act of practical knowledge and ignorance, which takes effect beyond consciousness and will and which may have conferred a "hypnotic power" to its manifestations (Bourdieu, 1998, p. 54).

It has often been questioned why these women of the Roman elite were victimised. Such questioning refers to the current idea that the lives of elite white women, who are well off economically, who society believes are well-married and therefore do not need to work, may be giving the impression that they are not abused. On the contrary, financial dependence can be a trigger for oppression. In fact, the action of Brazil's Maria da Penha Law commonly addresses complaints made against men without resources, since the same law has been opening up for lawyers paid by middle and upper-class men to refrain them from the complaint made by middle-class victims in women's police stations. It should be noted that the categories imposed to demonstrate female diversity show different difficulties, not leaving aside the fact that all women are likely to suffer some type of violence, regardless of such categories, which end up separating women into distinct groups. A real progress in this area will only occur through full unity, compassion, consciousness and understanding of each other.

Returning to Roman women, it must be thought that, probably, with the "institutionalisation" of Livia, there was an indirect reconceptualization of places, with new limits and new circumstances, in which the public had to be reorganised as a result of a private, which previously associated women with it. In this way, what could be considered private in Livia's time came as a result of her agency being public, at a time when it seemed no longer sensible to keep such activities private. In another way, this does not mean that masculine domination stopped acting on women, but it was renewed in a way that the actions of Livia and other women of the elite were part of the new prevailing order, which does not mean that there were no tensions between the parties.

The distinction of public and private could be seen as an explanation for women's subordination and a crucial factor in the construction and reaffirmation of gender inequality (Davidoff, 1998 apud Goddard, 2000, p. 12). This dichotomy, applied to historical and ethnographic studies, emphasised the constructed and contingent character of gender relations and their connections to wider relations of inequality.

In the last decades of the twentieth century, there was an increased interest in critiquing the Western view of what was private and its origins in modern capitalism, industrialisation and contemporary ideas of citizenship and good government. Models developed by Hannah Arendt and Jürgen Habermas were used in which public and private spheres were understood in Europe and America as a product of the eighteenth and nineteenth century, during republican hegemony and the development of the economic market. For Milnor, what makes the dichotomy between public and private meaningful in the present time is the current civil, economic, and social structures. However, "private" is a term that also existed in Antiquity (Milnor, 2005, p. 17-18), which makes one ponder about what its meaning was in the past, adding the fact that the analysis in the face of such a dichotomy may not truly elucidate reality.

Regarding its Latin meaning, the adjective *publicus* seems to have derived from *populus*, that is, "the people", which seems to have meant either "of the people" in general, or "of the people" who were especially governmental. The *res publica*, which would be "public thing", became "the State". Concerning *privatus*, the Romans used different words from the radical *privo*, "to cause to be separated (from), to deprive or steal (from)". There was also the adjective *privatus*, meaning "private", as in private or personal property; the name *privatus*, meaning "a private person", as opposed to a magistrate or an official; and the adverb *privatim*, meaning "privately" or "individually". The word *privatus* would have a meaning in opposition to the political sphere, which would be deprived of it. For the Romans, it would be "beyond" the community, the affairs of the state, the places of civic life. The term was used in political matters and must have continued with a meaning within the context of public life. During the Republic, *privatus* was the definition of a man without political or military position. In the High Empire, it was used for anyone who did not have a political or military position, in other words, for those that did not have a public role in the empire. However, in the time of Augustus, all good men, in and out of their public activities, were responsible for the functioning of the State and the safety of their fellow citizens (Milnor, 2005, p. 19-20 and 24).

The distinction between public and private is still important as an ideological tool, since this separation can be considered for the social, political, and economic interpretation of a certain group (Goddard, 2000, p. 13-14). However, this public/private division can restrict the interpretation of the society studied, in a way that would make believe in the existence of only these two types of places of action. However, the division should be seen here as merely didactic, as a way of limiting the focus of the object under study, since Roman society was probably much more complex, and the very designation "public/private" can itself bring a great tangle of intersecting parts, relying on the very example of Livia, who, in order to act publicly, needed to follow religious purposes, allowing the private (Livia) to intertwine with the public (Livia's agency). Some feminists have argued that this division is in itself a gender structure in which women and men come to be identified with different places and activities, and therefore also has certain ethics and values (Bahrani, 2005, p. 10).

This division can also be linked to the documentary sources we have access to and how they describe Antiquity. In this respect, the written sources show such a division, but it does not mean that it was followed in practice. Generally, Roman women are described in family environments, but there are also exceptions, forming an opposition between the public and private worlds. The house would be a place where they would be inserted most of the time. Men were described as those who are hardly associated with domestic places, with an image of toughness and manly rudeness.

Exceptions could bring tensions and an obligation to change within the places, since the Roman State itself prescribed institutional factors for the division of the genders, which ratified private and public patriarchy, with public patriarchy being inscribed in all the institutions charged with managing and regulating the daily existence of the domestic unit. Otherwise, private patriarchy guaranteed an ultra-conservative vision, which made the patriarchal family the beginning and model of the social order as a moral order, founded on the absolute pre-eminence of men over women (Bourdieu, 1998, p. 105).

The public sphere, in its fullness, would be where agency and change would happen, where the potential of human "freedom" could be employed and where it would be significant for people in this place to associate themselves with specific mindsets, with men being, in a sense, more likely to embody such types of thinking (Goddard, 2000, p. 13-14), given that, even with Livia, the public sphere was an arena for the creation and establishment of gendered assumptions, such as that a woman would not be well accepted.

When places are not neutral and are recognised as having gender differentiations, such as that men are linked to the public sphere and women to the private sphere, the redefinition of that space can be grand (Goddard,

2000, p. 17), which presumes that Livia, for example, needed to be very intelligent and skilled to deal with the advent of such place, as did Agrippina Minor and other women who were active in this environment and were potentially criticised, such as Fulvia. The examples of women of the Roman elite in public life can demonstrate an arena of the gender perspective of that time and a place of power. In this respect, the presence of women in public places created an agency to negotiate, directly or indirectly, the boundaries and ways in which these places were utilised. Consequently, such agency presumably led to a redefinition of the meaning and value of such places that were intended to remain separate, or that were seen as separate.

Possibly, the presence of elite women in the public sphere should have been seen as subversive to the traditions that legitimised politics as a male activity. Today, in relation to the social position of women, Márcia Barbosa, a professor at the Physics Institute of the Federal University of Rio Grande do Sul (UFRGS), Brazil, emphasises in an interview with the magazine called *Pesquisa Fapesp,* that at various events she had to listen in a mocking way to the fact that "science lived so well without women", and ended up replying: then "it would now be necessary to incorporate them" (Queiroz, 2020, p. 21), demonstrating their great presence and effectiveness in all academic fields.

As far as the past is concerned, Livia achieved various powers, as she had the support of the Senate. Her polished agency in dealing with social politics among its members seems to have been entirely resourceful, since the exclusion of women led them to reproduce divisions, as well as the hierarchical predispositions they themselves favoured as a way of being accepted in the prevailing system. Livia's position was shrewd in that, by having power, she had to maintain a hierarchy and strategically balance her agencies, in a masculine world, through a feminine position.

However, without a radical transformation of the domestic sphere, the limits of "maternal thinking" were evident in the public arena, for in the absence of changes in the private arena, the appropriation of feelings and images from the domestic sphere remained susceptible to what were conservative and hierarchical instance objectives (Goddard, 2000, p. 19). An example of this can be seen in the representations of these women on coins, where they start from the personifications of goddesses, emphasising *pudicitia*, to the presence of elements linked to fertility, such as the cornucopia, noting a dubious position, that is, of power, but submissive in other aspects.

The images of the women of the Roman elite would have to follow the assumptions of values of that time, boasting the sampling of the virtues of those women, to be a benefit to the ruler. The emperor, by consenting to the minting of coins with the female figure of his family, made sure that her virtues were in accordance with a moral, holding these images under his control. In this way, the coins confirmed a dimension of the historical variety of gender formation, which is a social construction and transmitted to a society through certain vehicles of meanings and symbols. The coins, together with the iconography present, reproduce the expected female domestic life, carrying symbolic meanings, which served to report the harmony of the imperial family. It was a means of expressing social rank and status within a society, demonstrating values, social norms, and functions in general, defining behaviours, with a long duration, as a constant and firm medium (Riess, 2012, p. 499-500).

Therefore, the minting of female figures on the coins of Rome had to pass to a governmental approval, related to the imperial and senatorial power, which led to the demonstration in this material culture the gender relations within the imperial family and the limits pertinent to female members in these coinages, thus marking the power of dominance of a male group over a female group, with the effect of a restrictive agency linked to a male imperial propaganda. Another event that also marked the agency for the production of coins with female figures was the Patronage activity carried out by these imperial women, which classified them as benefactors, but on behalf of a government and male dominance. However, the "freedom" that these women gained by having their images honoured should not be classified as "freedom" in fact, but it was made available to them to perform this activity, since in this way they would benefit the image of the emperor himself and his family. Consequently, they were used as key vehicles for imperial propaganda, which tended to spread religiously, economically, and socially.

In the meantime, their agencies represented a challenge to the boundaries between the public and the private and/or, in reality, such boundaries were not so blunt. However, it should be recognised that there may have been a reinvention of the domestic and a recognition of the importance of gender to cultural and political phenomena indirectly within a framework of male dominance. From this perspective, this study aimed to demonstrate, through coins and alongside textual sources, Roman identity constructions and the importance of agency in building complex processes of change. The focus on gender has helped to bridge the conceptual gaps between processes of change, public settings and the everyday lives of men and women (Goddard, 2000, p. 20). However, more comprehensive work is needed to establish the presence of the different women of this past in different locations and how they were perceived, counting with the subaltern world.

However, as power relations are not static and could also change as a result of different locations, there were tensions for the modifications, as female figures ended up being more called upon than the emperor himself. One example was the case of Livia and her son Tiberius, who had to restrict the honours paid to her by the Senate. Yet, the agency of Augustus linked to the adoption of Livia by the *gens Iulia,* giving her the title of Augusta, would also have an intention aimed at masculine dominance, since Livia's titles could be at the disposal of her son Tiberius. However, by the standard of the Roman ideal of the male and female role, which Tiberius probably had in mind, he did not allow to accept the status that his mother would pass on to him, even if it was for his own benefit.

Regarding the criterion of power relations, both the material culture and the written sources analysed together were essential to prove this issue, since the literature explains well the gender relations of the emperors and their wives. Material culture could demonstrate that coins of Fulvia seem to have been minted because of Mark Antony's performance and power, but also because she had gained public respect beyond what was expected of a woman. Octavian only minted coins of Octavia after marrying her to Antony and thus legitimised the Pact of Brundisium. Livia was minted because the Senate itself consented and she was worshipped as a goddess, and even as a "mother goddess", in the provinces for her actions as a patron, before being deified, so that the highest grade of her titration was "GENETRIX ORBI", minted only provincially, probably having a local circulation. It may be mentioned that Livia's rise was due to Augustus' actions and the visual propagation of the imperial family that he provided.

The images of Roman women mentioned here were generally minted to appear subordinate to their husbands or sons, that is, to the emperor, for example, when they were portrayed next to them on the obverse, behind their figure, or when the figure of the emperor appeared on the obverse and the female figure on the reverse. The caption demarcating the authority of the emperor also marks power relations in material culture, since male and female figures could appear on the obverse facing each other, evidencing a possible equality of positions. However, the captions directly emphasise the emperor, or mention the woman, but characterise her by her relationship with him. When the woman appears on a coin alone, made with the consent of the Senate, the caption includes the name of the emperor who minted it. In the case of Livia, her cult was also directly linked to the cult of Augustus. This contextual repertoire symbolises Roman gender relations and particularly their tensions, revealing a binary visual social identity, with some advantages for the female gender, which commonly had divine attributes. Women rarely had tiaras, but by receiving too many elements and titles, they clashed with the male gender, as in the case of Livia and Tiberius. On the other hand, imperial women accepted their position, because the more power the emperor had, the more advantages they got because of his position, so they could be active in manipulating them to get more power.

This study suggested a complexity of gender relations, with data that demonstrated an outdated dichotomy of thinking that the domestic was feminine, and the public was masculine, establishing a complex symbolic system of abstraction of gender relations within the representative conceptions of the social and political, but still possessing ideologies linked to the gender assumptions established by that society in the past. However, it can be mentioned that the new position of imperial women may have caused conflicts, but it was not able to shake the dominant patriarchal Roman social framework, and they were seen and used essentially for the success of the male imperial regime.

Analysing the position of these women in Roman society serves to understand the gendered nature of Roman society, as well as the relationship between gender and power, while also involving this aspect in the socio-political structure of Roman society. However, it should be understood that all societies construct images of groups existing within them according to values and interests of the dominant group. Characterisations of Roman women must be placed in a context of conflict between approved roles for women and those that place them in a position of threatening powerful women (Fischler, 1994, p. 116 and 127).

That said, it can be considered that Roman women were generally used as an abstraction to elucidate positive or negative judgements of their emperors. However, they were potentially active agents in aristocratic male formation, that is, in the public activities they became part of, helping to form the aristocratic male *virtus* of their family, through symbolic actions and gestures (McCullough, 2007, p. 76). In this sense, aristocratic men brought the private sphere and their women to benefit from their virtues.

These norms and values can be considered significant to the formation of the social identities that constituted the Roman society of that time. This work was concerned with demonstrating the difference attributed to men and women in the elite of Roman society. Thus, even if women have conquered a place and actions in public life, with their images and reputations, it must be taken into account that such positions were merely constructed according to their virtues, relying on an adherence to the traditional Roman female way of life. However, some flexibilizations seem to have been made to fit them into the new feminine attitudes within the virtues stigmatised by that society.

In view of this perspective, it is congruent to finalise this work by composing the fact that the major problematic found here was the female position in Roman society. This issue is not outside of the present concerns, since one of the 2020 issues of the magazine *Pesquisa Fapesp* was dedicated to demonstrating data on the presence of women in science. One of the articles reports that, since 2003, women have become the majority in the number of PhDs; in 2007, 54% of PhDs were women. In the 1990s, there were almost twice as many men as women leading research groups in Brazil; the most recent figures provided by the National Council for Scientific and Technological Development (CNPq), from 2016, show that the male advantage has fallen to 15% (Marques, 2020, p. 27).

However, according to biologist Jacqueline Leta of the University of Rio de Janeiro (UFRJ), who studies gender in science, equality is still a long way off. She adds that the most powerful positions in universities and funding agencies are held primarily by men and that the conception of science follows the same one formulated by the pioneers in each field of knowledge, generally men, aimed at publishing results in renowned journals (Marques, 2020, p. 27-28).

To get an international idea, the gender of authors from 15 countries who published articles in the *Scopus* database between 2014 and 2018 was analysed through the report entitled *The researcher's journey through the gender lens*, published by Elsevier on 5th March 2020. Brazil appears among the most equitable, with 0.8 women per man (compared to 0.55 in the period 1999-2003); surpassed by Portugal (0.9) and Argentina (just over 1 woman per man); ahead of the United Kingdom (0.6), the United States and Germany (0.5). However, even though the presence of women in science today is driven by their high participation, the places of power are still delimited, because while men win higher paid positions, women remain in the less prestigious positions (Marques, 2020, p. 28).

However, it can be concluded that women have for more than 2,000 years been mostly in a secondary social position[291], which, even if they reach positions of power or leadership, go through an arduous, abusive, and unsympathetic path. That said, the historicization of this female past is important to demonstrate the symmetry and diversity of historical contexts, highlighting the similarities of the past with those of the present, revealing and adding an awareness of the scope of masculine domination in both periods. It should be emphasised that the Roman female position proves to be an important instructive resource to be explored to raise awareness of current male and female agencies. In this perspective, the position of Roman women offers a counterpoint to think about the women of the present, which is very much guided by abuses, physical and symbolic violence, and even feminicides. Therefore, the critique of Roman patriarchy is also a consciential and educational resource for questioning gender agencies and their identities in contemporary times.

---

[291] See BEAUVOIR, Simone. **Le deuxième sexe**. Paris: Gallimard, 1949.

Bibliography

Ancient sources

ANONIMOUS. **Fragmenta Vaticana – Mosaicarvm et romanarvm legvm collatio**. 1890. Available at: https://archive.org/details/fragmentavatica00momm-goog/page/n8/mode/2up. Accessed: 03 nov. 2023.

APPIANUS de Alexandria. **Historia Romana – De bellis civilibus**. Translated Petrus Candidus Decembrius. Venice: Bernhard Maler, Erhard Ratdolt and Peter Löslein, 1477.

APULEIUS de Alexandria. **Metamorphoses and Golden Ass and Philosophical works**. Translated from original Latim to English by Thomas Taylor. London: J. Moyes, 1822.

ASCONIUS, Quintus. **Commentaries on five speeches of Cicero**. Simon Squires. Wauconda: Bolchazy-Carducci Publishers, Inc, 2006.

CASSIUS DIO, Lucius. **Roman History**. Published in vol. V of the Loeb Classical Library edition, 1917. Available at: https://penelope.uchicago.edu/Thayer/E/Roman/Texts/Cassius_Dio/48*.html. Accessed: 13 Jun. 2023

CASSIUS DIO, Lucius. **Roman History**. Edited by E. Cary, London: G. B. Putman, 1925.

CICERO, Marcus T. **Letters to Atticus**. Translated by: Winstedt, E. O., M. A. London: William Hernemann and New York: G. P. Putnam's son, 1912/1919.

CICERO, Marcus T. Epistulae Ad Familiares. Edition and translation by: Skackleto Bailey, D. R. Cambridge: Cambridge University Press, 2004.

CICERO, Marcus T. **La république**. Paris: Les Belles Lettres, 1989.

CICERONIS, Marcus T. **Orationes**: Pro Milone; Pro Marcello; Pro Ligario; Pro Rege Deiotaro; Philippicae 1-14. Notes and critics by Clark, A. C. Oxford: Oxford University Press, 1918.

CICERONIS, Marcus T. **Q. Asconii Pediani Orationvm Ciceronis Qvinqve Enarratio**. Notes and critics by Clark, A. C. Oxford: Oxford University Press, 1956.

GAIUS. **Institvtiones**. Translation and commentary by Edward Poste, M. A. Forth edition revised by E. A. Whittuck and introduced by A. H. J. Greenidge. Oxford: At the Claredon Press, 1904. Available at: http://files.libertyfund.org/files/1154/Gaius_0533.pdf. Accessed: 31 July 2021.

HESIODO. **Teogonia**: a origem dos deuses. Tradução de Jaa Torrano. São Paulo: Iluminárias Ltda., 1995. Available at: https://www.assisprofessor.com.br/documentos/livros/hesiodo_teogonia.pdf. Accessed: 14 Dec. 2021.

HOMERO. **Ilíada**. Translated by: Manoel Odorico Mendes. ebooksBrasil, 2009. Available at: http://www.ebooksbrasil.org/adobeebook/iliadap.pdf. Accessed: 14 Dec. 2021.

HORATIUS, Quintus. **The odes of Horace**. Book 1. Specimen of an attempt to give a closer English verse translation of The Odes than has Hitherto been done (1879). Translation by James John Lonsdale. Whitefish, Montana: Kessinger Publishing, LLC., 2010.

JUSTINIAN, Flavius. **The institutes**. Translation and notes by Thomas Collett Sandars, M. A. London: Longmans, Green, and Co., 1865. Available at: https://www.fd.unl.pt/Anexos/Investigacao/7877.pdf. Accessed: 31 July 2021.

JUSTINIAN, Flavius. **Digesto**. Tradução de Madeira, H. M. F. São Paulo: Thompson Reuters, 2013.

JUVENAL, Decianus. **The Satires**. Translated by A. S. Kline. 2011. Available at: https://web.ics.purdue.edu/~rauhn/Hist_416/hist420/JuvenalSatirespdf.pdf. Accessed: 31 July 2021.

LIVIO, Titus. **História de Roma**: Ab Vrbe Condita. Introduction, translation and notes by Paulo Farmhouse Alberto. Lisboa: Editorial Inquérito, 1999. v. 1.

LIVY, Titus. **Book I and II**. Edited by Warmington, E. H., M. A. The Loeb Classical Library. Cambridge, Massachusetts: Harvard University Press; London: William Heinemann LTD., 1919.

LIVY, Titus. **History of Rome**. English Translation by. Rev. Canon Roberts. New York, New York. E. P. Dutton and Co. 1912. 1.

LIVY, Titus. **Rome's Mediterranean Empire**. Books 41 - 45 and the Periochae. A new translation by Jane D. Chaplin. Oxford World's Classics. Oxford: Oxford University Press, 2010.

LUCANO, Marcus. **Pharsalia**. Translated to English by Nicholas Rowe. London: J. and R. Tonson and S. Draper, 1753.

OVID, Publius. **Consulatio ad Liviam**. LOEB Classical Library: Harvard University Press. Available at: https://www.loebclassics.com/view/ovid-poem_consolation/1929/pb_LCL232.325.xml. Accessed: 14 jun. 2021.

OVID, Publius. **The art of Love (Ars Amatoria)**. Book III. Translated by A. S. Kline. 2001. Available at: https://www.poetryintranslation.com/PITBR/Latin/ArtofLoveBkIII.php. Accessed: 14 July 2023

OVIDE, Publius. **Tristes**. Texte établi et traduit par Jacques André. Paris: Belles Lettres, 1987.

OVÍDIO, Publius. **Cartas Pônticas**. Translation, introduction and notes by Geraldo José Albino. Translation review by Zélia de Almeida Cardoso. São Paulo: Martins Fontes, 2009.

PLUTARCH. Caius Gracchus. **The Parallel Lives**. Tradução de Bernadotte Perrin. Cambridge, London: Loeb Classical Library, 1921. Available at: http://penelope.uchicago.edu/Thayer/E/Roman/Texts/Plutarch/Lives/Caius_Gracchus*.html. Accessed: 21 Jun. 2022.

PLUTARCH. Mark Antony. **Makers of Rome**. Translated and introduction by Ian Scott-Kilvert. London: Penguin Books, 1965.

PLUTARCO. Caesar. *In:* **Warner, Rex, Fall of the Roman Republic**. London: Penguin Books, 1958.

PROPERTIUS, Sextus. **Elegies**. Book III. Edited by: W. A. Camps. Cambridge: Cambridge University Press, 1966.

SALLUST, Gaius. **The war with Catiline**. Published in the Loeb Classical Library, revised in 1931. 1921. Available at: https://penelope.uchicago.edu/Thayer/e/roman/texts/sallust/bellum_catilinae*.html. Accessed: 15 Jun. 2023.

SENECA, Lucius A. **Annaeus. Moral Essays**: volume 2. John W. Basore. London and New York: Heinemann. 1932.

SUETONIO, Caio. **Da vida dos Césares**. Iul i.35.52, ii.17.

SUETONIUS, Gaius. **The Twelve Caesars**. Translation by Robert Graves. Harmondsworth: Penguin Books, 1957.

TACITUS, Publius C. **The Annals and The Histories**. Translation by A. J. Church and W. J. Brodribb. Great Britain: Penguin Classics, 1952.

TACITUS, Publius C. **The Germany and the Agricola of Tacitus**. The Oxford translation revised, with notes. With an introduction by Edward Brooks, Jr. Project Gutenberg Ebook. Produced by Anne Soulard, Charles Aldarondo, Tiffany Vergon, Eric Casteleijn and the Online Distributed Proofreading Team, 2013. Available at: https://www.gutenberg.org/files/7524/7524-h/7524-h.htm. Accessed: 31 July 2021.

ULPIAN, Eneo. **The Digest or Pandects of Justinian**. Translated by S. P. Scott. Cincinnati: The Central Trust Company, 1932.

ULPIAN, Eneo. **The rules of Ulpian**. Translated by S. P. Scott. 1932. Available at: https://droitromain.univ-grenoble-alpes.fr/Anglica/uipian_scott.html. Accessed: 16 jun. 2023.

VALERI MAXIMI. **Valeri Maximi Facta et dicta memorabilia**. Edited by J. Briscoe. Stutgardt: Teubner, 1998.

VELLEIUS PATERCULUS, Marcus. **The Roman History**. Published in the Loeb Classical Library, 1924. Available at: https://penelope.uchicago.edu/Thayer/e/roman/texts/velleius_paterculus/2c*.html. Accessed: 17 Jun. 2023.

VIRGIL, Publius. **The Aeneid**. Translated by Robert Fagles and with the Introduction by Bernard Knox. London: Penguin Classics Deluxe Edition, 2008.

Numismatic documentation

BRENNAN, Peter; TURNER, Michael; WRIGHT, Nicholas L. **Faces of Power**: imperial portraiture on Roman coins. Nicholson Museum. Sydney: University of Sydney, 2007.

CRAWFORD, Michael H. **Roman Republic coinage**. Cambridge: Cambridge University Press, 1976a. v. 1.

CRAWFORD, Michael H. **Roman Republic coinage**. Cambridge: Cambridge University Press, 1975b. v. 2.

HEAD, Barclay V. **Catalogue of Greek coins of Phrygia**. London: Oxford University Press, 1906.

NUMISMATIC Collection of the Aegean Numismatics. Available at: https://www.vcoins.com/en/stores/egean_numismatics/1/product/ionia_Esmirna_augustus__livia_27bc14ad_ae20/1349844/Default.aspx. Accessed: 19 May 2022.

NUMISMATIC Collection of the American Numismatic Society. Available at: http://numismatics.org/crro/results. Accessed: 17 Oct. 2022.

NUMISMATIC Collection of the *Bibliothèque Nationale de France*. Available at: https://www.culture.gouv.fr/Espace-documentation/Repertoire-des-ressources-documentaires/Bibliotheques/Bibliotheque-nationale-de-France-BnF-Site-Francois-Mitterrand. Accessed: 19 May 2022.

NUMISMATIC Collection of the British Museum. Available at: https://www.britishmuseum.org/collection. Accessed: 17 Oct. 2022.

NUMISMATIC Collection of the Classical Numismatic Group, LLC. Available at: https://www.cngcoins.com/. Accessed: 19 May 2022.

NUMISMATIC Collection of the Heritage Action: the world's largest Numismatic Auctioneer. Available at: https://www.ha.com/. Accessed: 25 Apr. 2022.

NUMISMATIC Collection of the KBR: cabinet des monnais et médailles. Available at: https://opac.kbr.be/coins-and-medals.aspx. Accessed: 18 Aug. 2022.

NUMISMATIC Collection of the Münzkabinett der Staatlichen Museen zu Berlin – Preußischer Kulturbesitz. Available at: https://www.smb.museum/en/museums-institutions/muenzkabinett/collections-research/collection/. Accessed: 25 Nov. 2021.

NUMISMATIC Collection of the Museums Victoria. Available at: https://museumsvictoria.com.au/. Accessed: 18 Aug. 2022.

NUMISMATIC Collection of the Pavlos S. Pavlou. Available at: https://www.vcoins.com/en/stores/pavlos_s_pavlou_numismatist-131/ancient-coins/Default.aspx?#!/Home. Accessed: 7 Nov. 2022.

NUMISMATIC Collectio of the Praefectus Coins. Available at: https://www.vcoins.com/en/stores/praefectus_coins-130/ancient-coins/Default.aspx?#!/Home. Accessed: 11 July 2022.

NUMISMATIC Collection of the WildWinds. Available at: https://wildwinds.com/coins/. Accessed: 11 July 2022.

PORTO, Vagner C. O culto imperial e as moedas do Império Romano. **Phoînix**, Rio de Janeiro, p. 138-154, 2018.

ROWAN, Clare. **Guides to the coinage of the Ancient World**: from Caesar to Augustus (c. 49 BC - AD 14), using coins as sources. Cambridge: Cambridge University Press, 2019.

Bibliographical references

ALFÖLDI, Andreas; GIARD, Jean B. Guerre civile et propagande politique: l'émission d'Octave au nom du Divos Julius (41 - 40 avant J.C.). **Numismatica e antichità classiche**, v. 13, p. 147-153, 1984.

ALMEIDA, Alexandra O. **Ciência, substantivo feminino.** Pesquisa Fapesp. São Paulo: Editora Fapesp, 2020.

ALVAREZ, Sonia E.; DAGNINO, Evelina; ESCOBAR, Arturo (ed.). **Cultures of Politics Politics of Cultures**. Re-visioning Latin American Social Movements. Boulder, Colorado: Westview Press, 1998.

AMANDRY, Michel. Le monnayage en bronze de Bibulus, Atratinus et Capito: une tentative de romanisation en Orient. **Revue Suisse de Numismatique**, v. 65, p. 73-85, 1986.

AMANDRY, Michel. Le monnayage en bronze de Bibulus, Atratinus et Capito. Part III. **Revue Suisse de Numismatique**, v. 69, p. 65-96, 1990.

AMANDRY, Michel; BARRANDON, Jean N. **Le genèse de la reforme monétaire augustéenne**. Del imperium de Pompeyo a la auctoritas de Augusto. Homenaje a Michael Grant, ed. M. P. García-Bellido, A. Mostalac and A. Jiménez. Madrid: Consejo superior de investigaciones científicas, 2008. p. 207-233.

ANDRADE, Vera R. P. A soberania patriarcal: O sistema de justiça criminal no tratamento da violência sexual contra a mulher. **Revista Sequência**: Estudos Jurídicos e Políticos, v. 51, p. 71-102, 2005.

ARENDT, Hanna. **On revolution**. New York: Viking, 1970.

ARIETI, James A. Rape and Livy's view of Roman history. *In:* DEACY, S.; PIERCE, K. P. (ed.). **Rape in Antiquity**: sexual violence in the Greek and Roman worlds. London: The Classical Press of Wales in association with Duckworth, 2002. p. 209-229.

ARJAVA, Antti. **Women and Law in Late Antiquity**. Oxford: Clarendon Press, 1996.

ASSMANN, Jan; CZAPLICKA, John. Collective memory and cultural identity. **New German Critique**, n. 65, p. 125-133, 1995.

AZEVEDO, Sarah F. L. Sexualidade e política à época de Augusto: considerações acerca da "Lei Júlia sobre adultério. *In*: CAMPOS, Carlos E. C.; CANDIDO, Maria R. (org.). **Caesar Augustus**: entre práticas e representações. Vitória/Rio de Janeiro: DLL-UFES/UERJ-NEA, 2014.

AZEVEDO, Sarah F. L. **O adultério, a política imperial e as relações de gênero em Roma**. Tese (Doutorado em História Social) – Faculdade de Filosofia, Letras e Ciências Humanas, Universidade de São Paulo, São Paulo, 2017.

AZEVEDO, Sarah F. L. Entre o presente e o passado: o conceito de "crimes sexuais" no estudo da sociedade romana, apontamentos sobre interdisciplinaridade e ensino de História. **Phoînix**, Rio de Janeiro, v. 29, n. 1, p. 114-133, 2023.

BABCOCK, Charles L. The early career of Fulvia. **The American Journal of Philology**, Baltimore: The Johns Hopkins University Press, v. 86, n. 341, p. 1-32, 1965.

BAHRANI, Zainab. **Women of Babylon**: gender and representation in Mesopotamia. London and New York: Routledge, 2005.

BAHRFELDT, Man von. Die Münzen der Flottenpräfekten des Marcus Antonius. **Numismatische Zeitschrift**, n. 37, p. 9-56, 1905.

BALANDIER, Georges. **O poder em cena**. Brasília: Edunb, 1980.

BALANDIER, Georges. **O contorno**: poder e Modernidade. Rio de Janeiro: Bertrand, 1997.

BALANDIER, Georges *et al*. **Civilizações**: entrevista do Le Monde. São Paulo: Ática, 1989. p. 147-153.

BALSDON, John P. V. D. **Roman women**. New York: The John Day Company, 1962.

BARBATO, Marta. The coins of Clovius and Oppius (RRC 476/1 and 550/1-3): new evidence from find-spots. **The Numismatic Chronicle 175 Offprint**, London, n. 175, p. 103-16, 2015.

BARKER, Graham. **Imperial legitimation**. London: Spink, 2020.

BARRETT, Anthony A. **Agrippina**: sex, power, and politics in the Early Empire. Yale, London: Yale University Press, New Haven, 1996.

BARRETT, Anthony A. **Livia**: first lady of Imperial Rome. New Haven: Yale University Press, 2002.

BARRETT, M. Word and Things: Materialism and Method in Contemporary Feminist Analysis. *In*: BARRETT, M.; PHILLIPS, A. (ed.). **Destabilizing Theory**: Contemporary Feminist Debates. Cambridge: Polity, 1992. p. 201-219.

BARTMAN, Elizabeth. **Portraits of Livia**: imaging the imperial woman in Augustan Rome. Cambridge: Cambridge University Press, 1999.

BARTMAN, Elizabeth. Hair and the artifice of Roman female adornment. **American Journal of Archaeology,** v. 105, n. 1, p. 1-25, 2001.

BARTMAN, Elizabeth. Early imperial female portraiture. *In*: JAMES, S. L.; Dillon, S. (ed.). **A companion to women in the Ancient World**. Malden, MA: Wiley-Blackwell, 2012. p. 414-422.

BAUMAN, Richard A. **Women and Politics in Ancient Rome**. London: Routledge, 1992.

BEARD, Mary; NORTH, John; PRICE, Simon. **Roman religion and roman empire**. Religions of Rome. Cambridge: Cambridge University Press, 1998. p. 313-363.

BEARD, Mary. The sexual status of Vestal Virgins. **The Journal of Roman Studies**. Cambridge: Cambridge University Press, v. 70, p. 12-27, 1980.

BEARD, Mary. Re-reading (Vestal) virginity. *In*: HAWLEY, Richard; LEVICK, Barbara (ed.). **Women in Antiquity**: new assessments. London: Routledge, 1995. p. 166-177.

BEAUVOIR, Simone. **Le deusième sexe**. Paris: Gallimard, 1949.

BÉLO, Tais P. **Boudica e as facetas femininas ao longo do tempo**: nacionalismo, feminismo, memória e poder. 2014. PhD (Doctorate in Cultural History) – Postgraduate program at the Institute of Philosophy and Human Sciences of the State University of Campinas, Department of History, 2014.

BÉLO, Tais P. Os estudos de gênero na Arqueologia. *In*: FUNARI, P. P. A.; CAMARGO, V. R. T. (org.). **Divulgando o patrimônio arqueológico**. Rio de Janeiro: Bonecker Acadêmico, 2018. p. 31-42. Available at: file:///Users/taispagotobelo/Downloads/Livro%20Divulgando%20o%20Patrimonio%20Arqueologico%20(1).pdf. Accessed: 6 Mar. 2019.

BÉLO, Tais P. **Boudica and the female facets over time**: nationalism, feminism, power and the collective memory. Manaus: EDUA; São Paulo: Alexa Cultural, 2019.

BÉLO, Tais P.; FUNARI, Pedro P. A. As romanas e o poder nos Anais de Tácito. **Classica**: Revista Brasileira de Estudos Clássicos, Belo Horizonte, Brazil, v. 30, n. 2, p. 75-90, 2017. Available at: https://revista.classica.org.br/classica/issue/viewIssue/39/53. Accessed: 6 Mar. 2019.

BERDOWSKI, Piotr. Some remarks on the economic activity of women in the Roman Empire: a research problem. *In*: BERDOWSKI, P.; BLAHACZED, B. (ed.). **Haec mihi in animis vestris temple**: studia classica in memory of professor Leslaw Morawiecki. Rezeszów: Institute of History at the University of Rezeszów & The Rezeszów Archaeological Foundation, 2007. p. 283-298.

BERENS, Edward. M. **The myths and legends of Ancient Greece and Rome**. Edited by S. M. Soares. Amsterdam: MetaLibri, 2009. v. 1.

BIELMAN, Anne. Femme et jeux dans le monde grec Hellénistique et impérial. *In*: JAMES S. L.; DILLON S. (ed.). **A Companion to women in the Ancient World**. Malden, Oxford, Chichester: Blackwell, 2012. p. 238-248

BILGE, Sirma. Théorisations féministes de l'intersectionnalité. **Dans Diogène**, v. 1, n. 225, p. 70-88, 2009.

BOATWRIGHT, Mary, T. Woman and gender in the forum romanum. **Transactions of the American Philological Association,** Baltimore, n. 141, p. 105-141, 2011.

BOBBIO, Norberto; MATTEUCCI, Nicola; PASQUINO, Gianfranco (org.). **Dicionário de política**. Brasília: Edunb, 1986.

BOURDIEU, Pierre. **O poder simbólico**. Rio de Janeiro: Bertrand, 1989.

BOURDIEU, Pierre. Novas reflexões sobre a dominação masculina. *In*: LOPES, M. J. M.; MEYER, D. E.; WALDON, V. R. (org.). **Gênero & Saúde**. Porto Alegre: Artes Médicas, 1996a. p. 28-40.

BOURDIEU, Pierre. **Razões práticas**: sobre a teoria da ação. Campinas: Papirus, 1996b.

BOURDIEU, Pierre. **A economia das trocas linguísticas**. São Paulo: Edusp, 1997.

BOURDIEU, Pierre. **A dominação masculina**. Rio de Janeiro: Bertrand Brasil, 1998.

BOURDIEU, Pierre. **A economia das trocas simbólicas**. São Paulo: Perspectiva, 1999.

BOURDIEU, Pierre. **Masculine domination**. Translated from the French by Richard Nice. Palo Alto: Stanford University Press, 2001.

BRADLEY, Keith R. **Discovering the Roman Family**: Studies in Roman Social History. New York and Oxford: Oxford University Press, 1991.

BRADFORD, Ernle. **Cleopatra**. São Paulo: Ediouro, 2002.

BRANNSTEDT, Lovisa. *Femina princeps*: Livia's position in the Roman State. Lund: Lund University, 2016.

BRASIL. **Lei n. 11340, de 7 de agosto de 2006**. Creates mechanisms to curb domestic and family violence against women, in accordance with § 8 of art. 226 of the Federal Constitution, the convention on the elimination of all forms of discrimination against Women and the inter-American convention to prevent, punish and eradicate violence against women; provides for the creation of courts for domestic and family violence against women; amends the Criminal Procedure Code, the Penal Code and the Criminal Execution Law; and takes other measures. Brasilia, DF: Presidency of Republic: Casa Civil, 2006. Available at: http://www.planalto.gov.br/ccivil_03/_ato2004-2006/2006/lei/l11340.htm. Accessed: 17 Jun. 2023.

BRENNAN, Corey, T. Perceptions of women's power in the Late Republic: Terentia, Fulvia, and the generation of 63 BCE. *In*: JAMES, S. L.; DILLON, S. (ed.). **A companion to women in the Ancient World**. Oxford: Wiley-Blackwell, a John Wiley & sons, Ltd, publication, 2021. p. 354-366.

BRENNAN, Peter. Faces of power. *In*: BRENNAN, P.; TUNNER, M.; WRIGHT, L. (org.). **Faces of power**: imperial portraiture on Roman coins. Nicholson Museum. Sidney: The University of Sidney, 2007. p. 7-8.

BRENNAN, Peter; TURNER, Michael; WRIGHT, Nicholas L. **Faces of Power**: imperial portraiture on Roman coins. Nicholson Museum. Sydney: University of Sydney, 2007.

BROOKS, Ann. **Postfeminisms**: Feminism, Cultural Theory and Cultural Forms. London: Routledge, 1997.

BROUWER, Herrik H. J. **Bona Dea**: the sources and a description of the cult. Leiden, New York, Kobenhavn, Köln: E. J. Brill, 1989.

BROWNMILLER, Susan. **Against our will**. London: Penguin, 1977.

BRUBAKER, Leslie; TOBLER, Helen. The gender of money: Byzantine empresses on coins (324 - 802). **Gender & History**, v. 12, n. 3, p. 572-594, 2000.

BRUUN, Patrick. Coins and the Roman imperial government. *In*: PAUL, G. M.; IERARDI, M. **Roman coins and public life under the empire**. Michigan: The University of Michigan Press, 1999.

BRYEN, Ari Z. Crimes against the Individual: Violence and Sexual Crimes. *In*: PLESSIS, Paul; ANDO, Clifford; TUORI, Kaius (ed.). **The Oxford Handbook of Roman Law and Society**. Oxford: Oxford University Press, 2016. p. 322-332.

BUCHWALD, Emilie; FLETCHER, Pamela R.; ROTH, Martha (ed.). **Transforming a rape culture**. Minneapolis: Milkweed Editions, 2003. (Trabalho original publicado em 1993).

BUENO, Samira; LIMA, Sérgio; PINHEIRO, Marina; ASTOLFI, Roberta; SANTOS, Thandara; HANASIRO, Olava. A polícia precisa falar sobre estupro: percepção sobre violência sexual e atendimento a mulheres vítimas nas instituições policiais. **Datafolha**, 2016. Available at: https://forumseguranca.org.br/publicacoes_posts/a-policia-precisa-falar-sobre-estupro-percepcao-sobre-violencia-sexual-e-atendimento-a-mulheres-vitimas-de-estupro-nas-instituicoes-policiais/. Accessed: 20 Jun. 2023.

BURNETT, Andrew M. The Authority to Coin in the Late Republic and Early Empire. **The Numismatic Chronicle** (1966), v. 17, n. 137, p. 37-63, 1977. Available at: http://www.jstor.org/stable/42666582. Accessed:18 Jun. 2023.

BURNETT, Andrew M. **Coinage in the Roman world**. London: Spink, 1987.

BURNS, Jasper. **Great women of imperial Rome**: mothers and wives of the Caesars. London and New York: Routledge, 2007.

BURSTEIN, Stanley. **The reign of Cleopatra**. Westport, Connecticut, London: British Library, 2004.

BUSINO, Giovanni. Propaganda. **Enciclopedia Einaudi**. Torino: Giulio Einaudi, 1980. v. 11. p. 275-295.

BUTCHER, Kevin. Information, legitimation, or self-legitimation? Popular and elite designs on the coin types of Syria. *In*: HOWGEGO, C.; HEUCHERT, V.;

BURNETT, A. (ed.). **Coinage and identity in the Roman provinces**. Oxford: Oxford University Press, 2005. p. 141-156.

BUTLER, Judith. **Gender troubler**: feminism and the subversion of identity. New York & London: Routledge, 1990.

BUTLER, Shane. **The Hand of Cicero**. London: Routledge, 2002.

BUTTREY, Theodore V. Thea Neotera on coins of Antony and Cleopatra. **Museum Notes (American Numismatic Society)**, v. 6, p. 95-109, 1954. Available at: http://www.jstor.org/stable/43573329. Accessed: 19 Jun. 2023.

CALLATAŸ, François de. Greek coin iconography in context: eight specificities that differentiate them from other visual media. *In*: BARRINGER, J. M.; LISSARRAGUE, F. (ed.). **Images at the crossroads**: media and meaning in Greek art. Edinburgh: Edinburgh University Press, 2022. p. 243-256.

CARLAN, Cláudio U. Os museus e o patrimônio histórico: uma relação complexa. **História**, São Paulo, v. 27, n. 2, p. 75-88, 2008.

CHARTIER, Roger. **A História Cultural**: entre práticas e representações. Rio de Janeiro: Difel, 1990.

CHARTIER, Roger. Diferença entre os sexos e a dominância simbólica (nota crítica). **Cadernos Pagu**, n. 4, p. 37-47, 1995.

CHASSEGUET-SMIRGEL, Janine. Freud and female sexuality. **International Journal of Psychoanalysis**, Abingdon-on-Thames, v. 57, p. 220, 1976.

CHEUNG, Ada. The political significance of Roman Imperial coin types. **Schweizer Münzblätter**, v. 48-49, p. 53-61, 1988-1989.

CHODOROW, Nancy. **The reproduction of mothering**. Berkley: University of California Press, 1978.

CID LÓPEZ, Rosa M. La matrona y las mujeres de la Roma antigua. Um estereotipo feminino através de las imágenes religiosas y las normas legales. Esther Martínez Quinteiro (coord.). **Mujeres em la Historia, el arte y el cine**: discursos de género, variantes de contenidos y soportes: de la palavra al auvisual. Salamanca: Ediciones Universidad de Salamanca, 2011. p. 55-70.

CLAES, Liesbeth. **Kinship and coins**: ancestors and family on Roman Imperial coinage under Principate. Enschede: Ipskamp Drukkers B. V., 2013.

CONKEY, Margaret W.; SPECTOR, Janet D. Archaeology and the study of gender. **Advantages in Archaeological method and theory**. London: Springer, 1984. v. 7.

CONNELL, Noreen; WILSON, Cassandra (ed.). **Rape**: the first sourcebook for women. NY: New American Library, 1974.

CONNELL, Robert. **Gender and Power**. Cambridge: Polity Press, 1987.

CRAIG, Christopher. Audience Expectations, Invective, and Proof. *In*: POWELL, J. G. F.; PATERSON, J. (ed.). **Cicero the Advocate**. Oxford: Oxford University Press, 2004. p. 187-214.

CRAWFORD, Michael H. **Roman Republican Coinage**. Cambridge: Cambridge University Press, 1974. v. 2.

CRAWFORD, Michael H. **Roman Republic coinage**. Cambridge: Cambridge University Press, 1975a. v. 1.

CRAWFORD, Michael H. **Roman Republic coinage**. Cambridge: Cambridge University Press, 1975b. v. 2.

CRENSHAW, Kimberle W. Demarginalizing the intersection of race and sex: a black feminist critique of discrimination doctrine, feminist theory and antiracist politics. **University of Chicago Legal Forum**, 1989. p. 139-167.

CRENSHAW, Kimberle W. Mapping the margins: intersectionality, identity politics and violence against women of color. *In*: FINEMAN, Martha Albertson; MYKITIUK, Roxanne (org.). **The public nature of private violence**. Nova York: Routledge, 1994. p. 93-118.

CRENSHAW, Kimberle W. Documento para o encontro de especialistas em aspectos da discriminação racial relativos ao gênero. **Estudos Feministans**, Los Angeles, v. 10, n. 1, p. 171-188, 2002.

CRENSHAW, Kimberle W. Beyond entrenchment: race, gender and the new frontiers of (un) equal protection. *In*: TSUJIMURA, M. (org.). **International perspectives on gender equality & social diversity**. Sendai: Tohoku University Press, 2010. p. 89-98.

CRISTOFOLI, Roberto; GALIMBERT, Alessandro; ROHR VIO, Francesca. **Dalla repubblica al principato**. Politica e potere in Roma antica. Roma: Carocci, 2014.

DAVIDOFF, Leonore. Regarding some "old husbands' tales": public and private in feminist theory. *In*: LANDES, Joan B. (ed.). **Feminism, the Public and the Private**. Oxford: Oxford University Press, 1998. p. 164-194.

DAUBE, David. **Roman law**: linguistic, social and philosophical aspects. by Daube David. Edinburgh: At the University Press, 1969.

DELANEY, Angelica E. Reading Cleopatra VII: the crafting of a political persona. **The Kennesaw Journal of Undergraduate research**, v. 3, issue 1, article 2, 2014. Available at: http://digitalcommons.kennesaw.edu/kjur/vol3/iss1/2. Accessed: 21 Jun. 2023.

DENIAUX, Elizabeth. Patronage. *In*: ROSENSTEIN, N.; MORSTEIN-MARX, R. (ed.). **A companion to the roman republic**. Malden, Oxford, Carltron: Blackwell Publishing Ltd., 2006. p. 401-420.

DIAZ-ANDREU, Margarita. Gender identity. *In*: ed. DÍAZ-ANDREU, Margarita; LUCY, Sam; BABIĆ, Staša; EDWARDS, David. **The archaeology of identity**: Approaches to gender, age, status, ethnicity and religion. London: Routledge, 2005. p. 13-42.

DIELEMAN, Jacco. Fear of women? Representation of women in Demotic wisdom texts. **Studien zur Altägyptischen Kultur**, Hamburg, v. 25, p. 7-46, 1998.

DIXON, Susan. A family business: women's role in patronage and politics at Rome, 80 - 44 B.C. **Classica et Mediaevalia**, Compenhagem, v. 34, p. 91-112, 1983.

DIXON, Susan. **The Roman Mother**. London: Routledge, 1988.

DIXON, Susan. **The Roman Family**. Baltimore and London: Johns Hopkins University Press, 1992.

DRAYCOTT, Jane. The symbol of Cleopatra Selene: Reading crocodiles on coins in the Late Republic and Early Principate. **Acta Classica LV**, v. 55, n. 1, p. 43-56, 2012.

DUNCAN-JONES, Richard P. The monetization of the Roman Empire: regional variations in the supply of coin types. *In*: PAUL, George M.; IERARDI, Michael (ed.). **Roman coins and public life under the Empire**. E. Togo Salmon Papers II. Ann Arbor: University of Michigan Press, 1999. p. 61-82.

DUQÚESNAY, I. M. Le M. Virgil's Fourth Eclogue. **Papers of the Liverpool Latin Seminar**, Tallahassee, v. 5, p. 25-99, 1976.

ELIAS, Nobert. **A sociedade de corte**. Rio de Janeiro: Jorge Zahar, 2001.

ELKINS, Nathan T. A note on Late Roman art: the provincial origins of camp gate and Baldachin iconography on the Late Imperial Coinage. **American Journal of Numismatics**, New York, v. 25, second series, p. 283-302, 2013.

ELKINS, Nathan T. **The image of political power in the reign of Nerva, AD 96 - 98**. New York: Oxford University Press, 2017.

ELKINS, Nathan T. Money, art, and representation: a look at the Roman world. *In*: KRMNICEK, S. (ed.). **A cultural history of money in Antiquity**. London, New York, Oxford, New Delhi, Sydney: Bloomsbury Academic, 2019. p. 105-121.

ERHART, Patricia K. A new portrait type of Octavia Minor (?). **The J. Paul Getty Museum journal**, Los Angeles, n. 8, p. 117-128, 1980.

EVANS GRUBBS, Judith. **Women and the law in the Roman Empire**: A sourcebook on marriage, divorce and widowhood. London: Routledge, 2002.

FANTHAM, Elaine. **Julia Augusti**: the Emperor's Daughter. London and New York: Routledge, 2006.

FANTHAM, Elaine. **Roman readings**: Roman response to Greek literature from Plautus to Statius and Quintilian. Berlim, New York: Walter de Gruyter GmbH & Co. KG., 2011.

FEARS, Jesse R. Princeps a diis electus: the divine election of the emperor as a political concept at Rome. **American Academy in Rome papers and monographs**, Rome: American academy, v. 2, 1977.

FEITOSA, Lourdes C. **Amor e sexualidade**: o masculino e o feminino em grafites de Pompéia. São Paulo: AnnaBlume, 2005.

FEITOSA, Lourdes. C. Gênero e sexualidade no mundo romano: a Antiguidade em nossos dias. **História**: Questões & Debates, Curitiba, n. 48/49, p. 119-135, 2008.

FILHO, Ernesto P.; VASCONCELOS, Edson. Foucault: da microfísica à biopolítica. *In*: RAGO, M.; MARTINS, A. L. (org.). **Revista aulas**: dossiê Foucault. Campinas: Unicamp, 2007.

FINLEY, Moses I. The silent women of the ancient world. **Horizon**, Dallas: American Heritage, v. VII, n. 1, p. 57-64, 1965.

FISCHLER, Susan. Social Stereotypes and Historical Analysis: the case of the imperial women at Rome. **Women in Ancient Societies**. New York: Routledge, 1994. p. 115-133.

FISCHLER, Susan. Imperial cult: engendering de cosmos. *In*: FOXHALL, L.; SALMON, J. (ed.). **When men were men**: masculinity, power and identity in Classical Antiquity. London: Routledge, 1998. p. 165-183.

FISHWICK, Duncan. **Imperial cult in the Latin West**: studies in the ruler cult of the western provinces of the Roman Empire. v. II. Leiden: Brill, 1991.

FISHWICK, Duncan. Coinage and cult: the provincial monuments at Lugdunum. Tarraco, and Eremita. *In*: PAUL, G. M.; IERARDI, M. (ed.). **Roman coins and public life under the empire**. Ann Arbor, MI: The University of Michigan Press, 1999. p. 95-122.

FITTSCHEN, Klaus; ZANKER, Paul. **Katalog der römischen portraits in den CapitolinischenMuseen und den anderenkommunalensammlunger der stadt Rom 3, Kaiserinnen und Prinzessinnenbildniss, Frauenporträts**. Mainz an Rhein: Verlag Philipp von Zanbern, 1983.

FLEMING, Maria I. D'A.; ABREU, Tatiana B.; BASTOS, Márcio T.; MARTIRE, Alex. S.; GREGORI, Alessandro. M. A importância das novas tecnologias para a Arqueologia e suas possibilidades de uso. A impressão 3D e os projetos do LARP: Vestígios. **Revista Latino-Americana de arqueologia histórica**, v. 11, p. 56-79, 2017.

FLORENZANO, Maria B. B. Anotações sobre a representação de monstros nas moedas gregas. **Revista do Museu de Arqueologia e Etnologia**, São Paulo: USP, v. 5, p. 223-234, 1995.

FLORENZANO, Maria B. B. A moeda romanana Antiguidade: uma introdução à história e aossignificados das emissões monetárias. *In*: FLORENZANO, M. B.; RIBEIRO, A. M.; MONACO, V. L. (org.). **A coleção de moedas romanas da Universidade de São Paulo, Museu Paulista, Museu de Arqueologia e Etnologia**. São Paulo: MAE/USP, 2015. p. 15-20.

FLORY, Marleen B. Livia and the history of public honorific statues for women in Rome. **Transactions of the American Philological Association (1974-)**, Baltimore, v. 123, p. 287-308, 1993. Available at: https://doi.org/10.2307/284333. Accessed: 22 Jun. 2023.

FLORY, Marleen B. The meaning of Augusta in Julio-Claudian period. **American Journal of Acient History**, Piscataway, v. 132, p. 113-138, 1998.

FOUCAULT, Michel. **The history of sexuality**. London: Allen Lane, 1979. v. 1.

FOUCAULT, Michel. **História da sexualidade I**: a vontade de saber. 14. ed. Rio de Janeiro: Graal, 2001.

FOUCAULT, Michel. **História da sexualidade I**: a vontade de saber. 13. ed. Rio de Janeiro: Graal, 1988.

FRANCO, Henar G. La imagen de la mulher "bárbara": a propósito de Estrabon, Tácito e Germania. **Faventia**, v. 21, n.1, p. 55-63, 1999.

FREITAS, Júlia C. C.; MORAIS, Amanda O. Cultura do estupro: considerações sobre violência sexual, feminismo e análise do comportamento. **Acta Comporamentalia**: Revista Latina de Análisis de Comporamiento, v. 27, n. 1, p. 108-123. Xalapa, Veracruz: Universidad Veracruzana, 2019. Available at: https://www.redalyc.org/articulo.oa?id=274560588008. Accessed: 24 Jun. 2023.

FREUD, Sigmund [1933]. **New introductory lectures on psychoanalysis**. Edited by L. Strachey. New York: Norton, 1966.

FRIEDRICH, Carl J. **Tradição e autoridade em Ciência Política**. Rio de Janeiro: Zahar, 1974.

FUNARI, Pedro P. A. Romanas por elas mesmas. **Cadernos Pagu**, Campinas, n. 5, p. 179-200, 1995.

FUNARI, Pedro P. A. **Arqueologia**. São Paulo: Contexto, 2003.

FUNARI, Pedro P. A.; GARRAFFONI, Renata S. **Historiografia**: Salútio, Tito Lívio e Tácito. Campinas: Editora Unicamp, 2016.

FUSTEL DE COULANGES, Numa D. **Les origines du système feodal**. Paris: Hachette 1890.

GALINSKY, K. Introduction. *In:* GALINSKY, Karl (ed.). **Memoria romana**: memory in Rome, Rome in memory. Ann Arbor: The University of Michigan Press, 2014, p. 1-12.

GARDNER, Jane F. **Women in Roman law and society**. London: Routledge, 1990.

GERO, Joan M.; CONKEY, Margaret W. **Engendering archaeology**: women in prehistory. New Jersey: Wiley-Blackwell, 1991.

GIDDENS, Anthony. **A transformação da intimidade**: sexualidade, amor & erotismo nas sociedades modernas. São Paulo: Editora Unesp, 1992.

GINSBURG, Judith. **Representing Agrippina**: Constructions of Female Power in the Early Roman Empire. Oxford and New York: Oxford University Press, 2006.

GLARE, P. G. W. (ed.). **Oxford Latin dictionary**. Oxford: Oxford University Press, 2012.

GODDARD, Victoria A. Introduction. *In*: GODDARD, V. A. (ed.). **Gender, agency and change**: Anthropological perspectives. London and New York: Routledge: Taylor and Francis Group, 2000.

GODECHOT, Jacques. La propagande. **Annales**, Paris, v. 34, p. 515-517, 1952.

GONÇALVES, Ana T. M. Poder e propaganda no período Severiano: a construção da imagem imperial. **POLITEIA**. Hist. e Soc., Vitória da Conquista, v. 1, n. 1, p. 53-58, 2001.

GONÇALVES, Ana T. M. **A construção da imagem imperial**: formas de propaganda nos governos de Septímio Severo e Caracala. PhD (Doctorate in History) – Postgraduate Program in Economic History, Department of History, University of São Paulo, 2002.

GONÇALVES, Ana T. M. Entre gregos e romanos: história e literatura no mundo clássico. **Revista Tempo**, Rio de Janeiro, v. 20, p. 1-14, 2014.

GONÇALVES, Ana T. M. Poder e propaganda no período Severiano: a construção da imagem imperial. **POLITEIA. Hist. e Soc.**, Vitória da Conquista, v. 1, n. 1, p. 53-58, 2001.

GRETHER, Gertrude. Livia and the Roman Imperial Cult. **The American Journal of Philology**, Baltimore and Maryland, v. 67, n. 3, p. 222-252, 1946.

GRIFFIN, Miriam T. **Nero**: The End of a Dynasty. New Haven and London: Yale University Press, 1985.

GRIFFIN, Susan. Rape, the all-American crime. **Ramparts**, New York, v. 10, p. 5-8, 1973.

GRUBBS, Judith E. **Women and the law in Roman Empire**: a sourcebook of marriage, divorce and widowhood. London and New York: Routledge: Frances and Taylor Group, 2002.

GRUEBER, Herbert A. **Coins of the Roman Republic in the British Museum**. London: British Museum, 1910. v. 1.

GRUEN, Erich S. **The Last Generation of the Roman Republic**. Berkley, Los Angeles, London: University of California Press, 1974.

HAHN, Ulrike. **Die frauen des Römischen Kaiserhauses und ibre Ebrungen im Griechischen Osten anhand Epigraphischer und Numismatishcher Zeugnisse von Livia bis Sabina**. Saarbrücken: Saarbrücker Druckerei und Verlag, 1994.

HALBWACHS, Maurice. **On collective memory**. Chicago: University of Chicago Press, 1992.

HALLETT, Judith P. **Fathers and daughters in Roman society**: women and the elite family. Princeton, New Jersey: Princeton University Press, 1984.

HALLETT, Judith P. Fulvia, mother of Iullus Antonius: New Approaches to the Sources on Julia's Adultery at Rome. **Helios**, Maryland, v. 33, p. 149-164, 2006.

HALLETT, Judith P. Women as Same and Other in Classical Roman elite. **Helios**, Maryland, v. 16, p. 59-78, 1989.

HANNESTAD, Niels. Roman art and imperial policy. **Jutland Archaeology Society publications** 19. Højbjerg, Århus: Aarhus University Press, 1986.

HANSEN, William. **Classical mythology**: a guide to the Mythical World of the Greeks and Romans. Oxford: Oxford University Press, 2004.

HARRISON, Jane E. **A study of the social origins of Greek religion**. Cambridge: Cambridge University Press, 1912.

HARVEY, Tracene. **Julia Augusta**: images of Rome's first empress on the coins of the Roman empire. London and New York: Routledge: Tayor & Francis Group, 2020.

HEAD, Barclay V. **Catalogue of Greek coins of Phrygia**. London: Oxford University Press, 1906.

HEAD, Barclay V. [1910]. **Historia Nummorum**: a Manual ef Greek Numismatics. London, reprint London: Spink and Son, 1963.

HEKSTER, Oliver. Coins and messages: audience targeting on coins of different denominations? *In*: BLOIS, L. de *et al.* (ed.). **Representation and Perception of Roman Imperial power**. Amsterdam: Gieben, 2003. p. 20-35.

HEKSTER, Oliver. **Emperors and ancestors**: Roman rulers and the constraints of Tradition. Oxford: Oxford University Press, 2015.

HELLY, Bruno. Actes d'affranchissement thessaliens. **Bulletin de correspondence hellénique,** Lyon, n. 99, p. 119-144, 1975.

HEMELRIJK, Emily A. **Matrona docta**: educated women in the Roman elite from Cornelia to Julia Domna. London and New York: Routledge, Taylor & Francis Group, 1999.

HEMELRIJK, Emily A. Masculinity and Femininity in the Laudatio Turiae. **Classical Association Jounals Board CQ,** Oxford, v. 54, n. 1, p. 185-197, 2004.

HEMELRIJK, Emily A. Priestesses of the imperial cult in the Latin West: titles and function. **L'Antiquité Classique,** Lyon, v. 74, p. 137-170, 2005.

HEMELRIJK, Emily A. **Hidden lives, public personae**: women and civic life in the Roman West. Oxford: Oxford University Press, 2015.

HEMELRIJK, Emily. Public roles for women in the cities of the Latin West. *In*: SHARON, James, L.; DILLON, Sheila (ed.). **A companion to women in the Ancient World**. Malden, Oxford, Chchester: Blackwell, 2012. p. 478-490.

HIDALGO DE LA VEGA, María J. **El intellectual, la realeza y el poder politico en el imperio romano**. Salamanca: Ediciones Universidad, 1995.

HIRATA, H. Gênero, classe e raça: interseccionalidade e consubstancialidade das relações sociais. **Tempo Social,** Revista de Sociologia da USP, v. 26, n. 1, p. 61-73, 2014.

HODDER, Ian. **Reading the past**: current approaches to interpretation in archaeology. Cambridge: Cambridge University Press, 1986.

HOLLAND, Lora L. Women and Roman religion. *In*: JAMES, S. L.; DILLON, S. (ed.). **A companion to women in the Ancient World**. New Jersei: Blackwell, 2012. p. 204-214.

HÖLSCHER, Tonio. **Römische Bildsprache als semantisches System**. (Abhandlungen der Heidelberger Akademie der Wissenschaften. Philosophisch-historische Klasse 1987, 2.), Heidelberg: Carl Winter, 1987.

HOPKINS, Keith. **Conquistadores y esclavos**. Barcelona: Península, 1978.

HORNBLOWER, Simon; SPAWFORTH, Antony; EIDINOW, Esther (ed.). The Oxford Companion to Classical Civilization. 2. ed. p. xxviii + 867, ills, maps. Oxford: Oxford University Press, 2014.

HOWGEGO, Christopher. Coinage and identity in the Roman provinces. *In*: HOWGEGO, C.; HEUCHERT, V.; BURNETT, A. (ed.). **Coinage and Identity in the Roman Provinces**. Oxford: Oxford University Press, 2005. p. 1-18.

HUICI MODENES, Adrián. **Estrategias de la persuasión**: mito y propaganda política. Sevilha: Alfar, 1996.

HUZAR, Eleonor G. **Mark Antony**: A Biography. Minneapolis: University of Minnesota Press, 1978.

INSTITUTO DE PESQUISA E ECONOMIA APLICADA [IPEA]. Tolerância social à violência contra mulheres. Sistema de Indicadores de Percepção Social. 2014a. Available at: chrome-extension://efaidnbmnnnibpcajpcglclefindmkaj/ https://assets-compromissoeatitude-ipg.sfo2.digitaloceanspaces.com/2014/04/ IPEA_sips_violenciamulheres04042014.pdf. Accessed: 23 jun. 2023.

INSTITUTO DE PESQUISA E ECONOMIA APLICADA [IPEA]. Estupro no Brasil: Uma radiografia segundo os dados da Saúde. 2014b. Available at: http://ipea.gov.br/portal/images/stories/PDFs/nota_tecnica/140327_notatecnicadiest11.pdf. Accessed: 23 jun. 2023.

JONES, Arnold H. M. Numismatic and History. *In*: CARSON, R. A. G.; SUTHERLAND, C. H. V. (ed.). **Essays in Roman coinage, presented to Harold Mattingly**. Oxford: Oxford University Press, 1956. p. 13-33.

KAHRSTEDT, Ulrich. Frauen auf aintiken Münzen. **Klio,** Berlin, n. 10, p. 261-314, 1910.

KAMPEN, Natalie Boymel. Between public and private: women as historical subjects in Roman art. *In*: POMEROY, Sarah B. (ed.). **Women's History and Ancient History**. Chapel Hill: University of North Carolina Press, 1991. p. 218-248.

KAPLAN, Abraham; LASWELL, Harold. **Poder e sociedade**. Brasília: Edunb, 1979.

KEARSLEY, Rosalinde A. Women and public live in Asia Minor: Hellenistic tradition and Augustan ideology. *In:* TSETSKHLADZE, Gocha R. (ed.). **Ancient West and East**. Leiden: Brill, 2005. v. 4, n. 1, p. 98-121.

KEMMERS, Fleur. **The functions and use of Roman coinage**: an overview of 21st century scholarship. Leiden, Boston: Brill, 2019.

KENNEDY, George A. **The Art of Rhetoric in the Roman World, 300 B.C. - A.D. 300**. Princeton: Princeton University Press, 1972.

KENT, Susan K. **Analyzing activity areas**: an ethnoarchaeological study of the use of space. Albuquerque, NM: University of New Mexico Press, 1984.

KERGOAT, Danièle. Ouvriers = ouvrières? Propositions pour une articulation théorique de deux variables: sexe et classe sociale. **Critiques de l'Économie Politique**, Lyon, n. 5, p. 65-97, 1978.

KIMMEL, Michael, S. Masculinidade como homofobia, medo, vergonha e silêncio na construção de identidade de gênero. Tradução de Sandra M. Takakura. **Equatorial**, Rio de Janeiro, v. 3, n. 4. p. 97-124, 2016.

KING, C. E. Roman portraiture: images of power? *In*: PAUL, G. M.; IERARD, M. (ed.). **Roman coins and public life under the empire**. E. Togo Salmon Papers II. Michigan: The University of Michigan Press, 1999.

KLEINER, Diana E. E. **Cleopatra and Rome**. Cambridge: Harvard University Press Mass, 2005.

KLEINER, Diana E. E. Politics and gender in the pictorial propaganda of Antony and Octavian. **EMC**, v. 36, p. 357-358, 1992.

KLOSE, Dietrich O. A. Festival and games in the cities of the East during the Roman Empire. *In*: HOWGEGO, Christopher *et al.* (ed.). **Coinage and identity in the Roman provinces**. Oxford: Oxford University Press, 2005. p. 125-133.

KOCKEL, Valentin. **Portrdtreliefs stadtriimischer Grabbauten**. Beitrdge zur ErschliejJung hellenistischer und kaiserzeitlicher Skulptur und Architektur 12. Mainz am Rhein: Philipp von Zabern, 1993.

KOORTBOJIAN, Michael. **The divinization of Caesar and Augustus**: Precedents, Consequences, Implications. Cambridge: Cambridge University Press, 2013.

KORMIKIARI, Maria C. N.; PORTO, Vagner C. Arqueologia como instrumento de aproximação aluno-Mundo Antigo: para além de uma visão eurocêntrica. **Revista Transversos**. Rio de Janeiro: UFRJ, n. 16, p. 45-69, 2019. Available at: https://www.e--publicacoes.uerj.br/index.php/transversos/article/view/44732. Accessed: 24 Jun. 2023.

KRAFT, Konrad. S(enatus) C(onsulto). **JNG**, v. 12, p. 7-49, 1962. Reprinted in Augutus, edited by W. Shmitthenner, Darmstadt, p. 336-403, 1969.

LANGLANDS, Rebecca. **Sexual morality in Ancient Rome**. Cambridge, New York, Melbourne, Madrid, Cape Town, Singapore, São Paulo: Cambridge University Press, 2006.

LAPLANTINE, François; TRINDADE, Liana. **O que é imaginário**. São Paulo: Brasiliense, 1997.

LEFKOWITZ, Mary R.; FANT, Maureen B. (ed.). **Women's life in Greece and Rome**: a source book in translation. Baltimore: The Johns Hopkings University Press, 1992.

LEVICK, Barbara. Messages on the Roman coinages: types and inscriptions. *In*: PAUL, G. M.; IERARDI, M. **Roman coins and public life under the empire**. E. Togo Salmon Papers II. Michigan: The University of Michigan Press, 1999.

LEVICK, Barbara. Propaganda and the Imperial coinage. **Antichthon**, Sydney, v. 16, p. 107- 108, 1982.

LEVICK, Barbara. Women and law. *In*: JAMES, S. L.; DILLON, S. **A companion to women in the Ancient World**. Oxford: Wiley-Blackwell. 2012. p. 96-106.

LININGSTON, Candace W. **Imperial cult, Roman**. New York: Springer.

LINTOTT, Andrew W. P. Clodius Pulcher. Felix Catalina. **Greece & Rome**, Cambridge, n. 14, p. 157-169, 1967.

LINTOTT, Andrew. **Imperium Romanum**: politics and administration. London: Routledge, 1993.

LUTTWAK, Edward N. **La Grande Strategia dell'Impero Romano**. Milano: BUR, 1997.

MAIA, Ana C. B. Identidade e papéis sexuais: uma discussão sobre gênero na escola. *In*: MAIA, A. C. B.; MAIA, A. F. (org.). Sexualidade e Infância. **Cadernos Cecemca**, n. 1. Bauru: Faculdade de Ciências: Cecemca; Brasília: MEC/SEF, 2005. p. 66-82.

MANDERS, Erika. **Coining images of power**: patterns in the representation of Roman emperors on Imperial coinage, A.D. 193 - 284. Leiden: Brill, 2008.

MARQUES, Fabrício. A desigualdade escondida no equilíbrio: mulheres conquistam espaço na carreira científica no Brasil, mas obstáculos no acesso a algumas áreas são desafio. **Pesquisa Fapesp**, São Paulo: Editora Fapesp, ano 21, n. 289, p. 26-31, 2020.

MARTINS, Paulo. **Imagem e poder**: considerações sobre a representação de Otávio Augusto. São Paulo: Edusp, 2011.

MATHESON, Susan B. The divine Claudia: women as goddesses in Roman art. *In*: KLEINER, D. E. E.; MATHESON, S. B. (ed.). **I Claudia**. Women in Ancient Rome. New Haven, CT: University of Texas Press, 1996. p. 182-195.

MATIĆ, Uroš. **Violence and gender in ancient Egypt.** London and New York: Routledge, 2021a.

MATIĆ, Uroš. Gender-based violence. *In*: AUSTIN, Anne; WENDRICH, Willeke (ed.). **UCLA Encyclopedia of Egyptology.** Los Angeles: California Digital Library, 2021b. Available at: http://digital2.library.ucla.edu/viewItem.do?ark=21198/zz002kp50h. Accessed: 25 Jun. 2023.

MAZZA, Mario. **Lotte sociali e restaurazione autoritaria nel III Secolo d.C. Catania**: Università. Laterza: Bari, 1970.

McCULLOUGH, Anna. **Gender and public image in Imperial Rome**. A PhD thesis presented at the School of Classics, of the University of St. Andrews, 2007.

McHUGH, Mary R. Ferox Femina: Agrippina Maior in Tacitus's Annales. **Helios**, Lubbock, v. 39, n. 1, p. 73-96, 2011.

MEAD, Margaret. **Sexo e temperamento.** São Paulo: Perspectiva, 1969.

MEADOWS, Andrew; WILLIAMS, Jonatham. Moneta and the monuments: coinage and politics in Republican Rome. **The Journal of Roman Studies**, v. 91, p. 27-49, 2001.

MELVILLE, Joy. Baby blues. **New statesman and society**. 1991. Available at: https://www.newstatesman.com/uk. Accessed: 25 Jun. 2023.

MESKELL, Lynn. **Archaeology of social life**: age, sex, class et cetera in Ancient Egypt. Oxford: Blackwell Publishers Inc., 1999.

MEYERS, Rachel. Female portraiture and female patronage in the high imperial period. *In*: JAMES, S. L.; DILLON, S. (ed.). **A companion to the women in the Ancient World.** Malden, Oxford, Chichester: Blackwell Publishing, 2012. p. 453-466.

MILNOR, Kristina. **Gender, domesticity, and the Age of Augustus**: inventing private life. Oxford: Oxford University Press, 2005.

MOORE, Henrietta L. Fantasias de poder e fantasias de identidade: gênero, raça e violência. **Cadernos Pagu**, Campinas, n. 14, p. 13-44, 2000.

MOORE, Katrina. **Octavia Minor and the transition from Republic to Empire**. A thesis presented to the graduate school of Clemson University, in partial fulfillment of the requirements for the degree of Master of Arts History. Clemson, South Caroline, USA, 2017. Available at: https://tigerprints.clemson.edu/all_theses. Accessed: 26 Jun. 2023.

MORGAN, David. **Discovering Men**. London: Routledge, 1993.

MØRKHOLM, Otto. **Early Hellenistic Coinage**. Cambridge: Cambridge University Press, 1991.

MUNSCH, Christin L.; WILER, Robb. (2012). The role of gender identity threat in perceptions of date rape and sexual. **Violence Against Women**, v. 18, n. 10, p. 1125-1146, 2012. Available at: https://doi.org/10.1177/1077801212465151. Accessed: 27 Jun. 2023.

MURRAY, Alexander S. **Quién es Quién en la Mitologia**. Madri: M. E. Editora, 1997.

NARRO, José. III Encontro Internacional de Reitores Universia, 2014.

NEILS, Jenifer. Athena, alter ego of Zeus. In: DEACY, S.; VILLING, A. (ed.). **Athena in the Classical World**. Leiden, Boston, Köln: Brill, 2001. p. 219-232.

NOBLE, Vicki. A helping hand from the guys. In: HAGAN, K. L. (ed.). **Women respond to the men's movement**. San Francisco: Harper Collins, 1992. p. 105-106.

NOLASCO, Sócrates. **O mito da masculinidade**. Rio de Janeiro: Rocco, 1993.

NOREÑA, Carlos F. Coins and communication. In: PEACHIN, M. (ed.). **The Oxford handbook of social relations in the Roman world**. Oxford and New York: Oxford University Press, 2011. p. 248-268.

NOREÑA, Carlos F. The communication of the emperor's virtues. **Journal of Roman Studies**, Cambridge, v. 91, p. 146-168, 2001.

NORONHA, Edgard M. **Direito penal**. São Paulo: Saraiva, 1990.

OMENA, Luciane M. Os Ofícios: Meios de Sobrevivência dos Setores Subalternos da Sociedade Romana. **Fenix**: Revista de História e estudos culturais, ano IV, v. 4, n. 1, p. 1-13. São Paulo: Universidade de São Paulo, 2007. Available at: https://www.revistafenix.pro.br/revistafenix/article/view/755. Accessed: 27 Jun. 2023.

ORRIOLS-LLONCH, Marc. La violencia contra las mujeres en el antiguo Egipto. *In*: SEGARRA, Marta (ed.). **Violencia deliberada**: Las raíces de la violencia patriarcal. Barcelona: Icaria, 2007. p. 57-70.

OSGOOD, Josiah. **Turia**: A Roman woman's civil war. Oxford and New York: Oxford University Press, 2014.

PEREIRA, Marcos E. **Psicologia social dos estereótipos**. São Paulo: EPU, 2002.

PERISSATO, Felipe. **Elêusis no Império Romano**: Monumentalização do santuário e o culto dos Mistérios Eleusinos no Período Antonino. Dissertação (Mestrado em Arqueologia) – Museu de Arqueologia e Etnologia, Universidade de São Paulo, São Paulo, 2018.

PERKOUNING, Claudia M. **Livia Drusilla-Iulia Augusta**. Vienna: Böhlau Verlag, 1995.

PISCITELLI, Adriana. Re-criando a (categoria) mulher? Textos Didáticos. Dossiê: ALGRANTI, L. M. (org.). **A prática feminista e o conceito de gênero**. Campinas: Editora Unicamp, 2002. p. 7-42.

POLLINI, John. Man or God: divine assimilation an imitation in the Late Republic and early Principate. *In*: RAAFLAUB, K. A.; BERKELEY, M. Toher (ed.). **Between Republic and Empire**. Interpretations of Augustus and his Principate. CA: University of California Press, 1990. p. 334-357.

POLLINI, John. A new portrait of Octavia and the iconography of Octavia Minor and Julia Maior. **Römische Mitteilungen**, v. 109, p. 11-42, 2002.

POMEROY, Sarah B. **Goddesses, whores, wives and slaves**: women in Classical Antiquity. Berlin: Schocken Books, 1975.

PORTO, Vagner. C. A cidade como discurso ideológico: monumentalidade nas moedas do Império Romano. **Revista do Museu de Arqueologia e Etnologia**, Supl., São Paulo, n. 18, p. 93-101, 2014.

PORTO, Vagner. C. As moedas romanas da Península Ibérica e da Síria-Palestina: uma tentativa de diálogo. **Mare Nostrvm - Estudos sobre o Mediterrâneo Antigo**, São Paulo, n. 3, p. 13-32, 2012.

PORTO, Vagner. C. Calígula, Agripa I e os judeus: entre conflitos, amizade e redes de sociabilidade. *In*: CARVALHO, M. M.; LEONI, A. M.; JOSÉ, N. F. (org.).

Impérios, imperadores e redes de sociabilidade na Antiguidade. Curitiba: Editora CRV, 2023.

PORTO, Vagner. C. O culto imperial e as moedas do Império Romano. **Phoînix**, Rio de Janeiro, v. 24, n. 1, p. 138-154, 2018.

PURCELL, Nicholas. Livia and the womanhood of Rome. **Proceedings of the Cambridge Philological Society (Second Series)**, v. 32, p. 78-105, 1986.

QUEIROZ, Christina. O gênero da ciência: diálogo com teorias feministas abre novas frentes de investigação em distintas áreas do conhecimento. **Pesquisa Fapesp**, São Paulo: Editora Fapesp, ano 21, n. 289, p. 18-25, 2020.

RADCLIFFE, Sarah; WESTWOOD, Sallie. **Remaking the Nation**. Place, Identity and Politics in Latin America. London and New York: Routledge, 1996.

RAWSON, Beryl. Finding roman women. *In*: ROSENSTEIN, N.; MARX, R. M. (ed.). **A companion to the roman republic**. Oxford: Blackwell Publiching, 2006. p. 324-341.

REIS, Kellen C. F.; MAIA, Ana C. B. Estereótipos sexuais e a educação sexista no discurso de mães. *In*: VALLE, T. G. M. (org.). **Aprendizagem e desenvolvimento humano**: avaliações e intervenções. São Paulo: Cultura Acadêmica, 2009. p. 137-154. Available at: https://repositorio.unesp.br/handle/11449/109318. Accessed: 27 Jun. 2023.

REVELL, Louise. **Ways of being roman**: discourses of identity in the roman west. Oxford and Philadelphia: Oxbow Books, 2016.

RIESS, Werner. Rari exempli femina: female virtues. *In*: JAMES, S. L.; DILLON, S. (org.). **A companion on women in the Ancient World**. Chichester: Wiley - Blackwell, 2012. p. 491-501.

ROHR VIO, Francesca. Dux femina: Fulvia in armi nella polemica politica di età triunvirale. *In*: ROHR, F.; LUCCHELLI, T. M. **Viris Militaris**: rappresentazione e propaganda tra Reppublica e Principato. Trieste: Edizioni Università di Trieste, 2015. p. 61-89.

ROLLER, Duane W. **Cleopatra**: A Biography. Oxford: Oxford University Press, 2010.

ROSE, Charles B. **Dynastic commemoration and imperial portraiture in Julio-Claudian period**. Cambridge: Cambridge University Press, 1997.

ROWAN, Clare. **Guides to the coinage of the Ancient World**: from Caesar to Augustus (c. 49 BC - AD 14), using coins as sources. Cambridge: Cambridge University Press, 2019.

SAFFIOTI, Heleieth I. B. **Gênero, patriarcado e violência**. São Paulo: Fundação Perseu Abramo, 2004.

SALES, Gladys M. S. **Estruturas de poder** – patronato, honra e prestígio nas representações discursivas das moedas de Aelia Capitolina e Cesareia no século III EC. 2018. Dissertação (Mestrado em Arqueologia) – Programa de Pós-Graduação, Museu de Arqueologia e Etnologia, Universidade de São Paulo, 2018.

SALES, Gladys M. S. **Estruturas de poder e negociações na Judeia-Palaestina do século I AEC ao II EC** - Análise de moedas em contexto urbano. 2022. Tese (Doutorado em Arqueologia) – Programa de Pós-Graduação em Arqueologia, Museu de Arqueologia e Etnologia, Universidade de São Paulo, 2022.

SALES, José C. **A moeda como meio de propaganda**: o caso paradigmático do Egito Ptolomaico. Lisboa: Academia das Ciências de Lisboa, 2017.

SALLER, Richard. *Patria potestas* and the stereotype of the Roman family. **Community and change,** Cambridge: Printed in Great Britain, v. 1, issue I, p. 7-22, 1986.

SAMPAIO, Ângela O.; VENTURINI, Renata L. B. Uma breve reflexão sobre a família na Roma Antiga. *In:* JORNADA DE ESTUDOS ANTIGOS E MEDIEVAIS – TRABALHOS COMPLETOS, 6., 2009. ISBN: 978-85-99726-09-9. Available at: http://www.ppe.uem.br/jeam/anais/2007/trabalhos/030.pdf. Accessed: 27 Jun. 2023.

SCHEID, John. **An introduction to Roman religion**. Bloomington; Indianapolis: Indiana University Press, 2003.

SCHMITT, Laurent; PRIER, Michel. **Les monnaies romaines**. Paris: Les Chevau-légers, 2004.

SCOTT, Eleonor. Women and gender relations in the Roman empire. *In*: RUSH, P. (ed.). **Theoretical Roman Archaeology**: second conference proceedings. Aldershot: Avebury, 1995. p. 174-189.

SCOTT, Joan W.; KAPLAN, Cora; KEATES, Debra (ed.). **Transitions, Environments, Translations**. Feminisms in International Politics. London and New York: Routledge, 1997.

SCOTT, Joan, W. La travailleuse. **Histoire des femmes en Occident, op. cit. t IV, Le XIXe. sicle**. Sob a direção de Genevive Fraisse et Michelle Perrot. Paris: Plon, 1991. p. 419-444.

SCHULTZ, Celia E. **Women's religious activity in the Roman Republic**. Chapel Hill: The University of North Carolina Press, 2006.

SEAR, David R. **Roman coins and their values**: the Republic and the twelve Caesars 280 BC - AD 96. The millennium edition. London: Spink, 2000. v. 1.

SHANKS, Michael; TILLEY, Christopher. **Reconstructing Archaeology**: theory and practice. 2. ed. London: Routledge, 1992.

SILVA, Debora C. da. Altar Belvedere culto dos lares augusti: reorganização do espaço sagrado da urbs (ca. 12 a.C.). **Plêthos**, Niterói, v. 2, n. 3, p. 36-46, 2013.

SILVA, Frederico de S. **Apocolocintose do Divino Cláudio**: tradução, notas e comentários. 2008. Dissertation (Master of Arts) – Department of Classical and Vernacular Literature, Faculty of Philosophy, Literature and Human Sciences, University of São Paulo, 2008.

SJÖBERG, B. L. The Greek oikos: a space for interaction revisited and reconsidered. *In:* KARLSSON, L.; CARLSSON, S.; KULLBERG, J. B. ΛΑΒΡΥΣ: Studies presented to Pontus Hellström. Uppsala Universitet, 2014. p. 315-327.

SKINNER, Marilyn B. Clodia Metelli. **Transactions of the American Philological Association (1974-2014)**, Baltimore, n. 113, p. 273-287, 1983.

SKINNER, Marilyn B. Woman and Language, in Archaic Greece, or Why is Sappho a Woman? *In:* RABINOWITZ, N. S.; RICHLIN, A. (ed.). **Feminist Theory and the Classics**. Londres: Routledge, 1993. p. 175-192.

SORDI, Marta (ed.). **Contributi dell'Istituti di Storia Antica**. Milano: Università Cattolica del Sacro Cuore, 1974.

SOUZA, Fabiana C. **Meninos e meninas na escola**: um encontro possível? Porto Alegre: Zouk, 2006.

SPAETH, Barbette S. **The Roman goddess Ceres**. Austin: University of Texas Press, 1996.

SPENCER-WOOD, Suzanne M. Gendering power. *In*: SWEELY, T. (ed.). **Manifesting power**: gender and the interpretation of power in archaeology. Londron and New York: Routledge, 1999. p. 175-183.

STAFFORD, Emma. The people to de goddess Livia: Attic Nemesis and the Roman imperial cult. **Kernos**, Liège, v. 26, p. 205-238, 2013.

STAPLES, Ariadne. **From good goddess to Vestal Virgins**: sex and category in Roman religion. London: Routledge, 1998.

STEWARD, Peter. **The Social History of Roman art**. Cambridge: Cambridge University Press, 2008.

STRATHERN, Marylin. **Before and after gender**: Sexual mythologies of everyday life. Chicago: HAU Books, 2016.

SUTHERLAND, Carol H. V. Compliment or complemente? Dr. Levick on Imperial coin types. **Numismatic Chronicle**, v. 146, p. 85-93, 1986.

SUTHERLAND, Carol H. V. Octavian's gold and silver coinage from c. 32 to 27 BC. **Numismatica e antichità**, London, v. 5, p. 129-157, 1976.

SYDENHAM, Edward A. **The Coinage of the Roman Republic**. London: Spink and Son, Ltd., 1952.

SYME, Ronald. **Roman revolution**. Oxford: Oxford University Press, 1939.

SYME, Ronald. **Sallust**. Berkeley: University of California Press, 1964

SYME, Ronald. **The Augustan aristocracy**. Oxford: Oxford University Press, 1986.

TAKÁCS, Sarolta A. **Vestal Virgins, Sibyls, and matrons**: women in roman religion. Austin: University of Texas Press, 2008.

TATUM, W. Jeffrey. **The Patrician Tribune**: Publius Clodius Pulcher. Chapel Hill: The University of North Carolina Press, 1999.

TAYLOR, Lily R. **The divinity of the Roman emperor**. Philadelphia: Porcupine Press, 1975.

TEMPORINI, Hildegard. **Die Frauen am Hofe Trajans**. Ein Beitrag zur Stellung der Augustae im Principat. Berlin: De Gruyter, 1978.

THE NATIONAL ARCHIVES. **Offences against the Person**. Act 1861. UK Public General Acts, 1861 c. 100 (Regnal. 24_and_25_Vict). Available at: https://www.legislation.gov.uk/ukpga/Vict/24-25/100/crossheading/attempts-to-procure--abortion, accessed: 3 Oct. 2023.

TJADEN, Patricia; THOENNES, Nancy. **Extent, nature, and consequences of rape victimization**: findings from the National Violence Against Women Survey: special report. Washington, DC: National Institute of Justice, 2006. Available at: http:// www.nij.gov/pubs-sum/210346.htm. Accessed: 27 Jun. 2023.

TREGGIARI, Susan. **Roman Marriage**: Iusti Coniuges from the Time of Cicero to the Time of Ulpian. Oxford: Oxford University Press, 1991.

TREGGIARI, Susan. **Terentia, Tullia, and Publilia**: The Women of Cicero's Family. London and New York: Routledge, 2007.

TRIMBLE, Jennifer. **Women and visual replication in Roman Imperial art and culture**: Greek culture in the Roman world. Cambridge: Cambridge University Press, 2011.

TUNNER, Michael. Foreword. *In*: BRENNAN, P.; TUNNER, M.; WRIGHT, L. (org.). **Faces of power**: imperial portraiture on Roman coins. Nicholson Museum. Sidney: The University of Sidney, 2007. p. 5-6.

VARELLA, Flávia. A proximidade feminina e a imagem Imperial: Nero, Tácito & os Anais. **Revista electronica**: Cadernos de História, ano I, n. 1, p. 1-12, 2006.

VARGAS, Joana D. Análise comparada do fluxo do sistema de justiça para o crime de estupro. **Dados**, v. 50, n. 4, p. 671-697, 2007. Available at: https://dx.doi.org/10.1590/S0011-52582007000400002. Accessed: 27 Jun. 2023.

VEIGA, Janio Celso Silva. **Lei das Doze Tábuas:** Linguagem e Contexto. 2008. PhD (Doctorate in Classical Literature) – Department of Classical and Vernacular Literature, Faculty of Philosophy, Literature and Human Sciences, University of São Paulo, São Paulo, 2008.

VEYNE, Paul. La famille et l'amour sous le Haut-Empire Romain. **Annales**, v. 33, n. 1, p. 35-63, 1978.

VIEIRA, Rafaela C. M. **A propaganda Augustana e a imagem de Cleópatra VII**: poesia e ideologia no século I a.C. 2012. Monograph (Specialization in Ancient and Medieval History) – Lato Sensu Postgraduate Program at the Institute of Philosophy and Human Sciences, State University of Rio de Janeiro, Rio de Janeiro, 2012.

VON HAHN, Brita B. **The characterization of Mark Antony**. Dissertation submitted in part fulfilment of the requirements for the degree of Master of Arts, with specialization in Ancient Languages and Cultures. University of South Africa, 2008.

VOSS, Barbara L. **Feminism, queer theories and the archaeological study of past sexualities**. Same-sex culture and sexuality: an anthropological reader. Oxford: Balckwell, 2008.

WADDINGTON, W. H. Mémoires et dissertations. *In*: CARTIER, Par E.; SAUSSAYE, L. (org.). **Revue Numismatique**. Paris: Chez E. Dézairs, 1853.

WALLACE-HADRILL, Andrew. Image and authority in the coinage of Augustus. **Journal of Roman studies**, Cambridge, v. 76, p. 67-68, 1986.

WEEDON, Chris. **Feminist Practice and Poststructuralism Theory**. Oxford: Basil Blackwell, 1987.

WEIR, Allison J. **A study of Fulvia**. A thesis submitted to the department of Classics, in conformity with the requirements for the degree of Master of Arts. Kingston, Ontario: Queen's University, 2007.

WEISS, Peter. The cities and their money. *In*: HOWGEGO, Christopher; HEUCHERT, Volker; BURNETT, Andrew (org.). **Coinage and identity in the Roman provinces**. Oxford and New York: Oxford University Press, 2005.

WELCH, Kathryn E. Antony, Fulvia, and the Ghost of Clodius in 47 B.C. **Greece & Rome**, Cambridge, v. 42, n. 2, p. 182-201, 1995.

WHITAKER, Dulce C. A. Menino - Menina: sexo ou gênero? *In*: SERBINO, R. V.; GRANDE, M. A. R. L. (org.). **A escola e seus alunos**: o problema da diversidade cultural. São Paulo: Unesp, 1995. p. 31-52.

WILDFANG, Robin L. **Rome's Vestal Virgins**: a study of Rome's Vestal Priestesses in the Late Republic and Early Empire. London: Routledge, 2006.

WILLIAMS, Jonathan. Religion and Roman coins. *In*: RÜPKE, J. **A companion to Roman religion**. New Jersey: Blackwell Publishing Ltd., 2007a. p. 143-163.

WILLIAMS, Jonathan. The Republican identity of Roman imperial coinage: 1st to mid-3rd centuries AD. *In*: CUNZ, Riner (ed.). **Money and identity**: lectures about History, Design, and Museology of money. Incomon: International committee of money and banking museums and Numismatische kommission. Hannover: 2007b. p. 57-64.

WILLIAMSON, George. Aspects of identity. *In*: HOWGEGO, C.; HEUCHERT, V.; BURNETT, A. (ed.). **Coinage and Identity in the Roman Provinces**. Oxford: Oxford University Press, 2005. p. 19-28.

WINKES, Rolf. **Livia, Octavia, Julia**: Porträts und Darstellungen. Providence, R.I.: Brown University, Center for Old World Archaeology and Art; Louvain-la-Neuve, Belgique: Département d'archéologie et d'histoire de l'art, Collège Erasme, 1995.

WINKLER, Lorenz. **Salus**: Vom Staatskult zur politischen idee, eine, Archäologische Untersuchung. Heidelberg: Verlag Archäologie und Geschichte, 1995.

WOLF, Eric. Distinguished Lecture: Facing Power - Old Insights, New Questions. **American Anthropologist**, v. 92, n. 3, p. 586-596, 1990. Available at: http://www.jstor.org/stable/680336. Accessed: 26 Jun. 2023.

WOLTERS, Reinhard. Nummi signati: untersuchunger zur römischen Münzprägung und Geldwirtschaft. **Vestigia 49**, Munich: Beck, 1999.

WOOD, Susan E. Diva Drusilla Panthea and the sisters of Caligula. **American Journal of Archaeology**, Chicago, v. 99, n. 3, p. 457-482, 1995.

WOOD, Susan. E. Memoriae Agrippinae: Agrippina the Elder in Julio-Claudian Art and Propaganda. **American Journal of Archaeology**, Chicago, v. 92, n. 3, p. 409-426, 1988.

WOOD, Susan E. **Imperial women**: a study in public images, 40 BC - AD 68. Leiden, Boston, Koln: Brill's Scholars' List, 1999.

WOOD, Susan E. **Imperial women**: a study in public images, 40 B.C. - A.D. 68. Leiden, Boston, Köln: Brill, 2000.

WOOD, Susan E. **Imperial women**: a study in public images, 40 B.C. - A.D. 68. Leiden, Boston, Köln: Brill, 2001.

WOOLF, Greg. Becoming roman staying Greek: culture, identity, and the civilizing process in Roman-East. **Proceedings of the Cambridge Philological Society**, v. 40, p. 116-143. Cambridge: Cambridge University Press, 1994.

WOOLF, Greg. Divinity and power in ancient Rome. *In*: BRISCH, N. **Religion and power**: divine kingship in the Ancient World and beyond. The Oriental Institute of the University of Chicago, Oriental Institute Seminar, n. 4. Chicago, Illinois, 2008. p. 235-251.

WORLD HEALTH ORGANIZATION [WHO]. **Sexual violence**. In World report on violence and health. Geneva: World Health Organization, 2002.

WORLD HEALTH ORGANIZATION [WHO]. **Global status report on violence prevention**. Geneva: World Health Organization, 2014.

WOYTEC, Bernhard. Heads and busts on Roman coins. Some remarks on the morphology of Numismatic Portraiture. **Revue Numismatique**, Lyon, v. 171, p. 45-71, 2014.

WYLIE, Alison. Gender theory and the archaeological record: why is there no archaeology of gender? *In:* GERO, J.; CONKEY, M. (ed.). **Engendering archaeology:** women and prehistory. Oxford: Basil Balckwell, 1991. p. 31-56.

YAVETZ, Zvi. **Cesar et son image**. Paris: Les Belles Lettres, 1990.

ZAGER, Ilona. **The political role of women of the Roman elite, with particular attention to the autonomy and influence of the Julio-Claudian women (44 BCE to CE 68)**. Submitted in accordance with the requirements for the degree of Master of Arts, in the subject of Classical Studies, at the University of South Africa, Pretoria, 2014.

ZANKER, Paul. **Augusto e il potere delle immagini**. Torino: Giulio Einaudi, 1989.

ZANKER, Paul. **Augustus und die Macht der Bilder**. Munich: Beck, 1987.

ZANKER, Paul. **Roman art**. Translation by Heitmann-Gordon. Los Angeles: The J. Paul Getty Museum, 2010.

ZANKER, Paul. **The power of images in the Age of Augustus**. Ann Arbor, MI: University of Michigan Press, 1988.

ZENHAS, Armanda. **Estereótipos de gênero**. 2007. Available at: https://www.educare.pt/opiniao/artigo/ver/?id=11982&langid=1. Accessed: 27 Apr. 2017.

ŽIŽEK, Slavoj. **Violence**: Six sideways reflections. New York: Picador, 2008.

APPENDICES

Appendix 1

Something that is very much questioned when it comes to coins is their value and their nomenclature. From 141/140 BC, the way the Roman government dealt with money was through the sestertius, with signs such as IIS or HS. However, in the provinces, other denominations were used, such as the drachm. The unit of value could also change, as indicated by captions from Thessaly, which show that the local drachm was exchanged for the denarius, used to indicate prices after an edict of Augustus (Helly, 1970, p. 120). The sestertius was initially made of silver and later of brass. The silver sestertius was rarely produced during the Republic; the unit of value was not necessarily identical to coins in common circulation (Burnett, 1987, p. 35). The value given to the sestertius may have actually been paid with denarius or through another denomination (Rowan, 2019, p. 2-3).

Table 1 – The main denominations of the denarius system after 141/140 BC

Name	Metal	Value in *asses*
Aureus	Gold	400 (= 25 *denarii*)
Denarius	Silver	16
Quinarius	Silver	8
Sestertius	Silver	4
As	Bronze	1
Semis	Bronze	½
Triens	Bronze	1/3
Quadrans	Bronze	¼
Sextants	Bronze	1/6
Uncia	Bronze	1/12

Source: Rowan (2019, p. 4)

Table 2 – The main denominations of the Roman monetary system during Augustus

Name	Metal	Value in *asses*
Aureus	Gold	400 (= 25 denarii)
Golden quinary	Gold	200 (= ½ aureus)
Denarius	Silver	16

Name	Metal	Value in *asses*
Silver quinary	Silver	8
Sestertius	Orichalcum[292]	4
Dupondius	Orichalcum	2
As	Copper	1
Semis	Orichalcum	½
Quadrans	Copper	¼

Source: Rowan (2019, p. 4)

Table 3 – Andrew Meadows' denominational system for Greek coins

Name	Value	weight
1 *obol*	-	0.72g
1 drachm	6 *obols*	4.3g
1 mna (*mnaieion*)	100 drachmas	430g
1 Talent	60 *mnas* = 600 drachmas	25.8kg

Source: Rowan (2019, p. 206-207)

---

[292] In Flavian times, orichalcum coins (also known as brass coins) were composed of a metal alloy with metals that are not known for certain, which could be a combination of gold and silver, copper and zinc or copper and tin. Among the orichalcum coins, the quinarius, the sestertius and the dupondius stand out at that time (Kormikiari; Porto, 2019, p. 60).

Appendix 2

At first, religion in the Roman forum involved women as well as men, but only women such as the Vestal Virgins had the duty to give protection and longevity to the State. However, the *aedes Vestae* itself was inaccessible to men, and the six Vestal Virgins would have exceptional status as women. Men and women, for religious purposes, could have accessed the forum (Boatwright, 2011, p. 111). Thus, only men could enter the Roman forum, except for the Vestal Virgins and other women linked to religion, so much so that the place considered to be the oldest one would be the sanctuary of Vesta. However, during the Late Republic and Early Empire, this conception seems to have changed, which may have helped in a variation in the concept of Roman masculinity (Boatwright, 2011, p. 109-110).

The characterisation known of the Vestal Virgins was shaped in the 3rd century BC, during the Punic Wars and the rule of Augustus. They were six in number and dedicated their lives to the goddess Vesta and the Roman State, as well as being able to make omens. Their behaviour and rituals served to benefit the city of Rome and the empire, ensuring prosperity and continued government. They were citizens of Rome, but their social status was not a factor in being chosen, and after AD 5 the daughters of any free man were also eligible. Augustus opened up the range of possibilities due to the lack of female candidates. A Vestal received a quantity of money when she entered the priesthood and an annual stipend for her services. They gained the right *ius liberorum* in Augustus' time, as well as a *lictor*, and could sit with the senators to watch the games. They dressed like married women, but could not marry and had to be virgins. However, they brought an ambiguity of roles between matrons and priestesses, as well as being in essentially masculine places (Takács, 2008, p. 80-83).

The connection with various fertility cults reaffirmed the status of matron and priestess and what masculinised them were independence and freedom in places. One of their duties was to keep the fire of the temple of Vesta burning. This fire symbolised procreation and fertility. The greatest crime that a Vestal could be accused of was being impure (*incestum*), since her attention could turn to some man and leave the State aside, however, this type of crime was rare. The Vestal who was accused had to prove her chastity, otherwise she was condemned to death and buried alive. Their burial place was near the *Porta Collina*, which was located at the northern end of the *Murus Servii Tullii* (Takács, 2008, p. 88-89).

Vestals could be selected at the age of six and became part of the Pontifical Priestly College. The number of Vestals was usually six and their work ended after thirty years. The first ten years were for them to learn their duties; the second decade for them to perform their duties; and the last for them to teach the next generation. During such occupations, they had to be chaste, but afterwards they were free to marry. They had a legal relationship with the Pontiff Maximus, as if they were married, and had to go through a religious ritual, called *captio*, which was performed by the Pontiff after the process of selecting the girls. In 1980, Mary Beard said that Vestals were both wives and daughters, according to modern interpretations. Like men, they could make their wills; like magistrates, they were accompanied by a *lictor*; and they were legally free from paternal control. Beard (1995) reconsidered her earlier interpretation and came to see them in relation to their sexual status, not in isolation, but in terms of a cultural system that had its own norms regarding gender categories and its own ways of negotiating them.

Ariadne Staples (1998) mentions that if they would be outside the social norms of gender, it was possible that they could represent the Roman people as a whole. Women priestesses could participate in their cults. Sarolta Takács (2008) interprets the Vestals as protectors of Rome. They could be burnt alive in times of crisis. The reason for burning the Vestals is stated according to Robin L. Wildfang (2006), who mentions that since the Vestals' first obligation was to be pure, this was vital not only for their health, but also for the health of the Roman State as a whole (Holland, 2012, p. 209). Therefore, if there was a crisis, it was the Vestals' fault.

Appendix 3

The deification of emperors became a common practice from contact with Hellenistic cultures as the Empire expanded into Greece, where hero and king worship was practised. The terminology of "imperial cult" is used to designate this practice in the study of the Roman Empire among members of the imperial family (Liningston, 2018, p. 1).

The divine kingship of Rome was a phenomenon characteristic of the early Roman Empire, the Principate, but it existed after that period as well. The cult of the emperor began with the belief that much of what had been the Roman monarchy was negative, as the Greek stories about the Age of Tyrants recall. However, there was also something positive from the tradition of the kings of Rome, especially in relation to their founders and their cults (Fears, 1977, 85-119). Romulus was believed to be the son of Mars and was taken to heaven at the end of his reign and worshipped as Quirinus. By Greek tradition, the Trojan refugee Aeneas was considered the son of Venus. Aeneas would have known the site of Rome and worship was done for him in a period before the Republic, at *Ara Maxima*, near the harbour, demonstrating the belief that he had also been deified after his death. During the Republic, many rituals were performed by the *rex sacrorum*, which suggests a sacral origin of kings, having for years an association of the divine with the monarchy (Woolf, 2008, p. 235-236 and 239).

Religious authority of various kinds was concentrated in the oligarchic authority of the aristocracy, which was replaced by kings. Divine ancestry came to be claimed by traditional aristocratic families, such as the *Iulii*, who claimed to be descendants of Venus via Aeneas and his son Julius. Religious authority, during the Republic of Rome, remained with the Senate, with a council formed by former magistrates, who approved or disapproved of some cults, such as the restriction made on the cult of Bacchus. Otherwise, other cults were authorised by the Senate, which involved only members of the more traditional elite. The types of rituals ranged from when a general arrived with his triumphs, the rituals of the Vestals, to banquets with members of the aristocracy (Woolf, 2008, p. 236) and others. The first Romans we have evidence of who received honours were: M. Claudius Marcellus, who had a festival in his honour in Syracuse, Sicily (212 BC); and, in the East, the consul Titus Quinctius Flamininus (191 BC), who received honours (Livingston, 2018, p. 1).

In the eastern Adriatic, the Romans encountered a great variety of ruler worship, descended from the religious fusion created by Alexander the Great and the generals who succeeded him. This fusion concerns the combination of a Macedonian kingship and an honour system developed by Greek cities, their Achaemenid iconography and rituals, which also incorporated Egyptian, Babylonian and other religious elements. Achaemenid kings were not gods, but they considered themselves to have direct relations with a number of gods and their territories. In Alexander's time, the honour to men in these rituals was greater than to the gods themselves. Many Greek cities elected their kings descended from gods due to the fact that their Heroic Age was remembered for mortal kings and deities who were more often on earth than in other periods, and many of these kings were connected with oracular shrines and places of worship. These features are similar to those of the Near East, with which the Greeks must have had contact (Woolf, 2008, p. 236 and 239).

Thus, it seems that the imperial cult was popular in the eastern provinces, since it suggested a receptivity based on local tradition, and this type of ruler worship could be a response to the collapse of a local religious system. Consequently, the imperial cult had its various forms both in the provinces and in Rome. In addition to the imperial cult, there was a family cult, in which relatives utilised the figure of a prominent ancestor within the cult of the Lares and Penates gods, who were household deities (Woolf, 2008, p. 237). In the Hellenised provinces of the Augustan period, living rulers were referred to in Greek as *theos*, a god. From the beginning, the imperial cult in the East was strongly orientated towards the actual, living ruler, with little regard for the official lists of *divi* published by the Senate (Livingston, 2018, p. 2).

Julius Caesar's desire to receive divine honours appears commonly cited as one of the reasons for his assassination. The Senate voted on a cult and a *flamen* for Julius Caesar, and shortly after his death he was officially deified. These divine honours served as a suitable model to be employed by emperors during the Roman Empire (Livingston, 2018, p. 2). In this way, similar honours were passed on to his heir, Octavian, including the title of Augustus and the proof of legitimacy of the new regime, which was also followed by a monumentalisation of the city of Rome (Woolf, 2008, p. 238). However, Anthony A. Barrett (2002) points out that Caesar should have received divine honours before his death. Only in 42 BC, after his death, divine honours were bestowed on him (Barrett, 2002, p. 14).

In order to become a *divus* or *diva*, it was necessary to go through a post-mortem *consecratio*, in other words, to a sacralisation. This process, taken as the recognition of an objective reality in relation to the deceased, served as an authorisation for public worship. Decisions regarding consecration were made by the Senate, but the deification of a relative of the emperor reflected a wish of the emperor. The first *divus* was Julius Caesar, which led Augustus to later claim his divinity as *divi filius*, with his 31 BC victory over Mark Antony at Actium. Augustus claimed descent from *Divus Iuliu*, Mars and Venus, as he had been adopted by the *gens Iulia*, which called itself the successor of Roman heroes (Woolf, 2008, p. 242-243). Augustus received honours in Asia and Bithynia while he was alive, which he accepted with the stipulation that the cult included Rome, as a partner goddess, a precedent that was followed by several of his successors. He refused deification in Rome during his lifetime, but allowed the establishment of the cult of *Genius Augusti* around 12 BC (Taylor, 1975 apud Livingston, 2018, p. 2).

Augustus reorganised the worship of the *Lares Augusti* together with the *Genius Augusti*. The associations were made by *vicomagistri*, who were usually former slaves who were allowed to wear the same clothes as a State magistrate when presiding over games, sacrifices and festivals. The cult of the emperor's *Genius* was also performed by families as part of a family's collective cult, which included the Lares (Woolf, 2008, p. 243).

The Romans honoured the *Genius* of a living man and/or the Juno of a woman. These terms denoted a divine force in each human being, which at the same time was distinct from human nature, and their worship was not considered equivalent to the worship of deified humans (Livingston, 2018, p. 1). During the empire, many worshipped *genius, iunno*, and eventually a deified dead person. Some members of the imperial family began to receive worship, especially in the Greek East, at the time of Augustus. The first woman to be deified was Drusilla, Caligula's sister, and then Livia, Augustus' wife (Holland, 2012, p. 212).

After Augustus' death in AD 14, he received honours similar to those granted to Julius Caesar, including a temple, a *flamen* and a set of priests for his cult (*Sodales Augustales*), who were appointed by the Senate (Livingston, 2018, p. 2). Thus, prayers to Augustus passed to Tiberius upon his death. This passage was as a means of expressing subservience to the Senate and of recognising a new *divi filius* (Woolf, 2008, p. 244), who in order to exist had to have his *Genius* sacrificed.

Claudius reversed the cult of Augustus and ended up deifying his grandmother, Livia, as he was not descended from any *divi*. After that, Nero, as Claudius' adopted son, secured his title. The word *divus* would be synonymous of *god*, but it seems to be the definition of a god who was once a human being. His consecration was done with symbols of the republican aristocracy and was a central component of succession rituals of Roman emperors (Woolf, 2008, p. 242-243).

Another relevant aspect of the imperial cult was its political nature. Emperor worship was an opportunity to show loyalty to the ruler in a formalised civic manner. Some emperors certainly encouraged this in order to give meaning to their power in locations far from the capital. In this way, the cult resulted in a system that was part of the local aristocracy, which used it to have a link to Rome and to publicly prove its loyalty, as well as to activate a recognition and social status in participation in priesthood. What appears is that emperor worship carried a religious aspect that was shared by all within the Empire. Consequently, the imperial cult provided suitable frameworks for a negotiating relationship between the Hellenised elite of the eastern provinces and the centralised power of Rome. With this, the *konia*, the leagues of cities, competed among themselves as to which would host the temples of imperial worship (Livingston, 2018, p. 2).

Appendix 4

The *nodus* hair style, as the name implies, is characterised by a knot or a roll above the forehead, which was the standard in Augustus' time (Harvey, 2020, p. 65), in other words, the hair was curled forward in the middle of the head and pulled back with the intention of forming a tuft. On the sides, the hair is rolled into braids that go to the back of the head, which are tied into a bun. Small strands of hair could appear on the forehead and temples, in front of the ears and at the nape of the neck (Barrett, 2002, p. 260).

In the *Marbury Hall* style, the *nodus* was wide and flat, and the hair on the side was woven in twisted plaits. It seems that this type was closest to the portraits of Livia on Alexandrian coins (Barrett, 2002, p. 260).

The *Albani-Bonn* style would be later than the *Marbury Hall* one, named for examples found in the Villa Albani in Rome and the *Akademisches Museum* in Bonn. In this hairstyle, the *nodus* was larger and the hair around the face was thicker. The *Marbury Hall* and *Albani-Bonn* types tended to show Livia with a somewhat elongated oval face (Winkes, 1995, p. 32; Fittschen; Wood, 1999, p. 94-95; Bartman, 1999, p. 144-145 apud Barrett, 2002, p. 260).

The *Fayum* type was the most representative in terms of surviving examples. This style tended to enlarge Livia's head and make the lower part more triangular, giving a facial shape much closer to that of Augustus, with his characteristically Julian triangular face, and allowing a fictionalised resemblance of Augustus to his adopted son, Tiberius (Barrett, 2002, p. 260).

In the *Zopftyp* style, it had two plaits covering the sides of the head, in addition to the usual twisted plaits of hair running along the same area. The earliest examples of this type were found on coins from Pergamum, on which Livia was clearly identified by name and represented a local creation from Asia Minor (Fittschen; Zanker, 1983, p. III, 4a - e; Winkes, 1995, p. 95-96; Bartman, 1999, p. 221 apud Barrett, 2002, p. 260).

There was hair from the Parted in the Middle group, which had a centre parting and fell on either side to frame the face in a series of waves. The locks at the back were pulled into a tight bun at the neck. The centre-parted hairstyle was widely used in portraits from AD 14, but the *nodus* style continued, as it could have happened that not all sculptors had access to the new type and many would simply have favoured the old-fashioned traditional style. It seems unlikely that Livia, in her sixties, would have applied for a new hair type; and sculptors could have adapted existing models. It is commonly referred to as the Salus group or type, the name being derived from the portrait of Salus Augusta from Tiberius' dupondius (Bartman, 1999, p. 115 apud Barrett, 2002, p. 261).

The *Kiel* style had locks on the side of the centre parting, which were more prominent than the rest of the hair and rose to create almost a halo effect. The ends were pulled back in a bun that was parted horizontally and was considered a relic of the *nodus* style. Others, possibly from this early group, were later arranged with waves in a series of parallel bands. This last style was the one utilised after Livia's death, following its consecration during Claudius' rule (Bartman, 1999, p. 116; Winkes, 1995, p. 46-48; Wood, 1999, p. 118 apud Barrett, 2002, p. 261).